MW00510515

Ministry
By His Grace
And For His Glory

Essays in Honor of Thomas J. Nettles

Ministry
By His Grace
And For His Glory

Essays in Honor of Thomas J. Nettles

Edited by
Thomas K. Ascol
and
Nathan A. Finn

 Founders Press

Committed to historic Baptist principles
Cape Coral, Florida

Published by

Founders Press

Committed to historic Baptist principles

P.O. Box 150931 • Cape Coral, FL 33915
Phone (239) 772–1400 • Fax: (239) 772–1140
Electronic Mail: founders@founders.org or
Website: http://www.founders.org

©2011 Founders Press

Printed in the United States of America

ISBN: 978–0–9833590–0–5

Portrait on Dust Jacket by Robert Nettles

Contents

Contributors

Daniel Akin received his PhD from the University of Texas at Arlington. He is president and professor of preaching at Southeastern Baptist Theological Seminary in Wake Forest, North Carolina.

Tom Ascol received his PhD from Southwestern Baptist Theological Seminary. He is senior pastor of Grace Baptist Church in Cape Coral, Florida and executive director of Founders Ministries.

David S. Dockery received his PhD from the University of Texas System. He has served as president of Union University in Jackson, Tennessee for the past sixteen years.

Matthew Emerson received his PhD from Southeastern Baptist Theological Seminary in Wake Forest, North Carolina. He is Assistant Professor of Christian Studies in the Online and Professional Studies Program at California Baptist University in Riverside, California.

Nathan A. Finn received his PhD from Southeastern Baptist Theological Seminary. He is associate professor of historical theology and Baptist studies at Southeastern Baptist Theological Seminary in Wake Forest, North Carolina.

Roy Hargrave received his DMin from Southeastern Baptist Theological Seminary in Wake Forest, North Carolina. He is senior pastor of Riverbend Community Church in Ormond Beach, Florida, and President of GraceWorx Ministries.

Michael A.G. Haykin received his ThD in Church History from Wycliffe College and the University of Toronto. He serves as Professor of Church History and Biblical Spirituality at The Southern Baptist Theological Seminary and is also the Director of the Andrew Fuller Center for Baptist Studies at Southern Seminary.

Tom Hicks received his PhD from The Southern Baptist Theological Seminary. He is pastor of discipleship at Morningview Baptist Church in Montgomery, Alabama.

Erroll Hulse is a graduate in architecture from Pretoria University, South Africa. He studied theology under Principal E. F. Kevan at London Bible College. He is editor of *Reformation Today*, a director of the African Pastors' Conferences and Associate pastor of the Leeds Reformed Baptist Church in the United Kingdom.

Fred A. Malone received his PhD from Southwestern Baptist Theological Seminary. He is senior pastor at First Baptist Church, Clinton, Louisiana, author of *The Baptism of Disciples Alone*, and an original board member of Founders Ministries.

Ben C. Mitchell received his PhD from the University of Tennessee in Knoxville. He is the Graves Professor of Moral Philosophy at Union University in Jackson, Tennessee.

Russell D. Moore received his PhD from The Southern Baptist Theological Seminary. He is Dean of the School of Theology and Senior Vice President for Academic Administration at The Southern Baptist Theological Seminary in Louisville, Kentucky.

Phil A. Newton received his DMin from Fuller Theological Seminary. He is senior pastor of South Woods Baptist Church in Memphis, Tennessee.

Jim Scott Orrick received his PhD from Ohio University. He is professor of literature and culture at Boyce College, the undergraduate school of The Southern Baptist Theological Seminary in Louisville, Kentucky.

James M. Renihan received his PhD from Trinity Evangelical Divinity School. He is Dean and Professor of Historical Theology at the Institute of Reformed Baptist Studies at Westminster Seminary California, Escondido, California.

Jeff Robinson received his PhD from The Southern Baptist Theological Seminary. He is pastor of Philadelphia Baptist Church in Birmingham, Alabama and is a writer and editor for The Council on Biblical Manhood and Womanhood.

M. David Sills received his DMiss and PhD from Reformed Theological Seminary. He is Associate Dean of the Billy Graham School of Missions and Evangelism and A.P. and Faye Stone Professor of Missions and

Cultural Anthropology at The Southern Baptist Theological Seminary in Louisville, Kentucky.

Kevin Smith is a PhD candidate at the Southern Baptist Theological Seminary. He is assistant professor of church history and pastor of the Watson Memorial Baptist Church in Louisville, Kentucky.

Geoffrey Thomas received his DD from Westminster Theological Seminary, Philadelphia, in 2011. He has been the pastor of Alfred Place Baptist Church in Aberystwyth, Wales since 1965.

Sam Waldron received his PhD from the Southern Baptist Theological Seminary. He is one of the pastors of Heritage Baptist Church in Owensboro, Kentucky and Professor of Systematic Theology at the Midwest Center for Theological Studies.

Gregory A. Wills received his PhD from Emory University. He is professor of church history and vice-president for research and assessment at The Southern Baptist Theological Seminary in Louisville, Kentucky.

Foreword

Thomas Julian Nettles:
Guardian of Baptist Conviction

Cemeteries, asserted Charles de Gaulle, are filled with indispensable men. Many have noted that de Gaulle's statement was perhaps not so humble as it seemed, given de Gaulle's confidence in his own indispensability. Nevertheless, he was right. There are few, if any, truly indispensable men. Thankfully, however, a few do exist.

One of these is Thomas Julian Nettles. He has always been ready when Baptists have needed him, and Baptists *have* needed him. Nettles' life and legacy have shaped generations of Southern Baptists, many of whom know who they are as Baptists only because Tom Nettles has taught them.

Born just months after the end of World War II, Nettles was shaped by the Baptist world from the start. His roots in Mississippi gave him deep reservoirs from which to draw and would leave an indelible imprint upon his life and work.

Educated at Mississippi College and Southwestern Baptist Theological Seminary, Nettles became both a preacher and a teacher. After earning his Doctor of Philosophy degree in church history, Nettles became assistant to the pastor at the Broadmoor Baptist Church in Shreveport, Louisiana, serving with pastor John Sullivan. But Baptists needed him, and he soon returned to Southwestern Seminary as assistant professor of church history.

Tom Nettles was born to teach. In the classroom, he is a dynamo of energy, learning, and ideas. He is, as many have noted, fully invested in his subject matter—as likely to break out into a hymn as into a discussion period.

But Nettles came into adulthood even as the Southern Baptist Convention was headed into its most significant period of conflict. He joined the faculty at Southwestern Seminary the very year that witnessed the publication of Harold Lindsell's book, *The Battle for the Bible*. Nettles had arrived just as the battle was about to break out in his own beloved denomination.

Tom Nettles is, by every visual observation, almost the model for the stereotypical mild-mannered professor. He is a man marked by gentility, kindness, and careful speech. But make no mistake, he is a man of deep conviction—driven by a love for Christ, the church, and the Word of God that will not allow him to remain silent when the times demand a defense of the faith.

My first introduction to Professor Nettles came with the publication of *Baptists and the Bible* in 1980. Co-authored with Southwestern Seminary philosophy professor Russ Bush, the book was, like Lindsell's, a blockbuster. For decades, Southern Baptist theological education had been drifting into theological liberalism and forms of neo-orthodoxy. By the time Tom Nettles arrived on the scene, liberal Baptists had told themselves their own version of Baptist history for so long that they had begun to believe it. Southern Baptist "moderates," long in control of the denomination's seminaries, had convinced themselves that Baptists had historically been little more than doctrinal libertarians with baptisteries. Nettles knew better. He openly and eagerly embraced the theological orthodoxy, doctrinal confessionalism, and confidence in the Bible that had marked historic Baptist conviction.

As the battle over the inerrancy of the Bible broke out among Southern Baptists, Tom Nettles and Russ Bush were serving together on the faculty of what was then the denomination's largest seminary. Bush defended biblical inerrancy in his classes on Christian philosophy. Nettles did the same, arguing from his deep knowledge of Baptist history—drawn from his knowledge of the primary sources.

Nettles and Bush wrote *Baptists and the Bible* to set the record straight—and they did. Their book was a brilliant defense of Baptist conviction and a devastating attack on liberal misrepresentations. As Bush and Nettles wrote, "Baptists have had their share of battles over the Word of God; not all of them have ended yet. But when such 'evil befalls the faith,' it seems appropriate to call our Baptist leaders together to hear their wise counsel. Our forefathers 'being dead yet speak,' and we shall do well to hear them."

Baptists and the Bible not only changed the terms of the debate among Southern Baptists, it also revealed the misrepresentations of Baptist life and thought that had become standard fare among many Southern Baptists. As Southern Baptist leader Paige Patterson later remarked, Bush and Nettles "have focused a brilliant light into the confused darkness of emotion and counter claims."

When Baptists needed Tom Nettles, he was there—and he provided historical scholarship that helped to change the course of the denomination and to recover its seminaries for the inerrancy of God's Word.

In 1982, Nettles left Southwestern and joined the faculty of Mid-America Baptist Theological Seminary in Memphis, Tennessee. Mid-America was born as a conservative alternative to the six seminaries of the Southern Baptist Convention. *Baptists and the Bible* had established Nettles' reputation as a scholar and a defender of Baptist conviction. In the midst of the hottest years of controversy within the Southern Baptist Convention, Nettles taught at a school that made its own commitment to biblical inerrancy clear.

Soon after arriving at Mid-America, Nettles continued his work of teaching, research, and writing. During those years, he began to write and speak more intensively about the historic shape of Baptist conviction, clearly more Calvinistic than many Southern Baptists then knew, or wanted to know. Eventually, Nettles would set the record straight in another major book, *By His Grace and For His Glory*, first published in 1986. Once again, Nettles was there when Baptists needed him. He brilliantly and conclusively traced the historic Baptist—and Southern Baptist—commitment to the Doctrines of Grace.

Once again, controversy ensued. Nettles left Mid-America Baptist Theological Seminary in 1988 and then accepted a position as Professor of Church History and Christian Thought at Trinity Evangelical Divinity School near Chicago. He remained there, a Southerner among the Northerners, until 1997, when Southern Baptists knew they needed Tom Nettles once again.

I was elected president of The Southern Baptist Theological Seminary in 1993, charged with the task of returning the denomination's mother seminary to her confessional commitments and theological accountability. Eventually, almost the entire teaching faculty would be replaced, and the process was epic in both drama and pain. There was the very real risk that I could remove faculty members who were teaching against the seminary's historic confession of faith and find no one to replace them.

Thankfully, this was not the case. When I needed him, Tom and Margaret Nettles left the safe environs of Trinity Evangelical Divinity School in order to come home to Southern Baptists—and to Southern Seminary.

Throughout his teaching career and ministry, Tom Nettles has been there when Southern Baptists needed him. He has been ready with pen, voice, and heart to defend the faith and to set the record straight. He has deployed his great gifts of teaching in the classroom and his gifts of encouragement and humor wherever he is to be found. He is a scholar, a teacher, a preacher, and a wonderful faculty colleague. Tom and Margaret Nettles are an unforgettable and indivisible couple, and I cannot imagine these years at Southern Seminary without them.

Tom Nettles was born to be a teacher, called to be a preacher, and trained to be a scholar. He has produced a library of scholarship and has shaped a generation of Baptist ministers and leaders. He has also done what few scholars ever have the opportunity or courage to do—he has reset the terms of debate for an entire denomination of churches. Thanks to Tom Nettles and his influence, there are important truths that are known and now cannot be denied.

This volume honors a man who is most worthy of the honor. The authors of these chapters represent a small sample of the lives greatly blessed and enriched by the life, thought, and friendship of Tom Nettles. It is my great honor to provide this foreword and to put my name at the top of the list of those who thank God for Professor Thomas Julian Nettles—guardian of Baptist conviction, teacher, scholar, and friend.

R. Albert Mohler, Jr., President
The Southern Baptist Theological Seminary, Louisville, Kentucky

Introduction

The histories of reformations and revivals are primarily stories about people. More accurately, they are stories of how God uses people to accomplish His renewing work in the world. This is true for the current doctrinal renewal being experienced within North American evangelicalism in general and Baptists in particular. Over the last fifty years God has raised up men on whom he has poured out his spirit with peculiar anointing. By his grace he has given them a firm grasp on the truth of his gospel and has caused them to feel its transforming power. He has made them bold and unwavering in their determination to make this gospel known. They have done so not out of personal ambition but out of zeal for God's glory.

This book has been published in celebration of the life and ministry of one such man.

Scholar

Tom Nettles is a man of many accomplishments. As a scholar he has effectively engaged the disciplines of history and theology on both the academic and popular levels. He has challenged prevailing opinions through original research that has brought to light information that had been long forgotten or overlooked by other scholars. This has been particularly true in the area of his primary expertise—Baptist history and theology.

At a critical period in recent Southern Baptist history Dr. Nettles, along with his late friend and colleague, Russ Bush, demonstrated from original sources that from their inception Baptists have held a high view of Scripture's authority. When other recognized experts were claiming that the idea of inerrancy was incompatible with historic Baptist—especially Southern Baptist—convictions, Tom led the way in uncovering documents that exposed that assumption as unfounded. He and Bush published those findings in 1980 in *Baptists and the Bible*.

When Southern Baptist historians, theologians and denominational leaders were decrying the revival of the doctrines of grace within the
Southern Baptist Convention (SBC) Dr. Nettles helped demonstrate that
these doctrinal views formed the theological consensus among those who
established the convention and gave it shape over the first eight decades of
its existence. He researched early Southern Baptist pastors and teachers,
reading their printed sermons and correspondence as well as their published writings. His numerous articles and presentations on everyone from
James Boyce to Lottie Moon to J. B. Gambrell support this view. His 1987
book, *By His Grace and For His Glory, a Historical, Theological and Practical
Study of the Doctrines of Grace in Baptist Life*, presents a systematic argument for this view; to date no one has attempted a serious, attempted
refutation.

Tom's work as a scholar has been guided by a strong confidence in
truth that arises from faith in the God of truth whose Son, the Lord Jesus,
is truth incarnate. This commitment has at times led him to walk lonely
paths and stand against pressure to conform when doing so would have diminished the testimony of truth. In the early years of the inerrancy movement within the SBC two history professors drafted a document decrying
that movement and urging all of their colleagues in the history departments of the six SBC seminaries to sign it. Tom received a call from his
department head at Southwestern Seminary explaining the situation to
him and asking him to sign the document. Tom disagreed with it and was
the only Southern Baptist seminary history professor who refused to add
his name to the document, despite dire warnings of the consequences of
such a stand.

At another seminary he refused to change his views on the biblical
doctrine of regeneration when the administration tried to persuade him
that his convictions were both unbiblical and contrary to the school's confession of faith. Tom had wisely written out and submitted his convictions on this subject prior to accepting a faculty position at the school. In
that document, which was accepted by the president of the institution,
he specifically spelled out his understanding of regeneration vis-à-vis the
seminary's confession of faith, showing the compatibility between the two.
After the president changed his mind Tom was forced to change seminaries, but he did so with both his doctrinal commitments and integrity intact.

Teacher

When a man has blood mixed with his convictions his teaching carries
a note of authority that mere theoreticians never attain. This combination
of belief and experience comes through Tom's classroom lectures. History

sometimes is charged with having a somniferous effect on people but that reputation owes more to detached teachers than to the actual subject matter. No one has ever accused Tom Nettles of having a detached demeanor in the classroom.

In fact, in thirty-five years of teaching, numerous stories have emerged that illustrate just how engaged he has been with his classes. It would be hard to find a former student of Tom's who did not experience the singing of God-honoring hymns in class. Most could speak of times when he simply burst into song during a lecture, or after entertaining a student's question or comment. As often as not those solos would be show tunes that betrayed his study of theater in college. His rendition of "Trouble in River City" is legendary.

It may be difficult for the rising generation of theological students to imagine a day when Calvinism was largely unknown and rarely discussed in seminary classrooms. However, only a few decades ago that was the case in Southern Baptist seminaries. It was the exception to find a seminary professor who had read the historic Baptist confessions of faith or was familiar with the names of Boyce, Mell or Dagg. When Tom began his teaching ministry at Southwestern Seminary in 1986, he was one of those exceptions. In those early years, in order to soften the shock that often came with introducing these doctrines, he was known to have employed a sock puppet to help explain theological categories. "Five Point Pup," as that visual aid was affectionately called, introduced many Southern Baptist ministerial students to the doctrines of grace and the importance of those teachings in the foundation of their denomination.

Everywhere Tom has taught he has been one of the most popular professors on campus. Comments from a website that records student evaluations of teachers underscore his effectiveness in the classroom. He is described as "a very funny guy," "brilliant," a "gentleman in class" and "great prof" who "has clearly thought out the implications of historical theology." On a scale of 1–5 he has a 4.3 for "overall quality" and 1.8 for "easiness." These observations are close to my own recollections from sitting in his classes over thirty years ago. He is quite simply the most influential teacher I have ever had.

Churchman

One of the challenges that modern evangelicalism has not met very well is the separation of the academy from the church. Too often the former has been regarded as the exclusive venue for serious study and biblical reflection and the latter has been seen as the place for piety. A tragic result is that too few academicians are also genuine churchmen. Tom Nettles

xiv
Introduction

shatters that stereotype. He loves the church and has not allowed his work as a seminary teacher to compete with his calling to be deeply and personally involved in the church.

He has done this not only by seeing his classroom work as carried out in service to the church (which is true) but also by being deeply involved in local churches. He and Margaret have taught Sunday School classes, led church ministries and been faithful members in local churches everywhere they have lived. Tom has served as an elder as well as a member of a pastoral search committee in churches where he has been a member. He has also served churches as an interim pastor.

For years Tom and Margaret have had a particular passion to minister to the elderly in nursing homes. Leading worship, reading Scripture, praying with and singing with and to those who are physically and sometimes mentally infirm display the truth of gospel that he believes. Because God has created people in His own image and because the Lord Jesus has died for sinners as sinners, every person should be treated with dignity and respect. As the ravages of sin near its culmination in an elderly person, the ministry of the gospel becomes all the more urgent. The elderly are more obviously near death than others. If they are in Christ they need to be encouraged in their faith as they prepare to face the final enemy of death. If they are not in Christ, then they need to be persuaded to trust Him and to find in His life, death and resurrection victory over death. I have heard Tom repeatedly give this rationale both privately and publicly for his involvement nursing home ministry.

A Personal Reflection

I had the privilege of meeting Tom in 1977 when he was a new professor at Southwestern Seminary and I was a college student struggling with a call to gospel ministry. His sensitive concern and wise counsel were used by God to direct my steps into pastoral ministry. His church history class was my first course at Southwestern in 1979, just weeks before Adrian Rogers was elected president of the SBC for the first time.

As a new seminary student and only months into my first pastorate, I went to his office and assured him that I intended to vote against Dr. Rogers in order to save the SBC and the seminary from those who wanted to destroy them. Tom stared across his desk at me with a look of disbelief. After asking me where I had gained such a perspective, he got up, closed the door to his office, and began to school me in the nature and authority of Scripture as well as in denominational history and politics. My real education had just begun.

The best piece of advice that I ever received in seminary came from Southwestern's Dean of Theology, Huber Drumwright. As a disillusioned first-year student who increasingly found myself at odds with professors over the newly initiated "conservative resurgence" in the SBC, I went to the dean hoping to find some encouragement. At the end of a two-hour private lesson on the Bible's inspiration and preservation, Dr. Drumwright leaned toward me and in a somewhat hushed but very deliberate voice said, "There are two young professors on this faculty who really understand the issues and are completely trustworthy: Tom Nettles and Rush Bush. You need to stay close to them and learn everything that you can from them." I heeded that counsel and have thanked God for it many times.

In the ensuing years I have had the privilege of serving with and learning from Tom in a variety of settings. As a young husband I sat in his den one evening and was enthralled as he and his wife, Margaret, catechized their children. It was the first time I had ever observed such an activity. I have also watched him respond to personal adversity and injustice with humility and grace time and again. In fact, I have heard him defend people whose words and actions have harmed him, refusing to allow his defenders to impugn motives or think the worst of his detractors.

In 1982 I joined Tom Nettles and six other men in a Euless, Texas hotel to spend a day in prayer, reading Scripture, singing hymns, dreaming and planning. The burden of our prayers was for reformation and revival within the SBC and beyond. The result was the first Southern Baptist Founders Conference that met the next year. From the beginning, Tom Nettles has been a major influence in shaping and guiding Founders Ministries to work for the recovery of the gospel and the reformation of local churches.

Celebrating 35 Years of Ministry

Over the course of his ministry, thus far, God has used Tom to challenge, correct, teach and exhort a generation of scholars, pastors and churches to think more deeply and biblically about the gospel and the church—particularly Baptist churches. His students are spread across the globe expending efforts to declare the lordship of Jesus Christ. His books will, by God's grace, be used for generations to come as markers for understanding the ways of God in unfolding His purposes across history.

Tom's work on Baptist identity has been seminal. He contends that Baptists are evangelical, orthodox, reformational and confessional with a theologically integrated ecclesiology. The cogency of his arguments has such force that the debate among Baptist historians over this crucial idea has shifted over the last thirty years to incorporate them.

Tom Nettles has a spirit that is contagiously catholic that extends from a heart that is unashamedly Baptist. Both arise from careful study of and deep submission to the inscripturated Word of God. Though history is his love, Christ is his Lord and it is in devoted service to Jesus that he has pursued his study of God's providential dealings with His world across the ages.

This year marks the thirty-fifth anniversary of the start of Tom's seminary teaching ministry. Those early years in Ft. Worth, Texas at Southwestern Baptist Theological Seminary were followed by positions at Mid-America Baptist Seminary in Memphis, Tennessee (1982–88) and Trinity Evangelical Divinity School (1989–97). Since 1997 he has served as Professor of Historical Theology at The Southern Baptist Theological Seminary in Louisville, Kentucky. It is fitting that a book of essays in his honor should be offered in conjunction with this milestone in his teaching career. The contributors include his students, colleagues and friends, all of whom have been positively impacted by Tom's life and ministry.

Though Tom has published a number of significant books (see the bibliography prepared by Nathan Finn and Matt Emerson on page 319) none provides a better outline of his ministry than *By His Grace and For His Glory*. As such, the editors have followed the structure of that book in organizing this one. The first section contains historical chapters followed by those that are more pointedly theological. The final section addresses practical issues related to the church.

The Apostle Paul commands us to give honor to whom honor is due (Romans 13:7). Sometimes this can be difficult to do because all honor praise and glory belong ultimately to God and God alone. I know of no one who understands this more clearly nor defends our Lord's honor more passionately than Tom Nettles. He would have been extremely uncomfortable with this project and most likely would have contended against it— had he known about it. That is precisely why we did not ask his permission and tried to keep it from him. I can think of few positions less desirable than standing against Tom Nettles when he is convinced God's honor is at stake! I am banking on his humble submission to divine providence to prevent such a debate now that the book is published.

So these essays are offered in honor of Tom Nettles with full recognition that our Triune God is the One who deserves all praise for his life and ministry. Our Lord is the One who gives "pastors and teachers to equip the saints for works of ministry" (Ephesians 4:11-12). We thank God for raising Tom up in our day and using him mightily in the effort to defend the authority of Scripture and recover the gospel that it reveals. Our hope is that this book, which addresses subjects that Tom himself has emphasized in his teaching and writing, will also prove useful in showing that all that we are and have is truly by God's grace and for His glory.

Tom Ascol, Senior Pastor
Grace Baptist Church, Cape Coral, Florida

Part One

Historical

I

Baptists and the Bible
THE HISTORY OF A HISTORY BOOK

Nathan A. Finn

In 1980, Southern Baptists were in the early stages of a fierce interne-cine controversy wherein activist conservatives wrested control of the denomination's ministries from theological progressives and those who were willing to tolerate progressive beliefs.[1] From the very beginning, the rallying cry of conservatives was fidelity to biblical inerrancy, a doctrine they argued was rejected by far too many paid denominational servants. Conservatives were inspired by the writings of men like Clark Pinnock, Bill Powell, and Harold Lindsell, each of whom argued that too many Southern Baptists leaders, especially seminary and college professors, were drifting away from a high view of Scripture.[2] Progressives countered that

---

[1] For the standard conservative treatment of the controversy, see Jerry Sutton, *The Baptist Reformation: The Conservative Resurgence in the Southern Baptist Convention* (Nashville, TN: Broadman & Holman, 2000). For a scholarly moderate interpretation, see Bill J. Leonard, *God's Last and Only Hope: The Fragmentation of the Southern Baptist Convention* (Grand Rapids, IL: Eerdmans, 1990).

[2] Clark H. Pinnock, *A New Reformation: A Challenge to Southern Baptists* (Tigerville, SC: Jewell Books, 1968); Harold Lindsell, *The Battle for the Bible* (Grand Rapids, MI: Zondervan, 1976); William A. Powell, *The S.B.C. (Southern Baptist Convention) Issue & Question* (Buchanan, GA: Baptist Missionary Service, 1977). Regrettably, Pinnock later modified his views and embraced an understanding of biblical inspiration and authority (among other doctrines) much more in accord with the very progressives he criticized in the 1960s. See Kenneth Keathley, "Pinnock' Pilgrimage: The Curious Quest of My Teacher's Teacher," in *Here I Stand:*

inerrancy was a recent concept among Baptists and that the word was really a political *shibboleth*. The Baptist Left had been making this argument for almost two decades, largely in response to conservative victories in the two "Genesis Controversies" of 1961–1963 and 1969–1970.[3]

As it turns out, progressives did not know Baptist history as well as they supposed. In 1980, Southwestern Baptist Theological Seminary professors Russ Bush and Tom Nettles published *Baptists and the Bible: The Baptist Doctrines of Biblical Inspiration and Religious Authority in Historical Perspective*.[4] They argued most Baptists have historically believed the Bible is fully trustworthy, even though the word "inerrancy" is of relatively recent vintage. In other words, Baptists have almost always affirmed the *doctrine* of inerrancy, even if the nomenclature itself has evolved over time.

Considered in its historical context, *Baptists and the Bible* proved to be as much a political broadside as it was a scholarly tome, galvanizing the conservative movement that eventually gained control of the Southern Baptist Convention. This essay tells the story of *Baptists and the Bible*, including how various present and former Southern Baptists in particular have responded to the book over the past thirty years. It is the history of a history book, one that highlights an important but often underemphasized contribution to a significant denominational transformation.

Initial Publication[5]

Both Russ Bush and Tom Nettles were natives of Mississippi, graduates of Baptist-related Mississippi College, and lifelong Southern Baptists. The two men became close friends while students at Southwestern Baptist Theological Seminary, where they each earned both their MDiv and PhD.

Essays in Honor of Dr. Paige Patterson, eds. David Alan Black, N. Allan Moseley, and Stephen R. Prescott (Yorba Linda, CA: Davidson, 2000), 51–67.

[3] See Ralph Elliott, *The Genesis Controversy and Continuity in Southern Baptist Chaos: A Eulogy for a Great Tradition* (Macon, GA: Mercer University Press, 1992), and Jerry L. Faught, "The Genesis Controversies: Denominational Compromise and the Resurgence and Expansion of Fundamentalism in the Southern Baptist Convention" (PhD diss., Baylor University, 1995).

[4] L. Russ Bush and Tom J. Nettles, *Baptists and the Bible: The Baptist Doctrines of Biblical Inspiration and Religious Authority in Historical Perspective* (Chicago, IL: Moody, 1980).

[5] The historical narrative in this section draws heavily upon Richard M. Daniels, "L. Russ Bush III: A Biography," *Faith & Mission* 19, no. 3 (Summer 2002): 59–61, and Douglas Baker, "Baptists and the Bible: 30 Years Later," *Baptist Messenger* (June 7, 2010), available online at http://baptistmessenger.com/baptists-and-the-bible-30-years-later/ (accessed December 14, 2010).

By the mid-1970s, both men had joined the faculty of their seminary alma mater; Bush taught courses in philosophy of religion while Nettles' expertise was in church history and Baptist history. Both men were theological conservatives who were troubled by the leftward theology of many Southern Baptist scholars, particularly the rejection of biblical inerrancy and the related claim that inerrancy was a modern aberration among Southern Baptists. Like many conservatives, they appreciated Lindsell's *The Battle for the Bible*, but they believed it needed to be complemented by a work that focused specifically on how Baptists have historically articulated biblical inspiration and authority. In 1976, Bush and Nettles began writing *Baptists and the Bible*. They hoped the book would debunk what they perceived to be theologically motivated, shoddy historical work on the part of progressive scholars.

Bush and Nettles initially wanted Broadman Press to publish *Baptists and the Bible*. Broadman, which was a ministry of the Southern Baptist Sunday School Board, had in recent years published several controversial books advocating a progressive position, most notably Ralph Elliott's *The Message of Genesis* (1961) and G. Henton Davies' critical commentary on Genesis in the Broadman Bible Commentary (1969).[6] But Broadman had also published W. A. Criswell's *Why I Preach the Bible is Literally True,* a popularly written defense of inerrancy, though Criswell's book was published against the wishes of Broadman's leadership and only after the editors included a caveat in the book's opening pages.[7] Unfortunately, though perhaps not unexpectedly, Broadman rejected *Baptists and the Bible*.

Unsure of how to proceed, Bush sought advice from Paige Patterson, then president of Criswell College and a key architect of the conserva-

---

[6] The publication of these books and the controversies that ensued are recounted in detail in Faught, "The Genesis Controversies." For Tom Nettles reflections on these controversies and their import, see *The Baptists: Key People Involved in Forming a Baptist Identity*, Volume III: The Modern Era (Fearn, Ross-Shire, Scotland: Christian Focus, 2007), 257.

[7] David S. Dockery, *Southern Baptist Consensus and Renewal: A Biblical, Historical, and Theological Proposal* (Nashville: B&H Academic, 2008), 191. Progressives reacted harshly to Criswell's book. The Association of Baptist Professors of Religion denounced the book as ignorant fundamentalism rather than thoughtful evangelical scholarship. See Clark W. Pinnock, "Southern Baptists and the Bible Controversy: Dr. Criswell and the Professors," *Sword of the Lord* (May 23, 1969): 1, 7. Left-wing Baptist scholars also formed the short-lived E. Y. Mullins Fellowship as a caucus to promote progressive views, including the historical-critical method, among Southern Baptists. See Lynn Edward May Jr., ed., *Encyclopedia of Southern Baptists*, vol. IV (Nashville, TN: Broadman, 1982), s.v. "E. Y. Mullins Fellowship, The."

tive takeover movement. According to Bush, Patterson did not read the manuscript, despite later erroneous accusations that Patterson or another conservative leader enlisted Bush and Nettles to write the book as propaganda for the conservative movement. Patterson put the authors in contact with Moody Press, a more mainstream evangelical publishing house based in Chicago, and Moody subsequently published *Baptists and the Bible* in 1980.[8] Appropriately, Criswell penned the book's foreword.

Summary of Contents

Baptists and the Bible was structured around an introduction followed by eighteen chapters. From the very beginning, the authors indicated their book was not intended to be an exercise in detached scholarship:

> Lack of historical awareness will lead a denomination to walk down some of the same roads they have walked before. A strong historical identity, on the other hand, should give them the ability to correct their directions where necessary and to move forward with strength and unity. The Baptist contribution to the Protestant community in the area of biblical authority can only benefit the people of God if it is clearly defined and expressed.[9]

Bush and Nettles then moved to their thesis: "Historically, Baptists have built their theology from a solid foundation. Holy Scripture was taken to be God's infallible revelation in words. What God said, Baptists believed…. Scripture has been the cornerstone, the common ground, the point of unity."[10]

The chapters in Part One of the book focused upon the first two-and-a-half centuries of Baptist history, from roughly 1609 to 1860. Bush and Nettles identified significant Baptist thinkers and confessional documents, all of which lent credibility to their thesis that most Baptists have historically affirmed the full truthfulness of Scripture. From the early General

---

[8] These events were confirmed in public remarks made by both Paige Patterson and Tom Nettles at Bush's memorial service, held in Binkley Chapel at Southeastern Baptist Theological Seminary on January 27, 2008.

[9] Bush and Nettles, *Baptists and the Bible*, 16.

[10] Ibid., 18. Though the controversial word "inerrant" is not used in this passage, Bush and Nettles later make clear that the concepts of inerrancy and infallibility are closely connected to each other and cannot be severed: "[Inerrant] is merely a nuance of 'infallible' and is implied by the term. Although the word has recently taken on an inflammatory character, it has significant historical precedent among Baptists" (401).

Baptists to the later, more doctrinally meticulous Particular Baptists, all of the key Baptist figures who helped shape the earliest Baptist movement(s) affirmed biblical inerrancy and infallibility. A high view of biblical inspiration and authority gave shape to Baptist ecclesiology, buttressed Baptist polemics against pedobaptist Protestants and heretical sects, provided the impetus for the Baptist-led modern missions movement among English-speaking Protestants, and was articulated by leading Baptist writing theologians in the American North and South. The views of John L. Dagg should be of special interest to Southern Baptists because Dagg was the first systematic theologian in that particular denominational family. Bush and Nettles demonstrated that Dagg, who especially influenced the earliest generation of Southern Baptist pastors and theologians, advocated a high view of Scripture similar to that espoused by Southern Baptist conservatives during the latter years of the twentieth-century.[11]

Part Two of *Baptists and the Bible* was devoted to the period from roughly the American Civil War to the middle of the twentieth-century. Having established that infallibility and inerrancy represent the historic position of the first several generations of Baptists, Bush and Nettles argued the following century was marked by a declension from the earlier standard. Some Baptist theologians held tightly to the older view (J. P. Boyce, Basil Manly Jr., Charles Spurgeon, B. H. Carroll), though others rejected the full truthfulness of Scripture in favor of progressive views influenced by Darwinism and higher biblical criticism (Crawford Toy, John Clifford, William Newton Clarke, Harry Emerson Fosdick). Still other Baptist scholars held to a fairly high view of Scripture, but were transitional figures from a more conservative posture to one at least open to progressive articulations of biblical inspiration and authority (A. H. Strong, Alvah Hovey, E. Y. Mullins, W. T. Conner).

The book's third and final section began by engaging with several historic American Baptist confessions of faith, with emphasis on their respective articles concerning the Bible. Bush and Nettles included confessions from northern Baptists and southern Baptists, Calvinistic Baptists and Arminian Baptists, denominational Baptists and fundamentalist Baptists, revivalistic Baptists and Landmark Baptists. These Baptists uniformly affirmed the full truthfulness of Scripture, despite their diversity concerning any number of other matters, though the authors noted that the 1963 edition of the Baptist Faith and Message was vague enough to allow for less conservative interpretations of biblical inspiration.[12] The section and book ended with Bush and Nettles offering their own views on the matter; like

---

[11] Ibid., 163–70.
[12] Ibid., 388–92.

other Southern Baptist conservatives and most Baptists throughout history, they affirmed the full truthfulness of Scripture.[13]

Reception and Reviews

James Leo Garrett argues *Baptists and the Bible* "was seemingly influential in evoking a recovery or acceptance of the doctrine of biblical inerrancy among Southern Baptists."[14] Many conservative Southern Baptists concur. Richard Land contends the book's publication "was a very important event. I think that it helped people to understand what our history had been, our true history as Baptists had been, as opposed to the revisionist history which many in the moderate movement were trying to perpetuate."[15] Albert Mohler argues in a similar vein: "Bush and Nettles offered far more than an argument from history, necessary as that argument is. They pointed to the biblical, theological, and epistemological foundations of biblical authority and biblical inerrancy.... We can now see that *Baptists and the Bible* was a critical part of the movement that led to [the Convention's] transformation."[16] Daniel Akin adds that *Baptists and the Bible* represents "the definitive treatment demonstrating that the 'Conservative Resurgence' was not the new kid on the block, but was a return to Southern Baptists' historical roots and heritage. From our beginning we were a people of the Book who affirmed its inerrancy, infallibility and sufficiency."[17]

Moderates, including those at Southwestern Seminary, were somewhat less sanguine concerning the new book. Nettles remembers that conservatives Curtis Vaughan and Hubert Drumwright were the authors' only Southwestern colleagues to thank Bush and Nettles for writing the

---

[13] Ibid., Chapter 18.

[14] James Leo Garrett, *Baptist Theology: A Four Century Study* (Macon, GA: Mercer University Press, 2009), 667.

[15] Jerry Sutton interview with Richard Land, August 28, 1997, cited in Sutton, *The Baptist Reformation*, 87.

[16] R. Albert Mohler Jr., "A Legacy of Conviction and Courage," blog post for AlbertMohler.com (January 23, 2008), available online at http://www.albertmohler.com/2008/01/23/a-legacy-of-conviction-and-courage/ (accessed December 14, 2010).

[17] Daniel L. Akin, "Remembering Dr. Russ Bush: A Tribute to a Mentor, Friend and Man of God," blog post for Between the Times (January 21, 2009), available online at http://betweenthetimes.com/2009/01/21/remembering-dr-russ-bush-a-tribute-to-a-mentor-friend-and-man-of-god/ (accessed December 14, 2010).

book.[18] David Dockery contends that Southwestern president Russell Dilday's 1982 book *The Doctrine of Biblical Authority* was a direct response to *Baptists and the Bible*.[19] In a volume titled *The Unfettered Word*, moderate editor Robison James introduces several essays with criticisms of the historical accuracy of *Baptists and the Bible*.[20] But for the most part, moderates simply ignored the book by refusing to engage or even acknowledge it, with the exception of a handful of formal reviews in scholarly journals.

Baptists and the Bible received both positive and negative assessments from scholars authoring critical reviews. Moderates were predictably unimpressed with *Baptists and the Bible*. In 1980, Dale Moody wrote a caustic review for Southern Seminary's faculty journal *Review and Expositor* wherein he accused Bush and Nettles of misusing historical information to support a fundamentalist insurgence against the historic Southern Baptist view of the Bible. Moody also seemed to believe that, at the end of the day, Bush and Nettles basically agreed with Southern Baptist moderates, despite the former's insistence on the word "inerrancy."[21] Fisher Humphreys of New Orleans Seminary wrote a more irenic review for the journal *Baptist History and Heritage*. According to Humphries, *Baptists and the Bible* oversimplified history and neglected any developments in Baptist views of the Bible save for departures from inerrancy. Humphries also noted that Bush and Nettles made numerous qualifications to inerrancy and he

[18] Tom J. Nettles, "Curtis Vaughan: A Personal Tribute," *Founders Journal* 60 (Spring 2005), available online at http://www.founders.org/journal/fj60/article1.html (accessed February 2, 2011).

[19] See Russell Dilday, *The Doctrine of Biblical Authority* (Nashville, TN: Convention Press, 1982). For Dockery's remarks about the relationship between Dilday's book and *Baptists and the Bible*, see David S. Dockery, "The Rebirth of Baptist Orthodoxy," address given at the Baptist Identity Conference, Union University, April 5, 2004. Audio available online at http://www.uu.edu/audio/detail.cfm?ID=140 (accessed December 14, 2010).

[20] See the relevant footnotes in Robison B. James, ed., *The Unfettered Word: Confronting the Authority-Inerrancy Question*, 2nd ed. (Macon, GA: Smyth and Helwys, 1994), 92, 108, 127. David Dockery argues that *The Unfettered Word* offered a counter-proposal to the thesis advanced in *Baptists and the Bible*. See David S. Dockery, *Christian Scripture: An Evangelical Perspective on Inspiration, Authority and Interpretation* (Nashville, TN: Broadman & Holman, 1995), 205. Interestingly, Nettles contributed a chapter to *The Unfettered Word*. See Thomas J. Nettles, "Creedalism, Confessionalism, and the Baptist Faith and Message," in *The Unfettered Word*, 143–54.

[21] Dale Moody, review of *Baptists and the Bible*, in Review and Expositor 77, no. 4 (Fall 1980): 565–66.

agreed with Moody that the position espoused in *Baptists and the Bible* was more or less the same view held by moderates.[22]

Non-Baptist evangelicals were generally impressed with the book. J. I. Packer, himself a staunch proponent of inerrancy, reviewed *Baptists and the Bible* for the *Southwestern Journal of Theology*. Though Packer lamented the absence of any discussion about the Spirit's witness to Scripture's truthfulness, he nevertheless commended the book as a fine example of historical theology. He also expressed his hope that Baptists would not depart from their historic commitment to biblical inerrancy.[23] David Priestly of Lutheran School of Theology reviewed the book for the *Journal of the Evangelical Theological Society*. Priestly noted a couple of important omissions and observed that Bush and Nettles may have attempted too much with their book. But Priestly also commended their work and thought it an excellent "first effort" at a historical theological study of the Baptist view of Scripture.[24]

Virtually no conservative Southern Baptists wrote reviews of *Baptists and the Bible* at the time of its initial publication. The one early exception was a favorable review by David Dockery in *Grace Theological Journal*.[25] It is possible *Baptists and the Bible* was not reviewed in some Baptist-related journals because of the denominational politics of the era. It is also true there were relatively few openly inerrantist scholars teaching at the SBC seminaries and state Baptist colleges, which may account for the paucity of conservative reviews. Though we cannot know with certainty the reasons why, *Baptists and the Bible* received little in the way of formal review from conservative Southern Baptist scholars.[26]

---

[22] Fisher Humphreys, review of *Baptists and the Bible*, in *Baptist History and Heritage* 16, no. 2 (April 1981): 43–45. Humphries later contended that the Chicago Statement of Biblical Inerrancy and SBC conservatives overqualified the concept of *inerrancy* to the point of emptying the term of all meaning. He also continued to maintain that virtually all moderates affirmed the idea of inerrancy, if not the term, when it is thus qualified. See Fisher Humphries, "Biblical Inerrancy: A Guide for the Perplexed," in *The Unfettered Word*, 47–60.

[23] J. I. Packer, review of *Baptists and the Bible*, in *Southwestern Journal of Theology* 24, no. 1 (Fall 1981): 104–05.

[24] David. T. Priestly, review of *Baptists and the Bible*, in *Journal of the Evangelical Theological Society* 25, no. 1 (March 1982): 120–21.

[25] David S. Dockery, review of *Baptists and the Bible*, in *Grace Theological Journal* 3 no. 1 (Spring 1982): 150–51. Though a graduate student at the time he wrote the review, Dockery later became a professor at Criswell College, academic vice president at Southern Seminary, and eventually president of Union University.

[26] Interestingly, conservatives failed to write formal reviews of *Baptists and the Bible* even after an expanded edition of the book was published in 1999. To date,

More often than not, conservatives have simply commended *Baptists and the Bible* and noted its importance rather than authoring critical reviews of the work. Mark Dever argues Bush and Nettles produced a convincing Baptist-specific rebuttal to the famous Rogers-McKim thesis that inerrancy was unknown before the nineteenth-century.[27] Trevin Wax concurs, arguing, "*Baptists and the Bible* was instrumental in that it makes a strong case for Baptist continuity between contemporary inerrantists and the forefathers of the Baptist heritage."[28] Several Southern Baptist conservatives offered brief assessments and commendations of *Baptists and the Bible* following Bush's untimely death due to cancer in 2008, including Al Mohler, Danny Akin, David Dockery, Alvin Reid, and Paige Patterson.[29] The most recent assessment was written by Douglas Baker, former editor of the *Oklahoma Baptist Messenger*. Baker's article, titled "*Baptists and the Bible*: 30 Years Later," includes an interview with Tom Nettles.[30]

Keith Collier has written the only significant critical review of the revised edition of *Baptists and the Bible* for Baptist Theology, a website affiliated with Southwestern Seminary. See Keith Collier, review of *Baptists and the Bible*, for Baptist Theology, available online at http://www.baptisttheology.org/BaptistsandtheBible.cfm (accessed December 15, 2010).

[27] Mark Dever, "Inerrancy of the Bible: An Annotated Bibliography," IX Marks Ministries, available online at http://sites.silaspartners.com/cc/article/0,,PTID314526_CHID598016_CIID1552716,00.html (accessed December 18, 2010). The aforementioned thesis is articulated in Jack B. Rogers and Donald K. McKim, *The Authority and Interpretation of the Bible: An Historical Approach* (New York: HarperCollins, 1979).

[28] Trevin Wax, "A Baptist Theology of the Bible," blog post for Kingdom People (September 24, 2009), available online at http://trevinwax.com/2009/09/24/a-baptist-theology-of-the-bible/ (accessed December 18, 2010).

[29] See Mohler, "A Legacy of Conviction and Courage"; Akin, ""Remembering Dr. Russ Bush"; David S. Dockery, "A Tribute to L. Russ Bush," Baptist Press (January 23, 2008), available online at http://www.bpnews.net/BPFirstPerson.asp?ID=27244 (accessed December 18, 2010); Alvin Reid, "A Tribute to L. Russ Bush III, (1944–2008)," blog post for AlvinReid.com (undated), available online at http://alvinreid.com/archives/306 (accessed December 18, 2010); Patterson is quoted in Keith Collier, "Southwestern Seminary mourns the passing of Baptist professor, author and statesman," Southwestern News (January 23, 2008), available online at http://www.swbts.edu/campusnews/story.cfm?id=A7888A1C-15C5-E47C-F98A80C2E0964372 (accessed December 18, 2010).

[30] Baker, "Baptists and the Bible: 30 Years Later."

Historical Assessments

In the last generation, dozens of monographs, journal articles, and other essays have been devoted to understanding The Inerrancy Controversy. Most interpreters thus far have been scholars with some sort of tie to the Southern Baptist tradition. Though some of these works have been published by secular university presses and other non-Baptist publishers, most of the relevant material has been published by explicitly Baptist presses, particularly Broadman & Holman (now B&H), Smyth & Helwys, and Mercer University Press. Most of the Baptist-related writers who have studied The Inerrancy Controversy are of moderate sympathies, though there are a handful of historical studies or memoirs authored by conservatives. Surprisingly few of these works mention *Baptists and the Bible*, though the book occasionally receives comment.

In their writings on The Inerrancy Controversy, conservative authors have engaged *Baptists and the Bible* in a variety of ways. Journalist Jim Hefley, who chronicled what he dubbed the "Conservative Resurgence" in six volumes between 1986 and 1991, only references *Baptists and the Bible* in his background research.[31] In their respective histories, Paige Patterson and Jerry Sutton each claim that Bush and Nettles made an important contribution to the conservative movement, but neither elaborate in detail.[32] David Dockery and Timothy George each concur with and frequently build upon the basic premise of *Baptists and the Bible*, but their respective writings are often constructive proposals rather than mere historical inquiries.[33] Dockery does credit *Baptists and the Bible* as the most

---

[31] For example, see James C. Hefley, *The Truth in Crisis: The Controversy in the Southern Baptist Convention*, vol. 1 (Dallas, TX: Criterion, 1986), 27–28. The name "Conservative Resurgence," which has become the preferred term for most conservative Southern Baptists, was included in the title of Hefley's final summary volume. See James C. Hefley, *The Conservative Resurgence in the Southern Baptist Convention* (Garland, TX: Hannibal Books, 1991). Jerry Sutton also uses the term in the subtitle to his book *The Baptist Reformation*. I have framed The Inerrancy Controversy as a Conservative Resurgence in my own constructive proposals for the future of the SBC. See Nathan A. Finn, "Priorities for a Post-Resurgence Convention," in *Southern Baptist Identity: An Evangelical Denomination Faces the Future*, ed. David S. Dockery (Wheaton, IL: Crossway, 2009), 257–80.

[32] Paige Patterson, *Anatomy of a Reformation, 1978–2004* (Fort Worth, TX: Seminary Hill, n.d.), 12, available online at http://www.paigepatterson.info/documents/anatomy_of_a_reformation.pdf (accessed December 14, 2010); Sutton, *The Baptist Reformation*, 86–87.

[33] "The Inspiration and Authority of Scripture in the Southern Baptist Convention (1845–1994)," appendix to Dockery, *Christian Scripture*, 177–215; Da-

important work written by conservative Southern Baptists during the 1980s in defense of biblical inerrancy.[34] In an article dedicated to Bush's role in the conservative transformation of Southeastern Seminary, Jason Duesing argues, "Bush and Nettles' thorough work virtually ended" the debate about whether or not Baptists have historically affirmed biblical inerrancy.[35] But because Duesing's article is focused upon Bush's tenure at Southeastern Seminary, he does not flesh out this claim nor does he argue to what degree *Baptists and the Bible* influenced SBC conservatives.

Most moderate scholars devote little attention to *Baptists and the Bible*. Bill Leonard simply mentions the book among a list of other works dedicated to the inerrancy debate in the SBC.[36] Dennis Wiles criticizes Bush and Nettles for simplistically identifying historic Southern Baptist figures with biblical inerrancy.[37] Jeff Pool argues that Bush and Nettles (as well as Dockery) do not adequately make the case that Baptists have historically affirmed inerrancy, but only that Baptists affirm biblical authority, a doctrine Pool claims all Baptists affirm.[38] David Morgan notes that *Baptists and the Bible* "gladdened the hearts of fundamentalists" in the SBC because it supported their argument that the Convention should be led by iner-

---

vid S. Dockery, "A People of the Book and the Crisis of Biblical Authority," in *Beyond the Impasse? Scripture, Interpretation, and Theology in Baptist Life*, eds. Robison B. James and David S. Dockery (Nashville, TN: B&H, 1992), 17–39; Timothy George, "Toward an Evangelical Future," in *Southern Baptists Observed: Multiple Perspectives on a Changing Denomination*, ed. Nancy Tatom Ammerman (Knoxville, TN: University of Tennessee Press, 1993), 276–300; Timothy George, "Introduction," in Basil Manly Jr., *The Bible Doctrine of Inspiration*, Library of Baptist Classics, eds. Timothy George and Denise George (Nashville, TN: B&H, 1995), 1–15.

[34] David S. Dockery, "Looking Back, Looking Ahead," in *Theologians of the Baptist Tradition*, eds. Timothy George and David S. Dockery (Nashville, TN: Broadman & Holman, 2001), 357.

[35] Jason G. Duesing, "The Reclamation of Theological Integrity: L. Russ Bush III and Southeastern Baptist Theological Seminary, 1989–1992," in *Christian Higher Education* 9 (May 2010): 187.

[36] Leonard, *God's Last and Only Hope*, 70. See also Bill J. Leonard, *Baptists in America*, Columbia Contemporary American Religion Series (New York: Columbia University Press, 2005), 138.

[37] Dennis J. Wiles, "Factors Contributing to the Resurgence of Fundamentalism in the Southern Baptist Convention, 1979–1990" (PhD diss., Southwestern Baptist Theological Seminary, 1992), 89, n. 21; 104, n. 55 and 56.

[38] Jeff B. Pool, *Against Returning to Egypt: Exposing and Resisting Creedalism in the Southern Baptist Convention* (Macon, GA: Mercer University Press, 1998), 154, 156.

rantists.[39] Interestingly, Dwight Moody argues a similar thesis as Bush and Nettles in an essay delineating changing Baptist views of the Bible, though he does not reference the latter's work.[40]

Expanded Edition

In 1999, Broadman & Holman published a revised and expanded edition of *Baptists and the Bible*. Paige Patterson wrote the new edition's foreword, in which he briefly framed the book's initial publication within the wider context of the SBC Controversy.[41] The only major addition to the first edition was a new chapter devoted to the ongoing Southern Baptist disputes concerning biblical inspiration and authority from the late 1960s to the late 1990s. In reflecting on The Inerrancy Controversy, Bush and Nettles noted that Southern Baptist conservatives had always believed biblical inerrancy was the historic Baptist position and argued "*Baptists and the Bible* had provided documentation for this contention in 1980."[42] They closed the new edition with a confident assertion that their book had made a tangible difference in the debate:

> The body of literature unearthed from the past and the primary sources examined in this book… give such richness to the affirmation of full biblical truthfulness in Baptist theological literature over the years, that none ever again need quibble over the presence or absence in the historical literature of the specific word *inerrancy*.[43]

The new edition carried with it considerable symbolic significance. The same denominational press that once rejected the book now republished it two decades later. The same man who helped the authors secure a publisher for the first edition now wrote the foreword to the second edition. Nettles now served on the faculty of The Southern Baptist Theological Seminary, the Convention's mother seminary and a bastion of progressive theology at the time the first edition of *Baptists and the Bible* was pub-

---

[39] David T. Morgan, *The New Crusades, The New Holy Land: Conflict in the Southern Baptist Convention, 1969–1991* (Tuscaloosa, AL: University of Alabama Press, 1996), 48.

[40] Dwight A. Moody, "The Bible," in *Has Our Theology Changed? Southern Baptist Thought since 1845*, ed. Paul A. Basden (Nashville, TN: B&H, 1994), 7–40.

[41] The foreword is found in L. Russ Bush and Tom J. Nettles, *Baptists and the Bible*, rev. and expanded ed. (Nashville, TN: B&H, 1999), xiii–xiv.

[42] Ibid., 375.

[43] Ibid., 387.

lished.[44] Bush now served as the academic dean at Southeastern Baptist Theological Seminary, arguably the only seminary to the theological left of Southern Seminary in the 1980s.[45] Patterson now served as the president of both Southeastern Seminary and the SBC herself, a denomination he had helped to reshape through his own conservative activism in the 1980s and 1990s.[46] One could argue that the republication of *Baptists and the Bible* is one important indication that the theological renovation of the Southern Baptist Convention's leadership was complete by the dawn of the twenty-first century.

Conclusion

Baptists and the Bible is a landmark study in Baptist historical theology, albeit one that elicited controversy during a period when controversy was par for the course within the Southern Baptist Convention. Besides its scholarly import, *Baptists and the Bible* is also significant because the book first introduced conservative Southern Baptists to Tom Nettles and Russ Bush. By the time a revised and expanded edition of *Baptists and the Bible* was published in 1999, both men had emerged as leading intellectuals within the now thoroughly conservative SBC. In many respects, the way the book was perceived among those considered Southern Baptist scholars and leaders at various points between 1980 and 2010 is a gauge of the denomination's rejection of a theologically center-left posture among its intelligentsia in favor of a vision decisively conservative, evangelical, and in continuity with the best of the Baptist tradition.

Though relatively few historians have heretofore addressed the influence of *Baptists and the Bible* among Southern Baptists, it seems unlikely this historical omission will long persist. As a new generation of historians study The Inerrancy Controversy, they will have the benefit of augmenting earlier sources with the recollections of first and second generation move-

---

[44] For a thorough historical examination of Southern Seminary during the height of The Controversy, see Gregory A. Wills, *Southern Baptist Theological Seminary, 1859–2009* (New York: Oxford University Press, 2009), chapters 11–13.

[45] For a collection of essays articulating the progressive emphases of Southeastern Seminary prior to the conservative takeover of the school, see Thomas A. Bland, ed., *Servant Songs: Reflections on the History and Mission of Southeastern Baptist Theological Seminary, 1950–1988* (Macon, GA: Smyth & Helwys, 1994).

[46] Though Patterson was president of Southeastern Seminary at the time he wrote the foreword, in 2003 he became president of Southwestern Baptist Theological Seminary, the school where Bush and Nettles both taught when the first edition of *Baptists and the Bible* was published in 1980.

ment conservatives, including many Southern Baptist scholars during the early years of the twenty-first century. The very fact so many contemporary Southern Baptist intellectuals and other leaders believe *Baptists and the Bible* was influential within the conservative movement virtually guarantees future historians will pay more attention to the book, its reception, and its long-term legacy among Southern Baptists. Hopefully, this essay has been a worthwhile initial attempt to do just that.

––––––––

On a more personal note, much like Bush and Nettles some thirty years ago, I am not a dispassionate scholar who writes without reference to the happenings (both good and bad) within the Southern Baptist family. I am a product of the conservative movement who has been significantly influenced by Bush and Nettles, both through their important book and their individual ministries. As a scholar of Baptist history and theology, I have learned much from Nettles' scholarship and greatly value our friendship. I am a professor at Southeastern Baptist Theological Seminary, an institution Bush served for seventeen years as vice president of academic administration and dean of the faculty before his death three years ago. I concur with the thesis of *Baptists and the Bible* and am thankful for the book's influence among Southern Baptists, even if the "paper trail" documenting that influence is just beginning to surface. And like Bush and Nettles, I praise God for the theological renaissance in the SBC during the last generation. I am profoundly grateful to have known Russ Bush, to be friends with Tom Nettles, and to be contributing to (and co-editing) this *festschrift* in honor of the latter.

2

Remembering Baptist Heroes
THE EXAMPLE OF JOHN GILL

Michael A.G. Haykin

Should Christians have heroes? It is very tempting in an age besotted with celebrities from the realms of entertainment and sport to answer this question with a resounding no, were it not for one fact—the Scriptures speak otherwise. The Bible is filled with narratives that are designed, among other things, to display patterns of life to emulate and ways of behaviour to avoid.[1] The author of the letter to the Hebrews, for example, has a lengthy section of his work devoted to past heroes of the faith—what we know as Hebrews 11—that calls upon the original readers to live wholeheartedly for God by encouraging them through the lives of past saints who were faithful to God through thick and thin.[2] And in Hebrews 13:7 the readers are urged to "remember" those who originally spoke the Word of God to them. They are to do this by spending time reflecting on aspects of these leaders' lives so that they might imitate their faith-filled character.[3]

---

[1] See, for example, Romans 15:4 and 1 Corinthians 10:6. Moreover, as historian Sean Michael Lucas has noted, we really cannot "swear off looking for heroes" since "we are wired to 'look up' to others, to search for models and patterns, to cherish dreams and aspirations inculcated by others" (*Sean Michael Lucas*, post May 19, 2006; http://seanmichaellucas.blogspot.com/2006/05/heroes.html; accessed May 13, 2010).

[2] One of the clearest windows into the situation of the original readers can be found in Hebrews 10:32–6, to which Hebrews 11 is linked by both textual context and theme.

[3] For *anatheōrountes* as the means by which we remember, see Luke Timothy Johnson, *Hebrews. A Commentary* (Louisville, KY: Westminster John Knox Press,

As John Piper has noted by way of this verse, "God ordains that we gaze on his glory, dimly mirrored in the ministry of his flawed servants. He intends for us to consider their lives and peer through the imperfections of their faith and behold the beauty of their God."[4] Hebrews 13:7 is thus nothing less than an exhortation to read church history through the lens of Christian biography.

Tom J. Nettles is no stranger to this way of reading history. His three-volume history, *The Baptists* is appropriately subtitled *Key People Involved in Forming a Baptist Identity*,[5] while his magisterial biography of James Petigru Boyce (1827–88) presents the faith of a winsome Christian theologian and educator as a model for Christian leadership today, while at the same time refusing to depict the subject as a flawless saint.[6] It is indeed a privilege to have this essay on remembering John Gill as a Baptist hero— albeit I do not always agree with Tom on his reading of Gill[7] —included in this Festschrift for a man I consider one of the greatest Baptist historians of our day, and with whom I have the deep joy of serving as a fellow church historian at The Southern Baptist Theological Seminary.

After an overview of the way Gill was regarded as a hero in his own day and a brief biographical sketch of the Baptist divine, this essay looks first at those areas where Gill's influence was applauded by some—namely his development of Calvinistic thought—but regarded with concern by others. This portion of the essay reveals that our heroes, even the best of them, are flawed individuals. The essay concludes, though, on a positive note, as Gill's piety is shown to be deserving of emulation and his robust defence of Trinitarianism is seen to be a critical factor in the preservation

2006), 346. For the possibility that *anatheōrountes* is imperatival, thus indicating a command in addition to remember, see George J. Zemek, "The Modeling of Ministers" in Richard L. Mayhue and Robert L. Thomas, eds., *The Master's Perspective on Pastoral Ministry* (Grand Rapids, MI: Kregel, 2002), 268, n.61.

[4] "Thanksgiving for the Lives of Flawed Saints" (*desiringGod* post, November 18, 1999; http://www.desiringgod.org/ResourceLibrary/TasteAndSee/ByDate/1999/1143_Thanksgiving_for_the_Lives_of_Flawed_Saints/; accessed May 13, 2010).

[5] *The Baptists: Key People Involved in Forming a Baptist Identity* (Fearn, Ross-shire, Scotland: Christian Focus Publications, 2005–7).

[6] *James Petigru Boyce: A Southern Baptist Statesman* (Philippsburg, NJ: P&R Publishing, 2009).

[7] For that reading, see especially his *By His Grace and for His Glory. A Historical, Theological, and Practical Study of the Doctrines of Grace in Baptist Life* (Grand Rapids, MI: Baker Book House, 1986), 73–107, *passim*; "John Gill and the Evangelical Awakening" in Michael A.G. Haykin, ed., *The Life and Thought of John Gill (1697–1771): A Tercentennial Appreciation* (Leiden: E. J. Brill, 1997), 131–70; *Baptists*, 2:194–202.

of the people he served for most of his life, the English Calvinistic Baptists.[8]

"The celebrated Baptist Minister"

In September, 1753, Samuel Davies (1723-1761), a Presbyterian minister from Virginia, left his home for Great Britain on what would turn out to be an arduous, though highly successful, fund-raising expedition for the then-fledgling College of New Jersey (later to be renamed Princeton University). He was gone for a total of eighteen months, and met quite a number of key British evangelicals and churchmen, among them the leading Baptist theologian of the era, John Gill.[9] In his diary he recorded some details of a visit he made to Gill on the morning of Wednesday, January 30, 1754. Describing him as "the celebrated Baptist Minister," he found Gill to be "a serious, grave little Man," who looked "young and hearty," though Davies guessed rightly when he estimated his age to be "near 60." Gill was

---

[8] In what follows I am drawing on two sources: my *"Eruditione pietate ornatus*:A Profile of John Gill (1607–1771)" in [Gary W. Long, ed.,] *Baptist History Celebration 2007* (Springfield, MO: Particular Baptist Press, 2008), 10–14—used by permission—and an unpublished paper, "Hyper-Calvinism and the Theology of John Gill," that I gave at the True Church Conference, Grace Life Church, Muscle Shoals, Alabama, on February 19, 2010. For the full version of the latter, see http://www.andrewfullercenter.org/wp-content/uploads/hyper-calvinism-and-the-theology-of-john-gill.pdf.

[9] The standard biographical sketch of Gill is John Rippon, *A Brief Memoir of the Life and Writings of the late Rev. John Gill, D.D.* (Repr. Harrisonburg, VA: Gano Books, 1992). For more recent studies of Gill and his theology, in addition to those noted above by Nettles, see John W. Brush, "John Gill's Doctrine of the Church" in Winthrop Still Hudson, ed., *Baptist Concepts of the Church* (Philadelphia,PA: Judson Press, 1959), 53–70; B.R. White, "John Gill in London, 1719–1729: A Biographical Fragment," *The Baptist Quarterly*, 22 (1967–1968), 72–9; Olin C. Robison, "The Legacy of John Gill," *The Baptist Quarterly* 24 (1971–1972), 111-125; Graham Harrison, *Dr. John Gill and His Teaching* (Annual Lecture of The Evangelical Library; London: The Evangelical Library, 1971); Richard A. Muller, "The Spirit and the Covenant: John Gill's Critique of the *Pactum Salutis*," *Foundations* 24 (1981), 4–14; Thomas Ascol, "The Doctrine of Grace: A critical Analysis of Federalism in the Theologies of John Gill and Andrew Fuller" (Unpublished PhD Thesis, Southwestern Baptist Theological Seminary, 1989); George M. Ella, *John Gill and the Cause of God and Truth* (Eggleston, Co. Durham: Go Publications, 1995); Haykin, ed., *Life and Thought of John Gill*; and Timothy George, "John Gill" in his and David S. Dockery, eds., *Theologians of the Baptist Tradition* (Rev. ed.; Nashville, TN: Broadman & Holman, 2001), 11–33.

quite willing to lend his support to the College, but he thought his "name would be of little service" and he warned Davies not to expect much from the English Calvinistic Baptists as a whole: "in general," he said, they "were unhappily ignorant of the Importance of learning."[10]

Davies was not the only one who considered Gill something of a celebrity. One of the members of Gill's congregation, Richard Hall (1728–1801), born and bred in Southwark and a hosier, had taken the time to write down all of Gill's sermons that he had heard over twenty-five years and had them bound for his own reading and edification. When Gill died in 1771, Hall commented:

> Great is his loss in the Church and much felt by me. It is a great afflic-
> tion when we know the worth of our privileges by the want of them,
> especially our spiritual mercies. It is possible to set too great an esteem
> on man—perhaps I did not prize my faithful Minister as I ought to have
> done. I wish I had improved more under his sound Ministry. I now will
> greatly miss him. Will the Lord be pleased, as a token for good to me,
> to bring me into a good fold and give me an appetite for His Word and
> Ordinances. I desire to be thankful I have my pastor's works to consult,
> which I much value.[11]

In fact, in the year following Gill's death Hall had printed, at his own expense—£1.14.6—200 copies of *What I remember of Dr Gill*, which he then proceeded to give to friends and acquaintances, but of which sadly there appears to be no surviving copy.[12]

Yet another fan of Gill was William Williams Pantycelyn (1717–91), one of the central figures of eighteenth-century Welsh Calvinistic Methodism and the author of "Guide me, O thou great Jehovah." When Williams was dying in 1791, he thanked God for the "true religion" that he had found particularly in the writings of "Dr. Goodwin, Dr. Owen, Dr. Gill, Marshall, Harvey, [and] Usher."[13] Four of these authors, are of course, Pu-

---

[10] *The Reverend Samuel Davies Abroad: The Diary of a Journey to England and Scotland*, 1753-55, ed. George William Pilcher (Urbana/Chicago, IL: University of Illinois Press, 1967), 65.

[11] This citation is from a diary of Richard Hall in the possession of one of his descendants and cited by Gary Brady, "Richard Hall 02" (*Benjamin Beddome*, post October 30, 2008; http://benbeddome.blogspot.com/2008/10/richard-hall-02. html; accessed May 5, 2010). In other posts on this blog that deal with Richard Hall, Brady gives details of other aspects of Hall's life as gleaned from the diary that Hall's descendant has allowed him to consult.

[12] Brady, "Richard Hall 02."

[13] Cited Eifion Evans, "William Williams of Pant Y Celyn", *The Evangelical Library Bulletin*, no.42 (Spring, 1969), 6.

ritan figures—the two leading Independent theologians, Thomas Goodwin (1600–79) and John Owen (1616–83), the Anglo-Irish Episcopalian James Ussher (1581–1656), and the English Presbyterian Walter Marshall (1628–80). "Harvey" is the Anglican Calvinist James Hervey (1714–58), one of the members of the Wesleys' Oxford Holy Club, famous in his day for a defence of Calvinism, *Theron and Aspasio* (1755), and a close friend of Gill. That Gill should appear in the company of four Puritans says much about his way of doing theology as well as the form of his publications. In a day when brevity was highly prized as a literary quality, Gill's works read and definitely looked like the massive tomes of the baroque print culture of the Puritan era. In part, this may have had something to do with Gill's character. As Rippon noted in his memoir of Gill, "The Doctor considered not any subject superficially, or by halves. As deeply as human sagacity, enlightened by grace, could penetrate, he went to the bottom of everything he engaged in."[14] In part, it also reflected Gill's deep love for the Word of God and the very Puritan conviction that all of divine revelation needed to be taught to the people of God.

But for some of his contemporary Christians, Gill's bent for systematic theology was off-putting. Surely it is this lack of interest in the systematizing that attracted Gill which lies behind the famous remark of the younger Robert Hall (1764–1831) about Gill's writings. Hall was once in conversation with the Welsh Baptist preacher Christmas Evans (1766–1838) when the latter expressed his profound admiration of Gill and said that he wished that Gill's works had been written in Welsh. Hall, ever the vivacious conversationalist, quickly retorted, "I wish they had, sir; I wish they had with all my heart, for then I should never have read them. They are a continent of mud, sir."[15] In point of fact, this is a singularly unfair remark that tells us more about Hall than it does about Gill. Few of those who read Gill in the eighteenth century would have described his work thus, even those who were critical of some of Gill's theological emphases, authors like Andrew Fuller (1754–1815). For many, he was "the great & good Dr Gill," as Augustus Montague Toplady (1740–78) described the London divine not long after his death.[16]

[14] Rippon, *Brief Memoir*, 137.

[15] Cited Olinthus Gregory, "A Brief Memoir of the Rev. Robert Hall, A.M." in his ed., *The Works of the Rev. Robert Hall, A.M.* (New York, NY: Harper & Brothers, 1854), 82. Hall expressed an identical opinion about the works of the Puritan John Owen. See John Greene, "Reminiscences of the Rev. Robert Hall, A.M." in Gregory, ed., *Works of the Rev. Robert Hall*, IV, 37–8, note *.

[16] Letter to William Lunell, October 25, 1771 (Thomas Haweis Collection, Center for Methodist Studies Collections, Bridwell Library, Southern Methodist University).

Eruditione pietate ornatus: A biographical sketch[17]

Gill was born in Kettering, Northamptonshire, in 1697, at the very close of the Puritan era. His early schooling at a local grammar school came to an abrupt end in 1708 when the school's headmaster demanded that all of his pupils attend Anglican morning prayer. Gill's parents were decided Dissenters and consequently withdrew their son from the school. Due to the fact that his parents had limited financial resources—Gill's father Edward was a woollen merchant—they could not afford to send their son to a Dissenting Academy and so Gill's formal education was over. But this did not check his hunger for learning.

Gill had acquired a good foundation in Latin and Greek before leaving school, and by the time that he was nineteen he was not only adept in both of these languages, but he was also well on the way to becoming proficient in Hebrew. Knowledge of these three languages gave him ready access to a wealth of Scriptural and theological knowledge, which he used to great advantage in the years that followed as he pastored Goat Yard Chapel, Southwark (later Carter Lane Baptist Church), in London from 1719 till his death in 1771.

During this long pastorate, Gill wrote a number of significant works. The first was a youthful exposition of the Song of Songs (1728), which approached this portion of Holy Scripture from the vantage-point that it was an allegory of the love between Christ and his church, a perspective that had a long pedigree all the way back to the patristic era, and which, according to John Rippon (1751–1836), who succeeded him as pastor, "served very much to make Mr. Gill known."[18] Then, in the late 1730s, Gill issued a robust defence of the so-called five points of Calvinism, *The Cause of God and Truth* (1735–8). Written at a time when English Calvinism was very much a house in disarray, it helped to make Gill known as a prominent defender of the Reformed cause and revealed his deep indebtedness to seventeenth-century Reformed thought.[19] The story is told that when Gill was about to send this defence of Calvinism to the press, one of the members of his church told him in no uncertain terms that publication of the book would lead to the loss of some of Gill's best friends as well as the loss of income. Gill's reply was terse and gracious, but very much to the point: "I can

---

[17] The Latin is a portion of the inscription carved onto Gill's tombstone. Translated it means "Adorned with piety [and] learning." For the full inscription, see Ella, *John Gill*, 246–7.

[18] Rippon, *Brief Memoir*, 24.

[19] For details of this indebtedness, see Richard A. Muller, "John Gill and the Reformed Tradition: A Study in the Reception of Protestant Orthodoxy in the Eighteenth Century" in Haykin, ed., *Life and Thought of John Gill*, 51–68.

afford to be poor," he said, "but I cannot afford to injure my conscience."[20] This anecdote says much about the man, in particular, his determination to stay the course when it came to cleaving to biblical truth. It also provides us with a central reason for his greatness as a Christian theologian, namely, his refusal to be shaped by pragmatic concerns. What mattered above all was the truth and its proclamation. Later in his life, when Gill published a solid critique of the views of John Wesley (1703–91) on the perseverance of the saints and predestination, Wesley referred to Gill as one who "fights for his opinions through thick and thin."[21]

The 1740s saw the publication of Gill's critical commentary on the entire New Testament—his profoundly learned *Exposition of the New Testament*, published in three folio volumes between 1746 and 1748. Gill's companion to this commentary, his four-volume *Exposition of the Old Testament* did not appear for another fifteen years or so (1763–66). Together, these two sets became a central feature of the libraries of Baptist ministers throughout the British Isles. Also occupying a prominent place in those libraries was Gill's *magnum opus, The Body of Doctrinal and Practical Divinity*, issued in 1769–70, which was the definitive codification of his theological perspective.

The *pactum salutis*

As a Reformed theologian, Gill inherited the theological concept of an intra-Trinitarian covenant of salvation called the *pactum salutis*, which was made in eternity past and which had been a feature of Reformed thought since the sixteenth century. However, Gill was also aware that while previous Reformed theologians like Johann Heinrich Heidegger (1633–98), Louis de Dieu (1590–1642), Johann Cocceius (1603–69), Hermann Witsius (1636–1708), and John Owen (1616–83) had treated this eternal covenant at some length, they had focused their attention only on the involvement of the Father and the Son in this covenant. Justification for this focus had been found by these theologians in Zechariah 6:13, where it is stated that there shall be a "counsel of peace" between the Lord of hosts and the priest-king, namely, the Lord Christ.[22] But Gill, who, as has been noted,

---

[20] Quoted C.H. Spurgeon, *Autobiography*, eds. Susannah Spurgeon and Joseph Harrald (Rev. ed.; Edinburgh/Carlisle, PA: Banner of Truth, 1973), 2:477.

[21] Cited George, "John Gill", 18.

[22] *A Complete Body of Doctrinal and Practical Divinity* 2.6 (1839 ed.; repr. Paris, AR: The Baptist Standard Bearer, 1989), 211. Subsequent references to this work will refer to it as either *Doctrinal Divinity* or *Practical Divinity*, and they will include book and chapter, and, in brackets, the respective pagination from this edition.

was a key defender of the complete sovereignty of God's grace, and was also robust in his advocacy of Trinitarianism in a day when rationalistic forces were seeking to undermine the biblical concept of the doctrine of the Trinity,[23] sought to interpret the eternal covenant from a distinctly Trinitarian perspective.[24] As Gill explained:

> [I]t was in Jehovah the Father's thoughts, to save men by his Son; he in his infinite wisdom saw he was the fittest person for this work, and, in his own mind, chose him to it… Now in the eternal council he moved it, and proposed it to his Son as the most advisable step that could be taken, to bring about the designed salvation; who readily agreed to it, and said, "Lo, I come to do thy will, O God", (Heb. 10:7) from Psalm 40:7, 8; and the Holy Spirit expressed his approbation of him, as the fittest person to be the Saviour, by joining with the Father in the mission of him,…and by forming his human nature in time, and filling it with his gifts and graces without measure.[25]

The Spirit was not "a mere bystander, spectator, and witness" of this eternal covenant, as previous theological discussions of the *pactum salutis* had implied since they did not clearly explicate his role in it. The divine Spirit was very much "a party concerned" in this everlasting covenant.[26]

Gill found support for this inclusion of the Spirit in the *pactum salutis* from such biblical assertions as the Spirit's involvement in shaping the humanity of Christ within the womb of Mary (Matthew 1:18–20), his empowerment of Christ during his earthly ministry (e.g., Matthew 12:28), and his enablement of Jesus to offer himself as a propitiatory sacrifice to the Father (Hebrews 9:14).[27] Gill also reasoned from the fact that since the Spirit is described in Ephesians 1:14 as the "Holy Spirit of promise," he must be the one who makes real in the lives of the elect all of the promises made for them in eternity, things such as justification, pardon of sin, and adoption. But this would not happen if the Spirit had not "approved of and assented to" those very promises in eternity past when, together with the Father and with the Son, he made the everlasting covenant.[28]

The Spirit, therefore, makes the blessings promised to the elect in eternity past by means of the everlasting covenant a reality in time. For exam-

---

[23] See discussion below.

[24] Muller, "Spirit and the Covenant", 4–14.

[25] *Doctrinal Divinity* 2.6 (213).

[26] *Doctrinal Divinity* 2.14 (244).

[27] *Doctrinal Divinity* 2.14 (244–6).

[28] *Doctrinal Divinity* 2.14 (244–5). See also Peter Toon, *The Emergence of Hyper-Calvinism in English Nonconformity 1689–1765* (London: Olive Tree, 1967), 113–4; Muller, "Spirit and the Covenant", 9–10.

ple, one of these blessings is the blessing of justification. The Holy Spirit brings this blessing into the lives of the elect by the preaching of the gospel and by setting it "in the view of an awakened sinner." The "illumination of his [i.e. the Spirit's] grace" then "works faith" in the elect "to receive it." The same is true with regard to forgiveness of sins and adoption.[29] And without the "special energy of the Spirit," the "most comfortable doctrines and precious promises of the gospel," even when preached with great vehemence, will be of no avail to the one who hears of them.[30] "In short," Gill emphasized, "all the grace given to the elect in Christ, before the world began, all the things that are freely given them of God in the covenant, the Spirit in time makes known unto them, and declares their interest in them."[31]

Richard Muller has pointed out that because the seventeenth-century expression of the eternal *pactum salutis* did not explicitly include the Spirit, it thereby allowed the elect to be involved in their conversion. They could not co-operate in the covenanting of the Father and the Son for their eventual salvation, for that was done in eternity past. But as the Spirit made this eternal plan a reality in time, the conversion of the elect did not take place without the exercise of their faith and the commitment of their will. Gill, however, wished to be consistent in setting forth a completely monergistic view of salvation. The explicit inclusion of the Holy Spirit within the eternal council of peace removed any possibility of synergism and the human response of the elect to divine grace.[32]

Eternal Justification

Gill's desire to exalt God's grace in his doctrine of salvation can be seen most clearly in the London Baptist's defence of the concept of eternal justification. According to Gill, just as God's determination to elect a people for salvation actually constitutes their election, so his purpose to declare them righteous in Christ is their actual justification.[33] The pro-

[29] *Doctrinal Divinity* 2.14; 6.8 (245, 506).

[30] *Solomon's Song*, 143 (commentary on Song of Songs 3:4).

[31] *Doctrinal Divinity* 2.14; 6.8 (245, 506). See Muller, "Spirit and the Covenant", 10.

[32] Muller, "Spirit and the Covenant", 10–12.

[33] *Doctrinal Divinity* 2.5 (203 and 205). On this concept in Gill, see especially George M. Ella, *John Gill and Justification from Eternity: A Tercentenary Appreciation* (Eggleston, Co. Durham: Go Publications, 1998); Peter Naylor, *Calvinism, Communion and the Baptists: A Study of English Calvinistic Baptists from the Late 1600s to the Early 1800s* (Studies in Baptist History and Thought, vol.7; Carlisle, Cumbria/Waynesboro, GA: Paternoster Press, 2003), 190–9; and Robert W. Oliver, *History of the English Calvinistic Baptists 1771–1892: From John Gill*

nouncement in time within the heart of a believer that he or she has been justified is simply then a repetition of "that grand original sentence of it, conceived in the mind of God from all eternity."[34]

Eternal justification thus precedes faith, and, in fact, a person's faith is a product of his or her being justified. As Gill forthrightly stated:

> Faith adds nothing to the *esse*, only to the *bene esse* of justification;… it is a complete act in the eternal mind of God, without the being or consideration of faith, or any foresight of it; a man is as much justified before as after it, in the account of God; and after he does believe, his justification does not depend on his acts of faith.[35]

In his tract *The Doctrines of God's Everlasting Love to his Elect, and their Eternal Union with Christ*, Gill simply stated that:

> union to Christ is before faith… Vital union is before faith. …Faith does not give us a being in Christ, or unite us to him; it is the fruit, effect, and evidence of our being in Christ, and union to him.[36]

If justification is actually antecedent to faith, though, why does the New Testament—for example, Galatians 2:16¬; Romans 5:1—regularly speak of faith as a pre-requisite to justification? Gill rejects the argument that faith *per se* is able to save anyone, for he knows that by faith "Christ, and his righteousness" is "apprehended, received, and embraced."[37] What these texts must mean, then, is that faith is needed to know that one is justified and to revel in this fact.[38]

The doctrine of eternal justification also means that the status of the person who is both among the elect and yet to be converted must be viewed from two different angles. On the one hand, this person is under God's condemnation and as such needs to be regarded as a child of wrath. But, as one who has been justified from eternity past, in Christ they are "always viewed and accounted righteous."[39] Theoretically this argumentation could

---

to C.H. Spurgeon (Edinburgh/Carlisle, PA: The Banner of Truth Trust, 2006), 6–8. Ella defends Gill's teaching on this issue, while both Naylor and Oliver are critical of it.

[34] *Doctrinal Divinity* 2.6 (209).

[35] *Doctrinal Divinity* 2.5 (204).

[36] *The Doctrines of God's Everlasting Love to his Elect, and their Eternal Union with Christ* (3rd ed.; London, 1752), 33 and 39.

[37] *Doctrinal Divinity* 6.8 (511).

[38] *Doctrinal Divinity* 2.6 (208).

[39] *Doctrinal Divinity* 2.6 (208).

open the door to genuine antinomianism. Little wonder that Gill had to fend off charges of antinomianism at a number of points in his ministry.[40]

With regard to spirituality, there is also little doubt that Gill's doctrine of eternal justification helped to foster a climate of profound introspection. To come to Christ for salvation, one first had to determine if one was among the elect justified in eternity past. The net effect of this teaching—though unintended by Gill—was to place the essence of conversion and faith not in believing the gospel, but in believing that one was among the elect. Instead of attention being directed away from oneself towards Christ, the convicted sinner was turned inwards upon himself or herself to search for evidence that he or she was truly elect and therefore able to be converted. And by making eternal justification so central to his soteriology, Gill essentially reversed the biblical order in which one must believe in Christ before one is capable of knowing that he or she is among the elect.[41]

It is also important to note that in the most influential Baptist confessional statement in Baptist history, the *Second London Confession of Faith* (1677/89), Gill's seventeenth-century Calvinistic Baptist forebears explicitly rejected the notion of eternal justification. In the article on justification, it is clearly stated that "God did from all eternity decree to justify all the elect, and Christ did in the fullness of time die for their sins, and rise again for their justification; nevertheless, they are not justified personally,

---

[40] For Gill's rejection of antinomianism, see his *The Necessity of Good Works unto Salvation Considered* (London: A. Ward, 1739) and *The Doctrine of Grace clear'd from the Charge of Licentiousness* (2nd ed.; London: G. Keith, 1751). And for a study of this area of Gill's thought, see especially Curt Daniel, "John Gill and Calvinistic Antinomianism" in Haykin, ed., *Life and Thought of John Gill*, 171–90. See also Alan P.F. Sell, *The Great Debate: Calvinism, Arminianism and Salvation* (1982 ed.; repr. Eugene, OR: Wipf & Stock, 1998), 79–80.

Chad van Dixhoorn has identified the concept of eternal justification as a key intellectual origin for various forms of seventeenth-century antinomianism ["Reforming the Reformation: Theological Debate at the Westminster Assembly 1642-1652", 7 vols. (Unpublished Ph.D. Thesis, University of Cambridge, 2004), 1:277]. I am indebted to Mark Jones and Gert van den Brink, "Thomas Goodwin and Johannes Maccovius on Justification from Eternity" (Unpublished paper, 2010), 9, for this reference.

[41] Andrew Fuller, *Strictures on Sandemanianism, in Twelve Letters to a Friend* [*The Complete Works of the Rev. Andrew Fuller*, revised Joseph Belcher (1845 ed.; repr. Harrisonburg, VA: Sprinkle Publications, 1988), 2:563–4)]; E.F. Clipsham, "Andrew Fuller and Fullerism: A Study in Evangelical Calvinism", *The Baptist Quarterly*, 20 (1963–1964), 103; Sell, Great Debate, 82; Pieter de Vries, *John Bunyan on the Order of Salvation*, trans. C. van Haaften (New York: Peter Lang, 1994), 109.

until the Holy Spirit doth in time due actually apply Christ unto them."[42] The strongest theological influences on Gill, however, came through the early eighteenth-century London Baptist John Skepp (d.1721), who participated in Gill's ordination and whose sole literary publication, *A divine energy* (1722), was an out-and-out rejection of the free offer of the gospel. Gill reprinted it with a recommendatory preface in 1751.[43]

The Free Offer of the Gospel

It should occasion no surprise that Gill's development of the doctrine of the everlasting covenant, in which he highlighted the role of the Spirit, along with his tenacious commitment to the notion of eternal justification should then lead to the rejection of the free offer of the gospel.[44] For example, in a tract that he wrote in response to a rejection of predestination by the Methodist leader John Wesley (1703–91), Gill considered biblical verses like Acts 17:30, which states that God "now commands all men everywhere to repent" and Mark 16:15, in which there is a command to "preach the gospel to every creature." Gill did not believe that either of these verses can be used to support the idea of the free offer of the gospel. He admitted that the "gospel is indeed ordered to be preached to every creature to whom it is sent and comes." But, Gill observed, it needs noting that God has not seen fit to send the gospel to every person in the world: "there have been multitudes in all ages that have not heard it." Therefore, Gill stated, "that there are universal offers of grace and salvation made to all men, I utterly deny." Not even to the elect does God make an "offer" of salvation. Rather, the proclamation of the gospel informs the elect that "grace and salvation are provided for them in the everlasting covenant, procured for them by Christ, published and revealed in the gospel, and applied by the Spirit."[45]

[42] *The Second London Confession of Faith* 11.4. See the comments of Oliver, *History of the English Calvinistic Baptists*, 6–7.

[43] On Skepp, see Walter Wilson, *The History and Antiquities of Dissenting Churches and Meeting Houses, in London, Westminster, and Southwark* (London, 1808), II, 572–4; Geoffrey F. Nuttall, "Northamptonshire and *The Modern Question*: A Turning-Point in Eighteenth-Century Dissent", *The Journal of Theological Studies*, n.s. 16 (1965), 117–8; Toon, *Emergence of Hyper-Calvinism*, 85–9; Sell, *Great Debate*, 78; James Leo Garrett, Jr., *Baptist Theology: A Four-Century Study* (Macon, GA: Mercer University Press, 2009), 91–2.

[44] Nettles believes differently; see his "John Gill and the Evangelical Awakening" in Haykin, ed., *Life and Thought of John Gill*, 131–70.

[45] *The Doctrine of Predestination Stated, and Set in the Scripture-Light* (2nd ed.; London: G. Keith, 1752), 28–9.

In his systematic theology, Gill suggests another way of dodging the plain import of such verses: they are really only speaking about "an external reformation of life and manners," not "spiritual and internal conversion."[46] Not surprisingly Gill warns gospel preachers to be careful lest, when they preach repentance, they give their hearers the idea that repentance is "within the compass of the power of man's will." To preach like this is what Gill calls the "rant of some men's ministry,… low and mean stuff, too mean for, below, and unworthy of a minister of the gospel."[47]

Gill and Hyper-Calvinism

Now, it would be easy to think that Gill had simply allowed his reading of the Bible on these issues to be determined by his theological system. But the truth is more complex than this. Guiding Gill, first of all, was a genuine desire to exalt God and his sovereign grace. What he said early on in his ministry shaped his entire life: "I would not willingly say or write anything that is contrary to the purity and holiness of God."[48]

Then, his was a day, when the doctrines of grace were under heavy attack from the rationalism of the Deists and the moralism in much of the Church of England. It would have been natural for Gill and his fellow Calvinistic Baptists to view themselves as one of God's last bastions of truth in England. In such a situation, it is easy to see how one's defense of certain biblical doctrines—in this case, the doctrines of grace—could become unbalanced, and even produce error.

It is noteworthy that Gill's day was the so-called Age of Reason, when men and women began to trust in their own abilities and wisdom to understand the world in which they lived and what was incumbent upon them as human beings. Gill would have been horrified to think that his theology was deeply shaped by this culture that was beginning to trust in human reason alone. But it seems to this reader of Gill's works, that the Baptist theologian takes Scriptural matters to a logical end beyond what Scripture clearly affirms. Like it or not, Gill was shaped by the rationalism of his day.

However, when all is said and done, Gill's theology did hamper passionate evangelism and outreach. And not surprisingly, there is a long tradition that regards Gill as the doyen of eighteenth-century Hyper-Calvin-

---

[46] Cited Oliver, *History of the English Calvinistic Baptists*, 9.

[47] *Doctrines of God's Everlasting Love*, 79–80. I owe this reference to Garrett, Jr., *Baptist Theology*, 99.

[48] *Doctrines of God's Everlasting Love*, 41.

ism.[49] But this is not all there is to Mr. Gill. If it were, it would constitute a dubious reason to see him as a Baptist hero.

The Piety of John Gill: a Glimpse

In the debates among historical theologians about whether or not Gill was a Hyper-Calvinist—not at all an unimportant question and one in which the man whom this essay seeks to honor has played no small part— there is a side of Gill that has been far too frequently forgotten, namely, his piety.[50] Richard Muller, for example, in his fine examination of Gill's

[49] See, for example, J.M. Cramp, *Baptist History: From the Foundation of the Christian Church to the Present Time* (London: Elliot Stock, 1871), 435–6, 443; A. C. Underwood, *A History of the English Baptists* (2nd ed.; London: Carey Kingsgate Press, 1956), 135; W.R. Estep, Jr., "Gill, John" in *Encyclopedia of Southern Baptists* (Nashville, TN: Broadman Press, 1958), I, 560; H. Leon McBeth, *The Baptist Heritage* (Nashville, TN: Broadman Press, 1987), 176–8; Donald Macleod, "Dr T.F. Torrance and Scottish Theology: a Review Article", *The Evangelical Quarterly*, 72 (2000), 57; Anonymous, "hyper-Calvinism" in George Thomas Kurian, ed., *Nelson's Dictionary of Christianity* (Nashville, TN: Nelson, 2005), 347.

For various definitions of Hyper-Calvinism, see Toon, *Emergence of Hyper-Calvinism*, 144–6; *idem*, "Hyper-Calvinism" in Donald K. McKim and David F. Wright, eds., *Encyclopedia of The Reformed Faith* (Louisville, KY: Westminster/John Knox Press/Edinburgh: Saint Andrew Press, 1992), 190; Garrett, Jr., *Baptist Theology*, 89. For problems with the use of the term "Hyper-Calvinism," see Muller, "John Gill and the Reformed Tradition", 51¬–6.

Geoffrey F. Nuttall ("Northamptonshire and *The Modern Question*", 101, n.4) prefers the term "High Calvinism" to "the now more usual Hyper-Calvinism as less prejudiced and question-begging." Nuttall also prefers this term since it was in use in the late eighteenth century. As support for the latter point, he refers to the English edition of the New England historian Hannah Adams' *A View of Religions*, which Andrew Fuller edited and to which he also contributed a few entries, where the term "High Calvinists" appears in an article written by Fuller himself ["Calvinists", *A View of Religions* (3rd ed.; London: W. Button, 1805), 111]. Yet, in the same book, in the article entitled "Puritans"—in a passage that appears to have been added by Fuller—it is stated that in the eighteenth century the Congregationalists and Baptists "first veered towards high Calvinism, then forbore to exhort the unregenerate to repent, believe, or do any thing spiritually good; and by degrees many of them settled in gross Antinomianism" (*A View of Religions*, 270–1). From this statement it seems that "high Calvinism" was seen as a step towards a form of Calvinism that had problems with the evangelization of all and sundry, but not exactly equivalent to the latter. I have, therefore, chosen to retain the use of the term "Hyper-Calvinism."

[50] See the extremely helpful study of Gill's piety by Gregory A. Wills, "A Fire That Burns Within: The Spirituality of John Gill" in Haykin, ed., *Life and*

thoughts on the *pactum salutis*, argues that "Gill's precise systematization…
of Christian theology" lacked "the warm piety of earlier Reformed and Puritan thought."[51] While Christopher J. Ellis, in an otherwise superb study
of the history of Baptist worship, contrasts the "warm evangelical spirituality" of the West Country Particular Baptists that was centred on Bristol
Baptist Academy with the dominant Hyper-Calvinist tradition of Gill in
London which was accompanied, according to Ellis, by "a deep suspicion
of the religious affections."[52] But the actual situation is far more complex.

An excellent entrance-point into Gill's piety is first of all found in his
poignant funeral sermon for his daughter Elizabeth, who died at the age
of twelve on May 30, 1738. After preaching on 1 Thessalonians 4:13-14,
Gill intended to give some details about his daughter's conversion, Christian walk, and final days, but the emotion of the moment appears to have
overwhelmed him and he added his remarks later.[53] Among the things
that Gill especially noted about his daughter was her "great desire after,
and a wonderful esteem of the grace of humility." And to acquire such, Gill
observed that his daughter would "retire into corners, to read good books,
and to desire of God to give her his grace."[54] Gill believed that God did
indeed answer her prayers, for, he remarked, "to the last she entertained
a mean and low opinion of her self."[55] In his *Body of Divinity* Gill noted,
in the section on humility, that humility entails, among other things, "a
man's thinking meanly and the worst of himself."[56] He may well have been
thinking of his daughter when he wrote this. For Gill went on to say, "pride
is the devil's livery; but humility is the clothing of the servants of Christ,
the badge by which they are known."[57]

This stress on the importance of humility in the Christian life connects Gill to a much larger Christian tradition of spirituality that goes
back to such early Christian authors as Basil of Ceasarea (c.330–79) and
his sermon *Of humility*,[58] or the emphasis by Augustine (354–430) that

Thought of John Gill, 191–210. Also see Oliver, *History of the English Calvinistic Baptists*, 12–15.

[51] Muller, "Spirit and the Covenant", 12.

[52] *Gathering: A Theology and Spirituality of Worship in Free Church Tradition* (London: SCM Press, 2004), 32.

[53] See *An Account of Some Choice Experiences of Elizabeth Gill in his A Sermon Occasioned by the Death of Elizabeth Gill* (London, 1738), 33–44.

[54] *Account of Some Choice Experiences*, 38–9.

[55] *Account of Some Choice Experiences*, 39.

[56] *Practical Divinity* 1.14 (801).

[57] *Practical Divinity* 1.14 (804).

[58] For a study of this sermon, see Michael A.G. Haykin, " 'Strive for Glory with God': Some Reflections by Basil of Caesarea on Humility", *The Gospel Witness*, 82, No.3 (September 2003), 3–6.

ultimately the City of God is a holy community that lives by faith, hope, and self-denying love, and is thus marked by humility and obedience to God.[59] But the major source of Gill's piety was, after Scripture, Puritan divinity. Evidence of this can be found especially in his early treatise on the Song of Songs, but also at various points throughout his voluminous corpus. For example, he himself practised and also recommended to his readers and hearers the Puritan discipline of meditation, which, when it forms a regular part of a believer's walk with God, will, according to Gill, "sweetly ravish our souls, raise our affections, inflame our love, and quicken our faith."[60] As he explained further:

> By meditation a soul feeds on Christ, on his person, blood, and righteousness; and finds a pleasure, a sweetness, and a delight therein;…by it a believing soul feeds upon the gospel, its truths, and promises, and receives much refreshment from thence;…being cleansed in some measure from their former filthiness and uncleanness of their minds, they ascend heavenwards in their thoughts, desires, and affections, which they employ by meditating upon pure, spiritual, and heavenly things;… Meditation fits a man for prayer, and fills him with praise…[61]

Gill's works would have helped, therefore, to nourish elements of a vital piety among Calvinistic Baptists even when other areas of their communal life—such as the free offer of the gospel—were in disarray.

On the Trinity

Moreover, it was this man's theology that was used by God when revival came to the Baptists at the close of the eighteenth century.[62] In a world in which men were abandoning the main contours of biblical orthodoxy—the infallibility of the Word of God, the doctrines of the Trinity, the incarnation and resurrection of Christ—Gill held fast to all of these and enabled the Calvinistic Baptists to weather the intellectual storms of the eighteenth century. And in so doing, his fidelity gave form and shape

---

[59] *City of God* 19.23.

[60] *An Exposition of the Book of Solomon's Song, Commonly called Canticles* (London: Aaron Ward, 1728), 32 (commentary on Song of Songs 1:4).

[61] *Solomon's Song*, 171 (commentary on Song of Songs 4:2).

[62] On this revival, see Michael A.G. Haykin, " 'A Habitation of God, Though the Spirit': John Sutcliff (1752–1814) and the revitalization of the Calvinistic Baptists in the late eighteenth century", *The Baptist Quarterly*, 34 (1991–1992), 304–19 and *idem, One heart and one soul: John Sutcliff of Olney, his friends, and his times* (Darlington, Co. Durham: Evangelical Press, 1994), *passim.*

to the coals of orthodoxy upon which the fire of revival fell later in the century through men like Andrew Fuller.

Take, for example, his robust defence of Trinitarianism. As William C. Placher and Philip Dixon have clearly demonstrated, the growing rationalism of the seventeenth and eighteenth centuries led to a "fading of the trinitarian imagination" and to the doctrine of the Trinity coming under heavy attack.[63] Informed by the Enlightenment's confidence in the "omnicompetence" of human reason, the intellectual *mentalité* of this era either dismissed the doctrine of the Trinity as a philosophical and unbiblical construct of the post-Apostolic Church, and turned to classical Arianism as an alternate perspective, or simply ridiculed it as utterly illogical, and argued for Deism or Socinianism.[64] Gill's *The Doctrine of the Trinity Stated and Vindicated*—first published in 1731 and then reissued in a second edition in 1752—proved to be an effective response to this anti-Trinitarianism. In it he sought to demonstrate that there is "but one God; that there is a plurality in the Godhead; that there are three divine Persons in it; that the Father is God, the Son God, and the Holy Spirit God; that these are distinct in Personality, the same in substance, equal in power and glory."[65] The heart of this treatise was later incorporated into Gill's *Body of Doctrinal Divinity* (1769), which, for most Baptist pastors of that day, was their major reference work of theology.[66]

In Chapter 9, for example, Gill seeks to prove the personhood and the deity of the Holy Spirit. According to Scripture, the Holy Spirit acts as a person when

> he is said to convince of sin, of righteousness, and of judgment [John 16:8]; to comfort the hearts of God's people [John 16:7]; witness their adoption to them [Rom 8:16]; teach them all things [John 14:26]; guide

---

[63] William C. Placher, *The Domestication of Transcendence. How Modern Thinking about God Went Wrong* (Louisville, KY: Westminster John Knox Press, 1996), 164–78; Philip Dixon, *'Nice and Hot Disputes': The Doctrine of the Trinity in the Seventeenth Century* (London/New York: T & T Clark, 2003). The quote is from Dixon, 'Nice and Hot Disputes', 212.

[64] G. L. Bray, "Trinity" in *New Dictionary of Theology*, eds. Sinclair B. Ferguson, David F. Wright, and J. I. Packer (Downers Grove, IL/Leicester: InterVarsity Press, 1988), 694.

[65] *The Doctrine of the Trinity, Stated and Vindicated* (London: Aaron Ward, 1731), 203–4. For a good example of the serious light in which Gill viewed deviation from the doctrine of the Trinity, see Sayer Rudd, *Impartial Reflections on the Minute Which The Author received, from The Ministers of The Calvinistical Baptist Board, by the hands of Mess. Gill and Brine* (London, 1736).

[66] *Doctrinal Divinity* 1.31.

them into all truth [John 16:13]; assist them in their prayers; make intercession for them, according to the will of God [Rom 8:26-7]; and seal them up unto the day of redemption [Eph 4:30].[67]

In his *Body of Doctrinal Divinity* Gill expands on some of these items. For instance, he notes that the Spirit is depicted in the Scriptures not only as "a Spirit of grace and supplication"—so Zechariah 12:10—and "an helper of the infirmities of the saints in prayer, but as making intercession for them, according to the will of God"—thus Romans 8:26-7. Gill continues: "Now as the advocacy and intercession of Christ, prove him to be a Person, and a distinct one from the Father, with whom he intercedes; so the intercession of the Spirit, equally proves his personality, even his distinct personality also."[68] Here Gill clearly departs from his Puritan theological heritage, for the Puritans had argued that Romans 8:26-7 cannot mean the Holy Spirit actually prays for believers, for that would obviate the need for Christ's intercessory work. It would also indicate, John Owen argued, that the Spirit is not fully God, for "all prayer... is the act of a nature inferior unto that which is prayed unto."[69] What the passage must then indicate is a parallel to the thought behind Zechariah 12:10: the Spirit is the creator of all genuine prayer. David Clarkson (1622-86), who assisted John Owen for a number of years, has a detailed analysis of this passage along these lines in a sermon entitled "Faith in Prayer." He speaks for the Puritan tradition when he states:

> It is his function to intercede for us, to pray in us, i.e., to make our prayers. He, as it were, writes our petitions in the heart, we offer them; he indites a good matter, we express it. That prayer which we are to believe will be accepted, is the work of the Holy Ghost; it is his voice, motion, operation, and so his prayer. Therefore when we pray he is said to pray, and our groans are called his, and our design and intent in prayer his meaning... Rom. viii.26, 27...[70]

It appears, though, Gill was never afraid to differ from his Reformed tradition when Scripture led him a different way.

---

[67] *Doctrine of the Trinity*, 192-3.

[68] *Doctrinal Divinity* 1.31 (167-8).

[69] *A Discourse of the Work of the Holy Spirit in Prayer* (1682) in *The Works of John Owen*, ed. William H. Goold (Repr. Edinburgh/Carlisle, PA: The Banner of Truth Trust, 1967), IV, 258.

[70] *The Practical Works of David Clarkson, B.D.* (Edinburgh: James Nichol, 1864), I, 207. See also Owen, *Work of the Holy Spirit in Prayer* (*Works*, IV, 288-290); Thomas Manton, *Several Sermons upon the Eighth Chapter of Romans* (Worthington, PA: Maranatha Publications, n.d.), XII, 226.

Personal properties are also ascribed by the Bible to the Spirit. "He is an intelligent agent," and thus he is said to search the depths of God (1 Corinthians 2:10) and "does all things according to his pleasure and will" (1 Corinthians 12:11).[71] He is the subject of "personal affections": he loves the elect (Romans 15:30)[72] and is grieved by "the sins and unbecoming conversation of the saints" (Ephesians 4:30).[73] Gill also discerns proof of his personhood in his eternal procession from the Father and the Son,[74] his being described by Jesus as "another Comforter" and thus distinct from him,[75] and his being mentioned alongside the Father and the Son in the baptismal formula—"was he a mere power, quality, or attribute, and not a distinct divine person, he would never be put upon an equal foot with the Father and the Son."[76]

Seeking then to set forth the Spirit's deity, Gill argues first from the names given to the Spirit. Gill rightly notes that his being called "Lord" in passages like 2 Corinthains 3:17 bears witness of his deity.[77] It is noteworthy that in this regard he also appeals to 2 Thessalonians 3:5. In Gill's words,

> [the Holy Spirit] is that Lord who is desired to direct the hearts of the saints into the love of God and patient waiting for Christ; where he is manifestly distinguished from God the Father, into whose love, and from the Lord Jesus Christ, into a patient waiting for whom, he is entreated to direct the saints.[78]

This Trinitarian reading of 2 Thessalonians 3:5 ultimately goes back to Basil of Caesarea, who makes the identical argument for the Spirit's deity in his classic defence of the Spirit's deity, *On the Holy Spirit*.[79] Gill also employs this text to prove that the Spirit is the object of prayer, and there-

---

[71] *Doctrine of the Trinity*, 193.

[72] Gill interprets the phrase "the love of the Spirit" as a subjective genitive. The interpretation of John Calvin, though, is to be preferred. He interprets the phrase as the love "by which the saints ought to embrace one another" [Commentary on Romans 15:30, trans. Ross Mackenzie, *The Epistles of Paul The Apostle to the Romans and to the Thessalonians* (Calvin's Commentaries; Grand Rapids, MI: William B. Eerdmans Publ. Co./Carlisle: Paternoster Press, 1960), 317].

[73] *Doctrine of the Trinity*, 194.

[74] Ibid., 194–5.

[75] Ibid., 195–6.

[76] Ibid., 196–7.

[77] Ibid., 197–8.

[78] Ibid., 198–9.

[79] See Basil of Caesarea, *On the Holy Spirit* 21.52.

fore divine.[80] There are also a few passages, Gill notes, where the Spirit is implicitly called God: Acts 5:3–4, where lying to the Spirit is equated with lying to God, and 1 Corinthians 3:16, where the saints are first described as "God's temple" and then Paul states that God's Spirit lives in them, thereby calling the Spirit "God."[81]

Divine attributes are also ascribed to the Spirit, such as eternity ("eternal Spirit," Hebrews 9:14), omnipresence ("Whither shall I go from thy Spirit? And whither shall I flee from thy presence?," Psalm 139:7), omniscience—here Gill has a number of texts—and omnipotence—he formed Christ's "human nature in the womb of the virgin."[82] The Spirit also does what only God can do: he creates, "all the miracles which Christ wrought, he wrought by the Holy Ghost," he regenerates and he sanctifies.[83] Finally, Gill notes that prayer is made to the Spirit (he adduces 2 Thessalonians 3:5 and Revelation 1:4–5)[84] and that Paul swears by the Spirit (Romans 9:1), "which is a solemn act of religious worship."[85]

John Rippon, who followed Gill as pastor, rightly noted in his biographical sketch of his predecessor:

> The Doctor not only watched over his *people*, "with great affection, fidelity, and love;" but he also watched his *pulpit* also. He would not, if he knew it, admit any one to preach for him, who was either cold-hearted to the doctrine of the Trinity; or who *denied* the divine filiation of the Son of God; or who *objected* to conclude his prayers with the usual *doxology* to Father, Son, and Holy Spirit, as three equal Persons in the one Jehovah. Sabellians, Arians, and Socinians, he considered as real enemies of the cross of Christ. They *dared* not ask him to preach, nor *could* he in conscience, permit them to officiate for him. He conceived that, by this uniformity of conduct, he adorned the pastoral office.[86]

He did more than "adorn the pastoral office." Through such written works as his treatise on the Trinity he played a key role in shepherding

---

[80] *Doctrine of the Trinity*, 203.

[81] Ibid., 199.

[82] Ibid., 199–201.

[83] Ibid., 202–3.

[84] Gill rightly understands the mention of the "seven spirits" to be a reference to the Holy Spirit. For modern identification of the "seven Spirits" as a symbolic allusion to the Holy Spirit, see Richard J. Bauckham, "The Role of the Spirit in the Apocalypse", *The Evangelical Quarterly*, 52 (1980), 75–7; G. K. Beale, *The Book of Revelation* (Grand Rapids/Cambridge, U.K.: William B. Eerdmans Publ. Co./Carlisle, Cumbria: Paternoster Press, 1999), 189–90.

[85] *Doctrine of the Trinity*, 203.

[86] Rippon, *Brief Memoir*, 127–8.

the English Calvinistic Baptist community along the pathway of biblical orthodoxy.

Like all heroes, Gill has flaws, as we have seen, but nevertheless D. Martyn Lloyd-Jones, a keen and ardent student of eighteenth-century church history, was surely right when he stated: "Dr. John Gill was a man, not only of great importance in his own century, but a man who is still of great importance to all of us."[87]

---

[87] See Harrison, *Dr. John Gill*, 31.

3

Crawford H. Toy

SOUTHERN BAPTISTS AND THE LESSONS OF CONTROVERSY

Gregory A Wills

The church has never been free of controversy for any substantial period. Sometimes it occurs when persons from the outside attack the church's teachings, practices or leaders. But more commonly controversy originates within. False doctrine emerges within the church and creates division and controversy. False teachers can be quite winsome in promoting their errors and gain substantial numbers of followers within the church.

This should not surprise us. Jesus foretold it. "Beware of false prophets, who come to you in sheep's clothing, but inwardly are ravenous wolves" (Matthew 7:15). Peter warned that "there will be false teachers among you" (2 Peter 2:1). The apostolic churches were afflicted with "false apostles" (2 Corinthians 11:13; Revelation 2:2) and "false brothers" (2 Corinthians 11:26; Galatians 2:4). And when the early church was beset by controversy over false teaching, Tertullian reminded his brethren that this should not shock them, since "it was an apostle that betrayed Christ."[1]

Controversy nevertheless is often unjustified. Not every difference of opinion, disagreement or discourtesy demands controversy. Indeed most do not. Most differences within the church are genuinely minor matters

---

[1] Tertullian, *The Prescriptions against the Heretics*, in S. L. Greenslade, ed., *Early Latin Theology: Selections from Tertullian, Cyprian, Ambrose, and Jerome* (Louisville, KY: Westminster John Knox, 1956; reprint 2006), 33.

that require only humble forbearance, or at most, gentle remonstrance followed by humble forbearance. We ought to abjure a controversial spirit. Delight in controversy can hardly be right. At times churches have entertained and encouraged controversy over relatively inconsequential matters. This is divisiveness and a failure to love and forbear. At times Christians have pursued controversy with a mean spirit or by such crooked means as deceit or slander. This is sin.

And controversy is always tragic. The presence of controversy reveals that error, immorality and divisiveness have already done considerable damage within the church. But the controversy itself also produces injury. And the injury generally extends in surprising ways to areas well beyond the actual field of battle.

Controversy however is all too often necessary. To reject controversy when the church is threatened by error, immorality or divisiveness is far more destructive than the war against it. The toleration of false teaching, immorality and divisiveness can exchange the true gospel for "a different gospel" (Galatians 1:6), can change the Lord's Supper into an observance in which "it is not the Lord's Supper that you eat" (1 Corinthians 11:20) and can bring upon a church the judgment of the Lord, who said to an ancient church, "I have a few things against you: you have some there who hold the teaching of Balaam, … So also you have some who hold the teaching of the Nicolaitans" (Revelation 2:14–15). The cost of controversy is high, but the cost of avoiding controversy is often far higher. Controversy damages the church, but failure to oppose error and sin dooms large portions of it. Better to cure the patient, even though it results in some scars, than to suffer the patient's death in the name of peace.

The absence of controversy therefore does not necessarily indicate a healthy state of affairs. Orthodoxy and righteousness have often suffered great loss without any controversy at all. When error begins to spread, there will be no controversy unless someone stands against it. If we fail to controvert the error and we shun controversy for the sake of unity and peace, not only will we fail to achieve unity and peace, but we will also be in danger of losing the gospel itself.

Christians therefore have a duty to engage in controversy, for it is our duty to controvert error and immorality. And we rightly honor those who have prevailed over heresy, even when it entailed considerable controversy. Athanasius stood "against the world" when he pressed the controversy to defend the full deity of Christ Jesus, and Christians still honor him for it. Southern Baptists rightly honor such leaders as Adrian Rogers, W. A. Criswell, Paige Patterson and Paul Pressler for their defense of the truth of the full inspiration of the Bible, despite the considerable controversy it involved.

Controversy produces a number of benefits to the church. Controversy tests us. When Paul corrected the errors and sins of the church at Corinth, he explained that the factions that existed among them were necessary to test the church: "There must be factions among you in order that those who are genuine among you may be recognized" (1 Corinthians 11:19). Controversy also serves to purify the church. If pursued in accordance with truth and righteousness, it drives from the church the error and unrighteousness that was corrupting it. Controversy additionally serves to elucidate and advance revealed truth. Augustine recognized that heretics, whose false teaching afflicts the church in every generation, nevertheless "train her in wisdom."[2] False teaching compels Christians to search the Scriptures thoroughly in order to ascertain, establish, and defend its true teachings.

Baptists and Controversy

Baptists have usually recognized they have a duty to engage in controversy. Although controversy was painful, they recognized also it ought to result in the establishment of truth. When a St. Louis pastor practiced open communion in 1879, a painful controversy ensued. The discussion served to clarify the denomination's position and to explain the reasons behind it. "The necessity for the controversy is unfortunate," Missouri editor William Ferguson reflected, "but I think good has already come out of the discussion. Baptists here are learning more about what they believe."[3] James P. Boyce, founding president and professor of theology at the Southern Baptist Theological Seminary, regretted controversy, but he recognized that it was sometimes necessary. He reflected that although he was opposed to controversies generally, "controversy is apt to elicit the truth."[4]

Baptists in fact have rarely shied from controversy. Controversy has so characterized them that the history of the Baptists can seem to be a history of controversy. In recent years Southern Baptists have been known especially for controversy, as they prosecuted an extensive public controversy in the 1980s and 1990s to make commitment to inerrancy and orthodox doctrine a condition of denominational service. Baptists can almost seem to have been born to strife.

[2] Augustine, *The City of God against the Pagans*, trans. R. W. Dyson (New York: Cambridge University Press, 1998), 898.
[3] William Ferguson to John A. Broadus, 12 Aug. 1879, box 8, John A. Broadus Papers, SBTS.
[4] James P. Boyce, "Our Correspondents," *Southern Baptist*, 21 Feb. 1849, 582.

Baptists of course have no monopoly on controversy. Most Christian churches, denominations, and institutions have experienced significant controversy repeatedly. History thus reveals that controversy besets all Christian denominations. The source of controversy is human sin—error, immorality, and divisiveness—and all human institutions suffer controversy.

It is unsurprising then that the study of the history of Baptists requires careful study of the controversies that have so often marked their history. And the study of controversy is especially useful to historians. Controversy compels church leaders to express their views on the issues at stake in the conflict. Controversies thus generally provide historians with evidence of the mind of the denomination on an array of issues relating directly to the matters under controversy. As churches, associations and conventions study, report and vote on issues in the controversy, and as editors and other writers publish their views in newspapers, diaries and personal letters, a picture emerges of the various positions of the denomination and their relative strength among them. But controversies generally involve much more than the bare issues in conflict. The conflict requires participants to set the controversy in context, and to show how larger issues may be involved. They thus provide historians with insight into many of their most basic commitments.

The Crawford H. Toy Controversy

The controversy that erupted over the dismissal of Old Testament professor Crawford H. Toy affords a number of lessons concerning the nature and results of religious controversy. Crawford Toy taught Old Testament and Semitic languages at the Southern Baptist Theological Seminary from 1869 to 1879, but the seminary's trustees voted to dismiss him after he embraced liberal views of the inspiration of the Bible. Among the lessons of the Toy controversy are the following: When controversy must be engaged, it is better to pursue it sooner rather than later; controversy brings beneficial results, often extending well beyond the immediate parameters of the conflict; controversy is tragic, and involves damage both from the advance of error and from collateral damage; controversy requires wise and dedicated leadership in order to rescue churches effectively from the advance of false teaching.[5]

---

[5] For more on Toy, see especially Tom J. Nettles, *James Petigru Boyce* (Phillipsburg, NJ: P&R Publishing, 2009), 317–83. See also Gregory A. Wills, *Southern Baptist Theological Seminary, 1859–2009* (New York: Oxford University Press, 2009), 108–49, from which I have adapted portions of this essay; Billy G. Hurt,

Crawford Toy was born in 1836 and was raised in Norfolk, Virginia, where he attended his parents' Baptist church throughout childhood. He professed faith at the age of twelve, but soon doubted the genuineness of his conversion—he did not then join the church and was not baptized. In 1854 Toy came under new conviction during an awakening at the University of Virginia, where Toy had matriculated in 1852. Toy professed his faith before the Charlottesville Baptist Church, which received and baptized him. The church's pastor, John A. Broadus, was Toy's mentor in the faith, and when Broadus preached a missionary sermon in February 1859, Toy responded by giving his life to missionary service. The Foreign Mission Board of the Southern Baptist Convention appointed Toy as a missionary to Japan in 1859 and consented to his request that he take one year of courses at the new Southern Baptist Theological Seminary in Greenville, South Carolina, in order to equip himself to teach accurately Christian truth among "the heathen."[6]

But the secession of the southern states and the ensuing Civil War forced the Foreign Mission Board to stop sending out new missionaries. Since it might be many years before the board could send Toy, he determined to equip himself to teach Semitic languages at Southern Baptist Theological Seminary or at the University of Virginia. Toy served in the southern army, but as soon as the war ended set his sights on studying languages in Germany, and matriculated at the University of Berlin from 1866 to 1868. One year after his return, trustees of the Southern Baptist Theological Seminary elected him as Professor of Old Testament Interpretation and Oriental Languages.

Within two or three years, Toy suffered a crisis of faith. He became dissatisfied with efforts to harmonize the Bible with science. He had long been convinced by geological science that the earth was quite old, but in the past had concluded that the Bible could be harmonized with an old earth. He now concluded that the creation account in Genesis asserted that God created the world in six twenty-four-hour days, and consequently he could no longer harmonize the Bible's account with geology and its fossil record. Toy's crisis deepened when he embraced Darwinism at this

"Crawford Howell Toy: Interpreter of the Old Testament," PhD dissertation, Southern Baptist Theological Seminary, Louisville, KY, 1965; Pope A. Duncan, "Crawford Howell Toy: Heresy at Louisville," in *American Religious Heretics: Formal and Informal Heresy Trials*, ed. George H. Shriver (Nashville, TN: Abingdon Press, 1966), 56–88; Pope A. Duncan, "Crawford Howell Toy (1836–1919)," *Dictionary of Heresy Trial in American Christianity* (Westport, CT: Greenwood Press, 1997), 430–38; Paul R. House, "Crawford Howell Toy and the Weight of Hermeneutics," *Southern Baptist Journal of Theology* 3 (1999): 28–39.

[6] C. H. Toy, "Sketch of My Religious Life," T. T. Eaton Papers, SBTS.

time also, for he could not harmonize any sensible reading of Genesis with evolutionary science. He faced a dilemma of vast consequences. Science taught that the Bible's statements relating to natural history were false. He could not abandon scientific conclusions without abandoning rationality itself. But if the Bible was false, he would have to give it up as a source of reliable truth. "What, then," Toy wondered, "would become of the Bible, its truthfulness, its helpfulness?"[7]

By 1875 Toy discovered a way to retain commitment to the Bible's authority and to evolution. The answer was religious liberalism. Liberalism predated Darwinism. It was developed in the early 1800s to harmonize modern philosophy and the Bible, but it served effectively to harmonize evolution and the Bible also. Its foundational commitment was to a new understanding of the character of the Bible based on a new view of its inspiration. Liberalism taught that the Bible was inspired in its spiritual meaning but not in its historical statements.[8] Toy embraced this view. He concluded that the Bible had many historical errors, but that its spiritual meaning was reliable truth. The errors concerned mere "externals," the "framework" of the Bible. The Bible's inner truth was independent of its outward form.[9]

When Controversy Delays

Throughout the history of the church, false teachers themselves have generally been attractive individuals, and Crawford H. Toy was no exception. His geniality, integrity and passion for truth made him a favorite among students at the seminary. Southern Baptists generally found his manner and speech immensely appealing.

In 1879 the trustees of the Southern Baptist Theological Seminary voted 16–2 to accept Toy's resignation as professor of Old Testament. The trustee action effectively dismissed him from the faculty. It came as a rude shock to the large numbers of Southern Baptists who held him in high esteem. Few realized however that James P. Boyce, the seminary's facul-

---

[7] C. H. Toy, "A Bit of Personal Experience," *Religious Herald*, 1 Apr. 1880, 1.

[8] The best and most thorough account of liberalism in America is Gary Dorrien, *The Making of American Liberal Theology: Imagining Progressive Religion, 1805–1900* (Louisville, KY: Westminster John Knox Press, 2001). Also helpful are William R. Hutchison, *The Modernist Impulse in American Protestantism* (Cambridge: Harvard University Press, 1976); and Kenneth Cauthen, *The Impact of American Religious Liberalism* (New York: Harper and Row, 1962).

[9] C. H. Toy to John L. Johnson, 16 Dec. 1879, John Lipscomb Johnson Papers, Southern Historical Collection, Manuscripts Department, Library of the University of North Carolina, Chapel Hill.

ty chairman, and John A. Broadus, the seminary's founding professor of homiletics, Greek and New Testament, had delayed this event by one or two years in the hope that they could correct Toy's errors. Delay seemed fully justified in the premises. Delay meant however that Toy continued to sow his errors among the seminary's students. In light of subsequent events, Boyce and Broadus would have done well to avoid the delay and acted on the matter a year or two sooner.

It is nevertheless easy to understand why they did not bring the matter to trustees sooner. Toy's views were still developing. When Boyce and Broadus discussed the matter with Toy, he told them that he had not come to definite conclusions. He was investigating matters relating to the findings of historical science, geology and evolution. He assured them his during his investigation he took it as a fundamental principle that the Bible was inspired. He told them that he had abandoned all man-made theories of inspiration, but that he was fully committed to the fact of the Bible's inspiration.

When Boyce first learned that Toy's views seemed to be changing, he urged Toy to consider carefully his position on inspiration. Boyce told Broadus in June 1876 that he wrote Toy and "broke into a gentle remonstrance and earnest entreaty on inspiration."[10] The following summer Boyce apparently asked Toy to explain his views of inspiration. Toy's humble response encourage Boyce to believe that now that the matter was opened freely between them, he and Broadus would be able to discuss the issues with him and perhaps prevent him from going astray and capsizing. Boyce reported his appraisal of the situation to Broadus: "I have a letter from Bro. [C. H.] Toy setting forth his theory, in itself well enough. In so doing, I do not know that he goes beyond the statements of others. The trouble is when he enters, as he did in Virginia, into the details and begins to knock away one part and another. I think however that the ice being broken we shall be able to keep all right. His letter to me was very kind, if anything too flatteringly so. I do hope we can keep all right for I prize Toy more than all. I love him very much. He is a noble fellow and adds greatly to the glory of our institution."[11]

Boyce and Broadus had great confidence in Toy's intelligence and piety. They were anxious concerning the outcome of his investigations, but they also believed that he was not likely to go astray, especially since they now had opportunity to urge upon him arguments suitable to prevent him

[10] James P. Boyce to John A. Broadus, 20 June 1876, quoted in Archibald T. Robertson, *Life and Letters of John A. Broadus* (Philadelphia: American Baptist Publication Society, 1901), 301.

[11] James P. Boyce to John A. Broadus, 22 June 1877, Broadus Papers.

from adopting false views. Toy seemed sincerely humble before their ad-monitions and eager to consider their arguments. He professed that his instincts were conservative and that he held in horror the prospect of fall-ing into error and leading others there by his influence. When Boyce and Broadus asked him to keep his new ideas out of his classroom teaching, he readily agreed. Toy's humble response and cooperative spirit encouraged Boyce and Broadus in their hope that Toy "might ultimately break away from the dominion of destructive theories."[12] The arguments and influence of Boyce and Broadus seemed to have a good effect on Toy.

Toy seems to have encouraged them to view the matter this way, for Toy was not entirely forthcoming. Toy assured Boyce and Broadus that he had complete faith in the fact of the Bible's inspiration, and that he reject-ed only the humanly constructed theories of inspiration. Such expressions suited the commitment of American evangelicals to common sense real-ism and to a Baconian scientific method, which emphasized that a careful observation of facts led reliably to truth. This suggested that the only thing that he had done was to dispense with all theories. His response obscured the fact that he had adopted a new theory of the character of inspiration. He told trustees in his 1879 letter of resignation that he objected to all theories, and submitted himself to the facts of Scripture alone. He claimed that the facts led him to this conclusion: "I believe that the Bible is wholly divine and wholly human. The scripture is the truth of God communicated by him to the human soul, appropriated by it and then given out with free human energy as the sincere, real conviction of the soul."[13] Toy did not admit that this was fundamentally a new theory of inspiration.

Toy's response also obscured the fact that he had dispensed with the traditional interpretation of many passages in the Bible. Indeed, by 1877 he had already completed a massive reinterpretation of the Scriptures. He taught that the Pentateuch was the work of the priests and of Ezra during the time of the exile, even though Moses provided the germ.[14] The Law, Toy told students, represented declension from the pure religion of the proph-ets—the Law "imprisoned" spiritual religion and produced formalism.[15] He taught that Isaiah was the work of three different authors.[16] He taught

[12] John A. Broadus, *Memoir of James Petigru Boyce* (New York: A. C. Arm-strong, 1893), 262.

[13] C. H. Toy, "Full Text of the 'Paper' Offered with the Resignation of Rev. C. H. Toy, D.D., as Professor in the Southern Baptist Theological Seminary," *Baptist Courier*, 27 Nov. 1879, 2.

[14] Hugh C. Smith, Lectures in Old Testament English by C. H. Toy, 130–32, Archives and Special Collections, SBTS.

[15] Smith, Lectures, 1–139, 132 (quote).

[16] Smith, Lectures, 68.

students that the traditional Messianic prophecies in the Psalms, Isaiah, Micah and Joel did not refer to Christ, but that Christ was the fulfillment of all truly spiritual longings, and in this sense only were the passages messianic.[17] Toy told students that a multitude of specific prophecies were not fulfilled and "never came to pass," but they were fulfilled in a general way by Christ, because he represented spiritual redemption.[18] The prophetic promises of Israel's national prosperity and the restoration of the Davidic dynasty were "not realized in fact." Such ideas reflected merely the "outward form," the "framework of the spiritual thought." The spiritual truth was underneath. The "true inward spiritual thought was wonderfully fulfilled in Christ."[19] The "outward framework of spiritual idea" was irrelevant, since the true spiritual thought conveyed within communicated God's plan for spiritual redemption, represented most fully in Christ.[20] This was the "great principle of exegesis," he told the students, to "pierce through the shell, framework" to discover the "real, religious, spiritual idea."[21]

Indeed, even when Toy explained his views of inspiration to the trustees in 1879, he kept the full extent of his reinterpretation of the Bible out of view. Just as he did in the classroom, he explained in a general way that he was fully convinced of the Bible's inspiration, but that this inspiration concerned the religious meaning of the Bible, and did not concern its external framework. The "outward form" of the Bible was subject to mistake but this did not jeopardize its religious message. Moses gave the Hebrews some basic laws which later generations developed into the "Mosaic" law of the Pentateuch. Certain prophecies of Isaiah and Hosea did not occur as they predicted, but these statements were the "mere clothing of their real thought." The Old Testament historical writers composed their histories as Christ composed parables, in order to teach religious truth rather than factual history. But the historical assertions constituted merely the "framework or vehicle of a religious truth." Such defects were of the human element only. The Bible was the outward record of Israel's inner experience of God's care and guidance. Because they experienced God, their writings had religious power to inspire, encourage, and guide. Because they had this religious power, Toy recognized in them "a divine element."[22]

[17] Smith, Lectures, 44, 49–51, 58–60, 67–69, 118–124.
[18] Smith, Lectures, 48, 56–57, 65–68, 108.
[19] Smith, Lectures, 108.
[20] Smith, Lectures, 124.
[21] Smith, Lectures, 125.
[22] C. H. Toy to the Board of Trustees, May 1879, Archives and Special Collections, SBTS; Toy, "Full Text of the 'Paper' Offered with the Resignation of Rev. C. H. Toy, D.D., as Professor in the Southern Baptist Theological Seminary," *Baptist Courier*, 27 Nov. 1879, 2. Also, Toy, "Dr. Toy's Address to the

Toy also minimized the extent of his differences with the old view of inspiration by claiming that his view of inspiration was orthodox and scriptural. He concurred fully, he asserted, with the article on the Scriptures in the *Abstract of Principles*, to which every professor subscribed as a condition of service. Therefore, he concluded, his views of inspiration were "lawful for me to teach as Professor in the Seminary."[23]

So although Boyce had some intimation in 1877 of the extent of Toy's errors, Toy effectively kept the most objectionable aspects of his new views hidden. He had been cautious in exposing his views to others. Toy's sincere assurances, humble spirit, and general circumspection kept the extent of Toy's error largely hidden from Boyce. It was only at the end of 1878 that Boyce and Broadus were able to conclude that Toy's views were sufficiently advanced that the time had come to bring the matter to the trustees for a formal judgment.

Conditions in the seminary had also complicated matters. Boyce was engaged in an extraordinary fight for the seminary's survival. It is difficult to appreciate now the precariousness of the seminary's existence throughout the 1870s and the extent of the sacrificial devotion of Boyce and Broadus in the struggle to secure its survival. Boyce's personal convictions made him determined that the seminary would not tolerate any professor who subverted the Bible's teaching, especially concerning inspiration. He also felt deeply the seminary's responsibility to the Baptists who had given to its endowment with the understanding that the seminary would promote and defend orthodoxy, and that it would not tolerate heterodoxy. To dismiss a professor for erroneous doctrine would reassure past and prospective donors in this regard, but it would also embarrass the seminary, since both its enemies and its false friends would use the episode to cast doubt on the wisdom of the entire enterprise.

Another more important complication deriving from the seminary's precarious affairs was the fact that Boyce was living in Louisville in the period when Toy's views were evolving. Boyce and the trustees concluded in 1872 that the seminary must move from Greenville, South Carolina, and raise a new endowment in a new state, or else it would not survive. They chose Louisville, Kentucky, and Boyce moved there in 1872 in order to raise the new endowment. Until the seminary moved to Louisville five years later, he did not have the personal and frequent interaction with Toy, the faculty and students that he would have enjoyed otherwise. He and Broadus corresponded regularly, but he had to rely heavily on Broadus and

Board of Trustees of the Southern Baptist Theological Seminary," *Religious Herald*, 11 Dec. 1879, 1.

[23] Toy, "Full Text," 2.

the rest of the faculty for the character and direction of the seminary. His presence in Greenville would have altered the course of the controversy. I believe that it is unlikely that he could have changed the direction of Toy's convictions. Toy did not seek counsel from Boyce and Broadus concerning his developing views, though Broadus has long been his religious counselor and though Boyce had shown him much kindness and held him in such high regard. And though Toy received their admonitions and arguments in a genial manner in 1877 and 1878 (and there is good evidence by early 1879 Toy's geniality was outward only—inwardly he came to scorn their efforts to maintain orthodoxy), he had kept the matter largely secret until he was well settled on fundamental questions by around 1876. Had Boyce been in Greenville, he might have pressed matters to a conclusion earlier than 1879.

Another factor that explains why Boyce did not press the matter earlier was that liberalism itself was only just beginning to emerge as a distinct movement in America. It did not initially appear very threatening. To many observers, outspoken liberals initially resembled Unitarianism more than anything else. In the 1870s few evangelicals worried that a new Unitarianism would have wide appeal. But most of the early liberals were not outspoken. They spoke in conservative tones with a decidedly evangelical accent. They did not seek to start a revolution so much as to enlighten and educate their own denominations. So they did not initially appear to threaten any major disruption of evangelical commitments. They seemed to be advocating only a new common sense view of inspiration.

It should be said that liberalism would have spread in the denomination even if Toy had been dismissed years earlier. Toy was the most important early source of liberal ideas among Southern Baptists, but he was not the only source. Even in the late 1870s, there were many sources of liberal ideas. By 1900, most educated Southern Baptists would have confronted liberal ideas personally and many would have embraced liberal ideas.

Beneficial Consequences of the Controversy

Indeed, in God's wise providence, the extent and difficulty of the Toy controversy actually resulted in good for the denomination—a result that could not have been anticipated at the time. The reason is this: If liberal views had not spread so widely in the denomination among Toy's students, there would have been little or no controversy among Southern Baptists at this critical period. The controversy over inspiration became intense because so many pastors had embraced Toy's views. And from this intense conflict emerged a denomination more deeply and decidedly committed to the full inspiration and inerrancy of the Bible.

This beneficial consequence ensued as the founding faculty of the seminary—Boyce, Broadus and Manly—confronted Toy's errors. Their leadership in teaching and urging the traditional plenary, verbal view of inspiration strengthened the denomination's commitment to orthodoxy and worked to limit the spread of liberal views among Southern Baptists.

Of first importance was the fact that the faculty taught verbal inspiration and inerrancy. Broadus for example taught that "the inspiration of the scripture is complete" and the "inspired writers have everywhere told us just what God would have us know."[24] The Scripture writers employed human abilities and judgment "under the aid and control of the Holy Spirit, giving it just as God wished it to be given." Verbal inspiration did not mean mechanical dictation of God's speech in subversion of human freedom and consciousness, but the Holy Spirit controlled the writing concursively with human freedom and consciousness. The inspired writers were "moved by the Holy Ghost" so that they "will not only say what He wishes, but say it as He wishes."[25] The Bible, Broadus said, "is the word of God" and does not merely contain the word of God, so that "wherever it undertakes to teach its teachings are true."[26] In one of his last statements concerning the Bible, his 1892 catechism, Broadus wrote that the Bible's authors "were preserved by the Holy Spirit from error" and that "there is no proof that the inspired writers made any mistake of any kind."[27]

Basil Manly Jr., who had been the seminary's first professor of Old Testament, and who then replaced Toy in 1879, taught the traditional view of inspiration in his Biblical Introduction classes and in 1888 published the *Bible Doctrine of Inspiration*, an able defense of plenary verbal inspiration. Manly rejected Toy's method of extricating the spiritual meaning from the external framework of human speech. The human and the divine elements, Manly held, make one inspired text and meaning. The Bible was "all written by man, all inspired by God." The divine and human elements, Manly said, could be distinguished but they could not be separated. The "twofold authorship extends to every part of scripture, and to the language as well as to the general ideas expressed." Toy and the new theology assumed that the presence of the human element in the Bible necessarily subjected its message to human fallibility. But it was a fallacy, Manly said,

[24] John A. Broadus, *Commentary on the Gospel of Matthew* (Philadelphia, PA: American Baptist Publication Society, 1886), 58.

[25] John A. Broadus, "Quotations in Matthew," ms. notebook, 23, Archives and Special Collections, SBTS.

[26] John A. Broadus, "The Paramount and Permanent Authority of the Bible," *Baptist Courier*, 23 June 1887, 1.

[27] John A. Broadus, *Catechism of Bible Teaching* (Philadelphia: American Baptist Publication Society, 1892).

to hold "that God can not inspire and so use a human being as to keep his message free from error."[28]

Boyce's view was similar. He held that God so inspired the Bible authors that they wrote "exactly" what God wished—"as if he had written every word himself."[29] He believed in the "verbal inspiration" of the Bible's writers, that they "were guided in their very language by Him to whom are 'known all His works from the beginning of the world.'"[30]

Boyce and Broadus left a lasting mark also by establishing belief in plenary inspiration and inerrancy a condition of denominational service, to the extent of their role in the matter. They first made sure that all candidates for teaching positions at the seminary were sound on the doctrine of inspiration as well as on other fundamental points. They also ascertained candidates' views on inspiration before agreeing to recommend them to any position of responsibility among Southern Baptists.

Through the seminary's confession of faith, the *Abstract of Principles*, and through their determined opposition to the new view of inspiration, and through their forthright teaching and writing, they established a standard of orthodoxy in the denomination that has endured to the present.

Southern Baptists responded positively to their arguments on inspiration and respected their conviction that those who embraced the liberal view of inspiration were disqualified from positions of denominational service and trust. Their efforts effectively hindered the further spread of liberalism in the denomination. As a result, many liberals left the denomination. Others, warned by the example of Toy and instructed by the response of the faculty, were dissuaded from following his teaching.

Among this last group, young preacher J. O. Lowry, for example, returned to a more conservative position after Broadus's predictions about Toy's naturalistic trajectory started to become reality. Toy's participation in a Unitarian ministers' institute in 1881 caused Lowry to retract his statement of "moral and intellectual sympathy" with Toy.[31] Lowry recoiled before the practical consequences of Toy's views: "Dr. Toy's views and mine

[28] See. Jerome R. Baer, Notebook for Biblical Introduction 1879–80, Archives and Special Collections, SBTS; Basil Manly Jr., *The Bible Doctrine of Inspiration Explained and Vindicated* (New York: A. C. Armstrong and Son, 1888), 29, 90, 30.

[29] James P. Boyce, *A Brief Catechism of Bible Doctrine* (Greenville, SC: Sunday School Board of the Southern Baptist Convention, 1864), 1.

[30] James P. Boyce, Three Changes in Theological Institutions (Greenville, SC: C. J. Elford's Press, 1856), 27.

[31] J. O. Lowry to John A. Broadus, 14 Sept. 1881, 4 Oct. 1881, 14 Oct. 1881, box 9, Broadus Papers.

part company now... because of the practical destructiveness, the grief to which they tend."[32]

Others followed a similar trajectory. J. Hartwell Edwards had sympathized with Toy's views, but he assured Broadus that Toy's "recent writings have occasioned a reaction... in my own mind."[33] George B. Eager, who in 1900 would join the faculty of the seminary, rejected the traditional view of inspiration under Toy's influence, but he likewise grew alarmed at Toy's deliverances: "I came to see how far he was going and drew back amazed and startled."[34] J. A. Chambliss similarly sympathized with Toy's rejection of the traditional view but rejected what he called Toy's speculative opinions: "He is in his speculative opinions entirely out of harmony with Jesus and Paul."[35]

The most recognizable representative of this group however is Lottie Moon. In 1879, around the time of his dismissal, Crawford Toy and Lottie Moon began exchanging a series of letters. They were old friends. Toy had served as a professor at the Albemarle Female Institute, a Baptist college for women, while Lottie Moon was a student there in the 1850s. She impressed him with her intelligence and skill in languages. Her sense of humor and indomitable spirit were likewise impressive.

Lottie Moon's first biographer, Una Roberts Lawrence, relying on the reminiscences of a friend of the Moon family, wrote that in the summer of 1861 Toy traveled to the Moon estate, proposed marriage to Lottie Moon, and departed unsuccessful.[36] It is quite possible that Toy visited the Moon family in order to court Lottie at that time. But it is more likely either that this was a different man, or that the dates have been confused. Toy's prospects for supporting a family were entirely uncertain in the summer of 1861. In 1859, the Southern Baptist Convention's Foreign Mission Board appointed Toy as a missionary to Japan, and permitted Toy to delay his departure by one year to study at the Southern Baptist Theological Seminary, then located in Greenville, South Carolina. In 1860 Toy courted Mary Mauldin, a young Baptist woman in Greenville, and proposed marriage. Her mother opposed the match, apparently because of the distance and

[32] J. O. Lowry to John A. Broadus, 29 Oct. 1881, box 9, Broadus Papers.

[33] J. Hartwell Edwards to John A. Broadus, 20 Mar. 1883, box 9, Broadus Papers.

[34] Eager to Broadus, 31 Dec. 1883, Broadus Papers.

[35] Chambliss to Broadus, 10 Jan. 1884, Broadus Papers.

[36] Una Roberts Lawrence, *Lottie Moon* (Nashville: Sunday School Board of the Southern Baptist Convention, 1927), 49–51. Lawrence does not name him, but she later identifies him as Toy on 91–93.

dangers of missionary life, and she finally refused Toy's proposal around January 1861. As the South began agitating for secession in late 1860, the mission board stopped sending out new missionaries and kept Toy at home.[37] Toy taught Greek at Richmond College in the spring of 1861 and then joined the Confederate army.

Whether or not Toy proposed in 1861, he renewed the relationship in 1879. Lottie Moon was deeply committed to missions and courting her apparently led him to consider missionary service. When seminary trustees dismissed Toy in May of 1879, he turned his attention his future sphere of labor. Toy apparently did explore the possibility of becoming a missionary and his contemporary conversations with the mission board's executive secretary, H. A. Tupper, likely served this end.

There was no reason for Toy to think that the board would not appoint him. Toy believed that his views of inspiration were strictly orthodox, and that they strengthened orthodoxy rather than weakened it. The board in fact appointed two of Toy's former students in 1880, despite the fact that they held his views of inspiration. When Boyce and other leaders challenged the board to consider whether they should appoint men with such views of inspiration, the board investigated the views of inspiration of the two men, and rescinded their appointment. But in 1879, Toy probably had complete confidence that he could serve as a missionary without objection. Toy's friends in Virginia encouraged him that he would be perfectly acceptable to Virginia Baptists, who would be expected to raise the money for Toy's support.

It is unclear how seriously Toy may have considered becoming a missionary in 1879. It is clear that his letters to Lottie Moon represented a renewed courtship. Thus he may indeed have considered joining her in China and taking up missionary work as her husband, restarting the missionary career he had abandoned twenty years earlier. Toy's election to the faculty at Harvard University in 1881 however led in him a different direction—he would teach Hebrew in Cambridge rather the gospel in the Orient. Toy continued the courtship however and apparently proposed marriage about the time of his election at Harvard. In 1881 problems were mounting at the Southern Baptist mission in north China as missionary personnel dwindled. At the annual meeting of mission, the other missionaries asked Lottie Moon to carry many additional responsibilities, since she was the only one remaining who could do it. She initially refused and resolutely told them that she had other plans: She planned to leave China and "take

---

[37] See Toy to John A. Broadus, 12 Sept. 1860, box 1, Broadus Papers, SBTS; Toy to Broadus, 13 Oct. 1860, ibid.; Toy to Broadus, 31 Jan. 1861, ibid.

the professor of Hebrew's chair at Harvard University in connection with Dr. Toy," by which she meant that she planned to marry him.[38]

The other missionaries were concerned for the future of the mission if Lottie Moon resigned, but they were also anxious for her on account her intention to marry a man whose religious views were likely to prove objectionable from her own point of view. They asked her to take more time to consider her course, and apparently urged her to study his religious views in particular. Although little evidence survives, it appears that she studied the matter and decided against Toy's views of inspiration. She did not marry and remained in China.[39] Had she married Toy, the history of Southern Baptist missions would be substantially different. Her example of sacrificial and zealous service to extend the reach of the gospel profoundly shaped Southern Baptists commitment to and understanding of the church's missionary task. And there would have been no Lottie Moon Christmas Offering for missions. The result, almost certainly, would have been a greatly diminished commitment to foreign missions on the part of Southern Baptists.

The Destructiveness of Controversy

The Toy controversy had destructive effects, resulting in no little injury and grief. Toy himself drifted first into Unitarianism and then into the practical agnosticism of William James's philosophical pragmatism. A significant number of young preachers embraced Toy's teachings with disastrous results.

Boyce and Broadus tried to win Toy's sympathizers to an orthodox view of inspiration. To their dismay, in a number of instances they failed, as in the case of David G. Lyon, a promising seminary student concerning whom Broadus and Toy both took an interest. Once Toy resigned, Broadus labored to prevent Lyon from following in Toy's steps. Lyon was an exceptional student who excelled especially in Greek and Hebrew. Broadus hoped that Lyon would teach in a Southern Baptist school and recruited him as a tutor in the seminary. Lyon aspired to study in Germany and in the weeks after Toy's resignation sought the advice of his two mentors. Toy advised him to go in order to gain advantage of the best scholarship. Broadus, who generally advocated study in Germany for the sake of scholarship, advised Lyon however to stay at the seminary because if he left at that time to go to Germany, it would embarrass the seminary, it would harm his

---

[38] The best account of this is in Catherine B. Allen, *The New Lottie Moon Story* (Nashville, TN: Broadman Press, 1980), 138.

[39] Ibid., 139. See also Lawrence, *Lottie Moon*, 91–96.

reputation and it would possibly injure his faith.[40] Broadus sensed Lyon's inclination to follow Toy's errors and hoped that by inviting him to return to the seminary as a tutor, Lyon could be prevented from adopting the new view of inspiration. When Broadus asked him whether his convictions would permit him "to teach, as to inspiration, in accordance with and not contrary to the opinions which prevail among intelligent American Baptists," Lyon answered in Toy's dialect. He said that he held no particular view of inspiration. "In general terms, I can say, that I view the Bible as the inspired Word of God, but in the details of the subject my opinions are not well enough matured for me to write anything definite."[41] The faculty were not satisfied with this indefinite statement and Boyce wrote Lyon for more detailed information.[42] Lyon's reply revealed that he held Toy's views and that settled the question for the faculty.[43] When Broadus wrote him the following year to discover whether he had "grown more conservative," Lyon responded that "I am not more conservative than I was a year ago." He relished the prospect of joining the faculty of Southern Seminary but knew that his views of inspiration precluded that: "You wish a man who can assent to the absolute infallibility of the biblical writers, and that I cannot do."[44] A year later Toy recruited Lyon for Harvard, where he established the Semitic Museum and spent his entire teaching career.[45]

There were other disappointments among seminary graduates. Broadus failed similarly to dissuade George W. Manly, another Toy sympathizer and the son of Basil Manly Jr., from his determination to study in Germany.[46] Lewis J. Huff withdrew from the ministry when he could no longer "preach what I did not believe," and joined George Manly in studies at Leipzig.[47] William J. Alexander took up Toy's defense, embraced Darwinism and utilitarian moral philosophy, and then followed Toy into

[40] Lyon to Broadus, 7 June 1879 and 18 June 1879, box 8, Broadus Papers.

[41] David G. Lyon to John A. Broadus, 22 May 1880, box 9, Broadus Papers.

[42] James P. Boyce to John A. Broadus, 15 July 1880, box 9, Broadus Papers.

[43] Basil Manly Jr. to John A. Broadus, 27 July 1880, box 9, Broadus Papers.

[44] David G. Lyon to John A. Broadus, 28 Mar. 1881, box 9, Broadus Papers.

[45] On Lyon, see "David Gordon Lyon, 1852–1935," *Journal of Biblical Literature* 55 (1936): iii–iv; "David Gordon Lyon, 1852–1936," *Biblica* 17 (1936): 389; David Gordon Lyon biographical card, in Biographical File, David Gordon Lyon, HUA.

[46] See George W. Manly to John A. Broadus, 29 Dec. 1882, box 9, Broadus Papers; Manly to Broadus 18 Jan. 1883, ibid.; Manly to Broadus, 29 Jan. 1883, ibid.

[47] Lewis J. Huff to John A. Broadus, 1 Jan. 1885, box 10, Broadus Papers; Huff to Broadus, 15 Mar. 1885, ibid..

Unitarianism. For this last offense the trustees of the University of South Carolina transferred him from the chair of moral philosophy to English.[48]

These defections grieved Boyce and Broadus. They could no doubt sympathize with Tertullian's reflections preferring persecution to heresy: "Persecution at least makes martyrs, heresy only apostates."[49] Tertullian too recognized that in fact controversy over heresy trained the church in truth, but in every age the defection of promising preachers and humble believers to heresy is tragic.

The Importance of Leadership

The fact that the Southern Baptist Convention did not follow the course of the northern Presbyterians and Northern Baptists was largely due to leadership of Boyce. Boyce's vision at this critical time was clearer even than Broadus's. His vigilance was more determined. Broadus played a critical role in advancing Boyce's vision and vigilance. And final responsibility for the character of the seminary, the selection of faculty and actions to false teachers and foes fell to Boyce.

The case of Abraham Jaeger illustrates the point well. Before the faculty became aware Toy's new views, they nearly appointed Abraham Jaeger to teach regular courses, despite the fact that Jaeger held the liberal view of inspiration. Jaeger was a Rabbi who converted to Christianity. He served for a time as a Southern Baptist home missionary before enrolling at the Southern Baptist Theological Seminary in 1873. Jaeger's knowledge of biblical Hebrew impressed Toy, who soon enlisted him as an assistant in the Hebrew courses. By 1874 Toy was paying Jaeger a salary to assist him in Hebrew instruction, and began soliciting money from wealthy Baptists to pay Jaeger $1000 annually for this work.[50]

In early 1876 professor William Williams became too ill to continue teaching, which required reassigning his departments—church history, systematic theology, pastoral duties, and Latin theology—to the other professors. Boyce was living in Louisville and could not help (Williams was

---

[48] See Gregory A. Wills, *The First Baptist Church of Columbia, South Carolina, 1809–2002* (Brentwood, TN: Baptist History and Heritage Society, 2003), 168–70; Gordon B. Moore to John A. Broadus, 16 Mar. 1888, box 12, Broadus Papers.

[49] Tertullian, *Prescription*, 33.

[50] Seminary Faculty, Joint Faculty Minutes, vol. 1, 27 Oct. 1873; ibid., 30 Jan. 1874; Abraham Jaeger to John A. Broadus, 11 Aug. 1874, box 5, Broadus Papers, SBTS; C. H. Toy to John A. Broadus, 11 Aug. 1874, ibid. Jaeger apparently did not remain a student for long.

already teaching both his own and Boyce's departments). Broadus could see no way to provide for all the classes between himself, Toy and William Whitsitt. He proposed to Boyce that the best solution would be to ask Jaeger to take over one or more departments. Boyce rejected the idea immediately. "I earnestly protest against putting Jaeger in charge of any of these." He had been willing for Jaeger to assist Toy in teaching Hebrew, but he feared the consequences of making him a regular professor. "Do you not feel that his sentiments are not accordant with our abstract of principles upon inspiration if on nothing else?"[51]

Students subsequently petitioned that the seminary appoint Jaeger. Toy supported the idea, and apparently so did Whitsitt. Broadus saw no alternative and apparently consented to the idea. But Boyce was unmoved: "We must be very circumspect as to the position of influence which we give to a man not thoroughly sound. I had rather put an ignorant orthodox man in the chair of a professor than the most gifted of men if unsound. Dr. [E. G.] Robinson could not have done Rochester more harm than he did had he been the veriest ignoramus. And in Jaeger's case his unsoundness comes in the most serious direction for scholarship to dread, that of inspiration." Boyce regretted opposing the will of the rest of the faculty, "but even if you are unanimous about it you must pardon me for saying, I must say 'nay.'"[52] Without Boyce's determination to oppose to Jaeger's candidacy, alone if necessary, the seminary would have had two of its five professors holding definitely the liberal view of inspiration.

Boyce exercised similar leadership in the case of two others who embraced Toy's view of inspiration. In 1881, the Southern Baptist Convention's Foreign Mission Board appointed John Stout and T. P. Bell to replenish the missionary forces in China, where personnel losses threatened serious losses in the Southern Baptist missionary effort. Boyce discovered their views and felt that it was his duty to advise the board against their appointment. He participated in the examination of another missionary candidate W. S. Walker in Columbus, Mississippi in May 1881. When Walker said he had no theory of inspiration, Boyce pressed him on the fundamental issue, the results of inspiration and the question of inerrancy: "But Brother Walker, do you think there are any mistakes in the Bible?" Walker replied, "Certainly not." But T. P. Bell, who was present at the examination and already under appointment by the board, told Boyce

---

[51] John A. Broadus to James P. Boyce, 9 Feb. 1876, Boyce Papers, SBTS; James P. Boyce to John A. Broadus, 11 Feb. 1876, Broadus Papers.

[52] James P. Boyce to John A. Broadus, 6 Dec. 1876, box 7, Broadus Papers. Boyce predicted in this letter that Jaeger would leave the Baptists to join the Episcopalians, a prediction which was soon fulfilled.

afterward that he could not answer as Walker had, and apparently implicated Stout in the same opinion.[53] Boyce wrote the board and urged them to investigate. Broadus told his wife that it was Boyce who "first insisted that the board should look into it," though she still wondered whether her husband had himself been the one.[54] When the mission board trustees discussed the matter in June 1881, secretary Tupper "read a letter from Dr. J. P. Boyce and also letters from Brothers John Stout and T. P. Bell with reference to their views on the inspiration of the scriptures."[55] Boyce's letter apparently exposed their views of inspiration and explained the reasons that their views were objectionable. Afterward Tupper asked Broadus to recruit two students to replace Stout and Bell, and Broadus found two with sounder theology.[56] Many Southern Baptists rightly believed that Boyce was the leading voice among those who complained.[57]

Had not Boyce and a few others raised these inconvenient objections, two very capable preachers would have had opportunity to spread their liberal views of the Bible with the endorsement of the Southern Baptist Convention by virtue of their missionary appointment. They would have done much good, no doubt, but they would also have sowed the seeds of the destruction of the faith through the new view of inspiration and would have done so all the more effectively on account their abilities and goodness. They would have taught it to Chinese pastors and established it as an acceptable and orthodox belief at the very foundation of Chinese Christianity in their region of labor. It is likely also they would have spread their views among the missionaries at this early stage. It is difficult to estimate how far the damage may have spread.

[53] James P. Boyce to Matthew T. Yates, 13 July 1881, Letterpress Book 7, June 1881–Nov. 1881, Archives and Special Collections, SBTS.

[54] Charlotte Broadus to John A. Broadus, 21 July 1881, box 9, Broadus Papers.

[55] Minutes of the Foreign Mission Board of the Southern Baptist Convention, 6 June 1881.

[56] The two students who replaced Bell and Stout were Cicero W. Pruitt and William S. Walker. See Cicero W. Pruitt, "Life of Cicero Washington Pruitt, Composed by Himself," 4, box 1, Ida Pruitt Papers, Schlesinger Library, Harvard University; Minutes, Faculty, Southern Baptist Theological Seminary, 18 Nov. 1881; Minutes, Foreign Mission Board of the Southern Baptist Convention, 19 Nov. 1881.

[57] W. C. Lindsay to John Stout, 27 May 1881, Lide-Coker-Stout Family Papers, South Caroliniana Library, University of South Carolina; George B. Eager to John Stout, 13 Sept. 1881, Lide-Coker-Stout Family Papers, South Caroliniana Library, University of South Carolina. But others besides Boyce raised concerns (see T. P. Bell to John Stout, 28 June 1881, ibid.).

The noble preachers and teachers who stood against the new liberal view of inspiration promoted by Crawford Toy deserve the honor that subsequent generations of Southern Baptists have accorded them. Boyce above all merits our gratitude. His leadership in the Toy controversy, by the grace of God, secured profound and lasting benefit. May our gracious Father raise up such leaders among us in every generation until the day of the Lord's visitation (1 Peter 2:12).

4

Evangelicalism from the Beginning

ENGLISH BAPTISTS OF THE SEVENTEENTH CENTURY

C. Jeffery Robinson, Sr.

Four weeks before his death in the fall of 1889, Henry Holcombe Tucker, Southern Baptist theologian and editor of the *Christian Index* of Georgia, printed on the front page of the *Index* a pithy comment, one he saw as "full of truth," culled from the *Southwestern Presbyterian* newspaper: "The greatest fact in evangelical Christianity to-day is found in the principles which we hold in common, and which unite us; the next greatest is found in the principles which establish our individuality and keep us separate." Tucker appended a note of his own, affirming his solidarity with the Presbyterian periodical's sentiment: "We have seldom seen so much thought in few words as in [this] epigrammatic sentence."[1]

During a previous tenure as editor of the *Index*, Tucker published an article from the *Associate Reformed Presbyterian* weekly under the headline "Old Truths," in an attempt to isolate core doctrines that define evangelical truth. The author of the piece argued concisely and forcefully that historic, orthodox Christianity has an irreducible, objective center that, if removed, eviscerates "the faith once for all delivered to the saints" of its vital organs: "There are certain truths which evangelical Christians of all ages and nations have professed. These, it may be, are few, but they are fundamental. They are such as a belief in the Creation, the Fall, Inspiration of Scripture, the Divinity of Christ, the Atonement, Justification, the Resurrection and

---

[1] Henry Holcombe Tucker, *The Christian Index*, 8 August 1889, 1.

Future Judgment. These are the essentials of religious belief."[2] Further, the writer, whom Tucker did not name, called these doctrines "tried truths, constituting as they do the prominent and central features of the various Creeds,"[3] and went on to point out that teachings at the heart of the evangelical faith had been "the object of continuous assault."[4] However, these truths "have stood the intellectual shocks of the centuries and today they have the lodgement as strong and deep and secure in the Christian heart as in the days of the Apostles."[5] For the Presbyterian author, as for the editor of the Baptist *Index* who chose to adorn his newspaper's correspondence page with this article, "these truths have been attested in the deepest feelings of those who have passed from death to life and in characteristics that are common to those who differ in everything else. They have formed Christian character and given peculiar uniformity which makes Abraham and Paul and Calvin brethren in moral attributes as well as in profession."[6] Moving from the indicative to the imperative, the article concludes by insisting that the entire body of Christ "bring these old truths to the front, for there is in them a majesty and power which will expel error as light expels darkness" because "they are true, mighty and enduring, the very words of God, which liveth and abideth forever."[7] Tucker appended an affirming comment: "I can hardly do any better a summary of true evangelical religion than this; thus, I will leave the piece with few words so that its force may stand alone."[8] Tucker, a man largely forgotten by twenty-first century Baptists, was one of the brightest stars in the Southern Baptist constellation of the era immediately following the Civil War, a man who counted among his most intimate friends James Petigru Boyce, John Albert Broadus, Patrick Hues Mell and his theological mentor, John Leadley Dagg. Not only was Tucker a Southern Baptist, he was also a self-professed evangelical and assumed that his Southern Baptist brethren fit in the same category as well. Though Tucker and many other Southern Baptists took for granted that to be one was to be the other, Baptists' historical relationship to evangelicalism has been as frequently debated as the very definition of evangelicalism itself. But from their beginnings in 1845, in spite of the presence of such popular movements as Landmarkism within

[2] "Old Truths," *The Christian Index and Southwestern Baptist*, 15 December, 1881, 2.
[3] Ibid.
[4] Ibid.
[5] Ibid.
[6] Ibid.
[7] Ibid.
[8] Ibid.

the denomination, Southern Baptists have largely identified with broader evangelicalism.

It remains so in the twenty-first century. Tom Nettles, along with a majority of modern-day Baptist historians and theologians agree with Tucker: to be a Baptist is to be an evangelical Christian.[9] In the first of his three volume work, *The Baptists*, Nettles proposes a "Coherent–Truth Model" of Baptist identity which stakes the tent of Baptist identity with four main pegs.[10] Nettles argues that Baptists have been typified historically by a commitment to orthodox Christian doctrine, a theologically integrated ecclesiology, confessionalism and evangelicalism.[11] Nettles' definition of Baptist identity encompasses the two main theological camps within Baptist history: Calvinistic, or Particular Baptists, and Arminian, or General Baptists.[12] This chapter will support the argument that Baptists are indeed evangelicals and will seek to show that Baptists have, from their humble beginnings in seventeenth century England, exhibited three attributes that describe evangelicalism: Word-centeredness, Christ-centeredness and Cross-centeredness, a paradigm that describes evangelicals as articulated by Nettles. These traits will be examined later in the chapter using seventeenth century Baptists in England to illustrate the thesis.

First, however, it is important to survey briefly two critical questions at the headwaters of the Baptist-Evangelical confluence and to establish the current debate. The two fundamental questions are: 1) Are Baptists Evangelicals? and 2) What is and Evangelical?

---

[9] This idea is especially prominent in the writings of current Southern Baptist leaders R. Albert Mohler, Jr., Russell D. Moore and David Dockery. Recent SBC presidents such as Johnny Hunt, Frank Paige, James Merritt and others have publicly called the SBC an evangelical denomination and such language has been prevalent in denominational publications and articles published by Baptist Press.

[10] In his book on Baptist Identity, R. Stanton Norman, frames the debate similarly and argues for a definition of Baptists closely akin to that of Nettles. Norman identifies the two differing camps as the "Enlightenment Tradition" and the "Reformation Tradition." Enlightenment Baptists are epistemologically driven by religious experience, while Reformation Baptists are animated by biblical authority. R. Stanton Norman, *More Than Just a Name: Preserving Our Baptist Identity* (Nashville, TN: B&H, 2001). Norman does not deal directly with the relationship of Baptists and evangelicals, but seems to distinguish Baptists as separate from broader evangelicalism.

[11] Tom Nettles, *The Baptists: Key People Involved in Forming a Baptist Identity*, Vol. 1, *Beginnings in Britain* (Ross-Shire, Scotland: 2005), 40–45.

[12] Ibid., 40.

Are Baptists Evangelicals?

The discussion over the precise nature of the relationship between Baptists and evangelicals has evolved in recent years such that three discernable camps have emerged, separated largely along lines of theology and historiography: 1. Theological moderates who deny that Baptists are evangelical largely from an impulse that rejects biblical inerrancy and embraces a doctrinal latitudinarianism; 2. Theological conservatives who deny that Baptists are evangelicals largely on grounds of separatism; 3. Baptist historians and theologians who affirm that Baptists are best understood to exist within the stream of a discernible evangelical tradition.

Baptists are not Evangelical (Theological Moderates)

Glenn Hinson is representative of a vision of Baptist identity that Nettles calls the "Soul-Liberty" party.[13] At its first point of departure from theologically conservative Baptists, the Soul-Liberty temperament rejects the inerrancy of Scripture and labels it an evangelical intrusion into the Baptist camp, a product of Protestant Scholasticism. Soul-Liberty prioritizes religious experience over the systematic expression of doctrinal formulation. In a landmark 1983 study/debate *Are Southern Baptists Evangelicals?*, co-written by Hinson, James Leo Garrett and James E. Tull, Hinson argues that the Baptist way is "that version of Christianity which places the priority on voluntary and uncoerced faith or response to the Word and Act

---

[13] There are many other sources that might be quoted which articulate with significant depth the Soul-Liberty vision of Baptist identity, including: Bill J. Leonard, *Baptist Ways: A History* (Valley Forge, PA: Judson Press, 2003); Fisher Humphries, *The Way We Were: How Southern Baptist Theology has Changed and What it Means to Us All* (New York: McCracken, 1994); William H. Brackney, *A Genetic History of Baptist Thought* (Macon, GA: Mercer, 2004). Interestingly, Brackney employs a "gene pool" methodology in his search of a Baptist identity which leads him to affirm as genuine Baptists a far-ranging assemblage of personages with seemingly divergent theologies from Reformed stalwarts John Bunyan and C.H. Spurgeon to the ultra-liberal Harry Emerson Fosdick and William Newton Clarke along with a number of Black Power and Liberation pastor/ theologians. On page 2, Brackney establishes a seemingly open-ended historiography: "I will also proceed on the hypothesis that any model of Baptist 'theology' worth its salt must begin with a polygenic base.... Implicit in this approach is that assertions of a dominant stream of Baptist theology are inadequate. Attempts to mandate a truncated version of Baptist theological identity are harmful to the very freedom Baptists of all kinds have historically affirmed."

of God over any objective Word and Act of God."[14] To defend his thesis, Hinson calls on the witness of E. Y. Mullins and his doctrine of soul competency. Mullins, Hinson argued, had embraced Friedrich Schleiermacher's emphasis on "feeling" and religious experience. This emerges, Hinson posited further, in Mullins' doctrine of the competency of the soul as the foundational Baptist principle, which, in turn, animated Mullins' rejection of the confessional Princeton theology that had governed the thought of his predecessors at The Southern Baptist Theological Seminary as incarnated in men such as J. P. Boyce and John Albert Broadus.[15] Like Hinson, other Soul-Liberty Baptists locate the Baptist genius in the doctrine of soul competency as expressed by Mullins in his 1908 work *The Axioms of Religion*. Mullins asserted that "the competency of the soul under God in religion is both exclusive and inclusive in a measure which sets forth the distinctive contribution of Baptists to the religious thought of the race."[16] Further, Mullins argued that the idea of soul competency demands that religion is a personal matter between the soul and God.[17] While Nettles and others have responded that Mullins was not seeking to establish an atomistic view of Baptist identity with this doctrine, moderate Baptists have adopted it as the fundamental axiom that defines Baptists, thus Nettles' label "Soul-Liberty."[18] In summarizing Mullins' teaching, moderate Baptist historian Bill J. Leonard asserted, "Subjective religious experience,

[14] Quoted in Nettles, *Beginnings in Britain*, 29.

[15] Ibid.

[16] E. Y. Mullins, *The Axioms of Religion*, comp. R. Albert Mohler; ed. Timothy George and Denise George (Nashville, TN: Broadman & Holman, 1997), 65.

[17] Ibid. It should be pointed out that Coherent-Truth Baptists also affirm the doctrine of soul competency (the biblical truth that each person will stand before God to give a personal account of their lives), but do not view it as a definitive Baptist distinctive.

[18] Nettles argues that with the doctrine of soul competency Mullins "intended to show that Roman Catholicism, built on the 'incompetency of the soul in dealing with God,' must give way to the Baptist vision as surely as dead leaves are pushed off a tree by the returning sap of spring-time." Nettles, *Beginnings in Britain*, 24. Indeed, Mullins himself admitted as much and viewed Baptists as being first and foremost in broad doctrinal agreement with other evangelical Christians throughout the ages: "Of course this means a competency under God, not a competency in the sense of human self-sufficiency. There is no reference here to the question of sin and human ability in the moral and theological sense, nor in the sense of independence of the Scriptures. I am not here stating the Baptist creed. On many vital matters of doctrine, such as the atonement, the person of Christ, and others, Baptists are in substantial agreement with the evangelical world in general. It is the historical significance of Baptists I am stating, not a Baptist creed." Mullins, *The Axioms of Religion*, 64–65.

according to Mullins, was the foundation of the faith."[19] For many in the
Soul Liberty party, Baptists are not evangelicals, but instead comprise a
unique conglomeration of Christians who gather around a libertarian view
of personal autonomy and individual religious experience.

Baptists are not Evangelicals (Conservative Separatism)

A more nuanced Baptist rejection of the evangelical label has arisen
in recent years among a minority of Southern Baptist conservatives, as
expressed most notably through the writings of Malcolm Yarnell, associate professor of systematic theology at Southwestern Baptist Theological
Seminary. Yarnell and others see Baptists as more narrowly defined in terms
of theology, ecclesiology and polity, while they argue that evangelicalism
continues to proliferate and broaden in a search for identity.[20] Yarnell, who
traces Baptist origins to the sixteenth century Swiss Anabaptists, sees this
as particularly exemplified in the doctrinal latitude that is found within the
membership of the Evangelical Theological Society.[21] In his 2007 work,
The Formation of Christian Doctrine, Yarnell makes a full case for his assertion that Baptists and others in the free church/believer's church tradition,
should be defined separately from evangelicalism as it is understood in the
present historiography.[22] Though it argues against the thesis of the present
author, the position which Yarnell represents is conservative in its doctrinal
orientation contra the Soul-Liberty party.

---

[19] Bill J. Leonard, *God's Last & Only Hope: The Fragmentation of the Southern
Baptist Convention* (Grand Rapids, MI: Eerdmans, 1990), 50.

[20] Similarly, D. G. Hart, in his provocative work *Deconstructing Evangelicalism: Conservative Protestantism in the Age of Billy Graham* (Grand Rapids, MI:
Baker, 2001) argues that evangelicalism is no longer a helpful term. He asserts
fundamentally that evangelicalism did not exist in nineteenth-century America,
but is rather an abstract construction that arose out of fundamentalism in the
1940s and is applied by scholars of the late 1900s to earlier generations. Elsewhere, Hart defines evangelicalism socially around anti-formalism and theologically around anti-traditionalism and the experience of the new birth (see D. G.
Hart, ed., Reckoning with the Past: Historical Essays on American Evangelicalism from the Institute for the Study of American Evangelicals [Grand Rapids,
MI: Baker, 1995], 18–19).

[21] Malcolm B. Yarnell III, "Are Southern Baptists Evangelicals? A Second
Decadal Reassessment," *Ecclesiology* 2 (2006), 195–206.

[22] Malcolm B. Yarnell III, *The Formation of Christian Doctrine* (Nashville,
TN: B&H Academic, 2007).

Baptists are Evangelical

Contrary to those above mentioned, James Leo Garrett asserts that Baptists do indeed exist within the main stream of historic evangelical Christianity, but should be properly categorized as "denominational evangelicals."[23] That is, Southern Baptists possess a distinguishing set of their own ecclesiological doctrines such as believer's baptism by immersion and regenerate church membership, but also "belong to and exemplify the great heritage… which is evangelicalism."[24] Garrett defines evangelicalism in terms of five doctrinal and practical emphases: "Scriptural authority, Christocentric doctrine, gospel proclamation, experience of grace, and evangelistic endeavor."[25] Thus defined, Baptists are indeed evangelicals. As Garrett, Nettles and other historical theologians have asserted, the majority of Baptists, since their birth out of English separatism in the early seventeenth century, have stood in this line alongside evangelicals of all denominations.[26]

What is an Evangelical? (The Bebbington Quadrilateral)

British historian David W. Bebbington, a Baptist, has offered what Mark Noll calls "the most serviceable definition" for Protestants who consider themselves evangelical.[27] Many scholars have found Bebbington's

---

[23] On the tenth anniversary of the publication of the Garrett/Hinson volume, a number of Southern Baptists considered the question afresh in a volume edited by David S. Dockery, *Southern Baptists & Evangelicals: The Conversation Continues* (Nashville, TN: Broadman & Holman, 1993). A diversity of essayists from within the SBC and in the broader evangelical world demonstrated significant disagreement over whether or not Southern Baptists are synonymous with evangelical Christianity. More recently, Dockery edited a book with a more suggestive subtitle: *Southern Baptist Identity: An Evangelical Denomination Faces the Future* (Wheaton, IL: Crossway, 2009). In his opening essay, "Southern Baptists in the Twenty-First Century," Dockery admits that Southern Baptists, due largely to factors related to Southern sectionalism, have operated apart from other Christian denominations, but do in fact comprise "the largest evangelical denomination in the country."

[24] James Leo Garrett, Jr., E. Glenn Hinson, and James E. Tull, *Are Southern Baptists "Evangelicals?"* (Macon, GA: Mercer, 1983), 126.

[25] Ibid. Tull, who more or less served as a moderator in the "biblio debate," took a mediating position, preferring to leave the definitions opened-ended.

[26] Nettles, *Beginnings in Britain*, 41.

[27] Mark A. Noll, *America's God: From Jonathan Edwards to Abraham Lincoln* (New York: Oxford University, 2002), 5.

"Evangelical Quadrilateral" compelling as a descriptor of the attributes of evangelicalism. Bebbington's four attributes of evangelicalism include: biblicism, or the reliance on the Bible as ultimate religious authority; conversionism, or an emphasis on the necessity of the new birth; activism, or energetic, individualistic engagement in personal and social duties; and crucicentrism, or a focus on Christ's redeeming work as the heart of true religion.[28] Bebbington's fundamental premise asserts that evangelicalism is a phenomenon that traces its genesis to the early decades of the eighteenth century, a movement birthed through factors tied to the Enlightenment.[29] While Michael A.G. Haykin and other evangelical scholars agree that evangelicalism may be linked to some of the more positive aspects of the Enlightenment, most root evangelicalism in the Protestant Reformation with the recovery of a Word-centered ministry over against the sacerdotalism of the Roman Catholic Church.[30] The remainder of this chapter will present English Baptists of the sixteenth century as further evidence that the major characteristics of evangelicalism existed before the early 1700s. The writer agrees generally with Bebbington's four attributes that characterize evangelicalism, but, along with Haykin, Nettles and others, locates the beginning of evangelical Christianity in the Reformation.

Nettles and Evangelicalism: Baptists are Evangelicals

In a series of posts published in the fall of 2008 on Gospel Blog, Nettles set forth his own defining traits of evangelicalism. Nettles' three bonds that tie evangelicals together are similar to those of Bebbington and Garrett. He concludes that evangelicals are: Word-centered, Christ-centered and Cross-centered.[31] Nettles' criteria for defining evangelicals is similar to others and will serve as a framework to illustrate this chapter's contention that Baptists were evangelical from their birth in seventeenth century England. The categories Dr. Nettles employs to describe evangelicals will be used to examine seventeenth century Baptists in England to show that Baptists were in fact evangelical from the beginning, albeit what James

[28] David W. Bebbington, *Evangelicalism in Modern Britain: A History From the 1730s to the 1980s* (London: Unwin Hyman, 1989), 2–17.

[29] Ibid.

[30] For a detailed critique of the Bebbington thesis, see Michael A.G. Haykin and Kenneth J. Stewart eds., *The Advent of Evangelicalism: Exploring Historical Continuities* (Nashville, TN: B&H, 2009).

[31] These brief essays are available in five parts and may be accessed at http://gospeldriven.wordpress.com/category/tom-nettles/.

Leo Garrett calls "denominational evangelicals," a slight nuance that rings clear in Baptists' application of the authority of Scripture.

Baptists and the Bible: Evangelical Baptists are Word-centric

In their landmark book *Baptists and the Bible*, Nettles and L. Rush Bush provide the rationale for their work with a quote from historian Robert G. Torbet on the first page, showing that Baptists have always been, if anything, "a people of the book." For Baptists and other evangelicals, the Reformation principle of sola Scriptura is central.

> Baptists, to a greater degree than any other group, have strengthened the protest of evangelical Protestantism against traditionalism. This they have done by their constant witness to the supremacy of the Scriptures as the all-sufficient and sole norm for faith and practice in the Christian life.... It may be said without hesitancy that Baptists generally have quite universally placed their uncompromising faith in the authenticity of the Sacred writings through divine inspiration of the writers by the Holy Spirit, and have stressed the necessity of Bible reading by every Christian for himself.[32]

Similarly, John Quincy Adams (1825–1881) argued that Baptists, because of their consistent and clear-headed application of *sola Scriptura*, carried the work of the Reformation to its purest and fullest extent. Adams viewed Baptists as what Garrett called "denominational evangelicals" who were distinguished by a purer fidelity to Scripture than other denominations in the area of ecclesiology, a reality that is particularly regnant in Baptists' insistence on believer's baptism by immersion, regenerate church membership and liberty of conscience.[33]

Baptists were born out of an adherence to the Bible as the inspired, inerrant and authoritative word of God. Thomas Helwys, father of the General Baptists, in 1611 wrote a confession of faith to defend the validity of his baptism at the hands of John Smyth and to clarify has position on original sin and the will.[34] Helwys' confession, like the numerous Baptist statements of faith that followed it, established Scripture as the unique source of Christian epistemology in Article 23.

---

[32] Quoted in L. Russ Bush and Tom J. Nettles, *Baptists and the Bible* (Nashville, TN: B&H, 1999), 1.

[33] John Quincy Adams, *Baptists Thorough Reformers* (New York: Backus, 1980), 52–54.

[34] William L. Lumpkin, *Baptist Confessions of Faith* (Valley Forge, PA: Judson Press, 1969), 114–115.

That the scriptures off the Old and New Testament are written for our instruction, 2 Tim 3.16 & that wee ought to search them for they testifie to CHRIST, Io. 5.39. And therefore to bee used withall reverence, as conteyning the Holie Word off GOD, which onelie is our direction in al thinges whatsoever.[35]

British Baptist comprehension of the doctrine of Scripture and their application of its regulative function grew as the decades of the seventeenth century passed. By the mid-1700s, English Baptists had grown in number sufficient to upset the established religious order and brought upon themselves charges of heresy and sinful living, namely, accusations of Pelagianism and anarchy.[36] Why? Both Particular and General Baptists rejected infant baptism in favor of believer's baptism, believing that Scripture supported believer's baptism by immersion and that, by necessary inference from that doctrine, the church should be composed of believers only. Both Baptist groups also dissented from the state church because they viewed Scripture, and not the magistrate, to possess ultimate authority in the saving and sanctification of sinners. Gospel preaching, and not governmental coercion, is the means by which God converts His people. Thus, leaders in the established Church of England viewed Baptists as dangerous heretics and uneducated rubes who held to heterodox doctrines. These charges drip with venom in the pamphlets that rained down upon Baptists from the pens of ministers in the established church. One of the most strident Baptist opponents was Daniel Featley, who wrote the inauspiciously titled *The Dippers Dip't or the Anabaptists duck'd and plung'd over head and ears.*

In answer of such charges and to demonstrate evangelical solidarity, Particular Baptists wrote two well-known confessions, the *First London Confession of 1644* and the *Second London Confession of 1689.*[37] Both established the priority and authority of Scripture. Both grounded Baptist distinctives of believer's baptism by immersion and the necessity of a regenerate church in Scripture. But both also sought to demonstrate solidarity with other evangelicals in matters central to the Gospel. The *Second London Confession*, the most expansive expression of theology ever penned

---

[35] Ibid., 122.

[36] Ibid., 144–145.

[37] Seventeenth century Baptists also proved vigorous in the pamphlet warfare, answering opponents' accusations with works such as that of Particular Baptist pastor John Spilsbury. His 1643 work *A Treatise Concerning the Lawfull Subject of Baptisme* replied to objections by paedobaptists against the new practice of believer's baptism by immersion. Similarly, Hanserd Knollys defended Particular Baptists in the 1640s in *A Moderate Answer unto Dr. Bastwicks Book, called Independency Not God's Ordinance.* There were many others.

by Baptists, was taken directly from the *Westminster Confession of Faith*, with the articles on ecclesiology altered to reflect distinctive Baptist beliefs. In other evangelical doctrines, particularly those centering around the gospel such as the Trinity, effectual calling, justification by faith, the person and work of Christ, the 1689 confession closely resembled the *Westminster Confession*. And like its Presbyterian cousin, the *Second London Confession* began with an article on Scripture, one that bespeaks English Particular Baptists' belief in the inerrancy, inspiration and authority of the Bible.

> The Holy Scripture is the only sufficient, certain, and infallible rule of all saving Knowledge, Faith, and Obedience; Although the light of Nature, and the works of Creation and Providence do so far manifest the goodness, wisdom and power of God, as to leave men inexcusable; yet are they not sufficient to give that knowledge of God and His will, which is necessary unto Salvation. Therefore it pleased the Lord at sundry times, and in divers manners, to reveal himself, and to declare that His will unto his Church; and afterward for the better preserving, and propagating of the Truth, and for the more sure Establishment and Comfort of the Church against the corruption of the flesh, and the malice of Satan, and of the World, to commit the same wholly unto writing; which maketh the Holy Scriptures to be most necessary, those former ways of Gods, revealing his will unto his people being now ceased.[38]

Baptists, like the fellow evangelicals, were regulated in doctrine, worship, polity and the Christian life by the Bible. In application, however, Baptists also proved to be deeply denominational, thus the term "evangelical Baptists," because their commitment to the principle of *sola Scriptura* led them to dissent from the established church. And this dissent, in turn, led the state church to persecute Baptists and other separatists.

Suffering for the Sake of Scripture

The ascension of Charles II to the throne and the restoration of the monarchy in 1660 ended two-plus decades of calm and relative prosperity for nonconformists in England, prosperity that came in spite of the pamphlet wars waged against Baptists. On the heels of the Restoration of the monarchy, Parliament enacted the Clarendon Code in attempt to stamp out separatism and enforce loyalty to the Church of England. The four acts of anti-Puritan legislation included the Corporation Act of 1661 which required a municipal office holder to swear allegiance to the church,

---

[38] Lumpkin, *Baptist Confessions of Faith.*, 248–249.

the Act of Uniformity of 1662, which made compulsory the use of the Book of Common Prayer, the Conventicle Act of 1664, which prohibited religious assemblies of more than five people, except under the auspices of the state church, and the Five Mile Act of 1665, which prohibited clergymen from coming within five miles of a parish from which they had been banished. On August 24, 1662, a day now known as "Black Bartholomew's Day," more than 2000 pastors, including many Baptists, refused to comply with the Act of Uniformity and were forcibly and officially ejected from dissenting pulpits. The restoration of the crown meant perilous times for Baptists and their non-conforming brethren.[39]

Baptists did not conform largely, because of their view of Scripture: the preaching of the Word is the means by which God makes converts, not government coercion. The domain of the church is wielding the sword of the Spirit, while the government is to yield the sword of steel. John Bunyan (1628–88) was one who suffered under the lash of official persecution and his story is well-known. Bunyan wrote most of *The Pilgrim's Progress* during the twelve years he was imprisoned in Bedford. Dozens of other, lesser-known Baptist ministers who refused to conform because their consciences were captive to Scripture also suffered, including Thomas Hardcastle (1636–78) and Abraham Cheare (1626–1668), both of whom died in prison.[40]

When it came to an affirmation of the divine inspiration, inerrancy and authority of Scripture, Baptists were and remain evangelical. But when it came to a thorough application of Scripture as a regulative principle, Baptists differed from other evangelicals on matters of ecclesiology and church polity to a degree that they were willing to suffer the consequences.[41] But Nettles' second mark of evangelicalism, Christ-centeredness, was shared fully by Baptists and their fellow evangelicals in the seventeenth century.

[39] B.R. White, *The English Baptists of the 17th Century* (Didcot, Oxfordshire: The Baptist Historical Society, 1996), 95–133.

[40] An excellent study of this period in Baptist history, the ministers who suffered grinding persecution and the writings they produced in prison is found in Keith E. Durso, *No Armor for the Back: Baptist Prison Writings, 1600s–1700s* (Macon, GA: Mercer, 2007).

[41] Seventeenth century Baptists also sparred with each other over the application of Scripture in the practice of the local church. This is particularly true in the communion controversy between William Kiffin and John Bunyan and in a controversy over the propriety of singing hymns during Lord's Day worship in the London congregation of Benjamin Keach.

Solo Christos: Baptists are Christ-centered

At the epicenter of the Gospel is the truth that Paul articulates in Romans 10:17 (ESV): "So faith comes from hearing, and hearing through the word of Christ." As Nettles explains, the fact that faith "comes" testifies to the necessity of conversion.[42] And faith finds its saving object, not in itself, but in Jesus Christ. So, just as the Protestant reformers such as Martin Luther and John Calvin reasserted for the church that salvation comes *sola gratia, sola fide, solo Christos*, "by faith alone, through grace alone, in Christ alone," Baptists in seventeenth century England insisted that a sinner is justified by faith alone. They viewed Scripture itself as centered upon the redeeming work of God in the death and resurrection of his son, who was and is fully God and fully man and who became sin for us. Rejecting Roman Catholicism that viewed salvation as being dispensed through the sacramental system of the church, evangelicals came to be defined by this "good news," which is, after all what the "evangel" means in the New Testament.

Such Christ-centeredness is *writ large* throughout the published works of John Bunyan. Volume I of his Works is largely Christological, containing such Christ-focused writings as *Jerusalem Sinner Saved, The Work of Jesus Christ as an Advocate, Christ a Complete Savior, Come and Welcome to Jesus Christ, Of Justification by an Imputed Righteousness or No Way to Heaven but by Jesus Christ, Saved by Grace* and numerous others that do not feature Jesus Christ or salvation in the title, but are nonetheless focused on the person and work of Christ.[43]

Confessionally, English Baptists were deeply committed to Chalcedonian Christology. The *First London Confession* of 1644 includes 13 articles on the person, work and offices of Christ, while a majority of the remaining 39 articles are tied directly to Christ and the gospel.[44] Similarly, the *Second London Confession* of 1689 enlarges on the articles of its predecessor and focuses on the person, work and offices of Christ as well as the doctrines related to salvation through Christ alone, including effectual call, regeneration, adoption, justification and perseverance, among others. Chapter VIII, Article I tells of Christ, the mediator.

[42] Tom Nettles, "Evangelicalism Part IV: Evanglicalism is Christ-Centered," Gospel-Driven Blog, 8 Sept. 2008.

[43] John Bunyan, *The Works of John Bunyan*, Vol. I: *Experimental, Doctrinal and Practical*, ed. George Offor (Edinburgh: Banner of Truth, 1999).

[44] Lumpkin, *Baptist Confessions*, 158–162.

It pleased God in his eternal purpose, to chuse and ordain the Lord Jesus his only begotten Son, according to the Covenant made between them both, to be the Mediator between God and Man; the Prophet, Priest and King; Head and Savior of his Church, the heir of all things, and judge of the world: Unto whom he did from all Eternity give a people to be his seed, and to be by him in time redeemed, called, justified, sanctified, and glorified.[45]

British Baptist pastor Benjamin Keach (1640–1704) emphasized the crucial soteriological doctrine of justification by faith in Christ and devoted several works to its defense and articulation: *The Marrow of Justification* (1692), *The Everlasting Covenant* (1693), *A Golden Mine opened; or, the Glory of God's rich Grace displayed* (1694), *Jacob's Ladder Improved (Christ Alone the way to heaven)* (1698), *A medium betwixt two Extremes* (1698) and *The Display of Glorious Grace; or the Covenant of Peace opened* (1698).[46] Keach participated in a famous debate with Puritan Richard Baxter over Baxter's "neonomian" doctrine of justification. Baxter's view of justification combined faith with some degree of works as putting a sinner into right standing with God. Keach, however, saw this as a dangerous and unbiblical innovation, a capitulation to the Roman Catholic doctrine of justification, and he defended the classical Reformation position that a sinner is reconciled to God through the imputation of Christ's righteousness utterly apart from works.[47] Keach, like Bunyan, Hardcastle and Cheare, also suffered frequent imprisonment and was once humiliated at the pillory for holding dissenting views.[48]

Keach and his Baptist brethren countenanced no rivals for the pure gospel, and they did not move from what they saw as the biblical doctrine of salvation coming to a helpless sinner by grace alone, through faith alone, in Christ alone. Thus, English Baptists, like other evangelicals, placed major emphasis on the cross of Christ.

---

[45] Ibid., 260.

[46] Michael A.G. Haykin, ed., *The British Particular Baptists 1638–1910*, Vol. I (Springfield, MO: Particular Baptist Press, 1998), 107.

[47] This is argued most strenuously in Benjamin Keach, *The Marrow of Justification* (Vestavia Hills, AL: Solid Ground, 2007).

[48] Keach embraced the doctrines of grace after initially holding Arminian views. Austin Walker has written an excellent biography on Keach, his context, his theology and his ministry: *The Excellent Benjamin Keach* (Kitchener, Ontario: Joshua Press, 2004).

Christ and Him Crucified: Baptists are Cross-centered

A fundamental disagreement over the nature of the transaction that took place on the cross on the original Good Friday divided early English Baptists into two camps: Particular Baptists, who argued that Christ's death was effectual for the elect only, and General Baptists, who asserted that Christ died for every single person without exception. Thus, Particular Baptists left largely unchanged the *Westminster Confession's* view of the atonement, articulating the effectual nature for the elect of Christ's death on the cross in Chapter VIII, Article 5, of the *Second London Confession*: "The Lord Jesus by his perfect obedience and sacrifice of himself, which he through the Eternal Spirit once offered up unto God, hath fully satisfied the Justice of God, procured reconciliation, and purchased an Everlasting inheritance in the Kingdom of Heaven, for all those whom the Father hath given unto him."[49]

When General Baptists met in assembly in London in March of 1660 to determine how best to answer accusations of heresy from the state church, they framed the Arminian view in the resulting *Standard Confession*: "No man shall eternally suffer in Hell (that is, the second death) for want of a Christ that dyed for them."[50]

Throughout Baptist history, Calvinistic and Arminians have existed together.[51] This was true at the beginning of Baptist life in England and it continued after Baptists came to America. The overwhelming majority of first Baptists in America were Calvinistic, but the Free Will Baptists were soon founded in the deep South in the first years of the eighteenth century.

In the same way, evangelicalism has traditionally been defined broadly to include Calvinistic and Arminian denominations. Evangelicalism has included both Jonathan Edwards and John Wesley, Presbyterians and Methodists, Baptists and the various Holiness movement churches, and numerous others from both theological perspectives. The common ground in the atonement for both theological camps has been the doctrine of sub-

---

[49] Lumpkin, *Baptist Confessions*, 262.

[50] Ibid., 225–26.

[51] In his book *By His Grace and For His Glory: A Historical, Theological and Practical Study of the Doctrines of Grace in Baptist Life* (Cape Coral: Founders Press, 2006), Tom Nettles shows that Particular Baptists was the far healthier and longer-lasting stream of Baptists. Further, he demonstrates that the Southern Baptist Convention, which today includes both Calvinists and practical, if not fully-theological Arminians, was born out the Particular Baptist stream. General Baptists in seventeenth century England were by and large weakened by Socinianism and other doctrinal errors within a century of their founding.

stitution. By and large, the two have agreed that Christ died as a substitute, though Arminians practically deny the effectual nature of Christ as a substitute by asserting that he died for every person in the same way. In the confessions, however, both Particular and General Baptists have embraced the notion of substitution. This is clear not only in the two London confessions, but is also expressed in perhaps the most robust Arminian confession ever written, the *Orthodox Creed* of 1678.[52] This statement of faith was published in the name of the more earnestly orthodox General Baptist churches of the British Midlands to "unite and confirm all true protestants in the fundamental articles of the Christian religion."[53] A further motivation for these General Baptists was perhaps to distance themselves from the Hoffmanite Christology which Matthew Caffyn, a general Baptist messenger, was preaching in Kent and Sussex.[54] Article XVII on the mediatorial office of Christ, speaks of the sinfulness of man being placed upon Christ as a substitute on the cross, while sinful man is reconciled to God through the imputed righteousness of Christ, the substitute.[55] Christ "willingly underwent [...] the punishment due to us," the article reads in part.[56]

Both Particular and General Baptist confessions speak of Christ's atoning death on the cross as being voluntary and substitutionary. An irreducible part of being an evangelical and a Baptist is an embrace of Christ's voluntary work on the cross as a substitute for sinners. This sits at the heart of what the New Testament calls the "evangel," the good news of the Gospel. And Baptists are, if anything, a gospel people as witnessed by their emphasis on the preached word and their later pioneering of the modern missions movement with William Carey, Andrew Fuller and Adoniram Judson in the early nineteenth century. Evangelical Baptists remain fixated on the gospel and its proclamation today.

[52] Ironically, as Lumpkin points out, the *Orthodox Creed* comes closest to embracing Calvinism than any other General Baptist statement of faith. This is particularly evident in articles on predestination and election (IX), the covenants (XVI), original sin (XV), perseverance (XXXVI) and the invisible church (XXIX). It is unique among Baptist confessions also in its inclusion of three creeds of the early church: the Apostles,' the Nicene and the Athanasian. See Lumpkin, *Baptist Confessions*, 296.

[53] Lumpkin, *Baptist Confessions*, 295.

[54] Ibid.

[55] Ibid., 309.

[56] Ibid.

Conclusion

In his commentary on Baptists and evangelicalism in the December 15, 1881 edition of the *Christian Index*, H.H. Tucker celebrated the notion that Baptists were a part of a river of evangelical Christianity that flowed into post-bellum Southern Baptist life from the era of the Reformation. He summarized the common doctrines as the inspiration and inerrancy of Scripture, the person and work of Christ and the necessity of a personal, individual experience of the grace of God.[57] These doctrines and the term that best describes them in summary form, "evangelical," "certainly applies to Baptists," he wrote, and they describe all Christians, irrespective of denomination, who are "holders of these views as to the way of salvation."[58] For Baptists and for all genuine Christians, they represented a concise method of describing the "evangelical way of salvation."[59]

Baptists of the seventeenth century differed with other orthodox believers on matters of ecclesiology, but when it came to doctrines at the heart of the Gospel they were, and remain today, staunchly evangelical.

[57] Henry Holcombe Tucker, "A Peculiar People," *The Christian Index and Southwestern Baptist*, 27 July 1882, p. 8.

[58] Ibid.

[59] Ibid.

5

A Distracted Piety

AFRICAN-AMERICAN BAPTISTS

Kevin L. Smith

Colored Baptists began to shape their own identities during the second half of the nineteenth-century. Prior to this they were generally, with few exceptions, nominally treated members of the larger white-controlled Baptist community in the United States.[1] However, after the 1845 division of America's Baptists over the issue of slavery and the 1863 signing of the Emancipation Proclamation by Abraham Lincoln, the prior arrangement was no longer acceptable to colored Baptists, particularly those in the South.[2] For several decades colored Baptists struggled to develop associations, institutions, and conventions to carry on their work.[3] Not until 1895 would they develop a national convention that represented the interests of most colored Baptists in America.[4] One year before the founding of

---

[1] There were at least three main categories: "balcony" Baptists, "plantation" Baptists, and the invisible institution.

[2] In the South, Baptists split over the issue of slavery following the Methodists (1844) and ahead of the Presbyterians (1857). See *A Documentary History of Religion in America to the Civil War*, ed. Edwin S. Gaustad (Grand Rapids, MI: William B Eerdmans Publishing Company, 1992), 491–502.

[3] This was extremely important to proving their independent competence and usability by God.

[4] On September 28, 1895, there was a joint meeting in Atlanta with the "Foreign Mission Baptist Convention" (established 1880), the "American National Baptist Convention" (established 1886), and the "National Baptist Educational Convention" (established 1893).

the National Baptist Convention of the United States of America, a new periodical appeared, *The National Baptist Magazine* (1894). It sought to represent the scholarship, opinions, and church business of colored Baptists nationwide.

Using the early years of *The National Baptist Magazine* as a source, one can see that early national colored Baptist identity, while being unique due to the existential reality of racism, was doctrinally consistent with that of white Baptists as expressed in their generally accepted confessions of faith of that era.[5] The early years of the magazine will be surveyed chronologically to determine the characteristics identified as being distinct among Baptists. This method gives priority to this earliest of national black Baptist literature as being representative of the "purest" notions of identity expressed by Negro Baptists, on a national level, during this formative period.[6]

Colored Baptist identity was not shaped solely in the context of theological controversy. Racism was an equally significant factor. The importance of America's "race problem" cannot be overstated. David W. Wills has argued that race ("the encounter of black and white") has been one of the three central themes of American religious history.[7] If race is such a significant part of the meta-narrative of American Christianity, certainly the Baptists in America did not escape its defining influence. Yet despite the potentially overwhelming presence of racism, early colored Baptists carved out an identity that was distinctively "Baptist" as compared to the colored Methodists, Presbyterians, other Protestants, and Roman Catholics.

[5] This author takes the position that confessionalism is a characteristic of historic Baptist identity. Prior to 1894, the representative confessions would have been The Philadelphia Confession (1742), the Articles of Faith of the Sandy Creek Association (1816), and The New Hampshire Confession (1833). See William L. Lumpkin, ed., *Baptist Confessions of Faith* (Valley Forge, PA: Judson Press, 1969), 347–67.

[6] In this era, "colored" and "Negro" were mostly used to describe those in America of African-descent. Additionally, a few references are made to "Afro-Americans."

[7] David W. Wills, "The Central Themes of American Religious History: Pluralism, Puritanism, and the Encounter of Black and White," in *African-American Religion: Interpretive Essays in History and Culture*, eds. Timothy E. Fulop and Albert J. Raboteau (Routledge: New York, 1997), 9–20. Wills' three themes are pluralism, Puritanism, and the encounter of black and white. He also makes geographical assignments noting that Puritanism characterized New England while pluralism was identified with the middle colonies. Finally, religion in the southern colonies was characterized by racial issues.

This chapter will seek to identify the theological continuity between black and white Baptists without discounting the social discontinuity. However, if the term "Baptist" is used to signify a theological and doctrinal designation rather than merely a social grouping, colored Baptists' identity mostly paralleled that of white Baptists. In Gayraud S. Wilmore's *Black Religion and Black Radicalism* and James Melvin Washington's *Frustrated Fellowship: The Black Baptist Quest for Social Power*, the religious identity of colored people, Baptist in particular, is described in the context of "radicalism," a term associated with black religious nationalism and Black Power.[8] This approach, without a consideration of black Baptists' doctrinal distinctives, has the potential to lead to a "contrived" identity for black Baptists that has no connection to the Baptist heritage that originated in seventeenth-century Europe. This historiographical adoctrinalism characterizes the phenomenological approach to religious studies and tends to undervalue the theological and doctrinal commitments of religious persons. Articles and sermons in *The National Baptist Magazine* reveal theological commitments that were not merely incidental to Baptist identity, but central.

It should be conceded that the radicalism approach to African American religious history rightly notes the outrage persons of color felt as they endured the scourges of racism, both from Christians and non-Christians. However, the Negro has often been sophisticated enough, and endowed with enough discernment, to distinguish, as Frederick Douglas said, between the "Christianity of Christ" and the "Christianity of the slaveholder [or segregationist]." Early issues of the magazine reveal no resolve among colored Baptists to jettison any part of the Christian tradition. Rather, these Baptists were hopeful that a full embrace of Christianity, and its radical social implications, would lead to a better Baptist denomination and a brighter America. The early contributors to the magazine did not hesitate to critique white Baptists, other Christians, and America in general. However, the ethics of those being critiqued were always compared to what should be the ethic of "authentic" Christianity. The failure to make such a distinction presents the colored Christian as expressing an inadequacy in authentic Christianity, such as when Wilmore argued,

---

[8] J. Deotis Roberts, book review of *Frustrated Fellowship: The Black Baptist Quest for Social Power* in the *Journal of the American Academy of Religion*, Vol. 57, No. 4, 882–83. See also Gayraud S. Wilmore, *Black Religion and Black Radicalism: An Interpretation of the Religious History of Afro-American People* (Maryknoll: Orbis Books, 1993), and James Melvin Washington, *Frustrated Fellowship: The Black Baptist Quest for Social Power* (Macon, GA: Mercer University Press, 1990).

Christianity alone, adulterated, otherworldly, and disengaged from its most authentic implications—as it was usually presented to the slaves—could not have provided the slaves with all the resources they needed for the kind of resistance they expressed. It had to be enriched with the volatile ingredients of the African religious past and, most important of all, with the human yearning for freedom that found channel for expression in the early black churches of the South.[9]

In the above quote, it is unclear whether the Christianity was inadequate, and in need of fixing, or whether it was something other than Christianity altogether. The outrage of these oppressed Christians is rightly expressed. However, the specific target of their outrage should be clearer. The radicalism approach also, often, chooses definitive characters from among those having political significance rather than ecclesiological importance. For example, Wilmore cites Nat Turner, the nineteenth-century leader of a slave rebellion, as a prototype "Baptist."[10] As Baptists are congregational and the pastor is prominent among the people, it seems more helpful to appeal to pastors and denominational leaders as definitive figures rather than political figures.[11] The leaders who led colored Baptists after Reconstruction were pivotal in establishing an identity for colored Baptist within the broader Baptist denomination.

Early colored Baptists made a "perspectival" contribution to the Baptist heritage—but so did non-colored Baptists. Of course, *The National Baptist Magazine* featured articles addressing race and racial progress as well as sermons and editorials calling for the development of one national convention. The humanity of the Negro was defended, both domestically and globally. However, this chapter will focus on elements in the magazine that address and seek to clarify Baptist distinctives. What is impressive in the early years of the magazine is the editor's ability to maintain a reasonable balance between articles addressing issues of theology and those addressing issues of race.[12] Unfortunately, as the years progressed, the articles in the magazine became less theologically definitive and more racially focused. Perhaps as time passed a clear understanding of Baptist

[9] Wilmore, *Black Religion and Black Radicalism*, 27.

[10] Ibid., 62–73.

[11] In the early nineteenth-century, colored Baptists would have been affiliated with white-controlled congregations and associations; therefore, no distinct colored Baptist identity would have yet emerged. Nat Turner, and others, was a good example of black outrage over inauthentic Christianity.

[12] This is a stark contrast to today, when many white Baptists merely want to focus on theology and many black Baptist merely want to focus on race.

identity was assumed among colored Baptists. However, a more likely explanation is that responses to America's social sickness, racism, simply truncated theological discussion in the pages of the first national colored Baptist publication.

Baptist Identity

The inaugural issue of *The National Baptist Magazine* was published in January 1894. Its editor was W. Bishop Johnson (b. 1858), pastor of the Second Baptist Church in Washington, D.C. It was governed by a publishing committee that included Rev. E.C. Morris (1855–1922), who became the first president of the National Baptist Convention, a position that he held for twenty-seven years. The magazine featured four main sections: essays and articles (called the "review section"), poetry, a "sermonic section," and finally an editorial section. The original idea for a national magazine for colored Baptist was originally put forth by William James Simmons (1849–1890), a very influential colored preacher from Kentucky.

The opening pages of this new magazine immediately attacked the practice of lynching based upon an exposition of the rape of Dinah in Genesis 34. The next essay, "The Elevating Tendency of Religion," rejected pluralism and affirmed the uniqueness of Christianity. These two articles clearly demonstrated a desire to inform a readership that was specifically Christian even as they experienced the perils of racism in America that was common to all colored people regardless of their religious creed.

Colored Baptist identity was no mere religious discussion. It had sociological and political implications. E.C. Morris said, in "The Demand for a Baptist Publishing House," that "colored Baptists represent about five eighths of the entire colored population of the United States." With such numerical strength, one wonders how much of the moral and ethical worldview of Negroes at the turn of the century was influenced by Baptists. Also, colored Baptists were leading citizens, as Morris noted that colored Baptists did not have educational disparities when compared to colored Methodists or Presbyterians. This could not be said about white Baptists when they were compared with white Presbyterians or Episcopalians. Colored Baptists' numerical strength was not the result of mere racial solidarity but was attributed to "the simplicity of our [Baptist] polity and the correctness of our doctrine." Colored Baptists did see themselves as having a distinct identity as Baptists. Yet their distinct Baptist identity was existentially "colored" by their experience in America.[13]

---

[13] *The National Baptist Magazine*, Vol.1, No.1 (January 1894), 6–11, 12–14, 18–21, 23–26, 47–49. Reflecting the theological and racial importance of pub-

Colored Baptists had never been allowed by white Baptists to forget that they were colored. Therefore, when the opportunity for independence came, they quickly left their white brethren and organized their own congregations. David O. Moore said, "Within four years [of the Emancipation Proclamation], the vast number of blacks who had come to be so large a part of white Baptists churches in the South had departed to form their own churches."[14] Moore further noted that departing Baptists never felt like "equal brothers" in either the flesh or "under God."[15] Emmanuel McCall described this phenomenon as the "inability of white churches and denominations to relate to black experiences with integrity."[16] Thus social circumstances in Baptist life in the South provided the impetus for the development of a unique colored Baptist existence and identity.

Had racism not been condoned, and in some instances practiced, by white Baptists, the impetus for separate colored institutions would not have existed. White and colored Baptists experienced two different realities in America. Therefore, the fact that they shared the same biblical understandings of doctrine and ecclesiology could not overcome the fact that they were as different as they were alike. For example, their evangelistic motives were sometimes different. James Melvin Washington has suggested, "increasing discrimination against blacks in areas such as education, public accommodations, and jobs mandated a broadening of the preacher's understanding of evangelism."[17] An evangelism or a gospel that did not, or would not, address these injustices was seen as inadequate by many. This was particularly true of those colored Baptists that still maintained

---

lishing for colored Baptists, Morris said, "The colored Baptists of America have come to the place, to set up a sign for their children, by building institutions and inaugurating enterprises, that their children can own and control as gifts [theological and racial] from their fathers, to be revered and perpetuated, until at least a broader American Christianity shall sign the death warrant of a long lived American prejudice" (20).

[14] David O. Moore, "The Withdrawal of Blacks from Southern Baptist Churches Following Emancipation," *The Journal of African American Southern Baptist History*, Vol. I (June 2003), 63. See also Edward L. Wheeler, "Beyond One Man: A General Survey of Black Baptist Church History," *Review and Expositor*, Volume LXX, No. 3 (Summer 1973), 309–19.

[15] Moore, "The Withdrawal of Blacks from Southern Baptist Churches Following Emancipation," 65.

[16] Emmanuel L. McCall, *Black Church Lifestyles: Rediscovering the Black Christian Experience* (Nashville, TN: Broadman Press, 1986), 33.

[17] James Melvin Washington, 'The Making of a Church with the Soul of a Nation, 1880–1889" in *African American Religious Thought: An Anthology*, eds. Cornel West and Eddie S. Glaude, Jr. (Louisville, KY: Westminster John Knox Press, 2003), 415.

the "holistic" African approach to religion, which allowed no convenient distinctions between the religious and the political or social.

The most unique characteristic of this "colorized" Baptist identity, when compared with white Baptists in general, was its hope for a better America. In 1894, decades after the Emancipation Proclamation and following the disappointments of Reconstruction, William Waring still possessed the "hope that the hour is drawing near when the gospel will have driven from its ranks race-hate, race-pride, and caste of every kind, and become in practice as well as theory the gospel of brotherly love."[18] This article, entitled "The Negro Preacher of the Twentieth Century," suggested that the Negro Baptist preacher had a unique comprehensive understanding of the gospel that had escaped his white ("European") Baptist colleague who could not "comprehend the desolation of a gospel without brotherly love."[19] Focusing on the civil rights era of southern history, Andrew M. Manis highlighted these differing black and white "civil religions."[20] Manis' categories are helpful as one considers the interactions between black and white Christians, particularly Baptists in the South, throughout American history. Lewis V. Baldwin's summary of Manis' point is just as applicable to the 1890s as it was to the 1950s.

> Manis challenges the notion that black and white southerners share a single, clearly-defined version of civil religion.... In other words, the black South's version of civil religion, which embraces universal rights, human equality, and interracial community under God, conflicts with that of the white South, which sanctions individual rights, white supremacy, and segregation on Biblical and theological grounds.[21]

These early colored Baptist viewed themselves as having a Baptist identity that was to serve a broader Christian function in American society as they waited in prophetic anticipation for the unfulfilled racial agenda of justice for the Negro.[22] The prophecy that "the white man of a hundred years hence" would repent of this unfulfilling of the gospel of love came to

---

[18] *The National Baptist Magazine*, Vol.1, No.1 (January 1894), 24.

[19] Ibid.

[20] Andrew M. Manis, *Southern Civil Religions in Conflict: Civil Rights and the Culture Wars* (Macon, GA: Mercer University Press, 2002).

[21] Ibid, xvii.

[22] *The National Baptist Magazine* (January 1894), 23–26. In a stunning quote, Waring suggested that "the most learned commentator that ever took up his pen did not understand the story of the man who fell among thieves on his way to Jericho as any decent Negro has had it ground into his soul by contact with Christian men and women of other races" (24).

pass in 1995 when the Southern Baptist Convention adopted a resolution on race that included a repudiation of its historical dealings with colored persons in America. This prophetic element of colored Baptist identity was vital and those lacking some type of race-consciousness were subject to severe criticism.[23]

William Creditt, pastor of the Berean Baptist Church of Washington, D.C., delivered his sermon, "Hindrances to Baptism," in late 1893. Sermons are useful in discerning colored Baptist identity because significant parts of the Negro population were illiterate and therefore oral discourse was their main epistemological mechanism. The sermon drew five principles from the story of the Ethiopian eunuch in Acts 8. The sermon could not have been more Baptist as it read, "the great prerequisite to proper baptism is personal belief." Personal belief must precede baptism and for Creditt this is the definitive element of Baptist identity for he said, "upon this principle the Baptist Church takes its stand." This doctrine was no contrived notion but merely the result of Baptist belief in an "open Bible without word or comment." Therefore when colored Baptists excluded Presbyterians from the Lord's Supper they were not (in their eyes) practicing "close" communion but rather "close" baptism that recognized nothing but believer's baptism and immersion as its proper mode.[24] These early colored Baptist distinctive beliefs and practices were consistent with that of their white brethren. For example, the Principles of Faith of the Sandy Creek Association stated, "That true believers are the only fit subjects of baptism, and that immersion is the only mode [...] That the church has no right to admit any but regular baptized church members to communion at the Lord's table."[25]

The managing editor's first editorial clearly stated his desire that the magazine communicate the distinctives of colored Baptists. W. Bishop Johnson wanted colored Baptist to set "forth their distinctive principles" and boldly stand upon those "principles and practices which differentiate Baptists from all the world and which have made them the 'sect everywhere spoken against.'" For Johnson, Baptist identity was something worth contending for. He said, "We shall also be firm in placing the denominational

[23] "The Negro preacher of that day [the twentieth century] will of necessity represent the religious thought of his people and the preacher who comes among them with the claim that he is nothing more than a Methodist, a Baptist, and Episcopalian, or a Presbyterian will be sent to minister unto those who, like himself, are a hundred years behind the age." *The National Baptist Magazine* (January 1894), 26.

[24] *The National Baptist Magazine* (January 1894), 47-49.

[25] Lumpkin, *Baptist Confessions of Faith*, 358.

tenets squarely before the world, aiming, first, last, and all the time, to stimulate pride in our doctrines by intelligent discussions and charitable controversy." It is significant that this inaugural editorial set forth an affirmation of Baptist identity in general rather than any specific contrived "Negro" Baptist doctrine.[26]

He further said, "We believe in Baptist principles, not from necessity, nor force of association, nor family connection, but absolutely and unqualified from conviction."[27] This, also, was an important statement as they staked out their racial independence, organizationally, yet freely and willingly maintained theological principles with their white Baptist brethren.[28] Finally, it was the editor's opinion that publishing was a necessary tool for disseminating Baptist distinctives, second only to the pulpit.[29]

The second issue of the magazine (April 1894) contained a doctrinal article affirming the humanity of Jesus Christ, an appeal for churches to support the work of the Sunday School, and a sermon affirming the need of vital religion—a valid regeneration-based faith in Christ. These writings placed colored Baptists, doctrinally, within the broad Christian family.

An article by William Phillips, pastor of the Shiloh Baptist Church in Philadelphia declared a Baptist distinctive with its title "Alien Immersion Not Valid Baptism in a Baptist Church."[30] Since those attempting to come into Baptist congregations from non-Baptist churches were the issue, Phillips began by discussing who was a "proper administrator" of baptism. Basically, the administrator must have been truly regenerate, "he must have been *immersed* [emphasis theirs] and held church membership in some other Baptist church," and he must have been ordained. All others were improper administrators.[31] Therefore those coming from Methodist, Presbyterian or any tradition lacking a "proper administrator" were not recognized as being baptized. In declaring those so-called baptisms invalid, this colored Baptist invoked the regulative principle when he wrote, "He [the one seeking to enter the Baptist congregation] does not believe

---

[26] *The National Baptist Magazine* (January 1894), 58–60.

[27] Ibid. Present day black Baptists would benefit from such convictions.

[28] It has been noted that "the move towards racially separate churches was not a matter of doctrinal disagreement, but a protest against unequal and restrictive treatment." C. Eric Lincoln and Lawrence H. Mamiya, *The Black Church in the African American Experience* (Durham: Duke University Press, 1990), 25.

[29] *The National Baptist Magazine* (January 1894), 58–60.

[30] *The National Baptist Magazine* (April 1984), 86–88.

[31] Specifically, Phillips said, "No regular Baptist church would permit a licensed minister to baptize. No church would allow a deacon to do its baptizing. No church would suffer a lay member to baptize, however pious the individual might be." The *National Baptist Magazine* (April 1984), 87.

in the scriptures as being the only authority for his conduct and practice in this matter as we do."[32] These early colored Baptists were aware of the need actively to maintain a clear understanding of Baptist distinctives. In a prophetic warning about the loss of Baptist identity that would be borne out in the twentieth century by white Baptists in the South and the North, Phillips warned,

> There is at the present day a strong desire for popular praise and applause, which is likely to pull our old Baptist ship loose from her moorings, and set her afloat upon the high seas of irregularity with the danger of foundering upon the rocks of skepticism and unfaithfulness.[33]

The lead article in the July 1894 issue of the magazine called for Baptists to pursue education with an eye towards influencing society. This call for more Baptist intellectuals was careful to avoid sanctioning rationalism. The role of education in the shaping of culture was noted in the belief that "Christian education [worldview] is the salt of civilization, the bulwark of human governments and institutions."[34] Another article fully supported the exercise of church discipline.[35]

R.H. Porter, pastor of the Third Baptist Church of Alexandria, Virginia, contributed the longest article in this issue, entitled "Why I Am a Baptist: Bible Reasons for Our Faith." After investigating the principles "that Baptists regard as important and vital," he adapted an article by a "Dr. MacArthur of New York." There was no indication as to MacArthur's race. The article listed six basic principles of Baptist life: (1) regenerate church membership, (2) belief precedes baptism which precedes the Lord's Supper, (3) "baptism is not necessary to salvation" but should be done unless one is physically unable, (4) "religious freedom, the tenet that the civil magistrate has no authority over a man's religious creed and usage", (5) "immersion is essential to baptism" therefore "immersion is prerequisite for the Lord's Supper", (6) "faith must be personal and no man can believe for another."[36] This article reflected an understanding of colored Baptist identity that is doctrinal and biblical, being ordered by the New Testament. Although the article was adapted from another author, it is significant that

---

[32] Ibid.

[33] *The National Baptist Magazine* (July 1894), 88.

[34] *The National Baptist Magazine* (July 1894), 150.

[35] Gregory A. Wills provides helpful insight into the practices of church discipline with and among colored Baptists. See his chapter "African-American Democracies" in *Democratic Religion: Freedom, Authority, and Church Discipline in the Baptist South 1785-1900* (New York: Oxford University Press, 1997), 67–83.

[36] *The National Baptist Magazine* (July 1894), 154–61.

such a doctrinal exposition of Baptist identity was the centerpiece article in this issue.

These Baptists thought critically about Baptist distinctives and the nature of American Christianity in general. An insightful article by M.W. Gilbert, president of Florida Baptist Academy, evaluated colored churches, especially those that were Baptists. In "Colored Church An Experiment" certain elements of Baptist identity were seen as being abused by some congregations of newly freed Negroes. While appreciating the "free congregations" that no longer were subject to the "supervision and surveillance of the whites," Gilbert critiqued some of the attributes of the churches that had developed since the Emancipation Proclamation. Highlighting "some of the faults observable in our colored churches," Gilbert first chided colored Baptists for "rarely resorting to" the use of associational counsel. In an excessive and abusive understanding of local church autonomy, these new "free" churches were too free as they neglected "the usage of consulting a council of sister churches for advice." This is a helpful illustration of the challenges these new congregations faced as they "came out" from under white Baptist supervision and association. Further the churches were chided for seeking counsel from ungodly ministers. In memorable rhetoric Gilbert said some of the so-called councils were composed of ministers that were "too rascally and unscrupulous to sit in a counsel of demons." The author sought a reasonable balance between autonomy, associationalism, and accountability. He pointed out "in too many instances since our emancipation have we taken liberty to mean license, and freedom to do right as freedom to do as we please."[37]

This was not a retreat from the Baptist distinctive of local church autonomy—just a rebuke of its excesses. Holding up an effective model, Gilbert said, "Among the white people it [autonomy] is 'a thing of beauty and a joy forever.'"[38] Actually, local autonomy was cast as favorable for the Negro's future rather than other forms of polity that were characterized as being oppressive. Mingling polity and race, he contrasted colored Methodists and Baptists.

> It is oftentimes supposed that the apparent peace and quiet observed among the colored Methodists argue a better form of church government for colored people than that existing among colored Baptists. But that which at first seems to be a reflection upon our denomination is at once to our credit. The Methodist's polity and that of all Episcopal bod-

---

[37] *The National Baptist Magazine* (July 1894), 165–68.
[38] Ibid, 167. Gilbert did not foresee what white Baptist would do with "autonomy" in the twentieth century.

ies is better adapted to secure the harmony and strength of the individual church *for the present*, because the Negroes are accustomed to having a master, a driver, or someone to dictate to him and to do his thinking for him. The *future* is more favorable to the Baptists, when in this free republic, with slavery unfelt and forgotten, the Negro will in reality be free.[39]

Besides autonomy, colored churches were critiqued for having "the demagogue or politician" in the pulpit,[40] toleration of "bad men in the ministry," power-hungry ministers, hasty and inconsiderate ordinations, too many church splits, and the multiplication of "feeble churches" that could not support a full-time pastor. The article leveled a particularly stinging rebuke at excessive building debt and its detrimental effect on missions, describing some as

a poor people almost baptized into pauperism vying with the wealthy white man—free for centuries—in building meeting houses.... The craze for fine meeting houses is upon us. State missions, home missions, education, must go to the dogs for the present. Africa and lost souls must wait fifteen or twenty years, until the debt is paid and the mortgage removed.[41]

Sacramentalism among colored churches is also pointed out as churches erroneously serve the Lord's Supper to individuals when it is a "church ordinance." Additionally, the "blessing" of infants by Baptists is criticized for being too akin to infant baptism as well as a violation of the regulative principle. Finally, the author was not too impressed with the "excessive emotionalism in our preaching and worship."[42] This extensive critique, which ran over two consecutive issues, reveals the importance of polity, ecclesiology, ordinances, holiness, and ministerial qualification to leading early colored Baptists.

In addition to continuing the article critiquing colored churches, the October 1894 issue sought to advance the cause of equality by examining the common origin of humanity, advocated the study of Baptist history, and passed a resolution on lynching which noted the significant efforts of

---

[39] *The National Baptist Magazine* (July 1894), 168.

[40] Some of this stemmed from the rejection of black politicians after Reconstruction ended, leaving concerned black leaders with no other avenue for exercising power except the one institution that now belonged to them – the colored churches. I liken this to the many theologically inadequate and indifferent clergy that entered pulpits during and after the Civil Rights Movement.

[41] *The National Baptist Magazine* (July 1894), 168.

[42] *The National Baptist Magazine* (October 1894), 209–12.

Ida B. Wells. In a brief reference to a soteriological matter, one columnist suggested, "Predestination and Election grow out of God's knowledge as to how men would exercise their free agency."[43] Although freedmen were anxious to pursue the independent development of various Baptist institutions and organizations, they had no desire to disassociate with their white Baptist brethren. When a colored preacher, T.D. Miller, was elected moderator of America's oldest Baptist association, the magazine rejoiced, "The Philadelphia Association has not only honored Dr. Miller, but the entire Negro race."[44] Finally, the magazine reported on the beginning efforts to unify, in one national organization, the work of colored Baptists that was now being carried out by at least three significant and separate conventions.

Missions and Denominationalism

The Foreign Mission Convention (1880) sponsored mission work in Africa. The National Baptist Convention (1886) examined "questions affecting the race and denomination"[45] and published *The National Baptist Magazine*. The National Baptist Educational Convention (1893) encouraged education (religious and non-religious) among colored Baptists. The article distinguished between the "conventions" and the "denomination." Despite their organizational boundaries, these were all Baptists and they knew it. Anticipating the events of the following year, the article noted, "an effort is now being made to amalgamate the three organizations into one grand body."[46] Thus the magazine's first year featured clear understandings of Baptist identity, reasoned outrage over the injustices of racism, self-critical evaluations of colored Baptists, and a call for national solidarity among colored Baptists. Subsequent years of the magazine reflected broader involvement in social concerns and unfortunately theological issues began to be eclipsed.

February 20, 1895 marked the death of Frederick Douglass. This event overshadowed much in black life that year. Reflecting Douglass' prominence, the vast majority of the magazine during the second and third quarters paid tribute to Douglass. There were pictures, articles, poems, and a variety of memorials in its pages. The magazine even attempted to raise funds by selling pictures of the famous American. Despite Douglass' Methodism,

[43] *The National Baptist Magazine* (October 1894), 239.
[44] Ibid, 263.
[45] Ibid, 241
[46] Ibid, 242.

he was honored and revered for an extended period of time in *The National Baptist Magazine*.

Concern for Africa by these colored Baptists led to constant appeals in the magazine for missions support. The missiological thrust of early colored Baptist is a stark contrast to the efforts of some black Baptist denominations today. Future president of the combined convention, E.C. Morris made "a stirring appeal" in the July 1895 issue. Pleas for missions were frequently made appealing to the reader's concern for the unbelieving soul. Alexander Moore, pastor of the Antioch Baptist Church of Cleveland, Ohio, appealed,

> Brethren, if we are ever to make a success of our Convention or of our denominational work, we must lay aside our selfishness and work from love to God and to poor suffering humanity. Think of the millions of precious souls who without God and without hope are rapidly passing into a long, long eternity, while some of us, under the pretense of helping them, are only seeking the gratification of some selfish desire.[47]

In order to pursue missions in a coordinated manner, colored Baptists needed a more efficient denominational structure. By 1897, after two years of the national organization, it was apparent that annual meetings were cumbersome venues to organize yearlong missionary efforts. Without any model present from their white brethren (this was before the Southern Baptist Convention's establishment of its Executive Committee), it was apparent that someone or some body needed to be able to "run" the Convention when it was not in annual sessions. Moore suggested that colored Baptists needed "a permanent headquarters, and salaried officers who could give their entire time and attention to the management of the different departments."[48] These early Baptists had no desire to organize nationally for sentimental purposes—they were called upon to organize efficiently in order to do the work of God as equal participants in Christian missions with their white brethren.

Part of equal participation involved being able to set missions priorities. Africa was the primary concern of colored missions-minded Baptists. Their understanding of theodicy meant God had allowed them to be brought to America as slaves for some redemptive purpose. Even as white racism was criticized, it was noted that "The evils of slavery were turned to gracious account... and in return placing the Negro Christians of this

[47] *The National Baptist Magazine* (combined October 1896/January 1897), 276.

[48] Ibid, 278.

great country under lasting obligation to the work of African evangelization."[49] Washington further noted that black Baptists doubted whether white Baptists were "seriously interested in evangelizing Africa."[50]

Changing Priorities

A subtle shift in emphasis took place in the magazine as the "sermon" section began to be irregular and finally full sermons were replaced by mere sermon quotes in a section called "Sparks from the Anvils of Afro-American Pulpits" as the new century loomed on the horizon. The magizine began to print Presidential addresses to the convention. These addresses often covered a wide array of topics. More than communicating the distinctives of Baptist identity to the faithful, these addresses usually surveyed the political, social, and cultural settings that were currently challenging colored Baptists. The addresses usually bore the weight of the Negroes' unfulfilled citizenship in America. The April 1899 issue of the magazine carried E.C. Morris' presidential address entitled "The Church as a Factor in Solving the Race Problem in America." He expressed regret that "many of the churches of our country have remained silent while the very foundation principles of our great country are being undermined."[51] For him, the churches were not being faithful to the principles of equality as expressed in America's civil religion, which were recorded in the Declaration of Independence and the Constitution. However, he must have recognized the limitations of civil religion for he noted that when the Bible "has been made the Alpha and Omega of our country, there will be no race problem to solve."[52] Despite Morris' appeals to civil religion and his description of America as a "Christian Nation," the essentiality of God's church was understood when he said,

> No legislative enactments, backed by a million armed men, can force recognition of the Negroes rights in this country until a moral sentiment has been created among the people to grant those rights, and that sentiment can only be created through and by the Church of God, which is the true exponent of all moral law.[53]

[49] Washington, "The Making of a Church with the Soul of a Nation, 1880-1889," 416.

[50] Ibid.

[51] *The National Baptist Magazine* (April 1899), 185.

[52] Ibid, 186.

[53] *The National Baptist Magazine* (April 1899), 187.

As the content of *The National Baptist Magazine* became more diverse, addressing problems of race as well as reporting on denominational agencies, specific articles delineating Baptist distinctives did not appear as in the magazine's first two years. However, colored Baptist were still able to somewhat contend for Baptist identity, within the broader Baptist family, as they sought peaceful recognition from their white brethren.

Apparently, as colored Baptists began to seek to organize after Reconstruction, some whites were either threatened or offended by such activity. In his 1899 presidential address, E.C. Morris assured his listeners that colored Baptist were a legitimate "wing of our great and invincible denomination."[54] Despite the racism, insensitivity, and paternalism that characterized the experience of black Christians in white-led churches, Morris declared that the National Baptist Convention bore no race-hatred towards white Christians. Seeking to clarify misunderstandings about the convention's purpose, he said,

> I wish to repeat what I have said on several occasions: that this Society entertains no ill will toward any other Christian organization in the world. It seeks to be on friendly terms with all, and the charge that this organization means to draw the color line, and thereby create prejudice in 'Negro' Christians against 'white' Christians, is without foundation.[55]

White Baptists were encouraged to learn from black Baptists who sought to "obliterate all sectional lines among Baptists" and establish a truly national organization.[56] White opposition was a serious obstacle to be overcome. James Washington captured the fear, necessity, and tension of the moment when he said,

> Many believed that a greater sense of racial solidarity was a prerequisite to forming a strong racial ecclesiastical bond. But they really did not know how to create a greater sense of race loyalty in a society that frowned on black solidarity, and among white denominational brethren who had a history of working against such unions.[57]

Opposition to colored denominational unity came on two fronts. First, hostile opposition sought to disrupt planning meetings and annual sessions of black Baptists organizations. One notable example was the attack

---

[54] *The National Baptist Magazine* (September/October 1899), 65.

[55] Ibid.

[56] Ibid, 66.

[57] Washington, "The Making of a Church with the Soul of a Nation, 1880-1889," 422.

on Emanuel Love, pastor of the First African Baptist Church of Savannah [GA] as he traveled to Indianapolis on the East Tennessee, Virginia, and Georgia Railroad.[58] Second, "friendly" opposition came from paternalistic white brethren as blacks rejected invitations to join Northern organizations that did "home missions" work in the South. Despite such opposition, colored Baptists pushed forward and established a national organization and institutions that were distinctly Baptist in their doctrine and experientially colored in their social and ethical outlook.

Conclusion

A survey of early issues of *The National Baptist Magazine* revealed a colored Baptist identity that was uniquely "colored" while initially desiring to be consistently Baptist. The early writings expressed outrage over racial injustice in America but maintained a balanced presentation of Baptist doctrinal distinctives. As it regarded issues of polity, immersion, the Lord's Supper, church membership, the regulative principle, associationalism, a host of other issues, and missions, colored and white Baptists believed the same thing and shared a common identity. However, the prominent issue of race, a pivotal marker in American religious history, forced colored Baptist to "come out from among them," who were mostly just like them, and be separate.

If early organizational black Baptist piety was distracted by the existential necessity of the struggle for freedom following slavery and Reconstruction at the turn of the twentieth century, then the mid-century Civil Rights Movement was likewise another necessary distraction. However, this latter distraction was more enduring and substantial because of the personality of Martin Luther King Jr. King was a distraction to black Baptist piety in at least three ways: (1) his call to "ministry," (2) his ideal preacher, and (3) his rejection of his Daddy's faith.

In his 1948 application for admission to Crozer Theological Seminary King was asked to describe his personal reasons for wanting to study "for the gospel ministry." His answer is incredibly void of any reference to "the gospel."[59] Unfortunately, this type of calling would be repeated by a gen-

---

[58] Ibid, 424–31.

[59] "My call to the ministry was quite different from most explanations I've heard. This decision came about in the summer of 1944 when I felt an inescapable urge to serve society. In short, I felt a sense of responsibility which I could not escape." Clayborne Carson, ed., *The Papers of Martin Luther King, Jr.* (University of California Press: Berkeley), 144.

eration of socially concerned individuals who determined that they were destined to be "reverends."

Martin Luther King once described Harry Emerson Fosdick as "the greatest preacher of the century."[60] This admiration led to King's appreciation of and appropriation of various hermeneutical and homiletical practices from Fosdick. At Crozer he drank from Fosdick's 1942 *The Modern Use of the Bible* and was commended by his professor because he had "grasped the theological significance of biblical criticism."[61] This would certainly bear fruit later as King served in a variety of denominational positions during his early years as a pastor.

Daddy King raised his son in what Martin called "a rather strict fundamentalist tradition."[62] The preacher's son would leave seminary rejecting the tradition of his childhood. Initially attracted to Liberalism, he found its doctrine of man inadequate in light of mankind's obvious bent towards sin. However, an "indelible imprint" was made on King's thinking by Walter Rauschenbusch's *Christianity and the Social Crisis*. Once his approach to the gospel was realigned, he studied social and ethical theory. A methodology was discovered in the life and teachings of Mahatma Gandhi, thus providing King with a peculiar approach as a Civil Rights advocate.[63] Incidentally, as it regards black Baptist piety, King also happened to be the best-known black Baptist in the world.

It is certainly noteworthy that black Baptist piety has not merely been affected by the major distraction of "race," but rather by multiple distractions: (a) no theology, (b) liberation theology, (c) the Health, Wealth, and Prosperity Gospel, and (d) the Social Gospel.

[60] Robert Moats Miller. *Harry Emerson Fosdick: Preacher, Pastor, Prophet.* (New York: Oxford University Press, 1985), viii.

[61] MLK Papers, vol. 1, 251–52. Two Fosdick quotes are demonstrative. "Ours is not the first generation that has found itself surrounded by new circumstances and using new modes of thought. Therefore, our is not the first occasion in history when folk who venerated and believed in a sacred book have been distressed and puzzled because so many things in it seemed unfitted to their modern world. In this recurrent situation there has been one supreme resource: allegory."(Modern Use, 65.) and "And turning his attention to the New Testament, Origen said that the Gospels taken literally contained discrepancies, contradictions, and impossibilities."(Modern Use, 75.)

[62] Martin Luther King, Jr. *Strength to Love* (Collins Publishers: Cleveland, 1963), 147.

[63] Ibid., 150–51. "I came to see for the first time that the Christian doctrine of love, operating through the Gandhian method of non-violence, is one of the most potent weapons available to an oppressed people in their struggle for freedom." And "Christ furnished the spirit and motivation and Gandhi furnished the method."

The term "distraction" is used to convey a lack of intentionality. Biblical orthodoxy was not rejected in light of higher criticism, nor was systematic and biblical theology rejected in light of naturalism. Rather than any rejection of biblical orthodoxy, black Baptist piety was too often depleted of intellectual, rhetorical, and literary resources because of the demands of the "freedom struggle." This failed to address vital theological matters, particularly theodicy and exclusivity.[64]

There are hopeful signs of clarifying elements in black Baptist life: (a) the influence of Pentecostalism, (b) greater educational opportunities for younger pastors and a generational shift from the MLK paradigm, (c) the emergence of black reformed or expositional pastor/theologians, and (d) the steady, if often a minority voice, of plain "simple" gospel preachers. Perhaps the twenty-first century will provide an opportunity for an undistracted black Baptist piety to emerge in a post-slavery, post-segregation, and post-Civil Rights era.

Black Pentecostalism has influenced black Baptist piety, particularly in the areas of worship and sanctification.[65] Its otherworldliness and christocentrism has been an appealing alternative to the worldliness sometimes associated with a black piety overwhelmed by current political and social challenges. In the post-Civil Rights era, more educational opportunities are available for the training of black ministers. Particularly, evangelical Bible-believing schools (that previously would have been all-white) have opened their doors to black students. This can provide the basis for a more New Testament guided understanding of mission and the local church for black Baptists heading forward. These diverse educational opportunities also provide wider models of ministry than the previously dominant social-gospel model of Martin Luther King Jr. Additionally, black Baptist piety is also being shaped by young, thoughtful new pastor-writers and well-known preachers.[66]

---

[64] Note "Joint Baptist Board Meeting Points of Agreed Action" of 2005.

[65] Pentecostalism refers to the movement associated with the Azusa Street Revival in Los Angeles, CA in 1906. Four historic denominations emerged from that movement: The Church of God, the Assemblies of God, the Church of the Foursquare, and the mostly black Church of God in Christ (the largest of the four). Although Pentecostals were influential, Baptists have rejected their distinctive doctrines of subsequence and initial evidence.

[66] Four examples of writers are Eric Redmond, Anthony Carter, Roger Skepple, and Thabiti Anyabwile. Two preacher examples would be Ralph West (Houston, TX) who has been a model of contemporary, urban ministry built upon expository preaching and the late E.K. Bailey (Dallas, TX) who developed the first black conference focusing on expository preaching. Bailey also led in the area of racial reconciliation in the Body of Christ.

Finally, black Baptists have always had those in their midst that felt called to nothing more (and nothing less) than "tell the old, old story" of the life, death, burial, and resurrection of the Lord Jesus Christ. These, often uneducated, grounded soldiers have always been present in every generation. As blacks sought to elevate themselves in the various freedom struggles in American history, these preachers were often ridiculed as being "simple" preachers. Actually, in the long story of black Baptists in America, these simple ones in every era were perhaps the most undistracted.

Part Two

Theological

6

The Authority of Scripture
THE BIBLE AND BAPTISTS

David S. Dockery

As hard as it is for me to believe, it has been thirty years since I first met Tom Nettles. I was an eager student at Southwestern Seminary; he was a gifted faulty member in the department of church history. One of the youngest professors at the seminary at the time, Tom had a way of bringing his enthusiasm about Baptist history to the classroom that made the subject inviting for others. It was my initial foray into this world, a world that has fascinated me now for three decades. That Baptist history class was augmented by the young professor's participation in the campus tricycle race and those times when he would stop lecturing in his class to break into singing, which might be a hymn or a show tune from a Broadway musical like "Oklahoma." While these things made class fun, it was his love for Baptist history that invited engagement.

Not long after that semester, I was invited to serve as a grader for his classes. During this time he and Russ Bush were writing *Baptists and the Bible*. I was invited to help with the indexing and proofreading. In thanksgiving for Tom Nettles and the many years of friendship we have enjoyed, it is a delight to participate in this project to honor him. To do so, I would like to address two themes important to him: "The Bible and Baptists."

A People of the Book

Baptists are "a people of the Book," who have historically viewed Scripture as a special form of revelation, a unique mode of divine disclosure. In many ways a commitment to the authority of Holy Scripture represents one of the key hallmarks of faithful Baptist identity. Yet, we recognize that scriptural authority has been challenged throughout the history of the church, and particularly since the rise of the Enlightenment. As we write these words we are aware that fresh challenges, in their post conservative, post liberal, and postmodern forms, abound. Current issues and struggles in Baptist circles are not dissimilar to parallel debates taking place in Christianity at large.

Today the mainline denominations are characterized by liberal ex-perientialists who make human moral experience the primary basis for the church's message. On the other hand, fundamentalists have tended to equate cultural norms and forms of philosophical rationalism with the truth of Scripture. I believe that if we are to see renewal in Baptist life then we must avoid both extremes in offering an understanding of inspiration, interpretation, and authority of Scripture.

We need unapologetically to reaffirm the complete truthfulness and absolute authority of God's Word for our day in line with the best of our Baptist heritage. Each generation must consider anew the relationship of the divine and human aspects of Scripture, the understanding of truth, the place of the reader or community in the interpretation, and the meaning of authority. Likewise, we want to reaffirm an understanding of Scripture that equally maintains the unity of Word and Spirit in line with the great heritage of the church. While stressing the divine and human aspects of Holy Scripture, we acknowledge that the Bible is the Word of God writ-ten, in which we find God's Word to his people for all times.

In Baptist life there are a great number of people who have been taught in their homes and churches to believe that the Bible is an inspired book written by godly men. The Bible as it stands is to be believed as God's revelation to men and women, and since it is God's revelation, it is to be studied and obeyed. As previously noted, others, influenced by Enlighten-ment philosophy, have great difficulty accepting biblical accounts as mi-raculous without reinterpreting or demythologizing them. Our challenge is to do justice to the mystery of Scripture's divine inspiration and still affirm its human authorship. It is our belief that the divine-human tension continues to be one of the most crucial issues in contemporary discussions concerning Scripture.

Scripture cannot rightly be understood unless we take into consider-ation that it has a dual-sided authorship. It is not enough to affirm that the Bible is a human witness to divine revelation because the Bible is also God's witness. An affirmation that Scripture is partly the Word of God and partly the words of humans is inadequate. What must be affirmed is that the Bible is entirely and completely the Word of God and the words of human authors (Acts 4:25).

It is not entirely appropriate to make a direct correspondence between Scripture and Jesus Christ, but, nevertheless, there is an observable analogy. Just as the conception of Jesus came by the miraculous overshadowing of the Holy Spirit (Luke 1:35), so Scripture is the product of the Spirit's inspiration (2 Timothy 3:16). Likewise, as Jesus took on human form through a human mother, so the Bible has come to us in human language through human authors. The result is that Jesus is the living Word of God, the God-man, and the Bible is the written Word of God, the divine-human Scripture.

An affirmation that Scripture is completely the Word of God and the very words of humans also points to its dual-sided nature. Because it is the Word of the infinite, all-knowing, eternal God, it speaks eternal truth that is applicable to readers of all time beyond the original recipients. Yet, at the same time, it is the word from godly men to specific communities addressing problems and situations within certain contexts and cultures.

How can it be affirmed that Scripture is the inspired Word of God when it is a collection of books by human authors? Can the words of the Bible be identified with the Word of God? Is some of the Bible God's Word or can this be affirmed for all of the Bible? How is it possible that the Bible can simultaneously be the Word of God and a human composition?

The Divine Authorship of Inspired Scripture

In the history of the church, the divine character of Scripture has been the great presupposition for the whole of Christian preaching and theology. This is readily apparent in the way the New Testament speaks about the Old Testament. Because of the divine origin and content of Scripture it can be described as "sure" (2 Peter 1:19), "trustworthy" (1 Timothy 1:15; 3:1; 4:9; 2 Timothy 2:11; Titus 3:8), "confirmed" (Hebrews 2:3), and "eternal" (1 Peter 1:24–25). As a result those who build their lives on Scripture "will not be disappointed" (Romans 9:33; 1 Peter 2:6). The Word was written for "instruction and encouragement" (Romans 15:4) to lead to saving faith (2 Timothy 3:15), to guide people toward godliness (2 Timothy 3:16b), and to equip believers for good works (2 Timothy 3:17).

The purpose of Scripture is to place men and women in a right standing before God and to enable believers to seek God's glory in all of life's activities and efforts. But Scripture is not concerned only with a person's religious needs, for the divine character, origin, and content of Scripture teaches us to understand everything *sub specie Dei* (which includes: humanity, the world, nature, history, their origin and their destination, their past and their future). The Bible is not only a book of conversion, but also a book of creation and history. It is a book of redemptive history, and it is this perspective that best represents and defines the divine character of Scripture.

We must recognize that central to Scripture is the unifying history of God's redeeming words and acts, of which the advent and work of Christ is the ultimate focus. Jesus Christ is the center to which everything in Scripture is united and bound together—beginning and end, creation and redemption, humanity, the world, the fall, history and the future. If this overriding unity is ignored, Scripture is denatured and can lose its "theological-Christological definition" and become abstracted from its peculiar nature and content. The entirety of Scripture is divinely inspired and is God's light upon our path and God's lamp for our feet. We now turn our attention to the nature of inspiration and the Bible's witness to itself.

Biblical Inspiration

The term *inspiration* (*theopneustos*) has a long heritage in the theological literature, but it is always used with further explanation and disclaimers. This is because *theopneustos* means "God-breathed." In contemporary usage the term *inspiration* suggests the idea of "breathing into." Secular emphasis is generally synonymous with illumination or human genius. But the New Testament emphasis is that God "breathed out" what the sacred writers convey in the biblical writings. The point that must be stressed when using this term is that it points to God as the source of Scripture.

The idea of inspiration primarily focuses on the product, though it also has implications for the process. What must be affirmed is the activity of God throughout the entire process, so that the completed, final product ultimately comes from him. It would be a mistake, however, to think of inspiration only in terms of the time when the Spirit moved the human author to write. The biblical concept of inspiration allows for the activity in special ways within the process without requiring that we understand all of the Spirit's working in one and the same way. Just as in the processes of creation and preservation of the universe God providentially intervened in special ways for specific purposes, so too we can say that, alongside and within this superintending action of the Spirit to inspire human writings in the biblical books, we can posit a special work of the Spirit in bringing God's revelation to the apostles and prophets.

When we discuss the inspiration of Scripture, we must take seriously the human factors in the composition of the Bible. Theologians have described the activity of the Spirit with the activities of the human writers through which the Bible was written as a concursive work. While this perspective of inspiration is consistent with a plenary view of inspiration, it avoids any hint that God mechanically dictated the words of Scripture to the human authors so that they had no real part in the Scripture's composition. Our approach to inspiration attempts to take seriously the circumstances of the human authors. We think it quite plausible to suggest that just a revelation was manifested in various ways (Hebrews 1:1–2), so the process of inspiration differed with each author. Even if inspiration differs and is somehow less recognizable to the readers in some places, the entire Bible (*pas graphē*, "all canonical Scripture") can be characterized as inspired (*theopneustos*).

Human Authorship of Inspired Scripture

The biblical writers employed the linguistic resources available to them as they wrote to specific people with particular needs at particular times. The human authors were not lifted out of their culture or removed from their contexts. They were not autonomous, but functioning members within communities of faith, aware of God's presence and leadership in their lives. Obviously, these writers were not unbiased historical observers, but men committed to faith. The concursive action of Spirit and human authorship is informed by the spiritual commitments of the writers.

The biblical text is indeed the words of human authors in temporal-cultural contexts, but this does not limit the plausibility that God's eternal revelation can be communicated through their writings to contemporary men and women. We fully recognize the humanness and historicity of the text but simultaneously acknowledge that God's revelation can be communicated through such situations. The fact that the biblical authors were men of faith informs the issue of concursive inspiration; in the same way, recognition that every person bears the image of God has implications for the possibility of communication across cultures and ages.

It is readily obvious that the Bible is composed of different types of literature. Likewise, the form in which the teaching is expressed is influenced by literary genre. Each genre, whether legal, prophetic, lyric, gospel, epistolary, or apocalyptic, has distinctive characteristics. It is from the various collection of writings that the basic prophetic-apostolic message is discovered.

Not only is there variety of genres, but there is often variety within a particular genre. For instance, the different theological emphases among the synoptic writers demonstrate that there is variety even within the genre of gospel. Matthew's kingdom theology differs from Mark's servant theology, and they are each different from Luke's stress upon Jesus as Savior of the world. Yet, the central unity of Jesus Christ and the developing history of redemption cannot be ignored.

There is variety in the expression of the central message of the gospel. Variety works within the limits of the gospel. The different writers, with their own emphases, varied their expression according to their unique purposes and settings. We recognize that variety does not imply contradiction. But within this very real and rich variety that evidences the humanness of Scripture, there is a genuine unity that is the result of the divine superintending work of inspiration.

Plenary Inspiration

The Holy Spirit's work of inspiration certainly influenced the writers, but the focus of the Spirit's work of inspiration is primarily on the writings. The work of inspiration extends to all portions of Holy Scripture, even beyond the direction of thoughts to the selection of words. Even though the words are those that God wants communicated, the human writer expressed this message in a way that evidenced the situation of the writing and the author's unique style, background, and personality. We must recognize the element of mystery involved in this process, which does not fully explain the how of inspiration.

This understanding seeks to do justice to the human factors in the Bible's composition and avoids any attempt to suggest that entire books of the Bible were dictated. We believe this view best accounts for the divine character of Scripture and the human circumstances of the Bible's composition.

Inspired Scripture: Normative for Today?

We believe that the teaching concerning God and matters relating to God and his creation (*sub specie Dei*) is normative for the contemporary church. When such matters are proclaimed and confessed in the 21st Century, however, mere repetition of early Christian beliefs may not be sufficient; a restatement that awakens modern readers to an awareness that the Bible speaks in relevant ways to contemporary issues in church and society is also necessary. When Scripture is approached from this perspective, it will be necessary to determine underlying principles for all portions of Scripture that address the contemporary situation, even if the direct teaching of Scripture is somehow limited by cultural-temporal factors (see 1 Timothy 5:23; 1 Corinthians 16:20; Ephesians 6:5).

Believers will recognize that this is the case because of the two-sided character of Scripture. Because it is authored by humans in specific contexts, certain teachings may be contextually limited, but because it is divinely inspired, the underlying principles are normative and applicable for believers in every age. When approaching the Bible, recognizing its authoritative and normative character, we can discover truth and its ramifications for the answers to life's ultimate questions as well as guidelines and principles for godly living in the contemporary world.

We thus commit ourselves afresh to the relationship of the divine and human aspects of Scripture, as well as the truthfulness and authority of inspired Scripture. We affirm an understanding of Scripture that equally affirms the unity of Word and Spirit in line with the great heritage of the church. Likewise we need to stress the divine and human aspects of Holy Scripture, while affirming that the Bible is the Word of God written in which we find the truthfulness of God's Word to his people for all times.

The Truthfulness and Authority of God's Inspired Word

If the words of Scripture are God-breathed, it is almost blasphemy to deny that the Bible is free from error in that which it is intended to teach and infallible in the guidance it gives. When faced by difficulties in and objections to the truthfulness of inspired Scripture, we will infer that the problem is our failure to comprehend God's testimony to make truth plain, and we will be driven back to a closer rethinking of the matter in light of a closer study of the biblical evidence. Thus in our dealings with the doctrine of Scripture or the doctrine of God or other theological challenges, it is the sifting and weighing of Scripture in light of the history of doctrine that shapes our convictions. Certainly we learn from the debates between Arius and Athanasius and between Pelagius and Augustine, all of whom appealed to Scripture, that our goal is the careful and faithful reading of Scripture that has ultimately shaped the consensus of faith through the ages. This is how all doctrinal advance has been made throughout the history of the church. This is also how a more true and full understanding of the theological challenges for the 21st Century can be reached as well.

While Scripture possesses a practical relevance for us today, it must be stressed that Scripture's authority is not grounded in such contemporary relevance. Scripture is truthful and authoritative whether its subjective dimension is appreciated or not. The unique authority of Scripture rests on the activity of the revealing God, both in relation to the biblical material and to a similar extent in the subsequent work of the Holy Spirit in interpretation and appropriation by the readers. As we have previously noted, an orthodox understanding of Scripture is not merely rational but must be one that includes Word and Spirit.

A confession of the Bible's full truthfulness is an important and necessary affirmation. We must recognize, however, that a statement about the Bible's truthfulness or its inerrancy is an insufficient statement for Baptists to maintain consistent evangelical instruction and theological method; which is needed for an orthodox confession in the essential matters of salvation, Christology, and the doctrine of God. We heartily confess that the truthfulness of the Bible, as a corollary of inspiration, is a foundational issue on which other theological building blocks are laid. Twenty-first century Southern Baptists must therefore choose to articulate a view of the Bible for the contemporary Christian community that is faithful to historic Baptist positions that have characteristically confessed that the Bible is the written Word of God, is truthful, infallible, and is the only authoritative rule of all saving knowledge, faith, and obedience.

The Bible and Baptists: A Brief Historical Overview

As early as 1611, Thomas Helwys, in Article 23 of the first Baptist confession, set forth the following view of Scripture:

> That the scriptures off the Old and New Testament are written for our instruction, 2 Tim. 3:16, and that we ought to search them for they testifie off Christ, Io. 5:39, and therefore to bee used with all reverence, as conteyning the Holy Word off God, which onlie is our direction in all things whatsoever.

The early London Confessions (1644, 1677) similarly confessed the Bible as the Rule of all knowledge, faith, and obedience. The 1678 Orthodox Creed, a General Baptist statement, confessed the Scriptures "are given by the inspiration of God, to be the Rule of faith and life" (Article 37). The Philadelphia Confession (1742), which so greatly influenced Baptists in America, followed the language of the Second London Confession (1677).

In 1833 the New Hampshire Confession, an altogether new document for Baptists in America, articulated a high view of Scripture with language that has been officially adopted by many other Baptist groups, including the Baptist Faith and Message of the Southern Baptist Convention (1925, 1963, 2000). Article 1 declares:

> We believe that the Bible is written by men divinely inspired, and is a perfect treasure of heavenly instruction; that is has God for its author,

salvation for its end, and truth, without any mixture of error, for its matter...

Readily apparent is the confidence that Baptists have and have had in the Bible, its inspiration and authority. Since 1845, when the Southern Baptist Convention (SBC) began, there have been hundreds of pastors and professors who have influenced the shape of Southern Baptists theology. We will take a brief look at some of these influential and shaping thinkers throughout the 165 year history of the SBC.

John L. Dagg

John L. Dagg (1794–1844) served as president and professor of theology at Mercer University from 1844–54. In his *Manual of Theology*, he explained, "to us in these last days God speaks in his written word, the Bible, which is the perfect source of religious knowledge and the infallible standard of religious truth."

Basil Manly, Jr.

In 1888, Basil Manly, Jr. (1825–92), a founding member of the Southern Seminary faculty, penned *The Bible Doctrine of Inspiration*, in which he contended that an uninspired Bible would furnish no infallible standard of thought, no authoritative rule for obedience, and no ground for confidence and everlasting hope. He maintained that every aspect of Scripture is characterized as infallible and divine truth.

B. H. Carroll

B. H. Carroll (1843–1914) was the founder and first president of Southwestern Baptist Theological Seminary. The Bible was the focus of Carroll's career. He emphasized that inspiration insured a perfect standard of instruction, conviction, and is a profitable work for correction and instruction in righteousness.

J. M. Frost

The first leader of the Baptist Sunday School Board, J. M. Frost (1848–1916), edited a major work in 1900 that represented Baptists at the turn of the century. In *Baptists Why and Why Not*, Frost wrote, "We accept the Scriptures as an all-sufficient and infallible rule of faith and practice, and insist upon the absolute inerrancy and sole authority of the Word of God." Similar affirmations can be found during this period in the writings of J. B. Jeter, J. M. Pendleton, John A. Broadus, J. P. Boyce, A. T. Robertson, R. L. Davidson, T. T. Eaton, F. H. Kerfoot, E. C. Dargan, and J. Van Ness.

E. Y. Mullins

E. Y. Mullins (1860–1928) served as the fourth president and professor of theology at Southern Seminary. Mullins remained very much in the mainstream of Baptist thought during his decades as the leading Southern Baptist theologian of the period. While engaging wide intellectual interests and contemporary theological formulations, he continued the united consensus regarding Scripture that existed in the Southern Baptist Convention during its first seventy-five years. Nowhere are his traditional emphases better seen than in his 1923 address to the Southern Baptist Convention on "The Dangers and Duties of this Present Hour," where he concluded that the Bible is "God's revelation of himself and is the sufficient and authoritative guide for all life."

W. T. Conner

The role that Mullins played at Southern Seminary was carried out at Southwestern Seminary by W. T. Conner (1872–1952). While Conner relegated discussions regarding theories of inspiration to theological obscurity, he unhesitatingly confessed the Bible as the product of God's revelation, with redemption its central interest and Jesus Christ as its center. He believed these themes were central to understanding the Bible's overarching unity. Conner did not recognize any errors in the Bible and emphasized the Bible's divine origin and absolute authority in all matters spiritual. Historic Baptist positions regarding biblical inspiration and authority during the middle decades of the 20th Century can also be found in the works of William B. Nowlin, H. E. Dana, J. J. Reeve, R. G. Lee, J. B. Tidwell, among others.

1950–present

Theology in the post-Mullins/Conner era introduced an innovative time in a denomination moving out of its Old South context. The mid-twentieth century Southern Baptist Convention struggled with questions regarding the rise of biblical criticism. Controversy surrounded the use of biblical criticism in publications like the *Message of Genesis* (1961) and the first volume of *The Broadman Bible Commentary* (1969). New approaches to biblical interpretation and new ways of describing the Bible's nature were articulated, ways contrary to historic Baptist positions. One of the most important works affirming the historic Baptist position on biblical inspiration was a book penned by Russ Bush and Tom Nettles called *Baptists and the Bible*.

The controversy in SBC life surrounding the nature of Holy Scripture is well known and needs no further commentary at this point. The 1992 doctrine study for the SBC, while interacting with modern thought, nevertheless reaffirmed the inerrancy of Scripture, echoing the consensus viewpoint reflective of earlier Baptist theologians. This work, *The Doctrine of the Bible*, maintained that the Bible attests to its own inspiration, which can be characterized as plenary and concursive. This understanding of Scripture characterizes and represents the viewpoints of most all leaders in Southern Baptist life in the 21st Century.

Conclusion

As Baptists, particularly Southern Baptists, move forward into the 21st Century, we must convictionally and unapologetically stand where Scripture stands and speak where Scripture speaks. We heartily affirm the Bible's full truthfulness, authority, and sufficiency, which means that its full message speaks prescriptively and normatively to us today. We acknowledge that Scripture speaks not just to pietistic and religious needs but to the truth of and about God, and to all matters related to life and godliness. We call on Baptists to articulate carefully a doctrine of Scripture that maintains with equal force both the human and divine aspects of the Bible. Moreover, we commit ourselves as "people of the Book" to inspired Scripture, placing our trust and confidence in the truthful, trustworthy, and reliable written Word of God.*

---

* Large portions of this chapter previously appeared in the books, chapters, and articles listed in the "Sources" section of this chapter and are herein used with permission. Full documentation regarding additional sources is available in these works.

Sources

Black, David A. and David S. Dockery. *New Testament Criticism and Interpretation*. Grand Rapids, MI: Zondervan, 1991.

Dockery, David S. *Biblical Interpretation Then and Now*. Grand Rapids, MI: Baker, 1992.

_____. *Christian Scripture: An Evangelical Perspective on Inspiration, Authority and Interpretation*. Nashville, TN: Broadman & Holman, 1995.

_____. *Southern Baptist Consensus and Renewal*. Nashville, TN: Broadman & Holman, 2008.

_____. "The Divine-Human Authorship of Inspired Scripture," in *Authority and Interpretation: A Baptist Perspective*, edited by Duane A. Garrett and Richard R. Melick, Jr. Grand Rapids, MI: Baker, 1987.

_____. *The Doctrine of the Bible*. Nashville, TN: Convention, 1991.

_____. "The Inerrancy and Authority of Scripture," *Theological Educator* 17 (1988):15–36.

_____, editor. *New Dimensions in Evangelical Thought*. Downers Grove, IL: InterVarsity, 1998.

_____, editor. *Southern Baptists and American Evangelicals*. Nashville, TN: Broadman & Holman, 1993.

_____, editor. *Southern Baptist Identity: An Evangelical Denomination Faces the Future*. Wheaton, IL: Crossway, 2009.

Dockery, David S. and E. Ray Clendenen, editors. "Preface." *New American Commentary*. Nashville, TN: Broadman & Holman, 1991.

Dockery, David S., Kenneth A. Mathews, and Robert B. Sloan, editors. *Foundations for Biblical Interpretation*. Nashville, TN: Broadman & Holman, 1994.

Dockery, David S. with David Nelson, "The Doctrine of Scripture," in *A Theology for the Church*, edited by Daniel Akin. Nashville, TN: Broadman & Holman, 2007.

George, Timothy and David S. Dockery, editors. *Theologians of the Baptist Tradition*. Nashville, TN: Broadman & Holman, 2001.

7

Without One Plea

HUMAN DEPRAVITY AND THE CHRISTIAN GOSPEL

Russell D. Moore

Whenever I think of Tom Nettles, I can't help but hear, off there somewhere in the background, the hymn "Just As I Am." While there are many moments that come to mind when I imagine Tom Nettles, perhaps one stands out over all the others, and it has joined the Baptist historian and that song forever in my memory. My wife and I were sitting in church in LaGrange, Kentucky, a congregation where Tom Nettles and I co-taught a Sunday school class. On Sunday evenings, such as this one, the minister of music would sometimes stop the congregational singing abruptly in the middle of a song and point to Nettles: "Tom, you sing the third verse."

Now I loved "Just As I Am" and I loved Tom Nettles, but the two seemed contradictory in my mind, and I found myself somewhere between the worlds represented by each. Charlotte Elliott's hymn, after all, was the anthem of twentieth-century revivalism. It had been Billy Graham's altar call song, and then trickled down to the closing song of countless invitations in Southern Baptist churches throughout the South and beyond. And here was Tom Nettles, the godfather of contemporary Baptist Calvinism, and perhaps the sharpest critic in history of revivalism in the Southern Baptist Convention.[1] I started to smile at the irony of it all. But not for long.

[1] See, for instance, Tom J. Nettles, *Ready for Reformation? Bringing Authentic Reform to Southern Baptist Churches* (Nashville, TN: Broadman and Holman, 2005), 51–63.

I heard that central Mississippi voice fill the sanctuary with the haunting notes of that grand old song: "Just as I am, tho' tossed about, with many a conflict, many a doubt, fightings within and fears without, O Lamb of God, I come, I come." Tears streamed down my face—as they almost always do when I hear that song. This, after all, is where I first heard lyrically of the grace of God in the gospel, a song that embedded the good news deep in my childhood consciousness through thousands of worship services in a little church on the Gulf Coast of Mississippi. My tears came even more rapidly this time though, because I was hearing those liberating words, that haunting tune, from the vocal chords of a man whose writings had convinced me, in the middle of a great internal conflict years before, that my home church had been right to teach me that the Bible is truth without any mixture of error.[2] All I could do is watch the tears fall to the page of the hymnal, and hope they wouldn't stain it.

Truth is, the more I've thought about it, that moment was not nearly as ironic as I initially took it to be. Neither "Just As I Am" nor Tom Nettles live up to the caricatures conjured up about them. Moreover, "Just As I Am" sums up much of what Nettles has been calling Baptists to reconsider about the mercy and faithfulness and power of the gospel of God. As a matter of fact, the hymn throbs with a consensus uniting Baptists around what some might consider the most depressing and divisive of all the doctrines Tom Nettles and others like him have emphasized: the depravity of the human race.

The invitation hymn melds together the hopeless guilt of the sinner— "Just as I am, poor, wretched, blind"—with the free offer of the gospel— "Just as I am, thou wilt receive, wilt welcome, pardon, cleanse, receive." That is precisely the reason Nettles highlights human depravity in his writing and teaching, and why he doesn't consider it isolated and in the abstract. That's why, in Nettles magnum opus on the doctrine of salvation, depravity doesn't stand alone, but is considered in a chapter together with the call to salvation.[3] For Nettles, depravity and the overcoming of depravity by the Spirit aren't ethereal ideas. They are instead matters of spiritual warfare, a conflict between this present darkness and the kingdom of Christ. As Nettles put it, reflecting on 2 Corinthians 4:3–4: "Since man is under captivity and blinded by such a powerful foe, his only hope is that God may

---

[2] It is difficult to overestimate the influence, especially on the second wave of resurgent Baptist conservatives, of Nettles' book (written with L. Russ Bush, his then-colleague at Southwestern Baptist Theological Seminary) *Baptists and the Bible* (Chicago, IL: Moody, 1980).

[3] Tom J. Nettles, *By His Grace and For His Glory: A Historical, Theological, and Practical Study of the Doctrines of Grace in Baptist Life* (Grand Rapids, MI: Baker, 1986), 285–96.

grant repentance."[4] It is here that I think Nettles' vision of depravity can benefit even those who do not wholly agree with his doctrinal synthesis at other points. If we can grasp the holistic nature of human depravity, we might be able to re-focus our churches on the holistic nature of our gospel and of our mission. This will mean recapturing a moral imagination that pictures human depravity as only part of the story, a story of God's invading reign in Christ Jesus.

Human Depravity and the Gospel of Christ

The concept of total depravity seems naturally repugnant to most human beings. At first we might, in an attempt to seem spiritually superior, announce that this proves the rightness of the doctrine. It isn't "man-centered," we might want to say, but "God-centered," and, after all, his ways are not our ways. The very fact that it dethrones a human sense of rightness and justice, some might conclude, is all the more in its favor as an aspect of biblical revelation. But that doesn't quite work. Yes, the Bible does say that a way that "seems right to a man" leads to death (Proverbs 14:12). And, yes, Jesus' call to discipleship often seems to completely upend our "normal" human expectations and sense of what is right and true (for example, Luke 14:25–27). Yes, the prophet Job and the apostle Paul, and even the humiliated tyrant Nebuchadnezzar, call on human beings to shut their mouths in awe-filled silence as they seek to interrogate God for what he does (Job 42:1–6; Daniel 4:35; Romans 9:20).

But, on the other hand, Jesus sometimes also affirms our basic human intuition of what seems right and true. The Pharisees, for example, ought to know that a devil vs. devil warfare, as they are suggesting in the picture of a demon-possessed Jesus casting out demons, is nonsensical (Matthew 12:22–26). A father's instinct—even that of a spiritually lost father—to feed his child is in sync with the way the universe is designed (Matthew 7:9–11). Paul acknowledges the fundamental rightness of the human intuition that holding someone accountable for a law he doesn't know is unjust (Romans 2:12–3:20). If so, then what if our experience of knowing that our non-Christian neighbors aren't utterly wicked—and that, in fact, many of them can be kinder and more compassionate than some professing Christians—is an indicator that we ought to reconsider a doctrine of total depravity?

Many have objected to the doctrine of total depravity not because of what the doctrine teaches but because of what the name implies. "Total depravity" is, to use contemporary marketing lingo, "branded" in a totally

[4] Ibid., 291.

unhelpful way. Baptist historian Timothy George correctly notes that the term "total depravity" suggests, by implication, a quantitative measure of wickedness, that all human beings are as evil as they can possibly be. Because, as George says, "The image of God in fallen human beings has not been completely destroyed," he suggests that Christians speak of a "radical" depravity rather than a "total" depravity.[5] Regardless of whether "radical"—referring to the "root" level of sin—gets more closely to the nub of the issue, George is almost certainly correct that "total depravity" is easily misunderstood.

The "total" in "total depravity," however, at least as it is in articulated in the Baptist confessional tradition, does not refer to a degree of wickedness but rather to its location. Human sin is not quarantined in a single aspect of our existence—our intellect, for instance, or our will. Our sin nature, rather, affects every part of what it means to be human—our intellects, our affections, our wills, our imaginations, our consciences, and so forth. No one is as wicked as he could possibly be, thanks to the restraining grace of God in this fallen universe. It is better, I think, to speak of our depravity as "holistic" rather than "total." It also means that we must consider personal sin in light of the overarching cosmic storyline of the gospel.

First, depravity only makes sense when we grasp that the Bible is not primarily a catechism of doctrine or a handbook of moral principles, but a war-plan. While I disagree with theologian Gregory Boyd's understanding of God as self-limited in knowledge and on a few other points, he is correct that the Scripture projects a "warfare worldview" of conflict between the triune God and a band of rebel spirits who have highjacked the creation through deception, sin, and death.[6] This mystery of iniquity is at the core of our Christian view of human depravity.

After all, the very beginning of the biblical story presents us with a reptile, a created beast that is morally fallen not only in his choices but also in his very character. He is, the Bible says, "more crafty than any other beast of the field" (Genesis 3:1). The rest of the canon fills in for us something of the mystery here: this snake is a dragon, and the dragon is an unclean spirit at war with the image of God embedded in the human creation (Revelation 12:1–17). Jesus has arrived in order to "destroy the works of the devil" (1 John 3:8)—by freeing us from accusation of sin through his blood (Revelation 12:10), by overcoming our sentence of death through his resurrection (1 Peter 3:22), and by renewing the image of God in hu-

---

[5] Timothy George, *Amazing Grace: God's Initiative—Our Response* (Nashville, TN: LifeWay, 2000), 72.

[6] Gregory A. Boyd, *God at War: The Bible and Spiritual Conflict* (Downers Grove, IL: InterVarsity, 1997).

man nature so that we can participate in "the freedom of the glory of the children of God" (Romans 8:21,29).

One does not need to believe the biblical revelation to understand that a human being doesn't make up his own nature as he goes along. In every life, and in every set of choices, there is a context. A Darwinian account of our origins gives us one reading of why we do what we don't want to do, and why we want what we don't want to want. Various psychological theories—from Freudianism on down—attempt to a further explanation. The Christian narrative, though, asserts that humanity, at the very beginning of the race, joined an already-existing insurrection. By listening to the word of an unclean spirit, rather than to the Word of God, we cut ourselves off from the only source of life, God himself. The immediate consequence was, of course, a sentence of death, but notice in the biblical text how comprehensive the Fall was, affecting humanity at the level not only of death but in terms of sexuality, communion, vocation, the family, and on and on (Genesis 3:7–24). By coming under the accusation of the one who had the power of accusation, we became his prey (Hebrews 2:14–15).

An account of human depravity, therefore, that ignores the devil is biblically deficient. The reign of the satanic powers explains the extent of depravity, and does not require that one surrender to the demons our own responsibility and guilt. Human nature was never intended to be autonomous. We were designed to be governed by the Word of God, a Word that governed our calling and our appetites (Genesis 2:15–16). Now in our fallenness, we are governed by the word of another god, one who rules us through the chaos of our own appetites. Yes, we are, apart from Christ, "dead in trespasses and sins" (Ephesians 2:1). We are, apart from the gospel, the walking dead, "following the course of the world, following the prince of the power of the air" (Ephesians 2:2), who guides us through "the passions of our flesh, carrying out the desires of the body and the mind" (Ephesians 2:3). As the Scriptures present the picture, we are part of a conspiracy between the satanic powers (our chosen rulers), the world system around us ("the course of this world"), and our own twisted desires (our "flesh"). With the world around us under the sway of the demonic, we can't even see what "normal" would be apart from sin. And with our desires bent away from God's purposes, our nature resembles that of the devil himself. This is critical to understanding the extent of the depravity of fallen humanity.

In an encounter with some skeptical crowds, Jesus locates the source of their unbelief to the very core of their nature. If they were Abraham's children, they would walk in his way, Jesus argues (John 8:39). But instead their rejection of the truth shows that they "are of your father the devil, and your will is to do your father's desires" (John 8:44). Clearly, the hearers are free in one sense. They are not being coerced, but are doing what they want to do. But Jesus speaks of them as "slaves" to their own sin (John 8:34) because they are bound, by nature, to satanic desire.

The devil, we would probably all concede, is "free." He is free in the sense we use the word in the sentence, "It's a free country; you can do what you want." He does what he wants to do. Therein precisely is the problem. There are some places in the world, I suppose, where I might be "free" to marry my sister, but the very idea is repugnant to me. The "freedom" to do what I want can't change my moral revulsion at the idea of it all. Nettles is correct to argue that free will is always contextual. We act freely in accordance with our natures, our environment, our experiences, and "all our actions are done as a part of a complex convergence of factors that we find persuasive in an unbroken continuum of thinking and doing."[7]

This is why none of us should stay awake at night wondering what will happen to biblical prophecies about the final defeat of Satan should the devil repent of sin and throw himself on the mercies of God. This, quite simply, will never happen—despite the fact that Satan knows both of the reality of God (James 2:19) and of his own impending doom (Revelation 12:12).

Satan's rebellion is not just at the level of his will or of his intellect, but also at the very root of his character. "He was a murderer from the beginning, and has nothing to do with the truth, because there is no truth in him," Jesus says. "When he lies, he speaks out of his own character, for he is a liar and the father of lies" (John 8:44). Jesus tells us that before our liberation by the word of truth, we shared a nature with the devil himself, and our desires mirrored his (John 8:44).

This is why the Scriptures present such a bleak view of human nature. It is not just that we were guilty in our actions but none of us understood God or wanted to seek after him (Romans 3:10–18). As a matter of fact, our fallen response to the light of Christ was not just cognitive rejection but moral revulsion. "And this is the judgment: the light has come into the world and people loved the darkness rather than the light because their works were evil," Jesus says. "For everyone who does wicked things hates the light and does not come to the light, lest his works should be exposed" (John 3:19–20). Because human beings are engaged in a conspiracy to "suppress the truth in unrighteousness" (Romans 1:18), our depravity reaches to every aspect of our being: to our intellects, our volitions, our affections, our imaginations, and so on.

---

[7] Tom J. Nettles, "John Wesley's Contention with Calvinism: Interactions Then and Now," *The Grace of God, the Bondage of the Will: Historical and Theological Perspectives on Calvinism*, vol. 2, ed. Thomas R. Schreiner and Bruce A. Ware (Grand Rapids, MI: Baker, 1995), 322.

This does not mean, again, that human beings are as wicked as can possibly be. Nor does it mean that fallen humanity cannot know truth. Every aspect of God's truth impinges upon human autonomy. But often we cannot clearly see how a particular aspect of that truth impinges on our autonomy. An unbeliever, therefore, can understand agriculture, architecture, music, science, psychology, and even theology or biblical studies up to the point that he sees clearly in it the light of Jesus that challenges his enslaved "freedom." At that point, he will shrink back into his make-believe world of the self-as-god.

Here is an important truth, not only (as we'll see momentarily) about how we engage with unbelievers, but also about how we personally seek to be transformed by the gospel in our sanctification. The depravity the gospel brings us out of isn't simply a cognitive ignorance. As a matter of fact, it is not that at all. We knew there was a God (Romans 1:18–32) and we knew his moral economy (Romans 2:12–16). It is not, as we suppose, that we had a deficient "worldview" and then committed sinful action as a consequence of that; quite the reverse. We wanted to sin, to indulge our fallen natures, and we constructed then a worldview that would justify the approval of our actions (Romans 1:32). First, we become idol-worshippers, and only then—with "darkened minds"—do we find reasons for why we find the idols persuasive (Romans 1:21). We are sinners first, and thinkers later.

What is it that pierced through our blindness and captivity? The convicting power of the Holy Spirit as laid out for us in the gospel, in the "open statement of the truth" that alone is able to let the light shine in the darkness of our bedeviled psyches (2 Corinthians 4:2,6). This is why the gospel is central not only in our initial conversion to Christ, but in every step of our sojourn toward sharing in his glory.

An understanding of human depravity demands a vision of the Christian gospel big enough to encompass all of life. If we know that our hearts—as they are being conformed to Christ's image—are coming from a place in which we couldn't even fathom the way our own affections would deceive us (Jeremiah 17:9), then we are going to be, in one sense, skeptical of the possibility of such deceit. This is why perfectionism and legalism are so morally corrupting. If our depravity were so easily dispensed with—through moral rules or spiritual experiences—we would not need the gospel we have received.

Because we are aware of our own fallenness, we subvert our own tendencies toward sin. The man with a particular vulnerability to pornography might then keep his computer files accessible to his wife. The serial adulterer might quit her job as a truck-driver, knowing that long distances away from her husband create an occasion for sin. The covetous one might leave that Wall Street job for one less likely to provoke him to love of money. Moreover, we live within the web of a church community, in which others are empowered to call us on our deceptions, and hold us account-able to life in the new creation (1 Corinthians 5:1–13; Galatians 6:1–3).

Most importantly, we live with a sense of gratitude. Human depravity ultimately boils down to ingratitude. At the root of our sin is the refusal to honor God as God and to give thanks to him (Romans 1:21). The gospel reminds us of our own fallenness not to lead us into despair but to point us to our identity in Jesus. A holistic doctrine of human depravity might seem to lead to a cynical, misanthropic view of human nature, but that is only if we assume that fallen human nature is "normal." It's not. Jesus is the norm of God's purposes for humanity. We've fallen short of that. But Jesus, without ever committing sin, took on himself the full measure of God's judgment against our fallenness. God now views us, not as we were, but as hidden in Christ Jesus. With this the case, God's response to us isn't condemnation but rejoicing (Zephaniah 3:14–20). And the purifying power of the blood of Jesus doesn't end at changing our intellects but won't stop until it's made it's blessings known, as the hymn says, "far as the curse is found."

Human Depravity and the Mission of Christ

I once heard someone ask Tom Nettles about a very prominent fig-ure in Southern Baptist life, a man who had been completely opposed to Nettles' basic theological framework. In fact, some said that this figure had worked to have Nettles removed from a ministry position he once held out of opposition to the historian's views. When asked about this leader, Nettles told his questioner: "He is one of the godliest and most faithful men I've ever known. He loves Jesus with an unparalleled intensity." This questioner—looking for some red meat controversy, I suppose—was taken aback, and pointed to the leader-in-question's outspoken Arminianism (except, of course, on the question of eternal security). "How can he love Jesus," the questioner asked, "and hate his gospel?"

Nettles turned on his heel, and with a flash in his eye said something along these lines: "He doesn't hate the gospel. He doesn't agree with me on some important matters but it's not because he rejects the gospel but because he embraces it. He doesn't see how my understanding of the gos-pel fits with what he knows to be true: the love of God, the impartiality of God, the free offer of the gospel, and so on. He is right about all of those things, and he doesn't see how they fit with other things I believe the Bible teaches. I don't agree with him, of course, but his opposition doesn't come from a rejection of the gospel but, from his point of view, from his belief in it."

I was stunned to see—especially in a man pictured to be such a controversialist—such empathy, such charity, such bigheartedness, and such humility. What I was hearing was Christlikeness. Nettles didn't identify the issues he found important with himself—as though disagreement with him were a personal attack. While not conceding at all that his view of God's way of salvation was important and biblically revealed, he recognized that an opponent who saw such doctrines as "total depravity" as undercutting the free offer of the gospel was, while mistaken, on the side of the angels.

One of the primary objections to a holistic understanding of human depravity is that such a view would render evangelism and missions meaningless. Baptist theologian Fisher Humphreys agrees that human beings are unable to save themselves by their own effort, but he rejects "total depravity" because, he writes, it suggests that "we cannot repent and have faith in Christ when the gospel is preached to us." This is, he argues, fundamentally opposed to a core Baptist conviction, one that is sung as much as it is preached: "Whosoever will may come."[8]

First of all, the holistic idea of depravity doesn't divide Calvinists and Arminians from cooperating with one another to carry out the mission of Christ. As a matter of fact, despite their differences over libertarian free will, Arminians and Calvinists historically have both held to a holistic understanding of human depravity. The universal church anathematized, after all, both Pelagianism and semi-Pelagianism, any concept that the will was unaffected by the Fall. Jacob Arminius and the Wesley brothers—the most prominent historical proponents of what we now call Arminianism—believed strongly in total depravity, as did the General Baptist (Arminian) wing of the Baptist movement. The Orthodox Creed of the English General Baptists (1679) strongly affirms that in the Edenic Fall man "wholly lost all ability, or liberty of will, to any spiritual good, for his eternal salvation, his will being now in bondage under sin and Satan, and therefore not able of his own strength to convert himself nor prepare himself thereunto."[9] The General Baptists, like other Arminians before them, posited a special act of God's preventing grace (a "special grace," the Orthodox Creed puts it) that overcomes this total depravity and thus allows human beings to decide for or against the gospel.

---

[8] Fisher Humphreys, *The Way We Were: How Southern Baptist Theology Has Changed and What It Means to Us All* (Macon, GA: Smyth and Helwys, 2002), 70–71.

[9] The Orthodox Creed, Article XX, "Of Free-Will in Man," in W.L. Lumpkin, ed., *Baptist Confessions of Faith* (Valley Forge, PA: Judson, 1959), 312.

This is consistent with contemporary expressions of orthodox Arminianism, especially in Baptist life.[10] It is hard to imagine a more definitive statement of total depravity than that by Free Will Baptist theologian Leroy Forlines: "Fallen humanity has no ability or power to reach out to the grace of God on its own."[11] This is a far cry from the "optimistic" view of a neutral or perfectible human nature presented by liberal Protestantism or by some forms of revivalistic "easy-believism." Calvinists then ought not to caricature (orthodox) Arminians as Pelagians, and Arminians shouldn't caricature (evangelical) Calvinists as destroying the personhood of human beings. All of us hold that human nature was depraved in every aspect of its existence in the Adamic Fall; we simply differ on the extent and efficacy of God's overcoming grace to combat this depravity.[12] That's an important argument, but it's an argument that starts with a commonly "pessimistic" view of fallen human freedom. But pessimism doesn't equal passivism.

First of all, the holistic extent of our depravity does not excuse us from our moral responsibility before God. It would be hard to improve on Nettles' assessment of this argument:

> One must never draw the conclusion that moral perversion serves as sufficient excuse for immorality. A kleptomaniac cannot be tolerated in his thievery simply because it is "uncontrollable,' a megalomaniac cannot be indulged simply because his ego is "insatiable," and a man who has cheated his way into an unpayable debt cannot be absolved simply because he is an "incurable" swindler. Likewise, none may excuse himself before God by proclaiming, "I was so steadfastly and unalterably opposed to your will that only omnipotent power could change me."[13]

If we understand our own depravity this way, in light of the gospel, we will reframe our view of the lost in our neighborhoods and around the world. The gospel's insistence, after all, that there is "none righteous, no not one" is not simply a plank in a Roman road evangelistic presentation. It is an ongoing question to everyone in Christ: "For who sees anything different in you? What do you have that you did not receive? If then you received it, why do you boast as though you did not receive it?" (1 Corin-

---

[10] See, for instance, Roger E. Olson, *Arminian Theology: Myths and Realities* (Downers Grove, IL: InterVarsity, 2006), 155–57.

[11] F. Leroy Forlines, *The Quest for Truth: Answering Life's Inescapable Questions* (Nashville, TN: Randall House, 2001), 159.

[12] For an analysis of the idea of prevenient grace from the Wesleyan/Arminian tradition, see J. Gregory Crofford, *Streams of Mercy: Prevenient Grace in the Theology of John and Charles Wesley* (Lexington, KY: Emeth, 2010).

[13] Nettles, *By His Grace and For His Glory*, 294.

thians 4:7). Nettles' vision of depravity consistently emphasizes this. "The gift aspect of justification is highlighted when one realizes that there is no distinction between people," he writes. Since all are "equally sinful," there is no place for boasting. This, Nettles argues, necessitates a dynamic work of the Spirit since, if there is any other factor at work, then "one must conclude that an actual difference exists in the characters or wills of the two respective individuals who responded in different ways to the gospel."[14]

Our understanding of depravity means that we must stop our "culture war" rage against unbelievers, as though the difference between they and us were our moral superiority. The Darwinist behind the lectern in our college class, the sexual liberationist next door, the Buddhist atheist next to us on jury duty, these are not our enemies. They are, like we were, captives to the principalities and powers. Our depravity may have expressed itself in different ways. Perhaps our passions clamored for religious zeal rather than unrestricted orgasms, but the root was the same—a sinful heart—and the outcome would have been the same—exile from the presence of God. The only difference between us and the most hardened unbeliever or the most notorious sinner is the grace of God in Christ Jesus.

This is where the doctrine of holistic depravity becomes crucial to our mission. A holistic vision of human depravity doesn't undercut the free offer of the gospel; it instead makes it possible. After all, what is the foremost obstacle for most unbelievers in keeping them from coming to Christ? Some of them believe themselves to be too good for the gospel; justifying themselves in their own righteousness, they conclude they don't need redemption. Others believe themselves to be too bad for the gospel; shrinking back like Adam and Eve in the bushes, fearful of the sound of God's presence. The concept of holistic depravity does away with both notions. The gospel insists that you are, in fact, a rebel and that there is no rebellion that cannot be washed away by the regenerating power of the Spirit of Christ (1 Corinthians 6:9–11). It doesn't matter who you are—or who your neighbor is—or what you or they have done. We share a common depravity—and it doesn't surprise or thwart the purposes of God.

This means that in our mission we understand that the obstacle to the gospel is moral not ultimately cognitive or cultural. We don't mark off some ethnicities or cultures as "by nature" unresponsive to the gospel. We are all "by nature" unresponsive to the gospel, and so we carry the gospel everywhere. We don't coerce conversions by political pressure or emotional manipulation because such things can never get at the root of the human predicament. We advocate for every person's freedom to worship or not to worship, and we freely offer them the gospel. We don't give up on that

14 Ibid., 287.

unbelieving loved one, just because "she's already heard it all." So had most of us. Think about it for a moment. Did you believe the gospel the first time you ever heard it? Perhaps some of you did, but I'd venture that most of you—like me—heard the gospel over and over again until one day, for some reason, it was different. What was different? Was it some other piece of information ("Ah, I didn't know there was archaeological evidence for the existence of the Hittites. What must I do to be saved?")? Probably not. You probably—like me—heard the same gospel message you'd heard before, but this time you cried out, "Oh my God! That's me!" What made the difference? The convicting power of the Holy Spirit was freeing you from your captivity to the powers and to your passions. Our vision of depravity can teach us never to give up, until death itself, on even the most hardened and distant prodigal.

Conclusion

After Tom Nettles sang the third verse of "Just As I Am" that night, the rest of us joined in with the fourth. I couldn't help but think about how many times I'd heard it, and about how grateful I was for the little congregation that sang it when I was filled with fightings within and fears without. The people in my home church might not have known much about what Tom Nettles would be talking about, if he'd have delivered a lecture on total depravity to them in those days. But we would have understood it if he had sung it.

We would have understood that the core of it is that we are fallen—fallen even in ways we can't even see that we're fallen—but the grace of can reach us, no matter how far in this life we have wandered. The ex-drunk and the ex-adulterer and the ex-embezzler and the ex-Pharisee would have recognized a gospel that told us the truth about who we were, and, through the shed blood and risen body of Jesus, invited us in anyhow. We would have understood, somehow, that we stand before God not because of anything that was intelligent or commendable or moral in us. We would have known, somehow, that even in our looking for Jesus, he was first looking for us. We might not have known the word "depravity," but we would have known that we'd been utterly lost. And, in the final analysis, that's the point of telling ourselves the truth about our depravity. It is not in order to argue a system or to defend a tradition. It is to reframe, constantly, our gospel and our mission toward the good news that we have been saved, by His grace and for His glory, just as we are.

8

God's Sovereign Election

Erroll Hulse

Election is an extremely relevant subject for all Christians. It is so because it lies at the heart of our experience of salvation. Does God save
us or do we save ourselves? Clearly it is by my repentance from sin and my
faith in Christ that I am saved. On Pentecost day Peter proclaimed to all
the assembly, "Save yourselves from this corrupt generation" (Acts 2:40).
That faith that I exercised, was it me, or was it a gift? This is what we need
to explore.

The outline we will follow is, Election as an experience, Election challenged, Election defended, Election and Baptists, Election—its present
condition in the USA and finally, Election is always relevant.

Election as an experience

The most intense spiritual experience of my life has centred on the
biblical doctrine of election. I was born and brought up in Pretoria, South
Africa. My background was nominally Christian. I was invited a fellow
student David Cowan to an evangelistic campaign in which the preacher
was Ivor Powell, a Welsh evangelist. That was the first time I heard the gospel clearly preached. I responded to the altar call and registered in public
my faith in Christ. There is no doubt in my mind that that day was the day
of my new birth.

About the same time as my conversion my girl friend Lyn was inde-
pendently and suddenly converted on her own during a thunder-storm
in which she was terrified at the thought of our Lord's return. We were
baptized together at Pretoria Central Baptist Church. Almost all the Bap-

tist churches in South Africa are united together in a Baptist Union in which the battle against liberal theology was won way back in the 1920s. In the 1950s the churches were vibrantly evangelical and many were fundamentalistic. Although not written into stone or even on paper the way of spiritual holiness was to name, shame and forbid specific practices. These were smoking, drinking alcohol, attending cinema, dancing and, for ladies, wearing make-up. Anyone involved in these worldly practices would hardly be passed for baptism and church membership.

The gospel was faithfully preached. Election was understood to be by foreknowledge. God elected those who he foreknew would believe in Christ. In other words the Baptist churches were Arminian. I was firmly of this Arminian persuasion. I graduated and we married. Sensing a need for theological education we left South Africa in 1954 to study extra-murally at the London Bible College. E. F. Kevan was principal and tutor in systematic theology. Under Kevan we were taught the doctrines of grace. These doctrines were further powerfully preached by the renowned Dr. Martyn Lloyd-Jones at Westminster Chapel where we attended every Lord's Day. We lived at the Foreign Missions Club where we met the founder of the Banner of Truth publishing house, Iain Murray. He further endorsed the doctrine of election by pointing to Ephesians chapter one. At first we were entirely opposed to this free grace teaching. We especially resented Dr. Lloyd-Jones strong assertion that fallen sinners have lost free will and are at enmity toward God. With free grace teaching and preaching coming from all sides the issue had to be settled. I determined therefore to make an intense study of Paul's letter to the Romans. Looking back it was Romans 3:10–12, especially the words, "there is no one who understands, no one who seeks God," that settled it all. Once I grasped total depravity all the other points of the well-known five points of Calvinism fell into place. It was not easy. Foreknowledge was perplexing. It took my wife five years to come to terms with the implications of the doctrines of grace. For both of us this was an intense spiritual experience but ultimately coming to the doctrines of grace was like a second blessing. There is a very real challenge to election. To that we now turn.

Election challenged

Frederic Louis Godet (1812–1900) was a seminarian and scholar of considerable ability. He wrote a number of exegetical commentaries including one on Romans. On chapter 8 verse 29, "For whom he did foreknow," Godet writes, "Some have given the word *foreknow* the meaning of elect, choose, destine, beforehand. Not only is this meaning arbitrary, as being without example in the New Testament and as even in profane

Greek the word *ginōskein* to know, has the meaning of *deciding* only when it applies to a thing, as when we say: *connaitre d'une cause*, to judge of a case and never when applied to a person."[1] Here is a heavyweight theologian insisting that foreknowledge in Romans 8:29 is strictly knowing beforehand and that it is not people that are foreknown but their faith and decision that is foreknown.

In examining this challenge that election is God's foreknowledge of those who believe, as against those who do not believe, we need to examine the toughest proponents of the Arminian view. The weakest proponents are those who take the "Open Theism" position. According to Clark Pinnock, "God does not control everything that happens. Rather, he is open to receiving input from his creatures. In loving dialogue, God invites us to participate with him to bring the future into being."[2] It is hard to imagine committee meetings constantly gathered together and consulted in order to assist the Lord by giving him advice and counsel. Isaiah reveals a God of very different character. He is not a negotiator who is feeling his way forward as we gather from this statement in Isaiah:

> Remember the former things, those of long ago;
> I am God and there is no other;
> I am God and there is none like me.
> I make known the end from the beginning,
> from ancient times, what is still to come.
> I say: My purpose will stand,
> and I will do all that I please.
> From the east I summon a bird of prey;
> from a far-off land, a man to fulfill my purpose.
> What I have said, that will I bring about;
> what I have planned, that will I do (Isaiah 46:9–11).

The God of Open Theism bears no resemblance to the God of the Bible. We can safely by-pass this option and turn to the position maintained by Frederick Godet as stated above. This option is the one that has always prevailed among Baptists and continues to prevail, namely that God knows ahead of time who will believe in his Son and these are the ones he chooses. According to Jack Cottrell, 'God predestines to salvation those individuals who meet the gracious conditions which he has set forth.' Thus election is conditional, not unconditional. Therefore, when God foreknows

---

[1] Frederic Godet, *Romans* (Grand Rapids, MI: Kregel, 1979), 324.
[2] Cited in John Frame, *No Other God* (Phillipsburg, NJ: Puritan and Reformed, 2001), 20. See also article by Peter Barnes, "Election according to the foreknowledge of God" in issue 485 of *Banner of Truth*.

a sinner, he foreknows whether that individual will meet the conditions for salvation which he has sovereignly imposed. These conditions are faith (Galatians 3:26; Ephesians 3:17; Colossians 2:12), repentance and baptism (Acts 2:38; Galatians 3:27; Colossians 2:12). Hence Cottrell writes that, "God foreknows from the beginning who will and who will not meet them. Those whom he foresees as meeting them are predestined to salvation."[3] To Cottrell, "Only the doctrine of conditional election, where God elects to salvation those who comply with his graciously given and announced terms of pardon, can preserve the justice and impartiality of God."[4]

To Cottrell, regeneration comes through faith, not *vice versa*. He writes: "Just as God does not force a person to sin, neither does he force anyone to accept grace."[5] God's foreknowledge is not a distinguishing love: "The fact that God foreknows what that choice will be does not mean he caused it."[6] According to this teaching, God does not elect us, we elect Him.

Election defended

We now take up the text discussed above, namely, "For whom he foreknew" (Romans 8:29). Of course God knows all things and he knows everyone in the universal sense. Romans 8:28–30 describes five actions of God and the first of these is an action of love. A specific people are in view, not events and certainly not faith foreseen. Merely to know about is not an action. To possess knowledge about someone is not an action. In his commentary on Romans, Professor John Murray writes: "Many times in Scripture 'know' has a pregnant meaning which goes beyond that of mere cognition. It is used in a sense practically synonymous with 'love,' to set regard upon, to know with peculiar interest, delight and action."[7] The Hebraic meaning of foreknowledge is implicit in New Testament usage. It is the idea of an intimate relationship. *To know* refers to covenantal love. The meaning of intimate knowledge is conveyed by Amos 3:2: "You only have I known of all the families of the earth" (NKJV). Also Hosea uses the term *to know* to refer to a marriage relationship: "I knew you in the wilder-

---

[3] Jack Cottrell, "Conditional Election" in Clark Pinnock (editor) *Grace Unlimited* (Bloomington, MN: Bethany Press, 1975), 57.

[4] Ibid., 67.

[5] Ibid., 69.

[6] Ibid. I am indebted to Peter Barnes and his article in the *Banner of Truth*, issue 485, for these observations regarding Jack Cottrell whose view is representative of the Arminian position.

[7] John Murray, *The Epistle to the Romans* (Grand Rapids, MI: Eerdmans, 1997), 317.

ness, in the land of great drought" (Hosea 13:5, NKJV). In that terrible experience in the wilderness, Jehovah was joined to his people. The verb *jada*, love, often carries considerable depth of meaning in the Old Testament conveying the idea of a deep relationship of love. The Lord said to Jeremiah, "Before I formed you in the womb I knew you, before you were born I set you apart" (Jeremiah 1:5). There is a lament when this kind of knowledge of love is absent (Hosea 4:1; 6:6). This fact of love is expressed in 1 Peter 1:20 where Christ is described as foreknown: "For he was foreknown before the foundation of the world, but has appeared in these last times for the sake of you' (NASB). The NIV translates it as: "He was chosen before the creation of the world." Peter speaks of God's foreknowledge of Christ in terms of choosing and appointing him to be our Redeemer. In the introduction Peter describes the elect as those "who have been chosen according to the foreknowledge of God the Father" (1 Peter 1:2). In other words they are beloved of God the Father. *To know* means to know intimately. Jesus says, "I know my sheep and my sheep know me" (John 10:14). Thus Paul strongly rejects the idea that the Lord has cast away a people that "he foreknew" (Romans 11:2). That does not mean a people whom he merely knew about—it means a people upon whom *he set his love.*

Foreknow focuses attention upon the distinguishing love of God whereby the children of God were elected. In this way we understand Paul when he declares of the Father, "he chose us in him before the creation of the world to be holy and blameless in his sight" (Ephesians 1:4). The next action is predestination: "In love he predestined us to be adopted as his sons through Jesus Christ" (Ephesians 1:5). The grace given to us has its spring in the love of God the Father (2 Thessalonians 2:16). The Father has given a people to Christ (John 6:37). Christ's love for his people is concurrent with that of his Father. It is this love that sustained Christ in his determination to go through with the crucifixion (Romans 5:6–8; 8:37; Galatians 2:20; Hebrews 12:2).

This truth is practical. The context of Romans 8:18 concerns our present sufferings. We are comforted by the knowledge of the eternal electing love of God and that we are chosen to be in Christ. That love is a superlative love! It is the *so loved.* The Father *so loved* that he gave his one and only Son to be the propitiation for our sins. How can we respond to this great love? The answer: "Beloved, if God so loved us, we also ought to love one another" (1 John 4:11, NASB).

Paul writes to the Ephesians, "In him we were also chosen, having been predestined according to the plan of him who works out everything in conformity with the purpose of his will" (Ephesians 1:11). The love of God the Father is active and this is the source of his foreordination of his people to eternal life. Here, predestination focuses on God's people and, in particular, the purpose that they should be conformed to the likeness of Christ, "that he might be the *firstborn* among many brothers" (Romans 8:29). The term firstborn reflects the priority and supremacy of Christ (Colossians 1:15–18; Hebrews 1:6; Revelation 1:5).

Predestination means that, from all eternity God decreed all that should happen in time and this he did freely and unalterably, consulting only his own wise and holy will. Yet in so doing he does not become in any sense the author of sin, nor does he share responsibility for sin with sinners. Neither, by reason of his decree, is the will of any creature he has made violated; nor is the free working of second causes put aside; rather it is established. Predestination points to the origin of all things while providence points to the direct control of the Holy Spirit over all things in creation and in human affairs. To cite the *1689 Confession*: "Nothing happens by chance or outside the sphere of God's providence. As God is the first cause of all events, they happen immutably and infallibly according to his foreknowledge and decree, to which they stand related."[8]

The predestination of the Father is the second action in the five described in Romans 8:28–30 and is the only one that is elaborated further. The great end of the Father's purpose is our sanctification: "He predestined us to be conformed to the image of his Son that he might be the firstborn among many brethren" (Romans 8:29). Predestination concerns all the plans necessary to bring wayward sinners to repentance and faith in Christ.

Wayne Grudem in his *Systematic Theology* defines election as follows: "Election is an act of God before creation in which he chooses some people to be saved, not on account of any foreseen merit in them, but only because of his sovereign good pleasure." He goes on to affirm that election in the New Testament is presented as comfort to believers (Romans 8:28), as a reason to praise God (Ephesians 1:5–6) and as an encouragement to evangelism as Paul says, "I endure everything for the sake of the elect, that they may also obtain salvation in Christ Jesus with its eternal glory" (2 Timothy 2:10).[9] To this we can add the instance when Paul was faced with much opposition in Corinth. Paul was encouraged by the doctrine of election: "One night the Lord spoke to Paul in a vision: 'Do not be afraid; keep on speaking, do not be silent. For I am with you and no one is going to attack and harm you, because I have many people in this city'" (Acts 18:9–10).

Many shy away from the doctrine of God's election because they believe it destroys the truth of human responsibility. This is not the case.

---

[8] *A Faith to Confess: The Baptist Confession of 1689* (Leeds: Carey Publications, 1975), 3:1.

[9] Wayne Grudem, *Systematic Theology* (Grand Rapids, MI: IVP, Zondervan, 1994), 669–687.

Divine sovereignty and human responsibility have engaged the minds of theologians throughout the centuries. Perhaps the best way to grasp the combination of human responsibility in which everything seems to depend on us and divine sovereignty in which everything depends on God, is to study texts such as Philippians 2:12–13: "Continue to work out your salvation with fear and trembling (our responsibility), for it is God who works in you to will and to act according to his good purpose (divine sovereignty)." Divine sovereignty precedes human responsibility. Every spiritual act we perform which is acceptable to God can be traced back to the divine initiative of grace. Both sovereignty and responsibility must be fully asserted. We must never make an excuse of God's sovereignty as the Jews did in captivity in Babylon. They did this in a subtle way, blaming their predecessors for the mess they were in and implying that God had been harsh. But they were really avoiding the fact that they themselves were to blame for their evil behavior. Ezekiel drives home the fact that every individual is fully responsible for his own sin (Ezekiel 18). Indeed the Bible teaches everywhere that every person is responsible for his thoughts, words and deeds—*everyone* will be held to account. Ecclesiastes concludes with this declaration: "For God will bring every deed into judgment, including every hidden thing, whether it is good or evil" (Ecclesiastes 12:14). Revelation 20 describes the great judgment day and says that "each person was judged according to what he had done" (Revelation 20:13; see also Matthew 21:31–36). Largely fuelled by books published by the Banner of Truth publishing house (Edinburgh, Scotland), the doctrines of grace spread widely in the UK and America from about 1958 onwards. Suddenly, interest was quickened and the issue of where divine sovereignty and human responsibility meet ascended to the top of the theological agenda. The doctrines of grace have a profound impact on the way Christians evangelize and J.I. Packer addressed this subject at a series of meetings organized by a Christian Union in London in 1959. These papers were gathered together and appeared in print as a paperback with the title Evangelism and the Sovereignty of God. Chapter two of this small book is titled, *Divine Sovereignty and Human Responsibility*. Packer suggests that we have to deal with an *antinomy*, which the *Shorter Oxford Dictionary* defines as "a contradiction between conclusions which seem equally logical, reasonable or necessary." Packer writes,

> For our purposes, however, this definition is not quite accurate; the opening words should read 'an *appearance* of contradiction." For the whole point of an antinomy—in theology, at any rate—is that it is not a real contradiction, though it looks like one. It is an *apparent* incompatibility between two apparent truths. Antimony exists when a pair of principles stand side by side, seemingly irreconcilable, yet both undeniable. There

are cogent reasons for believing each of them; each rests on clear and solid evidence; but it is a mystery to you how they can be squared with each other. You see that each must be true on its own, but you do not see how they can both be true together. Let me give an example. Modern physics faces an antinomy, in this sense, in its study of light. There is cogent evidence to show that light consists of waves and equally cogent evidence to show that it consists of particles. It is not apparent how light can be both waves and particles, but the evidence is there and so neither view can be ruled out in favor of the other.[10]

Election and Baptists

Historical theology is a subject of foremost importance. We are edified by the study of theological understanding and development through the course of history. Biographies enrich historical theology. Professor Tom Nettles is an outstanding teacher of historical theology. His book *By His Grace and for His Glory* was written during a sabbatical spent in England in 1985 and published by Baker Book House in 1986. During 1985 we were moving from Haywards Heath in Sussex to Liverpool. Tom and Margaret Nettles stayed in our home which took a long time to sell. As the title suggests *By His Grace and for His Glory* is about the doctrines of grace and traces out the place of election in Baptist churches from the mid-seventeenth century up to the mid twentieth-century. The word *election* is used as a heading for several leaders such as John L. Dagg, J.P. Boyce, J.B. Tidwell and B.H. Carroll. In each case Professor Nettles describes the manner in which these leaders propounded the doctrine of election.

Later Dr. Nettles wrote three volumes each of which bore the title: *The Baptists, Key People in Forming a Baptist Identity*. These were published as hardback volumes in Scotland by Christian Focus. The first volume of 382 pages describes the beginning of modern Baptist history in England. The second volume of 510 page traces out the beginnings and development of Baptists in America. The third volume of 462 pages tells the story of Baptists through the 19th Century up to the end of the 20th Century.

Professor Nettles divides the first of these volumes into three parts. In the first he suggests a model for conceiving Baptist identity in comprehensive theological commitments in addition to the distinctives of regenerate church membership and liberty of conscience. He describes the competing Baptist models in the current American Baptist cosmos. Second, he outlines the General (Arminian) Baptist history of England. Third, he narrates the history of the Calvinistic (Particular) Baptists. Accounts of

[10] J. I. Packer, *Evangelism and the Sovereignty of God* (Downers Grove, IL: Inter-Varsity Press, 1961), 18–19.

leaders such as John Spilsbury, Knollys, Keach and Kiffin are portrayed. Section two consists of an overview of English Baptist history made most readable by focusing on three leaders. There is the story of John Smyth (d. 1612), Thomas Grantham (1634–692) and Dan Taylor (1738–1836). These talented leaders were of Arminian persuasion. Smyth began as a robust Puritan of Reformed persuasion. He took the road to separatism and in the process departed from historic Calvinism. Nettles comments: "The tendency of Arminianism to liberalism does not in each instance become incarnate, but the frequency of such decline in Baptist history is enough to serve as a warning."

In the second volume in the series Dr. Nettles takes up the subject: "What is a Baptist Church?" What are the main features that constitute the identity of Baptists? Leaders of the first generation of Particular Baptists compiled the Second London Baptist Confession of Faith now popularly known as the 1689 Baptist Confession. The Particular Baptists united in regional associations and so a very clear character or identity marked them which identity has re-merged strongly in various parts of the world in the late 20th and first part of the 21st century. Zambia and the Philippines are examples.

There are several characteristics which are peculiar to Baptists. One of these is a belief in religious freedom, liberty of conscience and the separation of church and state. This is where Nettles begins in this second volume which he divides into three sections. He shows how John Smyth and Thomas Helwys contended that it is not for civil magistrates to minister the 'new creature'. Christ's church is not created by force and by persecution. The church is God's creation by the preaching of the Word. Helwys boldly petitioned King James I to give up his power to appoint bishops and archbishops. Christopher Blackwood sent a book to the press with the title *The Storming of Antichrist in his two last and strongest garrisons; of compulsion of Conscience and Infant Baptism.* In young America Roger Williams and John Clarke were foremost in running with the same baton of religious freedom. Williams illustrated the ludicrous nature of religious coercion by pointing to the fact that under the Tudors each succeeding monarch imposed a different religion from Half-Papist to Protestant to Papist and back again to Protestant (p.43). Following were Isaac Backus (1724–1806) and John Leland (1754–1841) both from Congregational background and both leaders of exceptional preaching and intellectual ability who used their pens to effectively establish Baptist principles especially in the disestablishment of a state church. John Leland was privileged to witness powerful revivals. In one year alone he baptized 300. His theology of salvation accorded entirely with that of Jonathan Edwards. He was fiercely opposed to manipulation on the basis that the new birth can be achieved by self-exertion which later was to be associated with Charles Finney. Backus calls Jonathan Edwards "the greatest writer against a self-determining power in man that our age has seen" (p. 454). Leland records that on one occasion in the home of Deacon Wood he experienced great liberty and thought that of all his sermons that one was the best he ever delivered. Yet it was followed with 'small effects' and only one young woman was "divinely wrought upon." Yet thirty years later he recorded he had been privileged to baptise fifty-seven grand and great-grandchildren of the said Deacon Wood.

Section two addresses the subject of unity and co-operation among Baptist churches as seen in the development of associations, the Philadelphia Association, the Charleston and the Sandy Creek Associations which bodies followed the *Second London Baptist Confession* with a few minor variations. The account of these associations and their influence is woven round fascinating biographies of leaders, Oliver Hart, John Gano, Richard Furman and Shubal Stearns. Matters of lively and vital interest fill these fascinating short biographies. The striking overall feature is that these pastors possessed the gift of preaching to a remarkable degree. It was through their gospel preaching that extensive church planting was accomplished. For instance such was Gano's unction in preaching that some of the young preachers when they heard him remarked that they felt that they could never undertake to preach again. The leaders were Calvinists. They were clear doctrinal preachers. None were decisionists. They preached the necessity of repentance. Nettles describes in detail the confessional doctrinal teaching of Richard Furman. Eternal punishment is clearly defined as not a ruin which culminates in annihilation "for the soul is declared to be immortal" (p.150).

Shubal Stearns moved south and planted a church at Sandy Creek which grew rapidly from 16 to 606. It was from there that revival spread all over the south. Stearns born in 1706 was converted under the preaching of George Whitefield and adopted the New Light understanding of revival and conversion. One part of that was the conviction that it was impossible to reform established churches from within. It was imperative to start new churches. A favourite text was 2 Corinthians 6:17, "Come out from among them and be ye separate." And so the Separate Baptists were nick-named "come-outers" or "separates." While following the Calvinism of Jonathan Edwards and Whitefield Stearns rejected infant baptism. Fervent evangelism characterized the Separate Baptists. The preachers were revivalist preachers often evoking tears, trembling, screams, shouts and acclamations. There were some idiosyncratic practices which led Gano to use the word *immethodical* to describe this group which belonged to the Sandy Creek Association which eventually split into three different associations. Specific conditions were described when women had the right to speak.

One lady, a sister of Stearns, frequently melted a whole concourse by her prayers and exhortations. In defence of the Separate movement one wrote, "Surely we ought to prefer a revival of religion, though dished with some irregularities to the death-like coldness of mere orthodoxy and form" (p. 162).

In section three Nettles turns his attention to world-wide Mission. The example of Adoniram and Ann Judson gripped the imagination of Baptists across America. Nettles explains the thinking of the distasteful and misguided reactions of the Anti-Mission Society Movement.

The story of the formation of the first Southern Baptist Theological Seminary is intertwined with splendid biographies of Basil Manly Sr. and John A. Broadus. Broadus never stopped laboring to improve the effectiveness of the Christian pulpit in America.

Manly's preaching was characterized as "always marked by deep thought and strong argument expressed in a very clear style and by extraordinary earnestness and tender pathos." Manly was gripped passionately by the subject of theological training and the provision of top rate preachers and pastors for the churches. "Dull, careless sinners can never be built up by lifeless oration, dispassionate praying and theatrical reading of Scripture" (p. 263). In 1859 Manly cooperated with James P. Boyce, William Williams and Basil Manly Jr. in establishing the first theological seminary among Baptists in the South in Greenville, South Carolina. This seminary moved to Louisville in 1877 and today is the foremost Southern Baptist Seminary in America. We learn from these pages of the considerable enterprise, energy and funding necessary to establish an institution of this nature.

The life of Lottie Moon (1840–1912), famous single lady missionary to China, is described in gripping style. Her time of service was marked by terrible defections from the faith. She would have liked to marry Crawford Toy, a brilliant academic who at one stage seemed heading for the mission field. Seeds of error were sown in Toy's mind when he studied in Berlin. These germinated and he embraced liberal theology. Eventually he gave up the Christian faith altogether. Lottie Moon, herself faithful to the end, often noted the destructive advance of the new theology which is a principal theme of volume three on Baptist Identity.

The volume concludes with some descriptions of Calvinistic Baptists on the international stage with excellent biographies of Robert (1764–1842) and James Haldane (1768–1851) of Scotland and Gerhard Oncken (1800–1880), a German who for widespread effectiveness in church planting knows few equals.

The Baptist subject is so extensive that discipline is required to keep main issues in focus. Many talented leaders make up the story and it is not possible to do justice to them all. Thus Nettles has resorted to information boxes of a page or two each. There are 22 of these. In this way leaders are described such as Luther Rice, John L. Dagg, Lott Cary, Jesse Mercer, P.H. Mell, David Bogue, Vasili Pavlov, Alexander Carson and John Jasper. The latter was a slave, the last of twenty-four children by his mother Nina. He drew both blacks and whites by his powerful preaching and his church grew to near 2000 members.

Volume three in the series begins with the battle of the downgrade: Spurgeon versus John Clifford whom Nettles nicknames "the irrepressible liberal." The story then turns to describe A.H. Strong and E.Y. Mullins who were weak in their resistance to Modernism and outright Baptist Modernists Shailer Mathews, William Newton Clarke and Harry Emerson Fosdick. The role of the fundamentalists of the early twentieth century is described with special attention given to the extraordinarily fiery and controversial John Franklyn Norris (1877–1952). The recently published book *Catch the Vision* by John J Murray,[11] is commended as a lucid account of the Modernist movement and the doldrums of the period from about 1900 to 1950, followed by the recovery of the Reformed faith in the 1960s. The Baptist preacher and writer A.W. Pink (1886–1952) lived through that barren period. The cause of free grace was strong among Baptists from about 1800 to 1900 but then for the next sixty years went into steep decline. A.W. Pink was a lonely propagator of the doctrines of grace. After a powerful soul-saving ministry in the USA Pink settled in Australia where he was first rejected by the General Baptists who were Arminian and then by a small Hyper-Calvinistic denomination. From these setbacks Pink never recovered. He returned to England which was the land of his birth and upbringing where he received no invitations to preach. He became isolated. When bombs began to fall in the Second World War Pink moved far north to the island of Stornoway which is a Presbyterian stronghold. Here he continued his ministry of writing. As the only editor of a paper called *Searching the Scriptures* he maintained a ministry of Bible exposition which eventually was taken up by publishers. These made A.W. Pink a well-known author. His was a lonely Elijah-like voice. Apart from small Strict and Particular Calvinistic churches and some Presbyterian denominations which did not succumb to liberal theology the main body of evangelical churches were Arminian.

Of all Baptists Charles Haddon Spurgeon is the best known. According to Nettles he "surpasses all other ministers of the gospel in the rare combination of biblical clarity, theological coherence, rhetorical zest, per-

[11] John J Murray, *Catch the Vision* (Darlington, Co. Durham: Evangelical Press, 2008). 180 pages.

spicuity of diction, universality of appeal and urgency of application." By many Spurgeon is esteemed as the "tallest and broadest oak in the forest of time." At a young age through time spent with his grandfather at Stambourne Spurgeon was introduced to the Puritan writings. The preaching of his grandfather made deep impressions on young Charles. "The dew of the Spirit from on high never left the ministry and wherever my grandfather went, souls were saved under his ministry."

Spurgeon's popularity was greatly increased by the publication of his weekly sermons. By the end of the 19th century these had multiplied into one hundred million copies in twenty-three languages. The sale of the sermons helped to finance the theological college which he founded in 1856. His writings extended to 135 titles. The theology of the Puritans which he imbibed at a young age permeates his sermons and his books.

If we take Spurgeon as the exemplar of Baptist identity there is no doubt that we would embrace with him the *1689 Confession of Faith* which he adopted when he began his ministry at New Park Street. Spurgeon was clear about the value of this Puritan legacy. When the Calvinistic confessions and catechisms of the 17th century had been abandoned, "there followed an age of drivellings, in which our Nonconformity existed, but gradually dwindled down, first into Arminianism and then into Unitarianism, until it almost ceased to be."[12]

This third volume tells the story of R. Albert Mohler Jr. (1959–present) who was born in Lakeland, Florida. He was brought up in a Southern Baptist home and attended all the meetings organized for the young from Sunbeams onwards. He attended vacation Bible school and youth camps. He was converted at the age nine at Southside Baptist Church in Lakeland, Florida. The family moved from there to Pompano Beach where Albert was exposed to pluralism and to thinking contrary to his beliefs. The writings of Francis Schaeffer and sermons by James Kennedy helped him through. He graduated with a MDiv from Samford University in Birmingham and then earned a PhD at Southern Seminary, Louisville. At both Samford and Southern Mohler observed a condescending attitude toward conservative evangelicals.

In 1993 at age 34, he was called to be President of Southern Seminary, Louisville. In writing he had already referred to "the inevitable consequences of decades of doctrinal neglect by the denomination at large." Mohler set out to attain confessional fidelity in the seminary. This led to a string of resignations from modernist tutors.

Mohler does not view Baptist identity in terms of separate entities but rather views truth as an organic body which is grounded in the Protestant

---

[12] *Metropolitan Tabernacle Pulpit*, vol. 29, p. 394.

Reformation and which reaches back to the classical orthodoxy of the early church councils, the orthodox tradition of Nicaea and Chalcedon. In other words Baptists are not disconnected from the body of Christ as that body has developed over the centuries. Mohler declares his indebtedness to Carl Henry and accords with Henry when he chides Southern Baptists for their "theological amnesia." Mohler writes: "Even the opponents of Calvinism must admit, if historically informed, that Calvinism is the theological tradition into which the Baptist movement was born. The same is true of the Southern Baptist Convention. The most influential churches, leaders, confessions of faith and theologians of the founding era were Calvinistic—it was not until well into the twentieth century that any knowledgeable person could claim that Southern Baptists were anything but Calvinists."

Whereas modernist teachers in their desire to dilute the truth are averse to the clarity of creeds Mohler insists that "theological education must be confessional in character" and "the confession must not only be declarative but regulative.' 'Apart from a confession a theological school has no warrant for its mission." Mohler has followed in the steps of James Pettigru Boyce who with J.A. Broadus founded Southern Seminary. Boyce (1827–1888) sacrificed much of his inheritance to establish the seminary which began in Greenville, South Carolina, but after the Civil War moved to Louisville.

The Doctrine of Election—its present condition in the USA

In 2008 Collin Hansen wrote a stirring book with the title *Young, Restless, Reformed*. The sub-title is *A journalist's journey with the new Calvinists*.[13]

Very few Reformed lights shone in the USA in the early 1960s. As for Baptist Calvinistic leaders in the USA in the 1950s they would hardly number enough to fill a rowing boat.

In contrast to those days we now learn of the present day Reformed resurgence in the USA. In journalistic and anecdotal style Collin Hansen provides a litmus test on the state of the Reformed Faith in the USA. In his tour Collin interviewed leaders in six states. Out of fifty states that is only a small proportion. However since he visited some of the best-known leaders his survey represents a fairly accurate picture of Calvinistic resurgence. Small Reformed denominations like the Orthodox Presbyterian Church are not mentioned. The growing association of Reformed Baptists (ARBCA) is omitted. Not mentioned are smaller seminaries like the

Collin Hansen, *Young, Restless, Reformed* (Wheaton, IL: Crossway, 2008), 160 pages, paperback.

Puritan Reformed Seminary in Grand Rapids whose leader is Joel Beeke. At the beginning of his book Collin Hansen makes it crystal clear that he grasps and holds personally to the five points of Calvinism known by the acrostic TULIP. That is what he means by the Reformed Faith.

So how do things stand now in the USA? To discover more about the Calvinistic resurgence Collin Hansen's first call was to the ministry of John Piper at Bethlehem Baptist Church in Minneapolis. Hansen describes Piper (whose signature book *Desiring God* has sold 275,000 copies) as the chief spokesman for the Calvinist resurgence among young evangelicals. In the year 2000 40,000 students gathered at a venue near Memphis to listen to John Piper on the theme "Don't Waste Your Life." Subsequently 250,000 copies of Piper's book with that title have sold. If Piper is the most influential living leader in the resurgence then Jonathan Edwards is the most read theologian from the past. In 2003 to celebrate the 300th anniversary of Edwards' birth, 2,500, mostly pastors, met for a three-day conference in Minneapolis.

Next stop was Yale University, New Haven, Connecticut. Here he met Josh Moody who is pastor of Trinity Baptist Church with 300 members. In 1999 there were fewer than thirty members. Josh Moody earned his PhD at Cambridge University in England with a thesis on Jonathan Edwards. While at Yale Hansen probed into the extent of the ministry of RUF (Reformed University Fellowship) which has increased from ministry on 35 campuses in 1998 to over one hundred today.

The next port of call in Collin's tour was Southern Baptist Theological Seminary, Louisville, Kentucky. The upgrade at Southern is now well known. We are accustomed to downgrades but Southern represents a phenomenal upgrade out of liberalism. This came about under the leadership of Albert Mohler Jr. who was only 33 when he was appointed to the presidency of Southern Seminary. Mohler began a purge at Southern. The liberals were outraged and predicted the demise of Southern which is the first and best known Southern Baptist Seminary out of six in the USA. This dire prophecy proved false. Southern with 4,300 students is now the largest seminary in America.

The historic roots of the SBC go back to the *Philadelphia Confession of Faith* which is a sister confession to the *1689 Confession*. The Founders' Movement represents a body within the SBC calling for a return to the roots. In late 2006, two thousand recent graduates from Southern Baptist seminaries were surveyed on their commitment to Calvinistic doctrines. Twenty-nine percent were discovered to be "five-point Calvinists." This research strongly suggests that the growth of Calvinism among Southern Baptists is being experienced primarily among the rising generation. This does not mean that one-third of all Southern Baptist pastors are Calvinists, only recent graduates. The alarmists however, would warn that eventually the Calvinists will take over the Convention if the seminaries continue to indoctrinate graduates with Calvinist leanings. We know that a number of Reformed Baptist churches have been formed as an outcome of splits. A considerable number of SBC pastors preach free grace in expository style without mentioning Calvinism. Some have succeeded in bringing their churches all the way back to their historic confessional foundations. An example of complete reformation is Capitol Hill Baptist Church in Washington, D.C. where Mark Dever is pastor. Dever earned his PhD at Cambridge with a thesis on the English Puritans. Capitol Hill was a dying Southern Baptist church which has revived greatly under Dever.

Turning northwards Hansen visited leader C.J. Mahaney, founder in 1977 of Covenant Life Church in Gaithersburg, Maryland, a charismatic church of 3,800 members. TULIP is treasured as much as the gifts of the Holy Spirit. Mahaney was converted when he was a hippie in Arminian charismatic circles. On conversion he had an immediate appetite to read and soon came to the doctrines of grace. He is an extraordinarily dynamic and lively personality—very attractive, charismatic and fervently Reformed, a preacher who tells everyone to read more books by dead people—especially John Owen on sin.

C.J. Mahaney is president of Sovereign Grace Ministries, a family of seventy-five churches. This grouping prioritises evangelism and have close ties with Spanish-speaking churches in Bolivia. Two years ago Mahaney handed leadership of the main Covenant Life Church to Joshua Harris aged 33. Harris has worked hard among the younger generation and has been the key individual in the sponsoring of the New Attitude Conferences. This gathering is for 15–24 year old singles. 6000 have attended in Louisville for the last two years.

In April 2006 a Gospel Conference was organized in Louisville, Kentucky, in which good friends Dever, Mahaney, Ligon Duncan and Albert Mohler invited three of their heroes, John Piper, John MacArthur and R.C. Sproul to be the preachers. 3,000 pastors attended. It was not easy to settle on the music style. There were differences among these leaders such as baptism and eschatology. TULIP was the cement that cemented unity.

In this new resurgence it is Baptists and Charismatics who are now sharing the leadership and who are at the cutting edge for theology and for missions. Two to three decades ago some Presbyterians thought that it was out of place for any but Presbyterians to call themselves Reformed.

Collin's tour took him to the North West corner of America to Mars Hill Church, Seattle, Washington State. This is the home of 38 year old Mark Driscoll. Driscoll's teaching is uncompromisingly complementarian on the man–woman issue and unflinching on the issues of homosexuality, inerrancy of Scripture, the eternal punishment of the wicked and penal substitution. The church began in 1996 and is now attended by 6,000. This is impressive since only ten percent in Seattle are regular church-goers. Mars Hill is mother church to about a hundred churches nick-named Acts 29 churches. Driscoll affirms his indebtedness to Wayne Grudem and of Grudem's *Systematic Theology* declares it is "the finest on the market and the standard for Mars Hill Church and many of the churches we are affiliated within the Acts 29 Network."

The above described centres of influence are described in this book which shows that many have become weary of churches that seek to entertain rather than preach the great truths of God's sovereign grace. The young especially have sought out places where they can be fed with spiritual meat. Examples of large churches have come under review. What about thousands of small places where the truth is adored and obeyed? What about 300 to 400 prisons in America where Chapel Library (Mt Zion Bible Church, Pensacola) has achieved an amazing network of hundreds of groupings in prisons where sovereign grace literature is loved?

We must hold the black churches on our radar screens. One of the leading black Reformed ministers in America is Eric Redmond. He serves a church in Maryland, not far from where Mark Dever is in DC. Also on our screens is the home school factor. The home school movement is extensive in the USA and has paved the way for many since much of the curriculum comes from a Reformed persuasion.

Collin Hansen has not forgotten small churches and rural areas. To round things off he visited his original home in South Dakota, a little place of his childhood called Dell Rapids. There he discovered a newly planted church with about fifty in attendance. Andy Wright is the pastor. He enjoys fellowship with a number of pastors in South Dakota who share his Calvinistic views. One of these is Pastor Ryan Franchuk, First Baptist Church, Emery, South Dakota (population 450). Ryan has published a booklet called, *The Handy Dandy Doctrines of Grace Bible Verse Reference Guide* which lists proof texts for TULIP.

Hansen's experience in South Dakota was positive. Other areas are hopeful. For instance there are seven Reformed churches in Rhode Island, twenty-three in Connecticut and no fewer than 61 in Massachusetts!

D.A. Carson in his endorsement of Hansen's book provides a timely warning, "This is not the time for Reformed triumphalism. It is time for quiet gratitude to God and earnest intercessory prayer, with tears, that what has begun will flourish beyond all human expectation."

Election is always relevant

Election is a practical matter. Preaching on the subject of sovereign election in 2010 in Alfred Place Baptist Church pastor Geoffrey Thomas illustrated the place of election in a local church like this:

> There are times when people stand here before us and they give their testimony before they are baptized and join the church and come to the Lord's Table. Their testimonies are usually fascinating sermons in themselves, but my point is that everyone thinking of confessing Christ and being baptized should read this testimony of Paul. Notice what he doesn't say, "When I decided to give God a chance…" No. Or, "When I opened my heart and let Jesus come in…" No. That is the way many people speak today. They don't go back before the creation of the world, but they start with themselves and what they did. But Paul says that God, working according to an eternal plan, set him apart from his birth, before he took his first breath and uttered his first cry, then God had a plan for him. That's how Paul saw his conversion, not "I had the courage to make the all-important decision to accept Christ." Where does anyone anywhere in the Bible talk like that? You will search in vain looking for it. Those men were full of the Spirit and so they knew that before the foundation of the world God had loved them and purposed that they were going to be his people.
>
> Imagine we had an actual baptismal service and a candidate got up and said, "I suppose that it all comes down to this: I'm a little better than other people. I have a more discernment and insight than most people. I was willing to give God a chance to save me and it was because of my willingness that God was able to save me." I could imagine seeing your faces drop and my own heart would sink. What was I going to do? Could I baptize a man who boasted in himself like that? No way. This man evidently had never seen the grace and power of God. He was glorying in auto-soterism, in self-salvation. I was told of a very different Christian who came from China; he was in an informal meeting and was asked to give his testimony. "How did you come to know the Lord?" He spoke modestly of how God had sought him and then the Lord had opened his heart to receive the truth and how the Holy Spirit had given him a new birth and made him a new creation. When he had ended the chairman smiled and said, "That was wonderful, but you left out what you did." The man from China said, "I don't know what you mean. There was nothing I did." The chairman said, "God did his part and then you must have done something. What was your part?" The Chinese brother's face finally was wreathed in a smile, "Oh, yes, my part! I ran and ran as far from God as I could. I tried to get away from him, but his part was to run faster, tackle me and totally overcome me by his mercy and love."

During many years as a pastor I have known some who have come from General Baptist churches. In the UK General Baptist often infers Arminian Baptist because since the mid-seventeenth century there have always been two Baptist groups, Particular Baptists who believe in election and particular redemption and General Baptists who are Arminian. These brothers and sisters came because they appreciated expository doctrinal preaching but struggled with the doctrines of grace. Since all Baptists tend to love and appreciate Charles Haddon Spurgeon it is my custom to give a copy of a sermon preached by Spurgeon early in his ministry at New Park Street on 2 Thessalonians 2:13–14. "But we ought always to thank God for you, brothers loved by the Lord, because from the beginning God chose you to be saved through the sanctifying work of the Spirit and through belief in the truth. He called you to this through our gospel, that you might share in the glory of our Lord Jesus Christ" (New Park Street, volume one, sermons 41-42). In his exceptionally lucid manner CHS answers those who say, "God elected them on the foresight of their faith." "Now God gives faith, therefore he could not have elected them on account of faith, which he foresaw. There shall be twenty beggars in the street and I determine to give one of them a shilling; but will anyone say that I determined to give that one a shilling, that I elected him to have the shilling, because I foresaw that he would have it? That would be talking nonsense."

Early in his experience as a believer Spurgeon reflected on this very issue. This is how he described it:

> One weeknight, when I was sitting in the house of God, I wasn't think-ing much about the preacher's sermon, for I didn't believe it. The thought struck me, "How did you come to be a Christian?" I sought the Lord. "But how did you come to seek the Lord?" The truth flashed across my mind in a moment—I shouldn't have sought him unless there had been some previous influence in my mind to make me seek him. "I prayed," thought I, but then I asked myself, "How came I to pray?" I was induced to pray by reading the Scriptures. How came I to read the Scriptures? I did read them, but what led me to do so? Then, in a moment, I saw that God was at the bottom of it all and that he was the Author of my faith and so the whole doctrine of grace opened up to me and from that doc-trine I have not departed to this day and I desire to make my constant confession, "I ascribe my change wholly to God."[14]

---

[14] Charles H. Spurgeon, *Autobiography*, Vol. 1, *The Early Years 1834–1859* (Edinburgh: Banner of Truth reprint, 1973), 165.

9

Limited Atonement
A Short Defense*

Geoff Thomas

Christ loved the church and gave himself up for her to make her holy, cleansing her by the washing with water through the word, and to present her to himself as a radiant church, without stain or wrinkle or any other blemish, but holy and blameless (Ephesians 5:25–27).

For fifty years I have believed that the Bible teaches the limited design of Christ's atonement, that is, that his purpose in dying was to effectually save every one of his people from their sin, taking them to heaven, and transforming them into his likeness for evermore. I remember half a century ago being part of a group of students discussing animatedly the purpose of the death of our Lord, and then we'd gone on to a meeting in which we had sung, 'Lo! He comes with clouds descending once for favoured sinners slain,' and at that line I had a moment of recognition and turned and exchanged a little smile with a student called David. We had been asking, "For whom had Christ died?" and we had just been confirmed in the answer as we sang to one another these words, "for favoured sinners slain."

We could ask the question in this way; "On the cross whom is Christ saving?" and the answer is, "All who are saved." Then we ask, "Did he do

* This chapter has been adapted, with permission, from the Banner of Truth Trust. The original version is available online at http://www.banneroftruth.org/pages/articles/article_detail.php?1397 (accessed May 3, 2010).

that on purpose, or was it an accident?" We can only say, "He did it on purpose."That is limited atonement; Christ purposefully shed his blood on Golgotha as the Lamb of God and effectually saved all for whom he died.

Every building has a design. You go to the architect with your plan; it's for a conservatory, or a single bedroom flat, or perhaps a four bedroom detached house, or even a 75,000-seat stadium. That is what you want and the architect must plan and accomplish your end. His work will be limited by your purpose. Every work of engineering has a plan, and in the engineering of redemption God had a plan when he sent his Son into the world, didn't he? It was the outworking of the covenant of grace he had made with Abraham, that Abraham's seed would be vast, blessing all nations of the world, every one of them receiving the Holy Spirit. God is going to accomplish that plan through his Son Jesus Christ.

The Old Testament Knew Only a Limited Atonement

The Old Testament only knew a limited design to sacrifice and atonement, didn't it? There was no universal purpose in the Mosaic sacrifices was there? The Egyptians who worshipped their gods, and the Babylonians similarly sacrificing to their idols, and the Assyrians, and the Canaanites, and the Medes, and the Persians prostrating themselves before figures of stone, gold and silver—none of them had their sins purged away by the Jewish sacrifices made at that altar erected outside the tabernacle and later at the temple in Jerusalem. Only Israel's sins were pardoned on the Day of Atonement when the High Priest entered the Holy of Holies with the blood of the sacrifice. Only the names of the twelve tribes of Israel were carried upon his breastplate. You look in vain for the names of Egypt, or Babylon, or Assyria and the rest. Full atonement was limited to the repentant, obedient, sacrificing people of God wasn't it? Were all who died in Noah's flood covered by the altar that Noah built and the sacrifice he made after the flood waters went down? Not at all! Just the eight who believed and got into the Ark were saved. The rest died because they rejected the message he had preached to them of the Seed of the woman who would come in the fulness of time and save sinners. Gentiles like Rahab and Ruth needed to turn from their gods and put their trust under the wings of Jehovah. Naaman the Syrian leper needed to consult the prophet of God and dip seven times in the Jordan to be cleansed. Jonah was sent to Nineveh not to confirm that the sacrifices the Ninevites made to their idols had atoned for their sins but to urge them to repent and call upon the name of the Lord.

In the 39 books of the Old Testament there is one strong exhortation and that is that the people should come and reason with God as he pleads,

"Be willing! Be obedient! Make sacrifice for your sins as I have made provision! Do you scorn the blood of sacrifice? Apply yourselves to the means of atonement, and then, though your sins be like scarlet, they shall be as white as snow." Whose sins were atoned for? Was it all the physical descendants of Abraham without exception? Is that right? No. It is wrong.

The false prophets were descendants of Abraham, and the people who worshipped the Baals, King Ahab and Jezebel, the drunkards and the sluggards, the liars and the careless – they also were circumcised sons of Abraham. Did they all have atonement for their sins merely because Abraham was their great-great grandfather? You'd better not believe it or such faith will take you into presumption and that is a step from hell.

Atonement was for those who took a lamb without spot and blemish and led it to the altar where they in faith put a hand on its head and then handed it over to the priest to be slain and have its blood sprinkled on the altar. Only such a person could have any assurance that his sins had been atoned for.

Atonement was limited to the one who sought it in God's way—not the careless; not the scorner; not the godless and unrighteous who were too mean and unbelieving to offer a lamb, who never made a sacrifice. Those people had to bear the weight of their own sins. They carried that guilt throughout their lives. Those who were merely the physical descendants of Abraham bore it to the throne of judgment and answered to God for it. No one and nothing had made any atonement for their sins. They had no provision by a sacrifice and by divine pardon. Their sins were all unredeemed; they all stood naked, in their guilt before God; they answered for all their sins.

The New Testament Knows Only a Purposeful, Definite Atonement

Consider in the very opening chapter of the New Testament, Matthew chapter one, the statement made there by the angel of the Lord to Joseph about the child that Mary would soon bear, "She will give birth to a son, and you are to give him the name Jesus, because he will save his people from their sins" (Matthew 1:21). Why the incarnation? To save his people from their sin. Why the virgin birth? To save his people from their sin. Why that life lived under the law of God? To save his people from their sin. Why the death on Golgotha's cross? To save his people from their sin. Why the resurrection? To save his people from their sin. Why does he continue to make intercession for us? To save us from our sin. Why has he gone to prepare a place for us? To save his people from their sin. As he said in Matthew 20:28, "The Son of Man did not come to be served, but to serve, and to give his life a ransom for many." He gave his life for many, yes for a company of people more than any man could number.

Or again consider the words of exhortation to the elders in Ephesus in that moving farewell address of Paul. The apostle tells them, "Be shepherds of the church of God, which he bought with his own blood" (Acts 20:28). Get out of your house and go searching for the sheep when they've gone astray. Why? Christ bought the church with his own blood. Feed them with the purest doctrine and holiest truths. Why? Christ bought the church with his own blood. Pray for them all without ceasing. Why? Christ bought the church with his own blood. Be an example to them in godliness and loving kindness. Why? Christ bought the church with his own blood. They are a purchased people, that is, a redeemed people and the price paid was not silver and gold, but the precious blood of Christ.

Again, think of the people whom Jesus was conscious God had given him in a glorious donation of grace before the foundation of the world. He refers to them in John chapter six and verse 37, "All that the Father gives me will come to me." He could see them coming to him, every single one of them; none would be lost! That was his confidence, and for those people he interceded; John chapter 17 and verse 9, "I pray for them. I am not praying for the world, but for those you have given me, for they are yours." There are some people for whom Christ does not pray. Think of it! Doesn't that give you a chill of fear, that you could be going through life without a mediator with God, no high priest, no one interceding for you, no one saying, "Father I plead my sacrifice for that woman. May it not be in vain. Bring that woman safely home. She is going through such difficulties; Satan is giving her such a hard time; she is beset with doubts and her faith is failing, but I am praying for her, Father, that she will not give up." Is Jesus Christ praying for you? How do you know? One way only, that your hope is in the blood of Christ. In other words, if I should ask you why God should let you into heaven to be with him forever then you would reply, "Because the Saviour died to make atonement for my sins." Right! Then for you the risen Saviour ever lives and he makes intercession for you. It is a limited intercession if you believe the words of Jesus, "I am not praying for the world, but for those you have given me, for they are yours."

Or again, let us consider the words of our text in Ephesians chapter five and verses 25 through 27: "Christ loved the church and gave himself up for her to make her holy, cleansing her by the washing with water through the word, and to present her to himself as a radiant church, without stain or wrinkle or any other blemish, but holy and blameless." Notice three things about these words:

1. *Christ loved the church.*

Who was the object of Christ's love? The church, that is, all the believing, repentant people of God, those who will be saved, those whom the Father had given to him. "Christ loved the church"; those are the exact words of Scripture, aren't they? All the Old Testament believers who made atonement for their sins did so by the sacrifices of bulls and goats and lambs and pigeons just as God prescribed. They knew perfectly well that the blood of an animal couldn't cleanse their souls of their guilt. They knew it was a picture, a figure pointing to a great divine atonement that one day would be proved by the promised Seed of the woman, their Messiah, the seed of Abraham. But they faithfully did what God told them, putting their hand on the head of the sacrifice. The Messiah loved them for doing that.

He also loved all the people who after his death would entrust themselves to him and would be saved. Saul of Tarsus, that cruel torturer and persecutor of the church who was converted, said it like this, "He loved me and gave himself for me." It was such a personal love. Christ did not love some amorphous blob! His affection was not focused on a crowd, on his fans! He loved his own people passionately. He knew everything about them. They were all individual men and women to him, no two of them identical, and he loved each one of those different personalities. He was their lover and their bridegroom, as you sing it in those familiar words from "The church's one foundation":

> From heaven he came and sought her
>   To be his holy bride.
> With his own blood he bought her
>   And for her life he died.

He was desperately in love with them. He had been given them by his dear Father. What a precious gift and so he would look after them; he would do nothing to lose a single one of them. He would live to make a robe of righteousness like a bride's robe with which he would cover them from head to foot. He would die to make full atonement for their sin that they might go at last to heaven saved by his precious blood. Why did he do all this?

Because of his immeasurable love for his people, all of whom had been loved with everlasting love. How glorious is the love of God! God's own infinite, eternal and unchangeable love, and it is focused upon favoured sinners. Remember it is love! It is not just his mercy, and kindness, or even his forgiveness that Paul is speaking about here but the passionate affection, the undying love of Christ for his own people. There can be no greater blessing than to feel one is loved by God. But Paul goes on …

2. Christ gave Himself up for her.

He did not say to an angel, "Gabriel, or Michael, give yourself up as a sacrifice for those people whom the Father has given to me." He did not address men and women saying, "Favoured sinners, my Father has given you to me, but you need to make atonement for your own sins. You have to suffer exhaustively for your sins until they are all paid for. You must all go to a place where you will submit to suffering until you have earned the right to come to heaven." No! There is nothing like that. Not angels and not men and women were asked to give themselves up. It was Christ who humbled himself! He chose to drink that cup. It was Christ alone! He loved favoured sinners and he gave himself up to this fallen world, to constantly contradicting sinners, so wearingly and wearying. He gave himself up to the utter loneliness of his last hours when God and men forsook him. He gave himself up to the whipping, the 39 stripes making a lattice work of his back, criss-crossing in ugly, raw, bleeding welts. He gave himself up to carrying his cross, to being stripped and nailed through his hands and his feet and lifted up, hanging suspended by those nails in the blaze of the middle eastern sun until it turned dark, facing the chanting mockery of the mob. He gave himself up to enter the anathema of his Father's wrath against all ungodliness and unrighteousness of man. He gave himself to the abandonment and the dereliction. He gave himself up to death. He did it and he did it alone.

There was none other good enough. There was no other way. God must maintain the righteousness of his nature, always to be absolutely fair and straight.

But God's heart longs to forgive, to pass by the transgressions of those he loves and pardon them all. How can it be done without God compromising his own integrity? This is the way. Christ Jesus, the Son of God stood in man's place. He gave himself so freely; he humbled himself upon Mount Calvary instead of man. He drank that cup of agony and damnation that was being brought to us. He drank all the suffering and misery and anguish such as only God knows, as he is the only one who knows what sin deserves, and Christ gives himself to bear the eternal torment of every one who shall at last stand in heaven justified. His death buys their redemption. He drank all the dregs in a great draught of love. He drank damnation dry when he gave himself up for us.

3. Christ made her holy.

You see what is the purpose of his loving her and of his giving himself up on the cross for her? Paul says, "To make her holy, cleansing her by the washing with water through the word, and to present her to himself as a radiant church, without stain or wrinkle or any other blemish, but holy and blameless." This was Jesus' purpose in dying the accursed death of the cross and this is what Jesus had achieved when he finally shouted out "It is finished." He had finished doing all this for his people. If Christ had loved her, and if he had given himself up for her then this was the necessary effectual consequence, that those for whom he'd died could not be anything but holy; they were cleansed by the word; they were presented to Christ radiant, without stain or wrinkle or any other blemish; they were righteous and blameless. If Christ had died in the place of a sinner then this is what must happen to him.

Do you understand what the death of Christ accomplishes? It is not that Calvary makes atonement possible. It is that Calvary makes atonement effectual; it is an accomplished atonement. You understand the difference between a possible deliverance and an accomplished deliverance don't you?

There is a chain of life-savers sitting on their high seats along the beach, one every hundred yards. See their presence there stretched out along the shore, sitting with their tanned bodies and sunglasses, looking out to sea, their life-saving certificates nailed to the side of their chairs. They are saying "The lives of all swimmers in difficulty may be saved." So will no one drown? Of course people are still going to drown; the presence of the lifeguards on their seats makes life-saving only possible. To actually save a life they must jump out of their seats, run along the beach, dash into the water, swim out to the drowning man and deliver him, keeping his head above water, bringing him to the shore and give him the kiss of life and artificial respiration. That is accomplished salvation. Their being there on the high chairs and looking out to sea presents to the drowning man only the possibility of salvation.

We have a fire-brigade in the town. There are twenty men and two fire engines and the firemen are all qualified in rescuing people from danger. So will no one die in a burning house? Of course they will die unless that possible salvation is transformed into accomplished salvation when the men slide down the pole and get into their suits as they clamber onto the fire engine and drive off, the warning siren of a fire-brigade speeding along sending the cars to the side of the road that they might hurry past. Then they get to the burning house and they train their hoses on it, and put their ladders against it entering it and rescuing the children from the burning building. Then it is not just the possibility of salvation that they are offering to the people of the town; it is the accomplishment of salvation.

Again, I can use the illustration of a local hospital in the same way. People are still going to die of curable diseases though there is a 240-bed hospital full of trained physicians and nurses and expensive equipment within half a mile. That building, and the qualified personnel with all their skill are there. The drugs and the X-ray machines are also there, but they simply make deliverance from death possible; they must be applied to you or you will die.

So it is with the redemption of Christ. What he has done is not to plan and build a vast redeemability plant – "Golgotha Redeemability Incorporated." It is not that everyone in the world has been placed in a redeemable state through Calvary. Rather what Paul is telling us in our text is that Christ's dying love for us has actually made all those for whom he died "holy" men and women, that is, they are now a people set apart to God. That is what our text says. Christ has cleansed all of them by the washing with water through the word. They are clean in God's eyes however filthy they've been. Christ has presented them to himself as a radiant church. Christ has so effectively redeemed them that they are without stain, or wrinkle, or any other blemish but he has made them all utterly holy and blameless. That is what the atonement of Christ has achieve—according to the Bible, not according to my theories or my theology, but according to the plain claims of Scripture. We are pleading with you to face up to what Scripture teaches.

The cross of Christ has obtained eternal redemption for all for whom Jesus died (Hebrews 9:12). Jesus has got it! The eternal redemption of favoured men and women is all in the hands of Christ who has all authority in heaven and earth. God has given him a name above every name. Where would be a better place for our redemption? It is all in the hands of King Jesus.

Again, Paul reminds Titus of this in chapter two of the letter that he sent to him in verses 13 and 14, writing of "our great God and Saviour, Jesus Christ, who gave himself for us to redeem us from all wickedness and to purify for himself a people that are his very own, eager to do what is good." That is what the cross of Jesus Christ has accomplished; he has not made possible a redemption from all wickedness. He is not now anxiously watching to see whether one or more will respond. He has in fact actually redeemed us from all wickedness, and purified for himself a people eager to do what is good. That is the achievement of the blood of Christ. Then you must ask the question, "for whom has he done this?", and the answer Paul gives Titus is "a people that are his very own." They are the ones who live a new life. They are the ones who have been redeemed from wickedness. They are the ones who have been purified, who are now eager to do what is good. They are the ones who will one day be in heaven, saved by his precious blood.

So here is the plain teaching of the New Testament concerning the accomplishment of the dying of Jesus. If Christ has actually died in my place on Golgotha then he has once and for all dealt with all the sins of my life, of my heart, and my nature; my original sins and my actual sins; my sins of omission and my sins of commission. They have all been nailed to that cross in Christ. Think of every sin that you are aware of, and if you are in Christ then he was made that sin for you. Take all the sins that you cannot be aware of now, and yet when he gave himself for you he was giving himself for those sins too. That means henceforth I cannot consider or acknowledge my sins in isolation. I can think of them only as they have been made Christ's. They are no longer mine alone, in this sense, that I will never answer for Christless sins to God, because Christ has comprehensively answered for them already. There are no un-dealt-with sins for the people of God.

It is a magnificent and even an incredible concept, that our sins no longer control or modify our relation to God today. It is as if they weren't there. There is no guilt at all; there is no defilement at all; there is no blame at all; there is no shame; it does not exist; they have all been removed by God and laid on his Son. He has been made sin for me. He has taken our sin, our past sin, our present sin and our future sin and he has put it all away forever. So we are washed; we are clean; we are as Paul says so astonishingly in our text, "without stain or wrinkle or any other blemish, but holy and blameless."

I am not sure that my conscience believes it. I am not sure that there is not in me something that wants to cling in self-pity to some remnants of my guilt so that I wallow in my past, and turn my eyes on my yesterdays and tell people how badly I have lived, and so can feel sorry for myself. I am pleading with you to let the truth of these words be the whole truth about the way things are between you and God today. There is no barrier whatsoever; there is no impediment; there is no closed or limited access.

It has all been forgiven; it has all been forgotten. There are people who cling to faith in the fantasy dark land of 'purgatory' where they themselves are going to deal with the pollution of their sins. There they are going to handle their outstanding sins until they are all finally dealt with. A result of that error is that it actually encourages them to sub-Christian living, a little less dedication, a little less commitment, a little less sanctification because they feel they themselves will have to deal with those sins and their consequences after they die. Ultimately they are going to be delivered from them by their own sufferings. So they are not perturbed to let out the occasional swear word and blasphemy, and display carelessness about the Lord's Day, and the odd explosion of anger and the occasional drunkenness and some sexual sins. They shrug because they'll have to face up to the consequences of their own sins on the fantasy island of purgatory. I am telling you that the only purgatory there is either in this world or the next is the Cross. Only there are our sins dealt with; only there you will find the blood of Christ. God has made no plans for a purgatory.

I am saying that the sins of all the people of God—as many people as there are sands on the seashore—have all been forgiven; he has borne them all, every speck, every spot, every such thing has been dealt with by Christ there. There is absolutely nothing left, do you know it? There is no condemnation to them that are in Christ Jesus. The single determinant today of your relationship with God is what happened on the cross. Nothing else matters; nothing else is relevant. There are only two factors in the equation, what God did and how Christ responded. God made Christ sin and he received that sin lovingly. And how you feel about your life, and how sometimes you doubt, and what you are doing for Jesus, and how you fail—that is not remotely relevant to Golgotha. The one thing that matters is that Christ loved us and gave himself for us there. And I don't for a moment believe that the heart that knows that will take advantage of it and go from this meeting to get drunk or steal or deceive or live a life without law because the cross won't let you.

I believe on the contrary that if substitutionary atonement has no place in your thinking, if you are living your life with the smallest consideration of what Jesus Christ did for you on Golgotha, and if you are feeling that God still has things against you, then that often serves as some unconscious grudge against God, that somehow justifies you from being less than perfect and permits a relapse here and a shortcoming there. I want to know in the depths of my heart that when God made Jesus Christ sin for us that Christ made a good and decent and proper job of that sin, that he dealt with it all 100%, that he cleared it all away, that he experienced its hell in my place, that he entered its outer darkness instead of me so that I shall never, never know the unquenchable fires. When God comes to me searching for my sin he finds it on the Cross of Jesus condemned and covered, and on that fact is my whole confidence of forgiveness grounded.

He does not find on Calvary the possibility of redemption; he finds redemption accomplished.

The New Testament Declares a Cosmic Atonement

In the Old Testament there was an atonement limited to the Jews. They alone made sacrifice for their sin by the spotless lambs which they chose whose throats were then cut. No atonement outside Israel under the old covenant; none at all; the nations were in darkness and in the bondage of Satan, but what a difference when the Messiah came! John the Baptist announced the ministry of Jesus of Nazareth like this, "Behold the Lamb of God who takes away the sin of the world." No longer is there redemption only for believers in Israel, but through Jesus Christ sinners in every part of the world are going to have their sins taken away.

1.   So sometimes in the New Testament the word "world" refers to the vast Gentile world where the good news of the cross of Jesus was going to take away the sins of many.

2.   Sometimes the word "world" refers to the moral wretchedness and depravity of men and women. Remember John's great words to his readers, in his first letter and the second chapter, "Do not love the world or anything in the world. If anyone loves the world the love of the Father is not in him. For everything in the world—the cravings of sinful man, the lust of his eye and the boasting of what he has and does—comes not from the Father but from the world" (1 John 2:15, 16). What is the world? It is not an arithmetic concept, it is a moral concept. It does not refer here to every single person without exception from Adam until today. It does not refer to the more than 6,000 million people living on this planet today. It refers to a fallen rotten age in rebellion against God and characterized by the lust of the flesh and the lust of the eyes and the pride of life. If you love the things this sin-crazed world loves—that which is seen in all the world's media and talked of with such giddy excitement by sinfully disturbed men and women—then the love of God is not in you. You are acting and speaking and enthusing just like the people of the world who have rejected God. Yet we are told –hear me—Oh "Amazing pity! Grace unknown! And love beyond degree!" (Isaac Watts)—that God loved the world.

What we are told never to love, God loved, and so loved it as to send his own Son to die for 'the world.' Oh what a good thing that he loved the world! There would be no hope for any of us if God had not loved us worldlings and sent his Son to deal with the sins of the world! So sometimes the word 'world' refers to an ethical state of sinful darkness and rebellion against God.

3.   Sometimes again the word "world" refers to the creation. God loves the world he has made. He will not give it over to the devil to turn

into hell. Some sinners are going to be lost, and yet the world is going to be saved. There is going to be a new heavens and a new world and righteousness is going to characterize it because Christ has dealt with cosmic sin when he hung on the cross. He has de-sinned the cosmos by his precious blood, so powerful is the sacrifice of the Son of God who made the world.

4. Again sometimes the "world" refers to the blessings of common grace which have come to all mankind through the love of God in Christ, blessings which continually fall upon all men and women, even sinners who go to the grave rejecting Christ. Yet these men and women show family love, and moral rectitude, and participate in caring ministries, and make our lives rich by their cultural, creative, medical and teaching skills. All this comes to them from God via his Son Jesus Christ and through the great work of atonement he has done. Christ by his precious blood has bought the blessings of common grace for a groaning world so that we might preach the gospel to all men.

5. Sometimes the word 'all' means all kinds of men and women. Think of Titus chapter two: "for the grace of God that brings salvation has appeared to all men" (Titus 2:11). There were millions of men who lived and died without ever hearing of the grace of God bringing salvation. But to all kinds of men that grace has appeared. No longer is there Jewish exclusivity but now all men, rich and poor, with all colours of skin, all nations and tribes, to them all the gospel has been preached and people of every kind or personality have been changed by the grace of God. God commands all men everywhere to repent.

Do you see how you have to look at the context of New Testament words like "all," "everyone," and "the world," and see what makes sense of that verse?

There is one thing concerning which there can be no argument, that the blood of Christ is powerful to save the very worst of men, the chief of sinners. It makes the foulest clean. It makes scarlet sins whiter than snow. We can never limit the power of the blood of Christ can we? If Christ has died for them then they are eternally saved. Then the only alternative interpretation is that we must limit the design and purpose of the atonement, that it was the people of God in all their billions that Christ loved and made atonement for on Calvary's cross.

The Grievous Error of a Universal Atonement

I was recently reading some words of a preacher preaching a universal atonement. He was trying to impose that faulty logic, that philosophical system, upon the New Testament. This is what he said, and it made me quite ill to read it. The speaker was a man named Rob Bell, the founding pastor of Mars Hill Bible Church in Grand Rapids, Michigan, one of the American mega-churches and a leader in the Emerging Church movement. He said this:

> When Christ died on the cross he died for everybody.
> Everybody.
> Everywhere.
> Every tribe, every nation, every tongue, every people group.
> Jesus said that when he was lifted up, he would draw all men to himself.
> All people. Everywhere.
> Everybody's sins on the cross with Jesus.
> Forgiveness is true for everybody.

And then Bell goes on ...

> And this reality extends beyond this life.
> Heaven is full of forgiven people.
> Hell is full of forgiven people.
> Heaven is full of forgiven people God loves, whom Jesus died for.
> Hell is full of forgiven people God loves, whom Jesus died for.
> The difference is how we choose to live, which story we choose to live in, which version of reality we trust. Ours or God's.

I find that so shocking because what good does this man think the blood of Christ has done for him or for anyone? He thinks that the blood of Christ actually saves no one from hell. Jesus can die for you but you can still go to the place of woe. The damned in hell were as much an object of Jesus Christ's forgiveness as the saved in heaven, and so for all those in hell Christ died in vain, so ineffectual was Jesus' dying. He loved them; he gave himself for them and yet they ended up in the lake of fire with the beast and the false prophet. Such an atonement I despise. I reject it. As Spurgeon once said, 'I had rather believe a limited atonement that is efficacious for all men for whom it was intended, than a universal atonement that is not efficacious for anybody, except the will of man be joined with it.' What a religion that magnifies the will of man above the power of God! What saves from hell according to Rob Bell? It is man's choice with his free will that did it. That man was a smart cat! That's what made the difference. He got to heaven because he made a good choice, and he will have eternity to preen himself on that. Heaven was not decisively gained by the blood of Christ but by human decision.

We have been taught by the Spirit and by the Bible of the power of the blood of God the Son who gave himself up that we saved sinners might be his bride. Jesus died to "to make her holy, cleansing her by the washing with water through the word, and to present her to himself as a radiant church, without stain or wrinkle or any other blemish, but holy and blameless."

That is what the dying love of Christ has accomplished. If he died to redeem a sinner by hanging in the place of a sinner, propitiating the wrath of God towards a favoured sinner, reconciling God to us by his royal death, then we shall never perish; not one of all these blood-bought sinners shall end in hell. The blood of Christ will forbid it.

> Dear dying Lamb Thy precious blood
>   Shall never lose its power
> Till all the ransomed church of God
>   Be saved to sin no more.

Men and women, cling to the Bible's teaching on the limited and definite and effectual purpose of the blood of Christ. That will then be your comfort both in life and in death.

10

Understanding Effectual Calling

Tom Hicks

I know a young man who once lived a deeply sinful lifestyle. His sinful actions put him at odds with the law, and he became quite proficient at avoiding law enforcement. Over the years, he pressed further and further into his sins, but a couple of years ago, a faithful man of God confronted him with God's law and called him to repent and trust the Lord Jesus Christ. The young man underwent an immediate and dramatic conversion. He experienced a radical and mysterious change of heart, which none of his friends or family understood or expected. He never wanted Christ before, but now he wants Christ. He used to love sin, but now he sees his sin as offensive to God and as bringing misery to himself and others. He once had no desire for holiness, but now he wants to be holy. The young man was not looking for redemption. In fact, he was running from it. He was not seeking the Lord, but God sought him and graciously and powerfully changed his heart.

The Bible's explanation of this man's experience is effectual calling. The experience termed "effectual calling" goes by different names. Sometimes it is described as "effectual grace" or "irresistible grace."[1] It is "gracious" because God extends it to sinners who deserve only condemnation and wrath. It is "irresistible," not because men never resist it, but because they cannot effectively resist it. The Synod of Dordt declared that effectual calling "does not treat men as senseless stocks and blocks, nor take away their

---

[1] "Irresistible grace" or "effectual grace" is the fourth point of Calvinism, or the "I" in the well-known T.U.L.I.P. acrostic.

will and its properties, or do violence thereto; but it spiritually quickens, heals, corrects, and at the same time sweetly and powerfully bends it, that where carnal rebellion and resistance formerly prevailed, a ready and sincere spiritual obedience begins to reign."[2] Every sinner naturally resists God's effectual call with all of his power, but no sinner can ever successfully resist the effectual call. That's because God's effectual call powerfully and certainly conquers human resistance and causes hardened sinners to embrace Jesus Christ freely and willingly. The Lord Jesus said, "I will build My church and the gates of hell will not prevail against it" (Matthew 16:18). The gates of hell try to keep God out of mens' hearts, but they cannot stop Him because His power is limitless. Some misunderstand the doctrine of effectual calling to teach that God forces men against their wills to come to Christ. But, the effectual call of God never works against the human will; rather, it changes the will, causing men to want to come to Christ, to trust and love Him, though they previously opposed and hated Him. Joel Beeke says that effectual calling means "that the Holy Spirit never fails in His objective to bring His own to faith."[3]

Historical Background

The precise nature of God's grace is a question that has been hotly debated throughout history. It was first explored extensively in the historical debate between Pelagius and Augustine. Pelagius (c. 354 – after 418) was a British monk who moved to Rome around 380, where he began to teach his understanding of grace (*Exposition of Paul's Epistles*). Pelagius believed that God graciously gives human beings the power to keep His commandments. He denied that men are fallen in Adam, and he denied that they inherit a polluted nature from Adam that is inclined to sin. Any sort of propensity to sin among human beings, in Pelagius's view, is merely the result of environmental and social factors, but not of any corruption in human nature. Pelagius taught that God's grace takes two main forms. First, God graciously gives everyone a nature that is capable of willing good. Human nature, which has the power to choose good, is itself grace, according to Pelagius. Second, God gives His Word to men, which graciously instructs them in His will. Pelagius believed that God's law is grace. Pelagius also believed in a lesser third kind of resistible assisting grace, which helps men to keep God's commandments, but only if they freely

---

[2] *The Canons of Dordt*, Third and Fourth Heads, Rejection of Errors, Article 16: Regeneration's Effect.

[3] Joel R. Beeke, *Living for God's Glory: An Introduction to Calvinism* (Orlando, FL: Reformation Trust, 2008), 102.

choose to access it and cooperate with it.[4] One result of this teaching is that some men remain sinless and good throughout their lives. For sinless men, there is no need of the gracious work of the Holy Spirit or the work of Christ on their behalf.

Augustine (354–430), the bishop of Hippo in North Africa, strongly opposed the teaching of Pelagius (*Enchiridion, On Nature and Free Will*). Augustine taught that when God first created Adam, Adam had the ability to sin (*posse peccare*) and the ability not to sin (*posse non peccare*). But, when Adam chose to sin, he sinned as the representative of the whole human race and the whole race fell in him. As a result, all men who descend from him by natural generation inherit a polluted nature that is only and always inclined to sin and never inclined to do good. Mankind in Adam lost the ability not to sin and retained only the ability to sin. Fallen men are not able not to sin (*non posse non peccare*). For Augustine, fallen human beings need special grace. According to Augustine, grace takes two forms. First, God graciously reveals the gospel of Jesus Christ, which declares what God does in His Son to redeem sinners. For Augustine, there is a contrast between law, which exposes human inability, and gospel, which declares God's redemptive purposes. Second, God graciously sends His Spirit effectually to restore human ability not to sin (*posse non peccare*). Augustine believed that human nature needs God's effectual and irresistible grace to cause it to keep God's commandments. He taught that God's grace must give fallen men the ability to keep His commands, since that ability is not inherent within human nature.[5] Augustine believed that because human nature is fallen, all men need the work of Christ and the work of the Spirit to change them.

Pelagius's doctrine was condemned by the First Council of Ephesus (431), but men such as John Cassian, Vincent of Lerins, and Faustus of Riez, continued to oppose Augustine's doctrine of effectual calling because they understood that it is inextricably connected to the doctrine of predestination, which they vehemently opposed. After years of controversy, there was an attempt to settle the matter at the Synod of Orange (529) where "election was recognized, unconditional election was not mentioned, grace was not seen as irresistible, and predestination was expressly anathematized. The synod advocated cooperative salvation from an Augustinian perspective."[6] The Synod of Orange upheld Augustine's doctrine of human nature, but denied his doctrine of irresistible grace in favor of a semi-Augustinian understanding of resistible grace, which declared that

---

[4] John D. Hannah, *Our Legacy: The History of Christian Doctrine* (Colorado Springs: NavPress, 2001), 211–212.

[5] Ibid., 212–213.

[6] Ibid., 216.

God's grace is necessary but not sufficient to save. Augustine convinced the church that the fallen human nature is totally unable to do anything toward its own salvation, but he did not convince the church of the need for irresistible grace or effectual calling.

It was not until about one thousand years later during the Protestant Reformation that Augustine's views on effectual calling and grace were revived as a result of fresh reflection on the Scriptures. Stalwarts of the Reformation, including Martin Luther (1483–1546), Ulrich Zwingli (1484–1531), John Calvin (1509–1564) and John Owen (1616–1683), all affirmed the doctrine of effectual calling.

Effectual calling was not only taught by the major figures of the Reformation, but also in the churches of the Reformation and Post-Reformation periods. Early Particular Baptist confessions of faith clearly taught the doctrine of the effectual call.[7] For example, the Second London Baptist Confession of 1677/1689, Chapter 10: Of Effectual Calling, declares:

> **Paragraph 1.** Those whom God hath predestinated unto life, He is pleased in His appointed, and accepted time, effectually to call, by His Word and Spirit, out of that state of sin and death in which they are by nature, to grace and salvation by Jesus Christ; enlightening their minds spiritually and savingly to understand the things of God; taking away their heart of stone, and giving to them a heart of flesh; renewing their wills, and by His almighty power determining them to that which is good, and effectually drawing them to Jesus Christ.

> **Paragraph 2.** This effectual call is of God's free and special grace alone, not from anything at all foreseen in man, nor from any power or agency in the creature, being wholly passive therein, being dead in sins and trespasses, until being quickened and renewed by the Holy Spirit; he is thereby enabled to answer this call, and to embrace the grace offered and conveyed in it, and that by no less power than that which raised up Christ from the dead.[8]

Other influential Reformed confessions of faith also teach the doctrine of effectual calling, including the Dutch Reformed Canons of Dordt (1618), the Presbyterian Westminster Confession (1646), and the Congregationalist Savoy Declaration (1658).

---

[7] The First London Confession of 1644 (sections 5, 24), The Midland Association Confession of 1655 (section 5), The Somerset Confession of 1656 (sections 9, 11), and The Second London Baptist Confession of 1689/1677 (chapter 10). See William L. Lumpkin, *Baptist Confessions of Faith* (Valley Forge, PA: Judson, 1969), 144, 195, 200, 235.

[8] Ibid., 264–265.

Effectual Calling and the Trinity

To understand the doctrine of effectual calling in its proper theological framework, it ought to be viewed in light of its connection to the saving work of the Trinity. Effectual calling is based on the Father's unconditional election. Scripture teaches that in His eternal decree, God the Father unconditionally chose certain individuals for salvation (Ephesians 1:3–6). In order to accomplish His eternal purpose of election, the Father extends effectual calling to the elect in time so that they will actually be saved. Without God's effectual call, all men, including the elect, would continue to resist and reject Christ and would go to hell because of their totally depraved natures, and God's purpose would be thwarted. But, the Bible tells us "those whom He predestined, He also called" (Romans 8:30). God calls those who are predestined to be conformed to the image of Christ, guaranteeing that the elect will be saved. All who are called are justified and glorified (Romans 8:30).

Let us examine some of the biblical lines of evidence for the doctrine that the Father effectually calls the elect. Jesus said, "All that the Father gives to Me will come to Me" (John 6:37). The Father gives some individuals to the Son, and those given by the Father necessarily come to Christ. Jesus said, "You do not believe because you are not part of My flock. My sheep hear My voice, and I know them, and they follow Me" (John 10:26–27). Notice that believing in Christ does not make a person one of Christ's sheep. Jesus does not say, "You are not My sheep because you do not believe." Rather, the fact that a person is not one of Christ's sheep is the reason for that person's unbelief. In contrast, God's sheep always hear Christ's voice, and they always follow Him in faith (Acts 13:48). The Apostle Paul wrote, "God chose you as the first fruits to be saved" (2 Thessalonians 2:13), showing that those who are chosen by God the Father will be saved. The Apostle Peter wrote, "The God of all grace, who has called you to His eternal glory in Christ, will himself restore, confirm, strengthen, and establish you" (1 Peter 5:10). The Southern Baptist theologian James P. Boyce commented, "Here the Apostle is speaking of that effectual calling, which is the result of election, and tells us that it is a call unto eternal glory."[9] The doctrine of effectual calling is only properly understood against the background of the Father's unconditional election.

Unconditional election is not sufficient for salvation, however, because it does not answer the problem of how a holy God can justly save sinful men. For God to save His chosen people and still remain true to His own

[9] James P. Boyce, *Abstract of Systematic Theology* (1887; repirnt, Escondido, CA: den Dulk Christian Foundation, nd), 356.

perfect justice, the Son's atonement was legally necessary. Thus, God not only eternally elected some individuals for salvation, but He also entered into an eternal covenant of redemption among the persons of the Trinity to satisfy divine justice and to accomplish the redemption planned in His electing decree. This eternal covenant is sometimes called the "counsel of peace," the "everlasting council," the "covenant of grace," or the "covenant of redemption."[10] The Southern Baptist theologian John L. Dagg wrote, "That the covenant is eternal, may be argued from the eternity, unchangeableness, and omniscience of the parties, and from the declarations of Scripture which directly or indirectly relate to it," and "The reconciliation between God and men is provided for by the covenant engagement between the Father and the Son."[11] Thus, in eternity, Christ covenanted with the Father to merit eternal life for the elect and to bear their sins in His body on the tree (1 Peter 2:24). The Spirit also agreed to indwell Christ, while He accomplished His mission (Isaiah 42:1). Though formed in eternity, this covenant was actually executed in time, when "the Son appeared in human nature, in the form of a servant; and, after obeying unto death, was exalted by the Father to supreme dominion."[12]

The covenant of redemption has a close relationship to the doctrine of effectual calling. If Jesus Christ actually paid for the sins of the elect, and earned eternal life for them, then God is legally bound actually to give the experience and enjoyment of eternal life to the elect. When a debtor's fine is paid, the judge is obligated to release him from prison. Romans 5:10 says, "For if while we were enemies, we were reconciled to God by the death of His Son, much more, now that we are reconciled, shall we be saved by his life." The phrase "we were reconciled" refers to reconciliation that took place at the time of Christ's death. The result of that past reconciliation is that those for whom Christ died will be "saved." Since Christ's death actually reconciled the elect to God, divine justice requires God to save them so that they will enjoy the benefits of their reconciliation. It would be an injustice for men reconciled by Christ's death to remain in an unsaved condition, unable to enjoy or benefit from their reconciliation. Romans 8:32–33 says, "He who did not spare His own Son, but gave Him up for us all, how will He not also with Him graciously give us all things? Who shall bring

---

[10] For some texts traditionally used to support the doctrine of the covenant of redemption, see Psalm 2:8; 40:6–8; 89:3; Isaiah 49:3–12; 54:10; John 17:1–6; Hebrews 13:20; Titus 1:2.

[11] John L. Dagg, *Manual of Theology* (Harrisonburg, VA: Gano, 1990), 254–255. Texts Dagg believed demonstrate the eternality of the covenant include Hebrews 13:20, Ephesians 3:11, Titus 1:2, and 2 Timothy 1:9.

[12] Ibid., 255.

any charge against God's elect?" Paul's argument moves from the greater to the lesser. If God gave His Son to His people, then God would never withhold any other good thing from them. Some of the good "things" Paul has in mind are found in verse 30, which speaks of calling, justification, and glorification. Christ's payment for the sins of the elect guarantees that all of the elect will be effectually called and finally saved.

The Father's eternal choice and the Son's historical redemption are not sufficient for the elect to be saved. The Father's and the Son's objective actions must be brought subjectively into the minds and hearts of God's people. That is the work of the Holy Spirit. The book of Acts shows that God's Word and His Spirit come together when men are saved. Knowledge of God's Word without the work of the Spirit results in dead unbelieving orthodoxy. Subjective spiritual experiences without the Word result in mysticism and false worship void of the true knowledge of God. But, when the Word and the Spirit come together, God's people are saved and sanctified. The Word and the Spirit are parallel to the "external" and "internal" call of God.[13] The Word corresponds to the external call of God. The Spirit corresponds to the internal call of God, though since the Spirit inspired the Scriptures, He is also involved in the external call. According to Dagg, this distinction between the external and internal call is connected to the indirect and direct influence of the Holy Spirit. The external call, referring to the written or preached Word, "belongs to the indirect influence of the Spirit."[14] The internal call refers to the omnipotent regenerating and "direct" power of the Holy Spirit.[15] Greg Welty writes that advocates of effectual calling "make a distinction between the 'outer call' (which goes to all to whom the gospel is preached and which may not result in faith and repentance) and the 'inner call' (which goes to the elect alone and conveys the gift of faith and repentance)."[16] Scripture itself makes the distinction between the two kinds of calling in the parable of the wedding feast in Matthew 22:1–14. In that parable, the king sent his servants to call those who were invited to the wedding feast, but the invited guests refused to come. The king then sent his servants to "gather" people from the streets so that the "wedding hall was filled with guests." The conclusion of the parable is "Many are called, but few are chosen" (Matthew 22:14).

[13] Sometimes the distinction is referred to as "external call vs. internal call," "outward call vs. inward call," "outer call vs. inner call," or "general call vs. special call."

[14] Dagg, *Manual of Theology*, 332.

[15] Ibid., 332–333.

[16] Greg Welty, "Election and Calling: A Biblical Theological Study," in *Calvinism: A Southern Baptist Dialogue*, ed. E. Ray Clendenen and Brad J. Waggoner (Nashville, TN: Broadman and Holman, 2008), 234.

The External Call

The external call is the Word of Christ preached to all men. God's external call summons and commands all men everywhere without exception or distinction to come to Christ for salvation. The Lord Jesus said, "Come to Me all who labor and are heavy laden, and I will give you rest" (Matthew 11:28). Paul wrote, "The times of ignorance God overlooked, but now He commands all people everywhere to repent" (Acts 17:30). Revelation 22:17 says, "The Spirit and the Bride say 'Come.' And let the one who hears say, 'Come.' And let the one who is thirsty come; let the one who desires take the water of life without price." Thus, Scripture is clear that God's external call extends to everyone and no one is excepted. The Canons of Dordt, popularly known as the five points of Calvinism, articulate this biblical teaching: "The promise of the gospel is that whosoever believes in Christ crucified shall not perish, but have eternal life. This promise, together with the command to repent and believe, ought to be declared and published to all nations, and to all persons promiscuously and without distinction, to whom God out of His good pleasure sends the gospel."[17]

Non-Calvinists believe that the external call implies that all men can freely choose to obey the call or not. They reason, "The command to repent and believe implies that all people have the ability to choose to repent and believe when they hear the external call." The Bible does not say, however, that all sinners have the moral ability to obey gospel commands. To claim that they do on the basis of the commands/imperatives of Scripture is to read one's own assumptions into the text. Non-Calvinist Steve Lemke objects, "If He has extended a general call to all persons to be saved, but has given the effectual call irresistibly to just a few, the general call seems rather misleading."[18] But, Lemke cannot consistently hold that objection, since God requires obedience to the Ten Commandments. God's law is inflexible and requires perfect obedience, but no human being, believer or unbeliever, has the ability to obey it perfectly. Does this mean that God was "misleading" when He gave the Ten Commandments? Certainly not. Commands do not imply an ability to obey them. Paul said, "When the commandment came, sin came alive and I died" (Romans 7:9), and "For through the law, I died to the law" (Galatians 2:19). Part of the reason God

---

[17] *The Canons of Dordt*, Second Head, Article 5: The Mandate to Proclaim the Gospel to All.

[18] Steve W. Lemke, "A Biblical and Theological Critique of Irresistible Grace," in *Whosoever Will: A Biblical-Theological Critique of Five-Point Calvinism*, ed. David L. Allen and Steve W. Lemke (Nashville, TN: Broadman and Holman, 2010), 145.

gives commands is to show men their inability to keep them and need of God's grace. Apart from God's grace, "no one seeks for God … no one does good, not even one" (Romans 3:11–12). Similarly, the external call obligates everyone to come to Christ, but it does not imply that anyone has the ability to do so.

Historically, there was disagreement as to whether an external call obligates all men to come to Christ. In the eighteenth century, Calvinists debated what came to be called "The Modern Question," which asked, "Whether it be the duty of all men to whom the gospel is published, to repent and believe in Christ?"[19] Hyper-Calvinists claimed that since unregenerate men lack the power to turn to Christ, they are absolved of any responsibility to do so. Against hyper-calvinism, the Calvinistic Baptist, Andrew Fuller, answered the Modern Question with a clear and forceful "yes" in his work, *The Gospel Worthy of All Acceptation*. He argued that unregenerate men are responsible to repent and trust in Christ because they have the natural capacity to do so, even though they lack the moral desire. Even the unregenerate could turn to Christ if they only wanted to do so. The problem with the unregenerate is not that they lack the capacity to choose, believe, repent, come, etc. It is that they lack the desire, and it is for that lack of desire that God holds them responsible.

Regarding the free and promiscuous gospel call, John Murray affirmed that God genuinely desires men to obey commands that He does not necessarily decree that they obey: "In the free offer, there is expressed not simply the bare preceptive will of God but the disposition of lovingkindness on the part of God pointing to the salvation to be gained through compliance with the overtures of the gospel of grace."[20] In other words, Murray believed in a distinction between God's will of command and His will of decree. According to John Dagg, God's will of command "expresses what it would be pleasing to Him that [men] should do," and His will of decree is His "fixed determination as to what He will do."[21] In the external call, God commands and desires everyone who hears the gospel to repent and trust Christ for salvation, even if the command is heard by individuals who are not elected to salvation in the eternal decree.[22] Steve Lemke thinks that

---

[19] Thomas J. Nettles, *The Baptists*, vol. 1, *Key People in Forming a Baptist Identity* (Fearn, Scotland: Mentor, 2005), 248.

[20] John Murray, *Collected Writings of John Murray*, vol. 4, *The Free Offer of the Gospel* (Carlisle, PA: Banner of Truth, 1982), 114.

[21] Dagg, *Manual of Theology*, 100.

[22] If it is asked how God's desire for all to repent and believe is consistent with His decree to save only the elect, Murray says, "We have found that God himself expresses an ardent desire for the fulfillment of certain things which he has not decreed in his inscrutable counsel to come to pass. This means that there

Calvinists are absurd to affirm that God both has a will of command and a will of decree. He writes, "The God of hard Calvinism is either disingenuous, cynically making a pseudo-offer of salvation to persons whom He has not given the means to accept, or there is a deep inner conflict within the will of God.... This conflict between the wills of God portrays Him as having a divided mind."[23] However, non-Calvinists must also affirm that God has two wills. This is because they say that God sincerely desires all men to be saved, yet all men are not actually saved. Non-Calvinists have to explain why all men are not saved since God is powerful enough to save the whole world if He wanted to do so. The answer in every orthodox evangelical system is that God has a desire higher than the desire to save all men. Non-Calvinists believe that the preservation of man's free will is more desirable than saving everyone. God desires all men to be saved, but more than that, God desires to preserve the free will of all men. So, if Lemke's objection stands, then it stands against his system as well, since if Lemke affirms the Bible's teaching that some men go to hell, then God must have a desire higher than His desire to save all men. Calvinists who believe that God desires all men to be saved also believe that God has a higher desire than the salvation of all men. They believe that the display of the full range of God's own glory is more desirable than saving everyone. God desires all men to be saved, since He commands all men to repent and believe, but more than that, God wants to put all of His attributes on display, including His justice, mercy, grace, and wrath (Romans 9:21–23).[24]

The Internal Call

Even though God extends the external call to all who hear the gospel, not all men respond with obedience. Many people hear Christ appealing to them in His Word, inviting, commanding, and urging them to repent of their sins and trust in Him for salvation: "We implore you on behalf of Christ, be reconciled to God" (2 Corinthians 5:20); "We appeal to you ... Behold now is the favorable time; behold, now is the day of salvation" (2 Corinthians 6:1–2). But, no one will deny that large numbers of people stubbornly refuse to turn from their idols and come to Christ. The question is, "What accounts for the difference between the person who comes

is a will to the realization of what he has not decretively willed, a pleasure towards that which he has not been pleased to decree." Murray, *The Free Offer of the Gospel*, 131.

[23] Lemke, "A Biblical and Theological Critique," 145.

[24] Wayne Grudem, *Systematic Theology: An Introduction to Biblical Doctrine* (Grand Rapids, MI: Zondervan, 1994), 683–684.

to Christ for salvation and the one who refuses to come?" Non-Calvinists claim that the difference is rooted in different uses of free will after sinners receive a kind of prevenient grace that is necessary but not sufficient for salvation. Tom Nettles reasons, "If the bestowment of salvation arises from any factor beside the sovereign work of God's effectual grace, then one must conclude that an actual difference exists in the characters or wills of the two respective individuals who responded in different ways to the gospel. The one who received Christ must not have been as hard, rebellious, or captive as the one who rejected."[25] If God gives resistible grace to lost men that enables them to accept or reject the gospel when the external call comes, then people are saved because they are wiser, softer hearted, better, smarter, or possess some other favorable quality that would lead them to choose Christ for salvation, while others lack such a favorable quality and thus refuse Christ. Calvinists believe this to be salvation by human goodness or merit, which robs God of having all the glory in salvation, and prevents the redeemed from worshipfully giving all thanks to God for their salvation, since they deserve some credit for their own wise choice. Roger Olsen, an Arminian theologian, replies to this argument by saying that "the only 'contribution' humans make is non-resistance to grace. This is the same as accepting a gift."[26] He says there is no merit in "non-resistance." According to Olsen, God's grace does everything to save a sinner as long as the sinner relaxes his resistant will under the influence of divine grace. In reality, this defense does not solve the problem for the non-Calvinist because everyone who hears the gospel receives the same enabling resistible grace from God, which means that the determining difference or decisive (deciding) factor in human salvation is not God's grace alone, but only whether men choose to relax their resistance under God's grace or not. Here is the problem. This determining factor in salvation, "non-resistance," is either better or not better than "resistance." If "non-resistance" is better than "resistance," then some men go to heaven for all eternity because they made a better choice than other men, which gives them a ground of boasting and robs God of glory forever. If, however, "non-resistance" is not better than "resistance," then the situation is worse. Those who "resist" God's grace go to hell for all eternity even though their choice had the same or better value than the choice of "non-resistance."[27]

---

[25] Thomas J. Nettles, *By His Grace and For His Glory: A Historical, Theological, and Practical Study of the Doctrines of Grace in Baptist Life*, rev. ed. (Cape Coral, FL: Founders Press, 2006), 325.

[26] Roger E. Olsen, *Arminian Theology: Myths and Realities* (Downers Grove, IL: IVP, 2006), 165.

[27] Nettles, *By His Grace and For His Glory*, 325.

The only way to resolve this dilemma is to confess that all the choices of fallen human beings which move them toward God are the necessary result of God's effectual and irresistible calling. Every good thing a sinner does, including "non-resistance" is a gift of God's free and effectual grace. What makes a difference between sinners is not their uses of free will, but God's distinguishing sovereign grace.

The Word of God teaches that the internal call is an effectual call.[28] One of the key texts describing God's effectual call is John 6:44, which says, "No one can come to Me, unless the Father who sent me draws him. And I will raise him up on the last day." The first phrase of the text "no one can come to Me," is a statement of total inability. It universally excludes everyone from having the power or ability to come to Christ. But, the second phrase of the text provides an exception to the first phrase, "unless the Father who sent Me draws him." Notice the relationship between total inability and the drawing of the Father. Men are totally unable to come to Christ, unless the Father draws them. The Father's drawing is necessary to overcome human inability.

But some have suggested that the Father *draws* men to Christ in a resistible way. They think of the Father as *wooing* or *enticing* men to Christ, rather than actually bringing them to Christ.[29] However, the Greek word *elko*, translated *draw*, is often translated *haul in* or *drag*. John 21:6 says, "So they cast it, and now they were not able to *haul* it in, because of the quantity of fish." John 21:11 says, "So Simon Peter went aboard and *hauled* the net ashore, full of large fish." Acts 16:19 says, "They seized Paul and Silas and *dragged* them into the marketplace before the rulers." Acts 21:30 says, "They seized Paul and *dragged* him out of the temple, and at once the gates were shut." James 2:6 says, "Are not the rich the ones who oppress you, and the ones who *drag* you into court?" Clearly the Greek *elko* means something more than softly coax, woo, gently invite, enable, entice, or permit. *Elko* is a forceful term, communicating that what is drawn is actually moved and that the intended end of the movement is achieved. That powerful meaning is clear even when *elko* is best translated *draw*. For example, John 18:10 says, "Then Simon Peter, having a sword, *drew* it and struck the high priest's servant and cut off his right ear." Certainly Peter did not woo, coax, invite, or enable his sword to come out of his belt; rather, he pulled it out forcefully and succeeded in removing it.

[28] For descriptions of the effectual call, see Romans 8:30; 9:11–24; 1 Corinthians 1:9–26; Galatians 1:6–15; 1 Thessalonians 2:12; 5:24; 2 Thessalonians 2:14; Ephesians 1:18; 4:1–5; 2 Timothy 1:9; Hebrews 3:1; James 1:18; 1 Peter 2:9; 5:10; 2 Peter 1:3–10. Texts that speak of God's people as the "called" include Romans 1:6; 1 Corinthians 1:24; Hebrews 9:15; Revelation 17:14.

[29] R.C. Sproul, *Chosen by God* (Wheaton, IL: Tyndale House, 1986), 69–70.

Someone might still argue that even though the word *draw* means to *bring, drag*, or *haul in*, those who are drawn can still successfully resist God's drawing because God allows them to do so. All they need to do is "not resist" and God will drag them all the way to salvation. However, that understanding of *elko* in John 6:44 does not fit with the last phrase of the verse, which says, "And I will raise him up on the last day," which is a declaration of the perseverance of the saints. Every single person the Father "draws" will also be raised up on the last day. Therefore, we must conclude that the drawing of the Father is always successful. It is successful because God's effectual calling is rooted in His power. Dagg wrote, "In effectual calling, the Holy Spirit displays his omnipotence."[30] Lemke finds the doctrine that God powerfully draws men to Himself to be inconsistent with the Calvinist teaching that God never forces men against their wills. He writes, "If God compels persons with 'irresistible superiority,' in what way is it inaccurate to say that God is forcing people to choose Christ?"[31] The answer is that God does not force people to choose Christ because He never makes them choose Christ against their wills, inclinations, desires, preferences, etc. In His great love, God powerfully causes His people to choose Christ willingly, and never forces them to choose Christ unwillingly.

Practical Application

This doctrine of effectual calling is important in number of areas in practical theology, but consider its value in parenting and missions. A father and mother who understand the doctrine of effectual calling will not be shocked when their children sin or rebel. They will be grieved and disappointed, but not shocked because they understand the doctrines of human depravity and effectual calling. Sometimes Christian parents think that if they are faithful to teach their children the Word of Christ, then their children will turn out to be faithful and godly Christians. Parents who labor under this false assumption are sometimes confused and even discouraged when their children sin. This discouragement may even lead parents to give up on a biblical theology of child training or opt for different methods. But, parents who understand the doctrine of effectual calling will understand that they cannot change the hearts of their children. As parents, their responsibility is faithfulness to the gospel of Christ and to His Word, to teach the truth and to become like Christ to their children. Understanding effectual calling will help keep parents from becoming dis-

[30] Dagg, *Manual of Theology*, 333.
[31] Lemke, "A Biblical and Theological Critique," 113.

couraged or despondent because they will understand that they cannot make their children believe or obey from the heart. Parents will become more patient and prayerful because they understand that God must change the hearts of their children, or their hearts will not be changed.

Effectual calling is also important in mission work. It gives the missionary confidence because it teaches that God will certainly save His people. A missionary's work cannot fail because effectual calling cannot fail. When he was on mission to Corinth, the Spirit told Paul in Acts 18:9–10, "Do not be afraid, but go on speaking and do not be silent, for I am with you, and no one will attack you to harm you, for I have many people in this city who are My people." God was going to make certain that the elect in Corinth were saved. This is one of the greatest motives to mission work. Also, when missionaries understand effectual calling, they are well equipped to labor in cultures that are hostile to Christianity where there may be few if any converts for years. God saves His people in His timetable by His Word. They will not be tempted to adopt unbiblical techniques, methodologies, or messages to obtain converts or to improve the appearance of their success; rather, they will continue patiently to preach, teach, and live the biblical gospel, no matter what the apparent results, since God alone can change a man's heart and since God only changes men with the gospel. Finally, if missionaries experience many converts under their ministries, they will be humbled by the knowledge that God alone provides results. The numbers of conversions are not the result of their skill or strength, but only the result of God's power. May the Lord cause understanding and application of this great doctrine to grow in the minds and hearts of His people to His glory.

II

Perseverance
THE TRUE NATURE OF SAVING FAITH

Phil Newton

While often perverted into a very shallow, unbiblical, easy-believism
way of thinking, this doctrine [the doctrine of perseverance] teaches us
the true nature of saving grace, when properly presented in all its parts.
Through the window that perseverance provides into the grace of God,
one sees whether a person's repentance and faith have been prompted by
the fright of the moment or by the sovereign effectual working of the
Spirit.[1]

Perseverance, as part of Christian thinking and vocabulary, seems to hide
in the shadows of "once saved, always saved" in contemporary Baptist
life. Though still part of confessional language, many churches give little
attention to it, evident by carelessness in church membership rolls. Yet a
recovery of the biblical teaching on perseverance could help transform the
character of local churches as well as strengthen gospel witness.

Instead of perseverance as foundational to the believer's assurance,
some churches remain satisfied with promoting assurance as a decision
made in the past without perseverance in sight. New Testament writers
saw it differently. They taught assurance in light of the believers' perseverance. "The perseverance of the saints," wrote F.F. Bruce, "is a doctrine
firmly grounded in the New Testament (and not least in Pauline) teaching;

[1] Thomas J. Nettles, *By His Grace and For His Glory: A Historical, Theological
and Practical Study of the Doctrines of Grace in Baptist Life*, revised and expanded
20th anniversary edition (Cape Coral, FL: Founders Press, 2006), 360.

170

but the corollary to it is that it is the saints who persevere."[2] John Stott agrees: "...continuance or perseverance is the hallmark of God's authentic children."[3] Countless worship services issue calls to come forward to *receive* assurance of salvation. However, nowhere in Scripture do we find a hint that assurance is a snap decision, much less apart from ongoing perseverance. Assurance is not something that you do, nor the salvation itself, but the certainty of salvation as evidenced by a persevering faith. Genuine assurance cannot happen without corresponding perseverance.

First century believers, like many contemporary Christians, could be easily swept up in faulty teaching, such as that of Judaizers, Gnostics, or ascetics, thinking that legalism, on one hand, and sensationalism, on the other, would eliminate their doubts about salvation. To counter this, the Gospels and epistles are full of exhortations to persevere if one would count himself a Christian.

What is perseverance? While identifying one primary text on perseverance, Tom Nettles explained: "...the doctrine of perseverance involves the perfect confluence of divine sovereignty in preserving us and human initiative, work and energy in pursuing holiness."[4] His exposition of perseverance falls under three headings: "first, God's activity in preserving the believer; second, the believer's activity in persevering; third, the reality of the believer's continued sinfulness or 'perfectionlessness.'"[5] While numerous texts demonstrate his explanation, Romans 8:12–17 clearly demonstrates perseverance in the faith as foundational to the believer's assurance.

The Christian Has a New Obligation

Paul does not deal with a special category of Christians in Romans 8 which some have termed as "spiritual" as opposed to "carnal."[6] Instead, he shows what is true of all believers, referring to them as those "who are according to the Spirit," and consequently, indwelled by the Spirit with their minds set on the things of the Spirit (Romans 8:4–6).[7]

[2] F.F. Bruce, *Tyndale New Testament Commentaries: The Epistle of Paul to the Romans* (Grand Rapids: Wm. B. Eerdmans Publishing Co., 1963), 219.

[3] John Stott, *Romans: God's Good News for the World* (Downers Grove, IL: InterVarsity Press, 1994), 301.

[4] Nettles, *By His Grace*, 367.

[5] Ibid., 360.

[6] Cf. Ernest C. Reisinger, *What Should We Think of the Carnal Christian?* (Carlisle, PA: The Banner of Truth Trust, 1978), for an excellent treatment of the subject.

[7] Scripture quotations are from the *New American Standard Bible* unless otherwise noted.

"So then" (Romans 8:12) draws an inference from what has already been written. Basic distinctions between non-believers and Christians are clarified in Romans 8:9–11:

- Every Christian is "in the Spirit" (v. 9).

- "The Spirit of God dwells in you"—i.e. every believer (v. 9).

- Only those indwelled by the Spirit belong to Jesus (v. 9b).

- The believer's spirit is made alive through the righteousness of Christ applied by the Spirit (v. 10).

- The Spirit unites the believer to the death and resurrection of Jesus Christ, ultimately giving certainty to the Christian's bodily resurrection (v. 11).

"So then," because these things are evident in every believer, "brethren, we are under obligation, not to the flesh, to live according to the flesh" (8:12). "Obligation" implies a moral debt, something owed that one cannot let slide—"one's due."[8] Does this mean that the Christian stacks up points with God, by paying his "obligation" to God? It is obvious that Paul has nothing of this sort in mind, having spent the previous chapters proving that believers are justified in Christ alone and not through the works of the law.[9] So what does he mean when he tells us that we have a different obligation?

No longer obliged to the flesh

With a negative statement, Paul dismantles any *antinomian* view of the believer's assurance. The positive is so obvious that the negative will suffice to get the point across.[10] "We are under obligation, not to the flesh, to live according to the flesh." What does he means by "flesh?" It is unregenerate man: "the whole of our humanness viewed as corrupt and unredeemed, 'our fallen, ego-centric human nature,' or more briefly 'the sin-dominated self'"

[8] "Opheiletai," Walter Bauer, William F. Arndt, and F. Wilbur Gingrich, *A Greek-English Lexicon of the New Testament and other Early Christian Literature* (Chicago: The University of Chicago Press, 1957), 603.

[9] For example see Romans 2:28–29; 3:19–30; 4:1–8, 23–25; 5:15–21; 6:17–23.

[10] Leon Morris, *The Epistle to the Romans* (Grand Rapids: Wm. B. Eerdmans Publishing Co., 1995), 311, who quotes J.A. Bengel, "but this is elegantly left to be understood," *Gnomon of the New Testament* II (Edinburgh, 1873), n.p.

or what Luther described as "fallen human nature… 'deeply curved in on itself.'"[11] It is man without Christ, man without the experience of grace through Christ.

The flesh's authority is over—killed at the cross of Christ, made effective by union in Christ's death and resurrection (Romans 6:4–6). In one sense, this should be obvious. We should realize that if something has been put to death then it has no more power over us. Yet the reality is that the flesh, though killed by the cross, still bears influence upon us. How can this be? When someone has lived all his life under the authority of an evil tyrant, even at the tyrant's death it is difficult to be free from the iron hand of tyranny. Walking through the streets of Tirana, Albania, just a couple of years after their dictator Enver Hoxha was executed, I saw the faces of those trudging along still looking oppressed and fearful, as though the tyrant would come to life and haunt their steps. Though free from the dictator, they lived under his shadow, their minds still echoing his threats.

The flesh does that to us. It is an evil tyrant that exercised full authority over us until we died to the flesh through Christ. Yet we still hear its demands. Unlike Hoxha, the flesh is not eradicated. Its reign is broken but its presence lingers. The flesh even operates its tyranny in a religious way, telling us that we do not need a Savior but that we only need to try our best. It runs the gamut from *antinomianism*—law and obedience no longer matter; to *libertinism*—doing whatever our sinful desires want because we are "covered" by our decision for Christ; to *legalism*—doing what some law or standard requires apart from dependence upon Christ; to *perfectionism*—the lofty self-approval that ignores the reality of indwelling sin. It focuses on self-satisfaction. So what are we to do? Believe the gospel! "We are under obligation," even the flesh tells us that, but "not to the flesh, to live according to the flesh." It no longer holds the reins to the Christian's life. He died to the flesh when he died to the law as the means to righteousness. So as those persevering in the faith, "Let the word of Christ dwell richly in you," not the word of the flesh making sinful demands upon you (Colossians 3:16).

Now obligated to walk in the Spirit

"So then, brethren, we are under obligation" (8:12). We anticipate that Paul will say the new obligation is to walk in the Spirit, but the context

---

[11] John Stott, *Romans: God's Good News for the World* (Downers Grove, IL: InterVarsity Press, 1994), 222, also quoting Charles Cranfield, *A Critical and Exegetical Commentary on the Epistle to the Romans*, in *The International Critical Com-*

leaves it to be understood. The present tense calls for an ongoing obligation. So if we are *not* obliged to walk in the flesh, Paul's theology leaves only one other realm in which Christians can walk: "in the Spirit." He amplifies this call to walk in the Spirit and not in the flesh in Galatians 5:16–26. In that case, he gives examples of the flesh and its work contrasted with the Spirit and His fruit. But here, Paul suffices to remind us that "we are under obligation."

What is this new obligation? *It is to live out the gospel*, living out the righteousness of Christ that has been implanted in us. It is "imparted righteousness" as the Puritans called it: loving without hypocrisy, abhorring what is evil, clinging to what is good, being devoted to one another in brotherly love, giving preference to one another in honor, being diligent in our spiritual lives, fervent in spirit, serving the Lord, rejoicing in hope, persevering in tribulation, devoted to prayer, contributing to the needs of the saints, practicing hospitality (Romans 12:9–13). That's how the Apostle explains the obligation of the Christian: by paying attention to walking in the Spirit.

Yet what if a professing Christian gives no attention to the "obligation" to walk in the Spirit? Does his abandonment of walking by the Spirit give credence to the assertion that a believer can lose his salvation? Nettles does not see this as a denial of the believer's eternal security. He writes:

> That some who begin the journey leave the road before the final destination does not at all prove that the saved man may lose his salvation; that phenomenon does demonstrate that saving faith prompted by God's Spirit manifests an enduring qualitative difference from the spurious faith prompted by the temporary carnal excitement of the unregenerate man.[12]

On the other hand, can a person who gives no attention to the "obligation" to walk in the Spirit rightfully claim to be a Christian? Those holding an antinomian view of the believer's security would answer affirmatively. How do antinomians come to this belief? "…[T]hey radicalize eternal security by insisting that security in Jesus Christ guarantees that even those that fail to persevere in faithfulness to Christ and his gospel will never perish but are saved and will remain saved."[13]

---

mentaries, vol. I (London: T. and T. Clark, 1975), 372, and John Ziesler, *Paul's letter to the Romans*, in *The Trinity Press International New Testament Commentaries* (London: SCM and Trinity Press International, 1989), 195.

[12] Nettles, *By His Grace*, 365.

[13] Thomas R. Schreiner & Ardel B. Caneday, *The Race Set Before Us: A Biblical Theology of Perseverance & Assurance* (Downers Grove, IL: IVP Academic, 2001), 25.

In spite of the clear language in Romans 8:1–17 distinguishing believers and unbelievers, some evangelicals, under the banner of free grace, turn the other way when hearing Paul's language of "obligation." For instance, Zane Hodges excludes repentance as a necessary response to the gospel: "…the call to faith represents the call to eternal salvation. The call to repentance is the call to enter into harmonious relations with God."[14] He sees repentance as a condition of fellowship not relationship.[15] R.T. Kendall puts the weight on professing Christ even though some *professors* may pay no attention to the obligation to walk in the Spirit: "Such a person will go to heaven when he dies no matter what work (or lack of work) may accompany such faith.…In other words, no matter what sin (or absence of Christian obedience) may accompany such faith."[16]

So how do *antinomians* account for the sinful, unchristian behavior of so many professing Christians? They conveniently create a special category: "the carnal Christian." Charles Ryrie, in objecting to the teaching on the perseverance of the saints held by reformed Christians, rightly remarked, "Sometimes those who approach this doctrine [the security of the believer] from the viewpoint of perseverance deny the possibility of a Christian's being carnal."[17] Dr. Ryrie is correct! Unfortunately, he fails to see that Paul's only use of the term "carnal" in 1 Corinthians 3:1–4 addresses the "one problem of unwholesome division," rather than a secondary category of Christian.[18] Consequently, "the three-class theory," as Ernest Reisinger called it, "is prone to give assurance to those who were never really converted."[19]

The Christian Puts to Death the Deeds of the Body

Scholars debate whether Paul's use of body and flesh are synonymous.[20] If so, does putting to death the deeds of the body lead to perfectionism?

---

[14] Zane C. Hodges, *Absolutely Free! A Biblical Reply to Lordship Salvation* (Grand Rapids: Academie Books, 1989), 145.

[15] Ibid., 146.

[16] R.T. Kendall, *Once Saved, Always Saved* (Chicago: Moody Press, 1983), 49, 53.

[17] Charles C. Ryrie, *Basic Theology: A Popular Systematic Guide to Understanding Biblical Truth* (Chicago: Moody Press, 1999), 379.

[18] Reisinger, *Carnal Christian*, 10.

[19] Ibid., 17.

[20] For instance, James D.G. Dunn considers "body" (*soma*) "as a stylistic variant for the overloaded *sarz* [flesh], with its unusual negative force as the result"; *Word Biblical Commentary: Romans 1–8*, vol. 38a [Waco, TX: Word Books, 1988], 449. On the contrary, Charles Hodge asserted, "…it is very much to be doubted

Some Christians believe so. Paul made a clear distinction of "flesh" as unregenerate man, contrasted with those that no longer live according to flesh but "according to the Spirit" (Romans 8:4). "Flesh," in this context, clearly points to man as a fallen creature without the influence of the Spirit in his life. "For if you are living according to the flesh," the same phrase used in Romans 8:4–5, "you must die." The consequence of the flesh's rule in one's life is death in all its destructiveness and separation from God. The context does not allow us to present this as one who may be a Christian. Yet, does this suggest sinlessness or perfectionism?

The way Paul addresses the flesh in Romans 7–8, serves to remind believers of the ongoing conflict with it. Nettles refers to Paul's use of the conflict with *flesh* in Romans 8:4–5 and in Galatians 5:13–21, "as a principle of sin in opposition to the Spirit." It is "a moral and spiritual reality" that continues until Christians stand before Christ, rather than the clever posturing and theological denial, as in the errors of contemporary perfectionism.[21] *Perfectionism*, in any form, undercuts the biblical doctrine of perseverance, and consequently, those embracing it effectively deny the biblical teaching on assurance. Nettles identifies four errors in contemporary perfectionism that are either directly stated or consequently follow this line of thought. "The first error lies in the definition of sin and owes its content to contemporary existentialism and old-time Pelagianism." David Needham writes, "Sin is more pointedly the expression of man's struggle with the meaning of his existence while missing life from God," and in the Christian, sin is "the avoidable failure of the individual to fulfill the purpose for which he exists."[22]

"A second fundamental error is in the identification of 'flesh' with strictly material realities." Needham equates "flesh" and "body," leaning in the direction of a new Gnosticism. Instead, Nettles counters that, "flesh is an affection that focuses on enjoyment of the creature without primary reverence for and worship of the Creator. In the unregenerate man, this affection dominates all his activities; in the regenerate man, the flesh is

---

whether the word ever has this sense in the New Testament"; *Commentary on the Epistle to the Romans* (Grand Rapids, MI: Wm. B. Eerdmans Publishing, 1947, from 1886 edition), 265.

[21] Nettles, *By His Grace*, 380; Nettles explains the popularizing of perfectionism in David Needham's *Birthright* (Portland, OR: Multnomah Press, 1979) and Peter Lord's essay, "Turkeys and Eagles," *Fulness*, ed. Ras Robinson (Fort Worth, TX: Nov–Dec 1981), 8–11, both popular with Southern Baptists in the late 20th century.

[22] Nettles, *By His Grace*, 378–379, quoting Needham, *Birthright*, 25, 124.

ever-present as a hindering force but is more and more mortified and sub-jugated."[23]

Contemporary perfectionism's third error "consists of an unfortunate misunderstanding of 'righteousness'" that basically rejects "the doctrine of justification by faith" and approximates "the Roman Catholic doctrine of justifying righteousness."[24] Nettles quotes Needham's startling comment on regeneration: "It is an act so REAL that it is right to say that a Christian's essential nature is righteous rather than sinful."[25] He further demonstrates the tragic misunderstanding of imputed righteousness held by Peter Lord, who glosses over the judicial language claiming instead, an experiential righteousness.[26]

Fourth, contemporary perfectionism heads logically toward affirming sinless perfection. Though denying this, Needham ironically states, "Not only is sin avoidable, but righteousness is assumed to be the norm for every believer's behavior. ...Therefore, in some sense sinless perfection must be seen as a theoretical possibility."[27] Oddly, Lord made the claim, "Everything a Christian does, except the sins he chooses to do, is an act of righteousness." He claimed that the previous day he did "around 300" acts of righteousness and "0" sins.[28] Nettles traced this "new perfectionism" to "a truncated Darbyite anthropology." Rather than retaining the dual-nature of the believer in Darby's theology, the "new perfectionism" erases "the concept of the old nature and defines the Christian totally in terms of a Darbyite new nature. Therefore, sin, when it does recur, is an accident to be overcome simply by remembering and confessing who we are in our new nature."[29]

In reality, we still struggle with sin as long as we live in these bodies. Theologically, Paul distinguishes between flesh and body in order to make this clear. Flesh represents unregenerate man. "Body" refers to one's humanity without the *rule* (yet not the existence) of the sinful flesh. It is a body in which sin dwells as a squatter (Romans 7:17). The body is not inherently sinful, as is the flesh. It is the place where the war with sin rages. Paul explained the war that waged in "the members of my body...making me prisoner of the law of sin which is in my members" (Romans 7:23). So the body is the battlefield where the conflict takes place, not the enemy

---

[23] Ibid., 380.

[24] Ibid., 380.

[25] Ibid., 381, quoting Needham, *Birthright*, 25–30.

[26] Ibid., 381, quoting Lord, "Turkeys and Eagles," 11.

[27] Ibid., 382, quoting Needham, *Birthright*, 135.

[28] Ibid., 382, quoting Lord, "Turkeys and Eagles," 10.

[29] Ibid., 382.

assaulting the believer: "...the sense is that the actions of the flesh are expressed through the body."[30]

What does "put to death" imply?

The present tense verb (*thanatoute*) indicates: "putting to death the deeds of the body" as an ongoing aspect of the believer's perseverance. There's no one-time act that puts to death the deeds of the body (e.g. at conversion) but rather a constant, day-by-day, even moment-by-moment part of the believer's sanctification. "But if by the Spirit you are putting to death the deeds of the body, you will live" (Romans 8:13). Older writers such as John Owen called this action *mortification*. Owen describes its intentionality: "the mortification of indwelling sin remaining in our mortal bodies," is "the constant duty of believers...Be killing sin or it will be killing you."[31]

Mortification is "a clear-sighted recognition of evil as evil, leading to such a decisive and radical repudiation of it that no imagery can do it justice except 'putting to death.'" And what are Christians putting to death? Stott explains that it is "every use of our body (our eyes, ears, mouth, hands or feet) which serves ourselves instead of God and other people."[32]

Mortification emphasizes something that we do rather than something done to us. There's no passive, "let go, and let God"; no call for reaching a certain level of "full surrender" where sin is no longer an issue; no one-time act or decision in which the believer finally decides to enter into a life of fullness. Rather, Christians must attend to daily mortification because sin affects believers daily. "When the Spirit regenerates and indwells a person, the flesh begins to undergo a gradual process of being subdued," writes Nettles. "Thus dies the old man, and his deeds are gradually replaced with those of the new man—after true righteousness and holiness in accordance with proper knowledge. It is inevitable that what is alive and growing will overcome what is dead."[33] Without perseverance in mortification, one is not merely an immature Christian. In Paul's argument, he is not a Christian at all.[34]

---

[30] Thomas R Schreiner, *Baker Exegetical Commentary on the New Testament: Romans* (Grand Rapids: Baker Books, 1998), 421.

[31] John Owen, *The Works of John Owen: Temptation and Sin* (Carlisle, PA: The Banner of Truth Trust, 1967 from 1850–53 publication), vol. VI, 8.

[32] Stott, *Romans*, 228.

[33] Nettles, *By His Grace*, 368–369.

[34] Paul simply followed Jesus' teaching in Matthew 5:29–30.

Why should we mortify the deeds of the body? "But if by the Spirit you are putting to death the deeds of the body, you will live" (8:13b). Leon Morris explained, "Real life is not a possibility when we choose to luxuriate in the body's deeds. We must renounce all such deeds if we are to experience life in the Spirit." He clarified, "This is not because some meritorious achievement is required of us as a way of earning such life. It is because the two are incompatible. The one excludes the other. There is a living that is death and there is a putting to death that is life."[35]

The Spirit affects mortification by enabling and leading

The prepositional phrase clarifies: "But if *by the Spirit* you are putting to death the deeds of the body, you will live." Paul assures the believer, Nettles explains, "that the powerful presence of the Holy Spirit will cause him to mortify the flesh."[36] By the aid of the Holy Spirit, the believer puts to death the deeds of the body, especially by the Spirit bringing to mind biblical truths for applying to the particular sin-issue faced. He gives strength when our strength fails, urging us on to deal with sin by exposing it, calling it what it is as treason against God, and then pressing us to turn from it. Dependence on the Spirit's power to persevere removes any dependency on self through legalism.

"For all who are being led by the Spirit of God, these are sons of God" (8:14). Here is a marker, a defining point in the confluence of divine preservation and perseverance for all that are truly born of God: they are led by the Spirit of God.

Paul intends this to be a source of the believer's assurance: "these are sons of God." "These" is emphatic, indicating *these and these alone* are sons of God. Paul points to the Spirit's leading as a subjective experience, a definitive mark of the believer's salvation, evidenced by perseverance as the believer follows the Spirit's leading.

If you are being led—or continually led[37]—by the Spirit of God then you are declared a Christian. In the process of the Spirit at work in the believer he finds assurance that he truly belongs to Christ. Here is a fascinating mixture of preservation and perseverance: on one hand, the Spirit works, leads, influences, prods, and directs; on the other, the believer acts, presses on, humbles himself, conforms to the image of Christ, follows after God's commands. In the process, the Holy Spirit breathes assurance into the believer.

---

[35] Morris, *Romans*, 312.

[36] Nettles, *By His Grace*, 366.

[37] Greek present tense, so continual action implied.

What does this tell us about assurance? It is best experienced in the process of living out the gospel applied by the Spirit instead of sitting in a corner and trying to think deeply on assurance. Certainly, we want to read, study, and think about assurance. But we need not relegate assurance to our studiousness. It comes by persevering in the Christian life.

"As many as are being led (and continually led) by the Spirit of God, these ones are sons of God" (literal rendering of Romans 8:14). The Spirit leads consistently rather than sporadically. He leads believers to Christ and His sufficiency rather than depending on the law for righteousness (Romans 10:4). He leads clearly in the path of divine revelation in Holy Scripture.

The Spirit's leadership does not contradict the Word:

- He always leads Christians to glorify Jesus Christ—not self, not an idea, not a project, not a ministry, not an ideology, not a theology, not an image (John 16:14).

- He always leads Christians to truth—God's Word alone is truth (John 17:17; 14:17).

- He always leads Christians in the way of understanding and applying Scripture, never contrary to the eternal Word. (John 16:13; 1 Corinthians 2:6–10).

- He always leads Christians to more and more dependence upon the Father through the sufficiency of Jesus Christ demonstrated by the Spirit, as "the Spirit of adoption as sons, by whom we cry, 'Abba! Father!'" (Romans 8:15 ESV).

The Christian Belongs to the Father

In my hometown, most everyone knew everyone else. I could walk into Felton's Hardware or James Department Store, and I would overhear, "Oh, that's Joe Newton's boy." It gave me instant confidence that I was welcome in the store even if all I wanted to do was look without buying. I belonged to my dad.

Paul tells us of something far greater about the relationship between the Christian and God by using language that the Romans would easily grasp: *the language of adoption.*

What this is not

As he does so often, Paul begins with the negative in order to teach something positive. "For you have not received a spirit of slavery leading to fear again" (Romans 8:15).

A "spirit of slavery" indicates the contrast between the law as the means to righteousness and the righteousness in Christ applied by the Holy Spirit. "But now, we have been released from the Law, *having died to that by which we were bound*, so that we *serve* in newness of the Spirit and not in *oldness of the letter*" (Romans 7:6, italics added). The language of servitude and bondage was evident. Similarly, in Romans 8:2 the Spirit is shown to be a liberator. "For the law of the Spirit of life in Christ Jesus *has set you free from the law of sin and death*" (italics added). As long as one remains under the iron hand of the law as the means to righteousness, he remains a slave to it ending in death. But that is not what the believer received when he received the Holy Spirit.

Why does Paul bring up the subject of fear when talking about salvation? Because multitudes embrace various forms of legalism with hope of deliverance from their guilt, only to find themselves trapped in deeper bondage to fear. He explains, that if someone embraced another form of law for salvation, it would be a change in belief structure and liturgy but not a substantive change in his position. That happens with all who would by-pass dependence upon the crucified and risen Christ for their salvation. They claim to be Christian, but unless they turn from self-reliance and law-reliance for righteousness to trust in the Lord Jesus, then their Christianity is no different than their non-Christianity. They simply moved from one religion of fear that held them in bondage to self-performance of good deeds to yet another. But that is not what you received in Jesus Christ! With the negative assertion, Paul takes us back to the gospel, rooting assurance in the gospel.

Spirit of adoption

Yet another question arises concerning the word "spirit" in the phrase "spirit of adoption" (8:15b). Does that mean *spirit*—lower case and so used as a feeling of adoption; or *Spirit*—upper case, referring to the Holy Spirit as the deliverer of adoption? In this case, the ESV rendering of "the Spirit of adoption" seems likely since the context points to the Holy Spirit as the instrument of adoption. Otherwise, one might view this "spirit of adoption" as merely a legal transaction rather than a relational experience. "But you have received the Spirit of adoption as sons, by whom we cry, 'Abba! Father!'" (ESV).

"Adoption" was a common practice in both Greek and Roman worlds though not in Judaism. The Jewish structure of levirate marriages and the inter-connectedness of families virtually eliminated the need for adoption. However, that was not the case in the Roman world. F.F. Bruce explained:

> The term *adoption* may smack somewhat of artificiality in our ears; but in the first century AD an adopted son was a son deliberately chosen by his adoptive father to perpetuate his name and inherit his estate; he was no whit inferior in status to a son born in the ordinary course of nature, and might well enjoy the father's affection more fully and reproduce the father's character more worthily.[38]

When Paul wrote to the Romans and Galatians (4:4–7) about the Holy Spirit's role in adoption, it surely struck them with delight. What did this adopted child receive in the adoption?

(1) With great love and affection, the father intentionally chose him.

(2) The adopted child received a new identity.

(3) He would now be part of the father's inheritance.

But the one thing that the Roman fathers could not impart was their nature. Everything else, the adopted child received from the father.

What the Roman father could not do, God has done for those in Christ! The Father (1) chose us before the foundation of the world (Ephesians 1:4–6), (2) identified us as His very own by the marks of a new obligation to live according to the Spirit, a new impetus to put to death the deeds of the body, and the leading of the Spirit (Romans 8:12–14), (3) gave us His name ("sons of God," Romans 8:14), and (4) included us in His inheritance with all the saints (Romans 8:17). *He also gave us His nature.*[39] Peter explained that we are "partakers of the divine nature, having escaped the corruption that is in the world by lust" (2 Peter 1:4). The writer of Hebrews tells us that we "share His holiness" (Hebrews 12:10) so that He treats us as His children.

Adoption follows on the heels of redemption. "But when the fullness of time came, God sent forth His Son, born of a woman, born under the Law,

---

[38] F.F. Bruce, Tyndale New Testament Commentaries: The Epistle of Paul to the Romans (Grand Rapids, MI: Wm. B. Eerdmans Publishing Co., 1963), 166.

[39] J.I. Packer, *Concise Theology: A Guide to Historical Christian Beliefs* (Wheaton, IL: Tyndale House Publishers, 1993), 167–168.

so that He might redeem those who were under the Law, *that we might receive the adoption of sons*" (Galatians 4:4–5, italics added). The Holy Spirit does not by-pass the cross of Christ to make us sons of God! Through the suffering of death by the Son of God, the enmity was removed, and the Spirit gave us the new identity, name, inheritance, and nature in adoption.

Experience due to adoption

The context focuses adoption on the believer's assurance of salvation. Assurance leads to certainty and confidence, spurring perseverance. How does the Christian know that he truly belongs to Christ? He knows by the "Spirit of adoption." The Apostle speaks of a relationship of intimacy, enjoyment, and security pictured by the Roman understanding of adoption. He tells us that we have "received the Spirit of adoption as sons, by whom we cry, 'Abba! Father!'" (8:15b, ESV)

"Abba" is an Aramaic term of intimacy used by children when speaking to their fathers. It is akin to the American, "daddy" or the Italian, "papa." It's a term of endearment, full of familiarity, warmth, affection, tenderness, and the certainty of belonging to the one called "Abba."

Paul tells believers, "You have received the Spirit of adoption as sons." It is yours in union with Christ. The Holy Spirit makes this known so that, even as Christ did, the Christian can keep crying, "Abba! Father!" How do we know that we have received this Spirit of adoption? Objectively, the Father's *DNA* is evident in the believer's life by His nature and character rooted in the believer (2 Peter 1:3–4; Galatians 5:22–23). Subjectively, the Holy Spirit works in the believer a consciousness that he belongs to the Father. Here is the experience of the Spirit at work in the believer. Sometimes it is experienced while reading the Word or worshiping or singing a hymn. Other times we are conscious of adoption by the Spirit while thinking on the work of Christ. The intense, conscious reality that "you are not your own" (1 Corinthians 6:19) overwhelms the Christian, stirring worship and prayer, and motivating perseverance.

The Spirit's Witness as Preservation

Often, the motivation for pressing on in the faith has its roots in the inner witness of the Spirit. Here the reality of *divine preservation* is manifested. So deeply satisfying is this experience that it bolsters the believer's desire to persevere in the faith. Because of external trials and internal struggles, believers need the witness of the Spirit. Nettles explains, "The flip side of perseverance is preservation. We certainly persevere but only because God preserves."[40]

Just as with the Spirit of adoption, the witness of the Spirit is tangibly experiential though not easily explainable. It is similar to explaining the experience of love or joy. One can describe how it affects him, but he comes up short in defining it with clarity. Mystery surrounds those experiences, as does the witness of the Spirit. Yet Paul helps us to grasp it by three truths related to it.

Distinct experience

The present tense alerts us to the ongoing nature of the witness of the Spirit. "The Spirit Himself testifies with our spirit that we are children of God" (Romans 8:16). The witness is ongoing even though at times intermittent. From one period to another, from one need to yet another, the witness continues.

Does a believer always need the witness of the Spirit? Not necessarily, since he has the consciousness of the new obligation to live according to the Spirit, the Spirit's aid in mortifying the deeds of the body, the leadership of the Spirit, and the Spirit of adoption (Romans 8:12–15). However, there are times when he needs something more: times of great trial, suffering, opposition, Satanic oppression, or the normal strain of seeking to live faithfully as a Christian. The believer needs overwhelming assurance because he has been overwhelmed by the circumstances of life. And so the Holy Spirit *Himself* breathes into his spirit His testimony that the Christian is indeed a child of God.

While worshiping or contemplating Christ and the gospel, the witness of the Spirit comes. While singing, praying, and listening to biblical proclamation, the believer experiences a deep consciousness that what he is singing is true *of him*; what he hears expounded in the Word is true *of him*; and the One to whom he prays *affirms him as His own*. At other times the witness of the Spirit comes in meditating upon the Scripture or studying the Word or even talking of the gospel to others. Consequently, the believer is motivated to persevere.

---

[40] Tom Nettles, *The Baptists: Key People Involved in Forming Baptist Identity*, three volumes (Fearn, Ross-shire, Scotland: Mentor imprint by Christian Focus Publications, 2005), vol. 2, 146.

Affirming family

The Spirit testifies, "that we are children of God" or "that we are and continue to be children of God." Sometimes the Christian looks at his disobedience, spiritual disappointments and failures in perseverance, and wonders, "Can I really be a child of God?" Then the Spirit works in some setting: worship, meditation, service, witness, discussion, fellowship, Lord's Supper, etc. Each is a means given for strengthening perseverance in the faith. Through such means, He breathes into the believer's spirit the certainty: "I am His and He is mine."

The law cannot do this. It operates on the basis of performance: do this and live. That's why legalism ultimately fails. The Spirit bases His testimony, not upon *our* performance but upon the certainty of the work of Christ.

"And if children, heirs also, heirs of God and fellow heirs with Christ" (8:17). An "heir" has all of the privileges and resources that belong to the one of whom he is an heir. How does this affect the Christian facing a terminal illness or an unexpected trial or suffering for his faith in Christ? All of the suffering of the present is no longer "worthy to be compared with the glory that is to be revealed" (Romans 8:18).

Christians are not only heirs of God but also "fellow heirs with Christ." That which is Christ's belongs to all believers. What is the content of this inheritance? He does not tell us at this point but, "Indeed, 'it is difficult to suppress the richer and deeper thought that God himself is the inheritance of his children.'"[41]

Reality of family ties

The greatest test in our perseverance comes when we encounter various shades of suffering. Not only do we share in Christ's inheritance but we also share in His suffering and His glory. "And if children, heirs also, heirs of God and fellow heirs with Christ, if indeed we suffer with Him so that we may also be glorified with Him" (8:17). Here perseverance comes into view. Suffering denotes any of the effects of the fallen world that test our love, loyalty, and faithfulness to Jesus Christ. Christians face physical, mental, emotional, and spiritual suffering because of oppressive governments or critical co-workers; disease or injury or aging; emotional wiring or treatment by others; persecution for their faith; or the purifying effects of Fatherly discipline.

---

[41] Quoted by Stott, *Romans*, 234, from John Murray, *NICNT: The Epistle to the Romans*, (Grand Rapids, MI: Wm. B. Eerdmans Publishing, 1959–65, two vol.) vol. I, 298.

"The suffering is the necessary prelude to the glory."[42] It is the outward man perishing while the inward man is renewed day-by-day (2 Corinthians 4:16) until this mortal shall put on immortality, and this perishable shall put on the imperishable (1 Corinthians 15:54). Then death is swallowed up in the victory that is ours in union with Jesus Christ (1 Corinthians 15:54–57). All the while, the Holy Spirit encourages, assures, and comforts us with that inward testimony: "we are children of God." By God's grace, believers respond by joyfully persevering with confidence in Christ.

Conclusion

The doctrine of the saints' perseverance serves as a needed correction to the shallow teaching on assurance plaguing evangelicalism the past few decades. Tom Nettles explains the logic in perseverance. "The nature of grace and the glory of a faithful covenant God should never produce presumption." Then he quotes the remarkable 18th–19th century Baptist leader from South Carolina, Richard Furman, which provides a fitting closure to this chapter.

> The proof that we are of that number is best furnished to our own souls, as well as to the souls of others, not by our confidence that if we sin we shall be recovered; but by our resisting and hating every sin; by our taking heed lest we fall; by our mortifying the deeds of the body through the Spirit; and by our cleaving to the Lord with full purpose of heart, in faith, love and holy obedience. He, and *only* he, that endures to the end shall be saved. "If any man draw back," says the blessed God, "my soul shall have no pleasure in him."[43]

---

[42] F.F. Bruce, *TNTC: Romans*, 167.

[43] Nettles, *The Baptists—Beginnings in America*, vol. 2, 146, from Richard Furman, *The Crown of Life Promised to the Truly Faithful* (Charleston: Wm. Riley, 1822), 20–21.

12

Justification
THE USE OF GENESIS 15:6 IN ROMANS 4:3

Sam Waldron

Tom Nettles' ministry has been dedicated to the gospel of Christ. It is no surprise, then, that a review of his writing ministry reveals many treatments and defense of the traditional, Protestant doctrine of justification by faith alone.[1] This essay responds exegetically to current departures from the justification *sola fide* which he has loved and defended.

Thesis and Argument

This essay examines (1) the relevant uses of Genesis 15:6 and references to Abraham in a large group of ancient Jewish sources, (2) the immediate context of Romans 4:3, (3) the analysis of the Old Testament con-

---

[1] John Divito, a former student of Tom's, has discovered the following major treatments of justification in his books: Tom Nettles, *Ready for Reformation?* (Nashville, TN: Broadman and Holman Publishers, 2005); L. Russ Bush and Tom J. Nettles, *Baptists and the Bible* (Nashville, TN: Broadman and Holman Publishers, 1980); Thomas J. Nettles, *By His Grace and For His Glory* (Grand Rapids, MI: Baker Book House, 1986). The following articles in the Founders' Journal are also relevant: Issue 17, Summer 1994, "Missions And Creeds (Part 1)"; Issue 29, Summer 1997, "The Conserving Power of the Doctrines of Grace"; Issue 44, Spring 2001, "Ready for Reformation?". These journal articles may be found online. Not included in this listing are the many places where Nettles may mention the views of justification maintained by some historical figure which he is summarizing.

text of Genesis 15:6 and (4) the way in which Paul interprets and utilizes Genesis 15:6 in Romans 4:3. This essay contends that Paul's use of the text is a startling reaffirmation of themes original to Genesis 15:6 in its Old Testament context, contrasts starkly with the tendency of the Judaism of his day to read the Old Testament as supporting a soteriology of human achievement or "the works of the law" and undermines the central premise of the new perspective on Paul, all the while supporting the traditional doctrine of justification *sola fide*.

The Relevant Uses of Genesis 15:6 in Jewish Sources

A thorough examination of all the relevant data in the ancient Jewish literature is outside the scope of this paper. The influence of E.P. Sanders, James D.G. Dunn, N.T. Wright and the consequent debate over the new perspective on Paul requires, however, some reference to more extensive treatments of the data.[2] Das provides a balanced assessment when he remarks:

> Sanders may have gone too far when he denied that there are admonitions throughout this literature to observe perfectly what God enjoins in the law. If it is true that the Jews saw the law as requiring strict, perfect obedience, the key premise in "the new perspective on Paul" would be wrong.[3]

Das presents evidence that the new perspective is in need of corrective lenses. The evidence from Jewish literature now to be reviewed with regard to Abraham appears to confirm Das' general point of view.[4]

4 Ezra 9:7 says of Abraham:

> And it shall be that everyone who will be saved and will be able to escape on account of his works, or on account of his faith by which he has believed.

[2] A number of important studies may be cited that handle the data more comprehensively than this essay is permitted to do. Cf. A. Andrew Das, *Paul, the Law, and the Covenant* (Peabody, MA: Hendrickson Publishers, 2001), 12–69; D. Dixon Sutherland, "Genesis 15:6: A Study in Ancient Jewish and Christian Interpretation" (PhD diss., The Southern Baptist Theological Seminary, 1982), 73–135; Michael Thomas Irvin, "Paul's Use of the Abraham Image in Romans and Galatians" (PhD diss., The Southern Baptist Theological Seminary, 1985), 7–45.

[3] Das, *Paul, the Law, and the Covenant*, 13.

[4] Many of these statements were found with the help of Hermann Leberecht Strack, *Kommentar zum Neuen Testament aus Talmud und Midrasch* (Munchen: Beck, 1965), 4:186–201.

The Apocalypse of Baruch 57:2 says:

And after these things you saw the bright waters; that is the fountain of
Abraham and his generation, and the coming of his son, and the son of
his son, and of those who are like them. For at that time the unwritten
law was in force among them, and the works of the commandments were
accomplished at that time, and the belief in the coming judgment was
brought about, and the hope of the world which will be renewed was
built at that time, and the promise of life that will come later was planted.
Those are the bright waters which you have seen.

Aboth 5:3 in the Babylonian Talmud reads as follows:

With ten trials was Abraham, our Father proved, and he stood firm in
them all; to make known how great was the love of Abraham, our Father
(peace be upon him).

Genesis Rabbah, Parashah 44, in its comments on Genesis 15:1 contains this fairly typical view of Abraham:

Another matter: "His way is perfect" (2Sam. 22:31) refers to Abraham,
for it is written in his regard, "You found [Abraham's] way faithful before
you" (Neh. 9:8). Later in this same Parashah there is this revealing comment: "A. "After these things" (Genesis 15:1): There were some second
thoughts. B. Who had second thoughts? Abraham did. He said before
the Holy One, blessed be he, "Lord of the ages, you made a covenant
with Noah that you would not wipe his children. I went and acquired a
treasure of religious deeds and good deeds greater than his, so the covenant made with me has set aside the covenant made with him. Now is
it possible that someone else will come along and accumulate religious
deeds and good deeds greater than mine and so set aside the covenant
that was made with me on account of the covenant to be made with
him." Also note: "A. "But he said, 'O Lord God, how am I to know that
I shall possess it?" (Gen. 15:8): B. R. Hama bar Haninah said, "It was
not as though he were complaining, but he said to him, 'On account of
what merit [shall I know it? That is, how have I the honor of being so
informed?]" C. "He said to him, 'It is on account of the merit of the sacrifice of atonement that I shall hand over to your descendants. [5]

---

[5] This material is taken from Jacob Neusner, *Genesis Rabbah: The Judaic Commentary to the Book of Genesis: A New American Translation* (Atlanta, GA: Scholars
Press, n. d.), 125, 128, 129, 134, 135.

Jubilees 11:15–17 reads this way:

And in the seventh year of that week, she bore a son for him, and he called him Abram, after the name of his mother's father because he died before his daughter conceived a son. And the lad began understanding the straying of the land, that everyone went astray after graven images and after pollution. And his father taught him writing. And he was two weeks of years old. And he separated from his father that he might not worship the idols with him. And he began to pray to the Creator of all so that he might save him from the straying of the sons of men, and so that his portion might not fall into straying after the pollution and scorn." As the following context makes clear (11:18), Abram is viewed as 14 years old at the time of the above description.

Jubilees 17:17–18 says:

And the Lord knew that Abraham was faithful in all his afflictions, for he had tried him through his country and with famine; and had tried him with the wealth of kings, and had tried him again through his wife, when she was torn (from him), and with circumcision; and had tried through Ishmael and Hagar, his maid-servant, when he sent them away. And in everything wherein He had tried him, he was found faithful, and his soul was not impatient, and he was not slow to act; for he was faithful and a lover of the Lord." Irvin adds these relevant remarks to the above quotation: "Whatever might be offensive in the Genesis account was altered. No deception about Sarah occurred in Egypt (13:11–15), and when God told Abraham he and Sarah would have a son, Abraham rejoiced (15:17) instead of laughing (Genesis 17:17). At the age of fourteen, Abraham rejected idol worship, rebuked his father for worshipping them, and then boldly burned the idols (Jubilees 12). Abraham also endorsed the Torah's eternal validity and established cultic rituals. He reestablished the Feast of Weeks which had been discontinued since the time of Noah (6:18–20), he practiced circumcision, an eternal ordinance (15:25, 26), and he began the practice of tithing (13:25). Abraham even celebrated the Feast of Tabernacles exactly as the Torah later required (16:31).[6]

Jubilees 23:10 also describes Abraham:

For Abraham was perfect in all of his actions with the LORD and was pleasing through righteousness all of the days of his life.

[6] Irvin, "Paul's Use of the Abraham Image in Romans and Galatians," 11.

Jubilees 24:11 says of Abraham (cf. 24:10):

And all the nations of the earth will bless themselves by your seed because your father obeyed me and observed my restrictions and my commandments and my laws and the ordinances and my covenant.

Sirach 35:24 reads:

He that believeth in the Lord taketh heed to commandment; and he that trusteth in him shall fare never the worse.

Sirach 44:19–22 declares:

19 Abraham was the great father of a multitude of nations, and no one has been found like him in glory; 20 he kept the law of the Most High, and was taken into covenant with him; he established the covenant in his flesh, and when he was tested he was found faithful. 21 Therefore the Lord assured him by an oath that the nations would be blessed through his posterity; that he would multiply him like the dust of the earth, and exalt his posterity like the stars, and cause them to inherit from sea to sea and from the River to the ends of the earth. 22 To Isaac also he gave the same assurance for the sake of Abraham his father.

1 Maccabees 2:52 asks:

Was not Abraham found faithful when tested, and it was reckoned to him as righteousness?

Odes 12:8 affirms:

You, therefore, Lord God of the righteous ones, did not appoint repentance to the righteous ones, Abraham, Isaac, and Jacob, the ones who did not sin, but you appointed repentance to me the sinner. [*This is my translation of the Greek.*]

Much in the Jewish literature is not distinguishable from biblical ideas,[7] but in the passages cited themes emerge alien to the biblical canon. Abraham's righteousness is exalted in terms that exceed those of the Bible. He is perfect, passing all ten of the divine tests. Thus, we are told how

---

[7] Irvin, "Paul's Use of the Abraham Image in Romans and Galatians," 7–45, provides a much broader treatment of the Jewish sources than is possible here. His treatment and conclusions clearly support the necessarily more narrow treatment provided here and support its conclusions.

great Abraham's love was for God. Even before being called by God, when he was only fourteen, he recognized the idolatry of his father and sought God to save him from the idolatrous straying of men. Thus, Abraham had no need of repentance like ordinary men. Das adds that Philo said that "Abraham achieved perfect obedience of the law."[8] It is clear, furthermore, that this perfect obedience was seen as accruing merit to Abraham both for himself and his descendants. Abraham's faith is seen as obedience to God's commandments and as faithfulness in testing. Little mention is made of trust in God's promises. It is not for believing God's promises that Abraham is credited as righteous, but because he was found faithful when tested. The fact that God blesses His people for the sake of Abraham receives, therefore, a strange twist. God loves Abraham and blesses Israel for His sake as a response to works of Abraham. Paul likely knew that such viewpoints were current in Jewish circles when he cited Genesis 15:6 in Romans 4:3.

The Immediate Context of Romans 4:3

Romans 1:1–17 forms a comprehensive introduction to the letter. For our purposes the most significant aspect of this introduction is its repeated emphasis on the gospel which suggests that the theme of the epistle is the gospel which has for its power the righteousness of God (Romans 1:16–17). (Note threefold use of the word, gospel, $\epsilon\upsilon\alpha\gamma\gamma\epsilon\lambda\iota\upsilon\nu$ (in 1:1, 9 and 16) and the verb $\epsilon\upsilon\alpha\gamma\gamma\epsilon\lambda\iota\zeta\omicron\mu\alpha\iota$ meaning to preach the gospel in 1:15.)

Romans 1:18–3:20 concerns the ruin of man. More specifically, Paul is intent in this section of Romans on establishing the thesis he states in 1:18a, "the wrath of God is revealed against all ungodliness and unrighteousness of men." Paul does this by showing that both men in general (1:18–2:16) and Jews in particular (2:17–3:8) possessed a revelation of God's law against which they have sinned and in terms of which they are condemned. Paul brings this section of Romans to an emphatic conclusion through a long series of Old Testament quotations intended to demonstrate the depth and universality of human sin. Romans 3:19–20 is the summary conclusion of his argument. In this conclusion Paul asserts that "by the works of the law no flesh will be justified in his sight."

Romans 3:21–5:21 has for its theme the righteousness of God as the remedy to the wrath of God. 3:21 begins Paul's exposition of the righteousness of God which according to 1:17 is the power of the gospel.[9]

---

[8] Das, *Paul, the Law, and the Covenant*, 30.

[9] Interestingly enough, neither the noun, gospel, nor the verb, evangelize, is used again by Paul until chapter 10 where the verb is used in 10:15 and the noun is used in 10:16.

Romans 3:21–26 is Paul's initial identification of the righteousness of God. From the outset Paul is at pains to contrast this righteousness of God with "the works of the law." Verse 21 begins with the words, "but now without law." This righteousness of God is not by means of the law, but rather by means of redemption (v. 24) or propitiation (v. 25) achieved in and by God's act in Christ Jesus' bloody (v. 25) death.

This righteousness is, therefore, not something reserved for Jewish law-keepers. Since it is "without law" (3:21) and not "by the works of the law," (3:20) it is "for all those who believe; for there is no distinction" (3:22; cf. 1:16; 10:12). Thus, a polemic against Jewish ethnocentricity emerges in these verses, but one based on the universal inadequacy of the law to save.

Romans 3:27 commences a series of several questions and answers. There is, first, the two-part question about boasting in 3:27. There is, second, the two-part question about whether God is the God of the Gentiles in 3:29. There is, third, the question about the nullification of the law in 3:31. There is, fourth, the question about Abraham in 4:1. This series of questions in 3:27–4:1 seem to have for its purpose to draw out the implications of "the righteousness of God" revealed in the gospel as stated in 3:21–26.

Significant questions exist with regard to the internal connections of these questions with one another.[10] Though several considerations tie these four questions together,[11] it seems clear that the final question in 4:1 marks a significant turning point in Paul's argument. Romans 4:1 and following are Paul's summary response to each of the previous questions. Since the issue of boasting brackets this series of questions in 3:27 and 4:2, this suggests that the question of 4:1 is connected to the question of 3:27. Abraham's example is, then, intended to show why justification by works and boasting is excluded. The question of 3:29 also finds its definitive response in the answer to the question and answer found in 4:1–25. It seems clear then that 4:1 and following is really the extended response to each of the previous questions in the distinctive series of questions found in 3:27–4:1.[12] Romans 4:1–25 are the Old Testament confirmation of Paul's doctrine of the righteousness of God just laid out in Romans 3:21–26.

[10] John Murray, *Epistle to the Romans* (Grand Rapids: Eerdmans, 1959), 127–29.

[11] For instance, these questions are bracketed by the mention of boasting in 3:27 and then 4:2. This appears to indicate that there is some unifying thought that ties the four questions together.

[12] The οὖν of 4:1 is usually translated inferentially as *then* or *therefore* and suggests the possibility that Paul begins a new section of argument here. H. E. Dana and Julius R. Mantey, *A Manual Grammar of the Greek New Testament* (New York: The Macmillan Company, 1927), 252–58 argue that οὖν may also have an

Richard B. Hays has raised the question of how Romans 4:1 should be understood. He deviates from the mainstream of interpreters in two respects: the punctuation and the translation of the text. With regard to punctuation, Hays would make these words into two questions. He would punctuate as follows: Τί οὖν ἐροῦμεν; Εὑρηκέναι Ἀβραὰμ τὸν προπάτορα ἡμῶν κατὰ σάρκα;: *What shall we say therefore? Have we found Abraham to be our forefather according to the flesh?* Hays makes an alluring case for this approach to the text and in so doing furthers the agenda of the new perspective by focusing on the relation of Jews and Gentiles.[13]

Hays' proposal confronts, however, serious difficulties. Chief is the serious difficulty that Hays' translation creates with regard to the connection of Romans 4:2 and 4:1. Hays understands the problem and can only focus attention on 4:9–25 and away from 4:2–8. Romans 4:2–8 then becomes a "preliminary step" in Paul's argument the pivot of which is only reached in 4:9–18.[14] His view, however, simply does not provide a natural connection between 4:1 and 2 and must assume a significant distance between 4:1 and 2. In contrast the language shows a close connection between the two verses both by the repetition of the name, Abraham, and the use of the connective, γὰρ. The customary translation provides for such a close and more natural connection. "What then shall we say that Abraham our forefather according to the flesh has found?" Found with regard to what? The foregoing discussion supplies the ellipsis. Paul is asking, "What has he found with regard to the matter of the righteousness of God and justification?" Verse 2 follows naturally. He found, and we find with him, that we are justified not by works, but by faith.

Against the tendency of exegesis influenced by the New Perspective on Paul, 4:2–8 stands as abiding testimony to the emphasis and prominence in this context of the contrast between justification by works and justification by faith. Paul is interested in the fact that Jews and Gentiles are both justified in the same way, but he is more interested in this contrast between works and faith. It is a continuing feature of his exposition of the

intensive or even adversative force. The οὖν of 4:1 could be translated in one of these ways. The intensive translation would be as follows: "What indeed shall we say that Abraham our forefather according to the flesh has found?" The adversative translation is the most attractive, "What, however, shall we say that Abraham our forefather according to the flesh has found?" This translation is consistent with the idea that here in Paul's argument we come to a new point of departure or section of thought.

[13] Richard B. Hays, "Have We Found Abraham to Be Our Forefather According to the Flesh?" *Novum Testamentum* 27:1 (1985): 89.

[14] Ibid, 92–93.

righteousness of God revealed in the gospel (3:20, 21, 27–28). This contrast emerges again and explicitly in 4:2–8.

Romans 4:2 clearly emphasizes this contrast. There is some confusion, however, as to the exact force of Paul's reasoning here. At the root of the confusion is the meaning of the phrase, ἀλλ᾽ οὐ πρὸς θεόν *(but not toward God)*. Superficially read, this phrase appears to say that if Abraham was justified by works, he would have something to boast about before men, but nothing to boast about before God. But Paul has exclusively in view justification *coram deo*. In 3:27 Paul affirms that boasting is excluded not on general principles, but because of the principle of (justification by) faith. So here it is probable that ἀλλ᾽ οὐ πρὸς θεόν simply means, *but this is not the case with reference to God*. It is not the case, in other words, that Abraham was justified by works before God and has something to boast about toward God. Romans 4:3 supports this by showing that Scripture says that Abraham was justified by faith.

Romans 4:3 is, then, Paul's pivotal scriptural proof that Abraham was justified by faith and that his doctrine of justification does not nullify the Old Testament. Paul will cite the example of David in the Psalms in 4:6–8, but he immediately returns to the example of Abraham in 4:9–25 because Abraham is the pivot of Paul's argument. This is not surprising. Take the average American and combine his respect for George Washington, Abraham Lincoln, Billy Graham and the Pope into one person, and not even then do you understand how much the Jews respected Abraham. His example had a polemical weight beyond any other.

Romans 4:4–5 amplify a crucial assumption of Paul's interpretation of Genesis 15:6. Paul probably understood that Abraham's example was often used as an example of justification by works in Jewish thought. Paul, therefore, explains why he sees faith as opposed to the works of the law in 4:4–5.

Romans 4:4 likely echoes the LXX of Genesis 15:1 where God promises that the reward (ὁ μισθός) of Abraham will be very great. It is natural to ask about this reward how Abraham will come to possess it. Paul reasons that if a reward is given in response to works, it is given as the payment of a debt and not as a gift. Paul thinks this would give a ground of boasting to man. Thus, it is untenable both in terms of the relationship with God that it postulates and the gracious character of justification already affirmed in 3:21–26.

Romans 4:5 then places Genesis 15:6 in contrast to the way of working for reward explained in 4:4. Working is, however, contrasted not simply with the absence of work, but with believing in the promises made to the unworthy and ungodly. (The preposition translated in by the NASB is ἐπι which means literally upon and conveys in combination with the verb for believe the idea of resting on the promises of God.) The word *ungodly* implies that Abraham himself was not justified because he was the paradigm of obedience. He is rather the ungodly person justified by faith. In the quotation found in Romans 4:7–8 the crediting of righteousness is said three times to consist in the forgiveness of sin. This implies that not only David, but Abraham too had sins and lawless deeds and that his righteousness consisted in part of their being covered by grace.

Romans 4:6–8 by citing the example of David further clarifies that righteousness is credited apart from works. Righteousness is not a matter of being rewarded for faithful obedience, but having one's lawless deeds freely forgiven and not having one's sin taken into account.

Romans 4:9–12 contains one of the most brilliant of Paul's exegetical insights. Emphasizing what a plain reading of Genesis makes clear, he asserts that Abraham's faith was credited as righteousness while he was still uncircumcised. Abraham is already justified in Genesis 15, but circumcision was not required till Genesis 17. We must not forget that being uncircumcised and being a Gentile were equivalent.[15] Yet more, being a Gentile and being ungodly (ἀσεβῆ – 4:5) were also equivalent for Jews (Galatians 2:15). Since Abraham was an ungodly Gentile when he was justified, he certainly was not (Paul argues) justified by the works of the law.

Romans 4:13–22 enlarges on the fact that the promise of God to Abraham was not made in connection with the law, but in connection with the promises of God. Consequently, the fulfillment of the promise was not dependent on the weakness of the flesh, but on the power of the God who keeps His promises even if it means raising the dead or calling into existence that which did not previously exist (4:17, 21).

Romans 4:23–25 brings Paul's little sermon on Abraham in Romans 4 to its closing application. God's promise to Abraham is finally fulfilled by the delivering up of Jesus to death because of our transgressions and His resurrection from the dead (4:24–25). It is by believing the same promise that Abraham believed, only now in a fuller state of realization, that our faith—like his—will be credited as righteousness.

It is a gigantic mistake for Hays following Sanders and others to bring the concept of the merits of the patriarchs to the discussion of Abraham in Romans 4. He says, "Abraham's faithfulness was reckoned by God to the benefit not only of Israel (as in the rabbinic exegetical tradition) but also of the Gentiles."[16] To speak of "the vicarious effects of Abraham's faithfulness"[17] is to obscure or miss the whole point. Abraham is the ungodly man—not the faithful man—in Romans 4. He is not a Christ-figure with

---

[15] Cf., for example, Ephesians 2:11.
[16] Hays, "Have We Found Abraham," 96.
[17] Ibid, 97.

a treasury of merit, but a sinner with no merit in need of being justified himself. His faith is not admirable faithfulness, but empty-handed reliance on the promise of God.

The Analysis of the Context of Genesis 15:6

Reflections on Abraham in Scripture after the Conclusion of His Lifetime

Abraham is, as noted already, an enormous figure in both the Old Testament and the New. The reflections on Abraham in the Old and New Testaments must be examined in order to place Genesis 15:6 in its scriptural context.

THE REFLECTION ON ABRAHAM IN THE OLD TESTAMENT AFTER HIS LIFETIME

There are 216 references to Abraham and Abram in the Old Testament—forty-three of them outside of Genesis. Most are unremarkable for our purposes, but a number are relevant. God's undying love and friendship for Abraham are emphasized (2 Chronicles 20:7; Isaiah 41:8; Micah 7:20). There is mention of the fact Abraham kept God's covenant and commands and that therefore Isaac will be blessed (Genesis 26:3). The biblical emphasis on God's grace to Abraham, however, places this in a completely different theological context than it has in the Jewish literature cited. Mentions of Abraham's origin as an idolatrous Gentile emphasize God's power and grace in separating him from his evil background (Nehemiah 9:7; Joshua 24:2). As an encouragement to the faithful remnant there is reference to the fact that, though Abraham was only one, the power and grace of God multiplied him into a great nation (Isaiah 51:2). We also learn the wicked grounded a false hope in this same fact (Ezekiel 33:24).

THE REFLECTION ON ABRAHAM IN THE NEW TESTAMENT

There are 67 references to Abraham in the New Testament. Many are found in formulas mentioning God's covenant with Abraham or the God of Abraham. Some stress Abraham's obedience (Hebrews 11:8, 17; James 2:21, 23). Others stress that Abraham was justified by faith and not by works (Romans 4; Galatians 3).[18] The Gospels stress the false confidence

---

[18] Hebrews 6:13 approaches this same emphasis.

that the Jews placed in Abraham being their physical forefather (Matthew 3:9; 8:11; Luke 13:28; 16:23–31; John 8:39–58). One verse emphasizes that God appeared to Abraham in Mesopotamia before he lived in Haran (Acts 7:2). It likely teaches that God graciously appeared to him even while he was still living in idolatry (Joshua 24:2; Nehemiah 9:7). Paul emphasizes in Romans 4:9ff that Abraham was uncircumcised when he received God's promises and that this makes him the father of both Jews and Gentiles who believe in Christ.

Genesis 15 as the Immediate Old Testament Context of Genesis 15:6

Genesis 15:1–6

Ὁ μισθός in the LXX of Genesis 15:1, is used of wages in the other fifteen uses in the LXX of the Pentateuch. Nevertheless, we must not think that the term *reward* necessarily connotes something that is earned or strictly deserved. Genesis 15:1 indicates that God Himself is the reward of Abraham. Does Abraham deserve to have God Himself as his reward? Of course not! Paul also resists the equation of *reward* and *merit*. In Romans 4:4 Paul clearly assumes that a "wage" or "reward" may be credited either as a "favor" or "grace."[19]

The emphasis on divine promise is prominent in Genesis 15:1–6. The (apparently unsolicited) promises of verse 1 open the passage. The complaint of Abraham in verses 2 and 3 refers to the previous promise of a seed in Genesis 13:14–18 and Genesis 12:1–3 (which promises were also unsolicited). The promise of a seed is renewed in verses 4 and 5. The greatness of the seed promised (it is to be as the stars of the sky) serves to emphasize the glory of God's promise and the magnitude of His grace to Abraham. All of this orients Abraham's faith in verse 6 not to God's commandments, but Jehovah's promise. This orientation of Abraham's faith is in striking contrast to the orientation assumed in the Jewish literature cited above, but in striking conformity to the orientation of Abraham's faith in Paul (Romans 4 and Galatians 3) and even in Hebrews 6:13–20; 11:8–12.

---

[19] As will be noted below, the language of crediting used in Genesis 15:6 in other passages has the effect of reversing an idea—crediting something to be something that it is not. Perhaps, then, we are to think that God is credited as Abraham's reward (wages), when, in fact, He and all His gifts to Abraham are a matter of grace.

Genesis 15:7–21

The immediately succeeding context of Genesis 15:6 continues the striking emphasis of the chapter on the amazing promises of God to Abraham. In verse 7 Jehovah raises the issue of the land promise (Genesis 12:1) and connects it with his having brought Abram out of Ur of the Chaldees. Abraham in response in verse 8 asks for a confirmation of this promise of God. Without rebuking Abram, Jehovah orchestrates the strange ritual recorded in verses 9–21. Though debated by Old Testament interpreters, the issue most important for this essay is clear. The oven of smoke and torch of fire that passes through the split sacrifices is clearly a symbol of Jehovah himself. They seem to anticipate the appearance of Jehovah as a burning bush and as a pillar of fire and cloud. This identification is confirmed by the connection of verses 17 and 18. (See also the parallel passage in Jeremiah 34:18–19.) Passing through divided sacrifices symbolize making a covenant with someone. The oven of smoke and torch of fire passing through the split sacrifices indicate that "on that day the Lord made a covenant" (Genesis 15:18).[20] Jehovah passed through the divided sacrifices, but Abram does not. Jehovah pledges Himself in covenant to Abraham and takes the burden of the fulfillment of His promises wholly upon Himself. Leupold remarks:

> … the covenants God makes with men are not mutual agreements as between man and man. They are rather agreements emanating from God. For in the nature of the case here are not two parties who stand on an equal footing. In fact, in the instance under consideration God binds Himself to the fulfillment of certain obligations; Abram is bound to no obligations whatsoever. God's priority is a prominent feature of the covenants of this type.[21]

This much seems clear. God is pleased in the most graphic way to confirm the promise to Abraham by making a covenant with him. The grace

[20] G. J. Wenham, "The Symbolism of the Animal Rite in Genesis 15: A Response to G. F. Hasel, JSOT 19 (1981) 61–78," *Journal for the Study of the Old Testament* 22 (F, 1981): 135. Wenham here states, "It is surely agreed that the smoking fire pot and flaming torch symbolize the presence of God, as they do elsewhere in the Pentateuch." My own brief survey confirms that the generality of interpreters think that the oven of smoke and torch of fire symbolize Jehovah. Only John Calvin, *Commentaries on The First Book of Moses Called Genesis*, 420, of those I checked seems to differ.

H. C. Leupold, *Exposition of Genesis* (Grand Rapids, MI: Baker Book House, 1942), 1:489.

of this confirmation must not be overlooked. God's promises should never be doubted, but in condescension to Abraham's weakness and out of sheer kindness *and simply to assure his faith*, God *confirms* His promise with a covenant. Hebrews 6:13–18 is referring to another of God's dealings with Abraham, but its words apply.

> For when God made the promise to Abraham, since He could swear by no one greater, He swore by Himself, saying, "I WILL SURELY BLESS YOU AND I WILL SURELY MULTIPLY YOU." And so, having patiently waited, he obtained the promise. For men swear by one greater *than themselves*, and with them an oath *given* as confirmation is an end of every dispute. In the same way God, desiring even more to show to the heirs of the promise the unchangeableness of His purpose, interposed with an oath, so that by two unchangeable things in which it is impossible for God to lie, we who have taken refuge would have strong encouragement to take hold of the hope set before us (Hebrews 6:13–18).

Two related emphases in Genesis 15 are, then, highly significant for the meaning of Genesis 15:6: the emphasis of Genesis 15 on the magnificence of the promises of God and the emphasis on God's desire to confirm these promises to Abraham. Both emphases are intended to strengthen Abraham's faith. They serve to orient the faith of Abraham to the promises of God. Abraham's faith, then, must be defined in terms of reliance on God's magnificent and gracious promises. Paul exemplifies this orientation, but the Jewish literature does not.

The Larger Context of Genesis 15 (Genesis 11:23–25:11)

As one considers the life of Abraham recorded in Genesis, a number of features or emphases become clear. First, in these chapters the story of Abraham is the story of divine promise, grace and initiative. We hear of nothing (contrary to the Jewish literature) that commended Abram to God's choice and call. We hear of God making glorious (and apparently unsolicited) promises to Abram (Genesis 12:1–3; 13:14–18; 15:1–21; 17:1–22). God commands Abram to leave his native country and relatives likely to aid him in escaping from idolatry. We learn almost immediately of Sarai's barrenness. This emphasizes that a covenant seed depends wholly on God's promise and power.

Second, consistent with this the story of Abraham is the story of Abraham's believing response to God's promissory and covenantal approaches. He believes even when great promises are made to him (Genesis 15:6; Romans 4:3). The hiphil of אמן (translated *believed*) in Genesis 15:6 according to Keil and Delitzsch expresses "that state of mind which is sure of its object, and relies firmly upon it" and as "a firm, inward, personal, self-surrendering reliance upon a personal being..."[22] Abraham's faith then is here presented as trustful reliance upon the promise of God.

Third, Abraham is sometimes presented as an obedient man. Abraham obeys when called to leave his native country. He builds an altar to worship the God who has made such promises to him, allows Lot to leave peacefully to take the better land and delivers Lot at great personal risk and with considerable skill and bravery as a leader from those who had captured him. He is pictured as a man of hospitality, as a man of prayer who intercedes for Sodom for the sake of Lot, as careful not to allow his son to take a wife from the increasingly wicked people of the land. He observes the sign of the covenant God's makes with him. He even offers up Isaac when God requires this strange and difficult act of obedience.

Fourth, the story of Abraham's life is also checkered. It is the story of the forgiveness of an ungodly and sinful man (Joshua 24:2; Romans 4:5). In contrast to the glorification of Abraham as practically or completely sinless in the Jewish literature, the sins of Abraham are clearly recorded on the pages of Genesis. He is guilty of the questionable stratagem of deceiving others about the identity of his wife both early and later in his life (Genesis 13 and 20). Though Sarah was his half sister, the disaster that he almost brought upon those he deceived and the way in which Isaac repeated (without his excuse!) this same stratagem (Genesis 26) seems clearly to indicate the sinfulness of this stratagem. He is complicit in the unbelieving device of his wife when he takes Hagar as a concubine. The grace of God is peculiarly evident in this event. God keeps His promise of a seed in spite of Abraham's weakness in taking Hagar.[23]

---

[22] Carl Friederich Keil and Franz Delitzch, *Biblical Commentary on the Old Testament*, vol. 1: *The Pentateuch*, trans. James Martin (Edinburgh: T&T Clark, 1866), 212.

[23] Robert R. Gonzales, *Where Sin Abounds: The Spread of Sin in Genesis with Special Focus on the Patriarchal Narratives* (Eugene, OR: Wipf and Stock Publishers, 2009), 108–139. Gonzales through a careful exegesis of the key narratives of Genesis shows that even in the narrative of Abraham the author is emphasizing the spread of sin. His exegesis makes clear that we are not to attempt to exculpate Abraham from the sins he committed even after his being called by God or cover up the dark places in his checkered life recorded in Genesis 12 and following. As Gonzales remarks on pages 138–39, "Despite the fact that Abraham had aligned himself with Yahweh and committed himself to a life of faith, he was at times ensnared by remaining sin (Hebrews 12:1). Inded, his failure illustrates the lamentable truth that certain sins do not easily go away, and the true believer may "once more strike his foot against the same stone." Sin has not only spread to *all mankind*, but it has become so deeply entrenched that even the righteous cannot easily escape its grip."

The tension between Abraham the obedient (James 2:21–23) and Abraham the ungodly (Romans 4:3–5) must be considered. One strain of Judaism felt no tension whatever on this matter. Abraham was an obedient man and justified because of that obedience, period! There is a significant contrast here with the checkered character of the biblical picture of Abraham.

But questions remain. Some ask, "Does not Paul in Romans 4:5 refer to Abraham as ungodly at the point of Genesis 15:6?" Others wonder, "Does he not say that he was justified in Genesis 15:6?"

The second of these questions will be considered first. The peculiar form of the Hebrew verb describing Abraham's faith (וְהֶאֱמִן) is relevant to it. Leupold asserts:

> The form is unusual, perfect with *waw*, not as one would expect, imperfect with *waw conversive*. Apparently by this device the author would indicate that the permanence of this attitude would be stressed: not only: Abram believed just this once, but: Abram proved constant in his faith…[24]

Genesis 15:6 consequently is not a comment only or specifically on Abraham's faith in Genesis 15, but on his faith throughout his life. The writer rather says: *So we see here another illustration of that ongoing faith of*

---

[24] H. C. Leupold, *Exposition of Genesis* (Grand Rapids, MI: Baker Book House, 1942), 1:477; Gordon J. Wenham, *Word Biblical Commentary: Genesis 1–15* (Waco, TX: Word Books, 1987), 324. My friend and PhD in Old Testament, Bob (Robert) Gonzales, in private correspondence agrees with Leupold that the form of the verb used here is unusual. While the very scarcity of its occurrence makes him hesitant to be dogmatic, and while he notes examples of the use of this from which may not support Leupold's interpretation of it, he notes a number that do support him. He concludes: "Consequently, usage allows for Leupold's suggestion that Moses switches from the waw-imperfect consecutive, which normally functions as a preterite (i.e., discrete actions or events), to the plain waw-perfect in order to denote the durative or constantive idea, i.e., 'Abram proved constant in his faith.' That is, Leupold's view is linguistically and syntactically plausible. Not surprisingly, Leupold is not the only commentator to suggest a constantive or durative understanding of Abraham's faith in Genesis 15:6…. Kenneth Mathews has noted the anomalous construction and averred, 'The verbal construction "believed" (v. 6) and reference to a past event at Ur (v. 7) substantiate that Abram had already exhibited faith. The syntax of the verb [*wehe'emin*] diverts from the typical pattern found in past tense narrative. The force of the construction conveys an ongoing faith repeated from the past' [Genesis 11:27–50:26, vol. 1b of *The New American Commentary*, ed. E. Ray Clendenen (Nashville: Broadman & Holman Publishers, 2005) 166]," email message to author, May 2, 2004.

Abraham by which he was credited as righteous. Ungodly Abraham had been justified by this ongoing kind of faith years before as Hebrews 11:8 confirms. Before Genesis 15:6 there are clear evidences of faith. So the answer to the second question posed above, "Does he not say that he was justified in Genesis 15:6?" is no!

But what of the assertion that Paul in Romans 4:5 refers to Abraham as ungodly in Genesis 15:6? The plain record of Abraham's grievous failures after his calling are relevant to the question at hand. These grievous manifestations of remaining sin are a reminder of what Abraham had been, what he was by nature, and that his standing before God was not grounded on the very imperfect obedience which grew out of his faith in God's promises. Thus, for the purposes of being justified by God, Abraham was (from the standpoint of the stringent requirements of God's law) ungodly not only before his call but afterwards. This, however, is not contrary to saying that (from the standpoint of the gospel) he was justified and possessed the real, but imperfect, manifestations of evangelical obedience in his life.

The Way in which Paul Interprets and Utilizes Genesis 15:6 in Romans 4:3

In Romans 4:3, Genesis 15:6 is adduced as part of Paul's polemic against being "justified by works" and boasting before God. Verses 4 and 5 elaborate the contrast involved in this polemic. This means that both Abraham's believing in God and his faith being credited for righteousness are seen as contrasting with the view against which Paul polemicizes. It is clear with regard to both parts of the quotation that Paul is correct. As we have seen, Abraham's believing in God in Genesis 15:6 is exclusively oriented toward God's gracious and free promises in its Old Testament context.

But is Paul correct when he regards faith being reckoned as righteousness as not grounded on Abraham's own obedience. Yes, the context of Romans 4:3 shows that this means that *in some way* Abram's faith was a substitute or replacement for the righteousness before God which he did not possess. Psalm 32:1–2 is cited in Romans 4:6–8. This citation shows that reckoning as righteous even in the Old Testament consisted (partly) in the free and unearned forgiveness of sin. Is this, however, a possible meaning of the language of Genesis 15:6?

The answer is an unequivocal yes. In each of the other three uses of the verb translated, reckon or credit (חשׁב) in Genesis, the idea of "something being regarded as something it is not" is present. In other words, the word is used to refer to a kind of reversal of the normal state of affairs. The word for reckon is in bold and italicized in the English translations given below.

> Genesis 31:15 Are we not *reckoned* by him as foreigners? For he has sold us, and has also entirely consumed our purchase price.

> Genesis 38:15 When Judah saw her, he *thought* she *was* a harlot, for she had covered her face.

> Genesis 50:20 As for you, you *meant* evil against me, *but* God *meant* it for good in order to bring about this present result, to preserve many people alive.

With this evidence before him, O. P. Robertson remarks:

> Other Scriptures in the pentateuch employ the term חשׁב to indicate that a person may be "reckoned" or "regarded" as something that he himself is not. Leah and Rachel affirm that their father "reckons" or "regards" them as *strangers*, although they are his own daughters (Gen. 31:15). The tithe of the Levite is "reckoned" or "regarded" as the corn of the threshing-floor and as the fulness of the winepress, although it obviously is not these things (Numb. 18:27, 30). Their tithe-offering functions in a substitionary capacity.
>
> Even closer to the "reckoning for righteousness" described in Genesis 15:6 is the declaration concerning certain sacrifices as described in Leviticus 7:18. If a particular sacrifice is not eaten by the third day, its value shall be lost, and it shall not be "reckoned" to the benefit of the sinner. The verse envisions a situation in which righteousness could be "reckoned" to a person, even though the individual concerned admittedly is a sinner.
>
> In this setting it is quite appropriate to understand Genesis 15:6 in terms of God's accounting as righteous the person of the patriarch although he himself is unrighteous.[25]

But how can faith be a "substitute" for righteousness before God? Romans itself makes clear that that Abraham's faith considered in and of itself is not an adequate substitute for righteousness. Many things conspire to make this clear. Two of the most important are these. First, to make Abraham's faith in itself righteousness would in Romans mean that it is *the righteousness of God* (Romans 1:16–17). It would be strange, indeed, if Paul were to give Abram's or our weak faith the mighty name of the righteousness of God. Second, to identify faith in itself as *the righteousness of*

---

[25] O. P. Robertson, "New Covenant Expositions of an Old Covenant Text," *Westminster Theological Journal* 42:2 (1980), 265–66.

God would be to make superfluous the obvious attention that Paul seeks to draw throughout this entire context to the death and resurrection of Christ (3:21–26; 4:24–25).

We must, rather, remember that faith is oriented toward and, we may even say, shaped by the promise of God. Faith is what it is because of the promise of God. Its content is the content of the promise of God. Since Paul in Romans 4:23–25 finds the ultimate fulfillment of the promise of God to Abraham in the death and resurrection of Christ, it is not difficult to see that the content of faith for which it is credited as righteousness to Abraham and the believer consists in the death and resurrection of Christ. This, and not Abraham's faith in and of itself, is the righteousness of God. To use Luther's illustration, "The believing heart holds fast to Christ just as the setting of a ring grips the jewel: we have Christ in faith."[26] Christ is the value and righteousness of faith.

Conclusion

Romans 4:1–25 provides the Old Testament corroboration for the doctrine of the righteousness of God Paul enunciates in Romans 3:21–31. It is likely many times Paul had heard the objection that what he was teaching simply was not in accord with the teaching of the Old Testament. In Romans 4 Paul responds with a masterful and compelling three point defense of justification *sola fide*. In Romans 4:3–9 he shows that the Old Testament teaches that Abraham was justified by faith not works; in 4:10–12 that Abraham was justified while still an uncircumcised (and, thus, ungodly) Gentile; and in 4:13–22 that Abraham was justified long before the giving of the law by the simple believing of the promise of God. In the context of this argument Genesis 15:6 provides a pivotal, crucial and compelling testimony against Jewish legalism and the new perspective and for Paul's and the Protestant understanding of the righteousness of God!

---

[26] Paul Althaus, *The Theology of Martin Luther* (Philadelphia, PA: Fortress Press, 1966), 231.

Part Three

Practical

13

The Preacher on Preaching
WISDOM FROM A WISE WORDSMITH

Daniel Akin

When we stand to preach the infallible and inerrant Word of God, the glorious gospel of Jesus Christ and "the faith which was once for all delivered to the saints" (Jude 3), there is an essential and necessary plumb-line that must always guide the God-called messenger: "*What* you say is more important than how you say it. But, *how* you say it has never been more important."

This plumb-line, this dictum, this homiletical "must statement" has biblical warrant and support. We find it embedded in the wisdom of Solomon when he says in Ecclesiastes 12:9–10 that the wise Preacher "taught the people knowledge ...words of truth" (the *what*), and that "The Preacher sought to find acceptable (NASB, "delightful"; NIV, "just the right words") words ... words like goads, and ... well driven nails (the how)" (NKJV).[1]

Martin Lloyd-Jones said, "What is preaching? Logic on fire. Eloquent reason! Are these contradictions? Of course they are not!"[2]

Logic ⇨ what   Fire ⇨ how

Eloquent ⇨ how   Reason ⇨ what

---

[1] Unless otherwise indicated all Scripture quotations are taken from the NKJV.

[2] D. Martyn Lloyd-Jones, *Preaching and Preachers* (Grand Rapids, MI: Zondervan, 1971), 97.

Instruction

In this text, the Preacher, *Qoheleth*, addresses the proper means of teaching truth to the people of God. His primary focus may be on words that are written. However, written words of truth will also become spoken words of truth. Similar principles cohere for effectively delivering either a written or spoken message.

Solomon begins by saying, "because the Preacher (NIV, "teacher") was wise," he had a certain approach or strategy that shaped and guided his teaching ministry. It was "knowledge" and "truth" delivered with acceptable or delightful words that led his students to "fear God and keep His commandments" (v. 13). In other words, he faithfully taught his students the Word of God. God provided the message, He was simply the messenger. This goal for preaching is reflected in Article 25 of the "Chicago Statement on Hermeneutics" penned in 1982. It reads,

Article XXV

We affirm that the only type of preaching which sufficiently conveys the divine revelation and its proper application to life is that which faithfully expounds the text of Scripture as the Word of God.
We deny that the preacher has any message from God apart from the text of Scripture.

Because he is wise, the faithful preacher will be a faithful expositor, an engaging expositor. Now there are several essential elements necessary for engaging exposition.

The wise preacher will impart "knowledge" to his people. There will be content, what could be described as "theological exposition." Such a preaching agenda is the only reasonable and defensible strategy given the nature of the Bible as divine revelation.

John MacArthur is on target when he says, "The only logical response to inerrant Scripture… is to preach it expositionally. By expositionally, I mean preaching in such a way that the meaning of the Bible passage is presented entirely and exactly as it was intended by God."[3]

Good preaching always involves teaching just as good teaching will always have an element of preaching. Without it, our preaching is tepid and timid and our people malnourished!

---

[3] John MacArthur, *Rediscovering Expository Preaching: Balancing the Art and Science of Biblical Exposition* (Dallas, TX: Word, 1992), 35.

Walt Kaiser saw this malady almost 30 years ago when he wrote:

It is no secret that Christ's Church is not at all in good health in many places of the world. She has been languishing because she has been fed… "junk food."… The Biblical text is often no more than a slogan or refrain in the message… Biblical exposition has become a lost art in contemporary preaching. The most neglected of all biblical sections is the Old Testament—over three-fourths of divine revelation! … Motto preaching may please the masses in that it is filled with a lot of epigrammatic or proverbial slogans and interesting anecdotes, but is will always be a powerless word lacking the authority and validation of Scripture.[4]

Haddon Robinson reminds us, "When a preacher fails to preach the Scriptures, he abandons his authority. He confronts his hearers no longer with a word from God but only another word from men"[5]

Sidney Greidanus, in his book *The Modem Preacher and the Ancient Text* says, "Biblical preaching is a Bible shaped word imparted in a Bible-like way. In expository preaching the biblical text is neither a conventional introduction to a sermon on a largely different theme, nor a convenient peg on which to hang a ragbag of miscellaneous thoughts, but a master which dictates and controls what is said."[6]

The manner in which the preacher delivers the knowledge of God's Word is critically important. Three essentials are noted in Ecclesiastes 12:9:

1) *He pondered*—he weighed carefully what he wrote and said.

2) *He sought out*—he dug deep into the knowledge content he would present.

3) *He set in order many proverbs*—he considered how best to deliver wise sayings, wisdom words of truth. Here the word "proverbs" is broader in meaning than our word in English. It has the idea of wise sayings or teachings.

The faithful communicator of biblical truth will be gripped by the realization that the book lying before him is filled with wisdom, for it is the very Word of God. He will tremble at the thought of manipulating it or

---

[4] Walter C. Kaiser Jr., *Toward an Exegetical Theology: Biblical Exegesis for Preaching and Teaching* (Grand Rapids, MI: Baker, 1981), 7, 19, 37, 191.

[5] Haddon Robinson, *Biblical Preaching: The Development and Delivery of Expository Messages* (Grand Rapids, MI: Baker, 1980), 18

[6] Sidney Greidanus, *The Modern Preacher and the Ancient Text: Interpreting and Preaching Biblical Literature* (Grand Rapids, MI: Eerdmans, 1988), 10–11.

abusing it. He will carry out his assignment under a divine mandate to honor the text in its context as it was given by the Holy Spirit of God.

Indeed he will take to heart the wise admonition of Charles Koller, "In expounding the Word of God, there is a grave responsibility upon the preacher to convey the truth without distortion… With eternities at stake, the hearers can not afford to be in error, nor can the spiritual teacher whom he trusts… Every man has a right to his opinion, but no man has a right to be wrong in his facts… The integrity of the pulpit demands accuracy, thoroughness, and a scrupulous regard for text and context."[7]

A wise preacher will work hard to find the right words as he feeds the sheep under his protection. He will also deliver it in the best way. The phrase "acceptable words" in 12:10, means delightful or pleasing words.

In other words, not only is *error* a danger to the truth, *dullness* is a danger to the truth. Beautiful truth ought to be packaged and wrapped in an attractive style. Indeed, it is a sin to make the Bible boring!

Good preaching gives attention to form and content, structure and substance. It neglects neither and sees no need in sacrificing one for the other. John MacArthur well says, "The proper elements in an expository sermon may be summed up as follows:

Preaching is expository in purpose. It explains the text.

Preaching is logical in flow. It persuades the mind.

Preaching is doctrinal in content. It obligates the will.

Preaching is pastoral in concern. It feeds the soul.

Preaching is imaginative in pattern. It excites the emotion.

Preaching is relevant in application. It touches the life."[8]

But what about this issue of delivery? Lloyd-Jones provides wisdom and insight at this point: "Be natural; forget yourself; be absorbed in what you are doing and in the realization of the presence of God, and in the glory and the greatness of the Truth that you are preaching… that you forget yourself completely… Self is the greatest enemy of the preacher, more so than in the case of any other man in society. And the only way to deal with self is to be so taken up with, and so enraptured by the glory of what

[7] Charles Koller, *Expository Preaching Without Notes* (Grand Rapids, MI: Baker, 1962), 64–65.

[8] MacArthur, *Rediscovering Expository*, 289.

you are doing, that you forget yourself altogether."[9] He adds, "A theology which does not take fire, I maintain, is a defective theology; or at least the man's understanding of it is defective. Preaching is theology coming through a man who is on fire. A true understanding and experience of the Truth must lead to this. I say again that a man who can speak about these things dispassionately has no right whatsoever to be in a pulpit; and should never be allowed to enter one."[10]

The greatest preacher of the 19th century also understood the importance of wedding biblical content to an effective delivery. The faithful Baptist Charles Spurgeon noted:

> When I have thought of the preaching of certain good men, I have wondered, not that the congregation was so small, but that it was so large. The people who listen to them ought to excel in the virtue of patience, for they have grand opportunities of exercising it. Some sermons and prayers lend a color of support to the theory of Dr. William Hammond, that the brain is not absolutely essential to life. Brethren, … you will, none of you, covet earnestly the least gifts, and the dullest mannerisms, for you can obtain them without the exertion of the will … Labour to discharge your ministry, not with the lifeless method of an automaton, but with the freshness and power which will render your ministry largely effectual for its sacred purposes.[11]

Qoheleth, the preacher/teacher, instructs us in verse ten to communicate that which is "upright"—"words of truth." I cannot think of a better description of Holy Scripture: words that are upright, straight, words of integrity, because they are words of truth. I came across a marvelous statement concerning the Bible several years ago. Its source is unknown to me, but its affirmation is powerful. It is simply entitled:

THE BIBLE

This book contains: The mind of God, the state of man, the way of salvation, the doom of sinners and the happiness of believers. Its doctrine is holy, its precepts are binding, its histories are true and its decisions are immutable. Read it to be wise, believe it to be saved and practice it to be holy.

---

[9] Lloyd-Jones, *Preaching and Preachers*, 264.

[10] Ibid., 97.

[11] C. H. Spurgeon, *An All-Around Ministry* (reprint; Edinburgh: Banner of Truth, 1960), 316–17.

It contains light to direct you, food to support you and comfort to cheer you. It is the traveler's map, the pilgrim's staff, the pilot's compass, the soldier's sword and the Christian's charter.

Here, heaven is opened, and the gates of hell disclosed. Christ is its grand subject, our good its design, and the glory of God its end. It should fill the memory, rule the heart, and guide the feet.

Read it slowly, frequently, prayerfully. It is a mine of wealth, a paradise of glory, and a river of pleasure. It is given you in life, will be opened at the Judgment, and be remembered forever. It involves the highest responsibility, will reward faithful labor, and condemn all who trifle with its sacred contents.

> 'Tis the Book that has for the Ages,
> Lifted man from sin and shame;
> That great message on its pages,
> Will forever be the same.'

Never compare the Bible with other books. Comparisons are dangerous. Books speak from earth; the Bible speaks from heaven. Never think or say that the Bible contains the Word of God or that it becomes the Word of God. It is the Word of God.

Supernatural in origin, eternal in duration, inexpressible in value, infinite in scope, divine in authorship, regenerative in power, infallible in authority, universal in interest, personal in application, inspired in totality. Read it through. Write it down. Pray it in. Work it out. Pass it on. It is the Word of God.

J. I. Packer says, "... the true idea of preaching is that the preacher should become a mouthpiece for his text, opening it up and applying it as a word from God to his hearers, ... in order that the text may speak ... and be heard making each point from his text in such a manner 'that [his audience] may discern [the voice of God].'"[12]

Admonition

Solomon says in Ecclesiastes 12:11–12, the words of the wise are like goads which prick and nails that stick. They will move us into action; action that leads us to being conformed to the image of Christ. Koller writes, "The supreme test of all preaching is: what happens in the pew? To John

---

[12] J. I. Packer, *God Has Spoken* (Downers Grove, IL: IVP, 1979), 28.

the Baptist there was accorded the highest tribute that could ever come to a minister of the gospel; when they had heard John, 'they followed Jesus!'"[13]

Wise words are like goads, they prod the sluggish and hesitant into action. They have a power to provide a mental and spiritual stimulus, a spiritual shot-in-the-arm. Wise words of "the master of assemblies" are also like well driven nails. They stabilize on the one hand, and give us something to hang things on, on the other. H. C. Leupold notes, "they furnish a kind of mental anchorage."[14]

The end of verse 11 is a direct declaration of divine inspiration. The "knowledge" (verse 9) and the "words of truth" (verse 10) are given by one Shepherd, the Lord who is my Shepherd (Psalm 23), the Good Shepherd, Jesus Christ (John 10).

J. Stafford Wright warns the preacher, "It is possible to be a miser in accumulating knowledge instead of using it for the benefit of others."[15] Solomon the realist knows there is no end to book making. Just imagine if he were alive today! And yet he is not down on books and down on study or knowledge in principle. He is down on it as an end in itself. Knowledge is not the same as wisdom. It is possible to be smart but not intelligent. It is possible to know a lot but not be wise. God's design for our lives is not to make us smart sinners but godly saints!

If we are not careful and wise, we can linger too long at the "Vanity Fair of Knowledge," only to miss out on the wisdom of God and a life that is really worth living. Billy Barnes puts it well in colorful poetic expression. He gives us something to think about in "Have I Stayed Too Long at the Fair."

> I wanted the music to play on forever—
> Have I stayed too long at the fair?
> I wanted the clown to be constantly clever—
> Have I stayed too long at the fair?
> I bought me blue ribbons to tie up my hair,
> But I couldn't find anybody to care.
> The merry-go-round is beginning to slow now,
> Have I stayed too long at the fair?
> I wanted to live in a carnival city, with
> Laughter and love everywhere.
> I wanted my friends to be thrilling and witty,

[13] Koller, *Expository Preaching*, 19.

[14] H.C. Leupold, *Exposition of Ecclesiastes* (Grand Rapids, MI: Baker, 1952), 295.

[15] J. Stafford Wright, "Ecclesiastes," in *EBC* vol. 5 (Grand Rapids, MI: Zondervan, 1986), 1196.

I wanted somebody to care.
I found my blue ribbons all shiny and new,
But now I've discovered them no longer blue.
The merry-go-round is beginning to taunt me—
Have I stayed too long at the fair?
There is nothing to win and no one to want me—
Have I stayed too long at the fair?

Some of us have stayed too long at various vanity fairs in life (knowledge, power, sex, popularity, wealth). Let God's word guide your priorities. Let God's Word chart the course of your life.

Exhortation

John Piper reminds us, "It is not the job of the Christian preacher to give people moral or psychological pep talks about how to get along in the world; someone else can do that … most of our people have no one in the world to tell them, week in and week out, about the supreme beauty and majesty of God."[16]

And just where is this "supreme beauty and majesty of God" found? It is found in the glory of Jesus Christ who is the very face of God. When I preach I always ask 5 questions of each and every text:

1) What does this text teach us about *God*?

2) What does this text teach us about *fallen man*?

3) What do I want my people to *know*?

4) What do I want my people to *do*?

5) How does this text *point to Jesus*?

You see Jesus teaches us in Luke 24 that all of Scripture is about Him, all of it. We dare not treat the Old Testament, for example, like a Jewish rabbi. In this regard I have been greatly blessed by men like Vos, Gredanius, Goldsworthy and Keller. To gain just a taste of what Christo-centric hermeneutics and homiletics can do, listen to the insight of Tim Keller as he scans the redemptive storyline of the Old Testament.

---

[16] John Piper, *The Supremacy of God in Preaching* (Grand Rapids, MI: Baker, 1993), 12.

It's All About Jesus (slightly revised)

Jesus is the true and better *Adam* who passed the test in the wilderness not the garden, and whose obedience is imputed to us.

Jesus is the true and better *Abel* who, though innocently slain by wicked hands, has blood now that cries out, not for our condemnation, but for our acquittal.

Jesus is the better *Ark of Noah* who carries us safely thru the wrath of God revealed from heaven and delivers us to a new earth.

Jesus is the true and better *Abraham* who answered the call of God to leave all that is comfortable and familiar and go out into the world not knowing where he went to create a new people of God.

Jesus is the true and better *Isaac* who was not just offered up by his father on the mount but was truly sacrificed for us. And when God said to Abraham, "Now I know you love me because you did not withhold your son, your only son whom you love from me," now we can look at God taking his son up the mountain of Calvary and sacrificing him and say, "Now we know that you love us because you did not withhold your Son, your only Son, whom you love, from us."

Jesus is the true and better *Jacob* who wrestled and took the blow of justice we deserved, so we, like Jacob, only receive the wounds of grace to wake us up and discipline us.

Jesus is the true and better *Joseph* who, at the right hand of the king, forgives those who betrayed him and sold him, and uses his new power to save them.

Jesus is the true and better *Moses* who stands in the gap between the people and the Lord and who mediates a new covenant.

Jesus is the true and better *Rock of Moses* who, struck with the rod of God's justice, now gives us living water in the desert.

Jesus is the true and better *Joshua*, who leads us into a land of eternal rest and heavenly blessing.

Jesus is the better *Ark of the Covenant* who topples and disarms the idols of this world, going Himself into enemy territory, and making an open spectacle of them all.

Jesus is the true and better *Job*, the truly innocent sufferer, who then intercedes for and saves his stupid friends.

Jesus is the true and better *David* whose victory becomes his people's victory, though they never lifted a stone to accomplish it themselves.

Jesus is the true and better *Esther* who didn't just risk leaving an earthly palace but lost the ultimate and heavenly one, who didn't just risk his life, but gave his life to save his people.

Jesus is the true and better *Daniel*, having been lowered into a lions den of death, emerges early the next morning alive and vindicated by His God.

Jesus is the true and better *Jonah* who was cast out into the storm so that we safely could be brought in.

Jesus is the *real Passover Lamb*, innocent, perfect, helpless, slain, so the angel of death will pass over us. He's the *true temple*, the *true prophet*, the *true priest*, the *true king*, the *true sacrifice*, the *true lamb*, the *true light*, and the *true bread*.

The Bible really is not about you is it? It really is all about Him.[17]

Oh how this needs to be reflected in our preaching.

The phrase "Let us hear the conclusion of the whole matter," could be paraphrased for our day: "when everything is said and done." In other words, what is the bottom-line, the end-game? Solomon says it is two-fold: 1) fear God and 2) keep His commandments. Trust Him and then obey Him. The order is crucial.

"Fear God" means to put God in His proper place, us in our proper place, and all fears, hopes, dreams and agendas in their proper place. The clear and consistent teaching and encouragement of the Word of God is essential if this is to take place. "Fear God": what does the text teach me about God? "Keep His commandments": what does this teach me about me? "Keep His commandments": obey Him out of love and respect for *who* He is and *what* He has done. You see it is accepted: I obey! It is not I obey so that I can be accepted. "For this is man's all." The NIV says, "For this is the whole duty of man." Augustine (AD 354–430) said it well, "thou hast made us for thyself, and our heart is restless till it rest in thee." We will never find rest, until we come to rest in Jesus.

Therefore every thought and every action will be exposed to the search light of God's judgment. Not one thing will escape.

---

[17] Tim Keller, "It's All About Jesus," 4 December 2006, available online at: http://kaleobill.com/?p–264 (accessed 8 October 2009).

"Every work": our actions.

"Every secret thing": our thoughts.

"Good or bad": it will all come to light.

One of my spiritual heroes and friends in his last years was the great expositor Stephen Olford (1918–2004). On the wall of his private study there hangs a plaque containing a quote from one of Dr. Olford's heroes, Robert Murray M'Cheyne. On that plaque are the words, "Lord, make me as holy as a saved sinner can be!"[18]

This is a good word from a great preacher. This is a good word for any preacher who understands the exhortation of *qoheleth*, "Fear God and keep His commands, for this is the whole duty of man" (NIV).

Cotton Mather, the American Puritan, accurately assessed the nature of our holy assignment when he said, "The office of the Christian ministry, rightly understood, is the honorable and most important, that any man in the whole world can ever sustain; and it will be one of the wonders and employments of eternity to consider the reasons why the wisdom and goodness of God assigned this office to imperfect and guilty man!"[19]

The preacher has given us some wise words on preaching. We need to hear his counsel. We need to act on his instruction. Let's preach beautiful truth in a beautiful way all for the glory of a beautiful Savior whose name is Jesus.

---

[18] See Andrew Bonar, *Memoir and Remains of Robert Murray M'Cheyne* (Carlisle, PA: Banner of Truth, 2004), 159.

[19] Quoted in John Stott, *Between Two Worlds* (Grand Rapids, MI: Eerdmans, 1982), 31.

14

An Idol Called Evangelism
AND ITS REMEDY

Roy A. Hargrave

It is with a measure of fear and trepidation that I enter into what some may see as a volatile opinion involving such a sacred task as *evangelism*. Though I obviously leave each person to his own conscience, I submit that my own is thoroughly convinced of the conclusions herewith explained. These conclusions are not absolute as to their application concerning every Christian or congregation. However, it is my conviction that the subsequent fallacies presented in this treatise are widely accepted and appropriated among churches and individuals who profess Christ. If true, the trend is alarming, if not immensely disastrous, within the realm of external Christianity.

My faith in God's sovereignty both emboldens me and encourages me to stay the course, knowing that our God and His church will finally be gloriously triumphant though often assailed these days by the slings and arrows of the enemy. Two fundamental elements must be addressed if the disastrous effects of unbiblical evangelistic methods are going to be diverted from what may well be the primary cause of a prophesied apostasy of the church (2 Timothy 4:3).

The first element is of a practical nature. It involves the proper placement of evangelism's importance among all theological doctrines. Prioritizations of things important are to be carefully discerned and established if we are to keep our spiritual wits. Secondly, theological content must be examined critically as to evangelism's doctrinal purity. It must be sustained within biblical parameters. There is no room for pragmatic subtractions, additions or alterations. What follows is a treatise of the essential elements that by God's grace may further enable the reviving of evangelism's biblical intent.

It is not without reservation that a preacher of the gospel would call into question what the Holy Scripture declares to be a most profound exercise. This is especially true of a divine commission that has been irrevocably delegated to the church of the Living God.

Clearly, it would be heretical to lay an unwarranted claim against the very means that God has ordained in rescuing the perishing from their fallen state. Evangelism, as set forth in the divine revelation, is foundational to reaching the lost with the gospel of Christ. Any opposition to that prescription is tantamount to plotting the ruination of Zion. However, in light of a necessary sensitivity regarding the sacred charge of evangelism, as well as our hallowed duty to guard its purity, it seems unusual that we unwittingly allow for the multiplied mutations of it.

The church must be awakened to this matter lest we relinquish the saving message as taught in the Word of God. Sadly, too many Christians assume that the means of evangelism is never in danger of evolving into a hybrid form that is foreign to the practice prescribed in the New Testament. Thus, it is imperative that such apathy ceases as soon as possible. If it does not end quickly, preachers of the gospel may find themselves vulnerable to the practice of spiritual malfeasance—one that results, not in a temporal setback for the hearers, but in their eternal destruction.

Though it may appear to the unwary as an unlikely occurrence in the body of Christ, we must maintain vigilance in guarding the purity of this most sacred assignment of New Testament evangelism. To engage in anything less than the due diligence required in this matter is akin to spiritual homicide. What a travesty when medical doctors take greater care of their patients than the doctors of the soul take care of their hearers. While physical maladies are of a temporal nature, it must be emphasized that spiritual maladies involve eternal consequences.

My burden is to set before you what has become a burgeoning dismantling of biblical evangelism. It is being replaced in many quarters by an amalgamated semblance that is but a shadow of the true substance. The title of this chapter could be misleading, seeing that evangelism as established in Scripture is not an idol. Rather, the idol is evangelism that has been incrementally contrived by those who unwittingly seek an easier pill for the lost to swallow. The only problem is that it turns out to be a placebo that serves to placate the guilty conscience through a faulty diagnosis.

The ill-informed hearers of such a truncated gospel further exacerbate the case—seeing that they mistakenly, yea tragically, are convinced of their man-made remedy. This is a remedy that has only served to numb their consciences with a carnally inspired elixir of spiritual morphine.

The degree to which preachers of every ilk go into this emerging vacillation about the true nature of the biblical evangel varies greatly. However, this reality must not negate the necessity of being starkly awakened to a possible, if not probable, catastrophe—if left unattended.

The prioritization of evangelism in our churches today, above all else, furnishes ample illustrations of man's propensity to fall into the traditions of manufactured counterfeits. Clearly, we must set our hearts upon that which supersedes all other ideas or practices. Put another way, if we prioritize a vital component over another element, one exceeding that component in value, we are engaging in confusing carnal beliefs and practices. Understand that to value the means of evangelism above a most infinitely supreme end is to devalue both.

The church's primary purpose and goal should be, without controversy, to glorify God and enjoy Him forever (see Ephesians 1). Therefore, if evangelism, as a means, is prioritized, even in a fashion thoroughly biblical over its proper end, it becomes an idol that replaces its greatest end—the manifestation and enjoyment of God's infinite glory.

The irony of the prioritization of such a means as evangelism over the glory of God is that such promotion becomes the primary root of biblical evangelism's dilution, if not demise. When the greatest end is relegated to a lower position than the means to that end, the greater priority is slighted and the lesser is unduly magnified.

Placing this controversy in perspective, it must be generally accepted among the wise that ends are always superior to the means to those ends. Not that means are unnecessary, for according to the Word, God has decreed the ends as well as the means. Both are therefore absolutely necessary in the economy of God.

Furthermore, it is a most essential truth in spiritual matters that means are transitory while the ends are eternal. Evangelism by necessity will ultimately reach its own termination, while the glory of God will never end. This alone should provide sufficient knowledge about that which is to be as supreme in the church today as it will be throughout eternity.

This is not a mere polemical argument invented to disturb the unity of the church of God as to the necessary task of evangelism. It is, however, an essential, substantial defense against the covert departure from properly motivated and biblically prescribed means of evangelism. It is difficult to ignore that such means of evangelism as are commonly used in our present day are often absent within the biblical narrative.

If evangelism is the highest priority in the church, as many now propose, it opens a greater temptation to tamper with its approach in making it more palatable to the lost. If this is the priority, it is more likely to produce a compromised evangelism that promotes emotional responses, fire engine baptisteries and knee-jerk reactions toward those who possess an extremely shallow understanding of necessary truth.

This may temporarily increase our churches numerically while decreasing our true spirituality, as the glory of God is subsequently relegated to a lower position. However, if the glory of God is the ultimate goal of the church, we are more likely to seek those prescribed means of evangelism set forth by the Lord in His Word.

The gospel truth should be accepted and taught unashamedly, as it is in Scripture (see Romans 1:16). Remember, it is "the foolishness of the message preached" (1 Corinthians 1:21, NKJV) that intrigues those who believe.

The fruit of today's generally accepted means of evangelism among the churches of God effectively betrays its flaws. Noticeable is a reduction in the knowledge necessary to believe the truth. Christianity demands knowledge, for God's Word explicitly states that "… you will know the truth, and the truth will set you free" (John 8:32, ESV). Unlike all other religions (which are fatally flawed), Christianity demands truth taught and comprehended as foundational to its genuine nature.

To improve on our secure acquisition of the true nature of Christianity, we must often be reminded that knowledge isolated from understanding (rationally and spiritually) is of no eternal value. Misunderstood knowledge is not knowledge at all; it is just as damning as no knowledge. Partial knowledge of salvation equates to one with no saving knowledge. Granted, all necessary knowledge is not known at once, but, ultimately, it must be true that all necessary knowledge be known if salvation is to be wrought in the heart.

The false reaction against such reasoning often speaks of Holy Spirit work that overcomes what is lacking in proclaimed truth. Of course, this is extremely dangerous reasoning and thoroughly unbiblical, if not damnable. The Holy Spirit bears witness to the Word—not apart from the Word but through the Word properly proclaimed and understood. It is certainly not by way of a mystical manifestation separate from Holy Scriptures, as we have observed among Eastern religions that possess no objective or propositional reality.

The means of Holy Spirit illumination and the understanding of the mind to revealed truth are both necessary ingredients in saving a soul (see Colossians 1:3–6). To deny either is to deny the proper means as prescribed in Holy Scripture.

The believer's witness is a means whereby the Holy Spirit uses the gospel treasure within weak earthen vessels as though God Himself were beseeching sinful men through them (2 Corinthians 5:18–20) to turn from darkness to light, from Satan to Christ, from sin to salvation.

Paul states in Romans 10:14–15 (ESV):

> But how are they to call on him in whom they have not believed? And how are they to believe in him of whom they have never heard? And how are they to hear without someone preaching? And how are they to preach unless they are sent? As it is written, "How beautiful are the feet of those who preach the good news!"

The good news, of course, is not always proclaimed according to biblical imperatives. For instance, if you carefully peruse many of the tracts that are prevalent among evangelicals, you will discover quickly the unfortunate general disregard of essential elements of necessary gospel knowledge.

Tracts are not unavoidably faulty in nature, though their necessary brevity often produces some confusion. I have, however, read some very excellent tracts that do present, as much as possible, a rather thorough presentation of necessary truth. Though I do not find it necessary to condemn the concept, I do warn of their propensity to oversimplify truth, as well as dangerously condense vital matters.

For instance, how many tracts or contrived evangelistic approaches engage in a clear presentation of God's nature? Consider the prevalent lack of information within the general tone of most tracts or canned presentations. They often fail to expose and explain any portion of God's attributes or other fundamental truths concerning His nature. If they do, in fact, address God's holy nature, it is usually extremely superficial, if not incidental.

Is it readily known among the hearers of such approaches that God's throne is built upon the foundation of His justice? Is it clearly stated that such justice is infinitely holy, as well as inflexible? Does the sinner who listens to these incomplete presentations and contrived prayers know that God demands of them an absolute perfection according to His Holy Law?

You may answer that the Law is not the gospel, for God is also merciful. Of course, but the problem with teaching the sinner the mercy of God outside of the context of His divine justice is to paint a false picture of God's redemptive purposes, as well as to diminish the greatness of the Savior's infinite sacrifice.

First and foremost, the nature of God in His righteousness and holiness is a source of fear, which is the beginning of wisdom (Proverbs 1). Secondly, the sight of Mount Sinai, where the Law was revealed, was a most terrible and frightful scene for those who stood at the foot of it (Exodus 19). It was so much so that the people finally requested that Moses speak in the stead of God due to God's overwhelming holiness displayed before sinful beings. Though few have been to Mount Sinai physically, all of us have spiritually arrived there by way of conscience. It has transported us there to behold the awful smoke and fire of conviction that is set ablaze by the immutable demands of a holy God.

Is this really the God to whom lost sinners are usually introduced in these days of moralistic preaching and excessive practical applications in the context of horizontal relationships? Evangelism's priority over the glory of God reduces truth to a level of practical, palatable assertions. Such assertions produce no offense to the sinner and usually plant his carnal faith in an unknown god. It is purely the work of the Holy Spirit that produces a sorrow about one's sins, as Paul told the Corinthian church: "For godly sorrow produces repentance leading to salvation ..." (2 Corinthians 7:10a, NKJV).

If evangelism's external result is the goal, then God actually being made known to the sinner may be lost because of practical necessity. Another way to put it is that we often see sinners as potential notches on our evangelistic belts more than as potential worshipers of the One True God. It is plainly stated in holy texts that God is found when He is sought with one's whole heart, not the present abundance of half-hearted giddiness.

More must be made of the previous allusion to Mount Sinai. In the gospel of God, what role does the law of God play? Isn't it to be made known to the sinner? Do we assume today that the law is readily taught to the unconverted, seeing that the law "is perfect, converting the soul ..." (Psalm 19:7, NKJV)? Can a sinner be led to Christ when the sinner has never sat under the schoolmaster of the law (Galatians 3:24–25)? Doesn't the law alone teach the sinner his great sinfulness and unworthiness before the law's inflexible and holy justice (Romans 7:7–8)?

This is often set aside for lighter words of comfort to the sinner, though the sinner is in direct opposition to the ways of God and hostile toward His revealed will (Romans 8:7). Can an unbroken sinner ever desire to come freely to the Savior? Would he ever want to come to God, seeing that he seeks not this Holy One, according to God's own declarations (Romans 3)?

Evangelism's prioritization is the culprit here. Decisions are what evangelism as an end produces, and such decisions are often contrived within man instead of through God's mercy and regenerative work. Baptisms are exalted beyond measure when the glory of God is ignored. Results are the desired ends of a godless pragmatism that has wrapped its tentacles around those who were once loyal to a biblical model.

This model is often hard and slow in fruitfulness because the immediate result of such a forthright gospel is usually that of offense due to man's sinful pride. We know that the true gospel "... is the power of God for salvation to everyone who believes ..." (Romans 1:16, ESV). But Paul also states that the same gospel is also foolishness and an offense to those who are perishing (1 Corinthians 1:18).

Furthermore, we must not forget that God's judgment is to be proclaimed. Where are the hell-fire and damnation sermons today? They are generally relegated to the shelf for a more self-serving message of man's self-esteem and preeminence. Hell's fury is not the primary motivator of the lost to seek the Lord, for the Law has that duty. But it is well-intentioned that the Holy Spirit who inspired the Word of God through men intended for its contents to be preached faithfully and without apology. That, of course, applies to all doctrines, many of which may bring great offense against the Word of God and the preacher of it.

We have so bought into the self-improvement of man in place of the redemption of man that we naturally throw out all obstacles to man's carnal longings. This is more prevalent than most Christians believe in our day. We must fight the urge to be liked and lauded. We must preach again the whole counsel of God, which alone is used by the Holy Spirit in saving the lost.

One brief thought on repentance: When we preach to those who live together out of wedlock or are presently engaged in open godlessness, no decision can rid the soul of sin unless there has been wrought a change of habit through their faith in Christ (Matthew 3:8). To receive such sinners who have jumped through the evangelistic hoops we've contrived is not sufficient if there is no fruit displayed. We're playing games and infecting the church with lost converts when we play these games. True biblical evangelism is the only cure.

Our attempt at promoting evangelism to the throne of our church's assigned duties is to dethrone God Himself. Such misplaced priorities are the very root and foundation of the sheer silliness we observe in our churches across this land. When we will not apply necessary discipline in our churches toward sin, it suggests that numbers are more vital than true disciples (Matthew 28:18–20). Evangelism isolated from God's glory and His whole counsel is extremely dangerous, even deadly, since it promotes carnal practices in order to reach its goals.

When we suggest a million baptisms for the coming year, we are out of line. God is the one who saves, and those He saves are within the bounds of His secret will. Finney is still alive and well among us as we continue to contrive carnal methods of evangelism that will keep the waters in our baptisteries moving.

Think not that truly saved men do not desire the salvation of the lost. Not only that a few would come to Christ but that many would flood our churches and be saved. Those, however, who seek to plot such activity by carnal means are foolish in their efforts. Living a godly life, praying fervently and proclaiming boldly the whole truth of God's Word (publicly and privately) is the prescription set forth in the Scriptures.

Some suggest that the follow-up programs are at fault. I find that to be the fruit of misinformation. If the soul is saved by a supernatural work of the Holy Spirit, such a person will both desire and seek more food for His redeemed soul. We've got to stop wasting our time propping up dead corpses in our churches while the world is going to hell (1 John 2:19).

Let us press on toward the reconciliation of such hard justice and loving mercy. What about inflexible justice in light of gospel mercy? It must be understood that God's justice is absolute and irrevocable. Not one sin will go unpaid in the Holy One's economy. There it is, standing before us as an impregnable fortress around which no sinner can negotiate.

But we must not leave the poor sinner, even as we once were, before such hopelessness. After all, justice, righteousness and holiness are not alone in God's beauties. There is also mercy, which is not inflexible as in His justice but is bestowed according to God's own inimitable discretion. God owes no man such mercy, though He owes every man His divine retribution.

What is horribly absent from the message of many preachers in our day is that God possesses within His Holy nature no obligation to save any sinner. Otherwise, His bestowed salvation would be out of debt toward man, which is absurd. It is by grace that man is saved through faith. It is not by way of man's own strivings or will (Romans 9:16). It is all God (see Romans 9:15; Galatians 2:8–9). Failing to understand this truth hinders a man from being hedged into God's free mercy alone, since he, in his depraved heart (Jeremiah 17:9), may still contrive hopes of God's obligation toward him. Tragically, this is indeed false hope.

The wrath God owes to man is just and right, and God's mercy carries with it no obligation to sinful beings. This was clearly manifested when some of the holy angels, led by Lucifer, fell from their own habitation and God directed no hint of mercy toward them. Rather, He consigned some of them to chains until the consummation of the ages. He permitted others to roam the earth and engage in Satan's bidding against the Sacred Head and His offspring until their damnation is ultimately secured in the Lake of Fire. This should bring sufficient fear to the rebel who dares to oppose the purposes of the Most High God.

Where then do the justice of God and His mercy meet? When and where do they find reconciliation within the thrice-holy God? It is at the cross where we see justice and mercy kiss. But there is a precursor required for such apparent antithetical friends as justice and mercy to embrace. It was typified in the ceremonial laws of the Old Testament revelation.

We see there the foreshadowing by way of a spotless lamb without blemish. Abraham's foreshadowing revealed a substitute as of a ram caught in a thicket (Genesis 22:13). The substance of this substitution was found in one—and one only—who was worthy to take the scroll and open it. His name is Jesus Christ, the substance of past shadows who is both man and God—not co-mingled but retaining the nature of both God in fullness and man in fullness within the one person.

He was made man through the Holy Spirit's miraculous conception through the seed of a woman. His conception happened without Adam's imputed sin that rested upon all the rest of the race. He was God by divine right through His eternal procession from the Father. He was thusly qualified in His person as to this seemingly impossible task of attaining mercy for sinful rebels without marring the inflexibility of the divine justice of the blessed triune God.

Another vital element had to be displayed before all of God's creation for Christ to be thoroughly qualified for such ends. His perfect obedience, required by God, had to remain flawless. No sin in thought, word or deed before God and man could be indulged within the purity of necessary holiness. He had to retain His absolute holiness in all things, without even a hint of disobedience. This He accomplished, proving His impeccability through trials and temptations that were conquered through His Holy nature. Jesus was tempted "… as we are, yet without sin" (Hebrews 4:15, ESV).

Qualified in His Holy Person and through His impeccability, Jesus was ready for His supreme moment. It was to be the apex of human history when the blessed God-Man ascended by way of cruel hands upon Mount Calvary to fulfill what man could not fulfill at Mount Sinai.

The law was holy, but man's flesh was sinful and unable to attain righteousness based upon his own tarnished merits. Therefore, there must be an alien righteousness, outside of man's sinful self, that could pave the way to eternal glory. It was Christ who accomplished such mighty works. He became what was typified in the Old Covenant ceremonies. He gave Himself as a substitute in man's hopeless state and became a sin offering to God. He retained all holiness, yet was declared by His Father a proper and acceptable sacrifice to satisfy God's immutable justice and placate His holy wrath by bearing man's sin on the cross.

It was the Father who bruised Him and put Him to shame there, because He was, through the everlasting covenant, ordained within the Trinity as the Mediator of a New Covenant. It was through the mediation of Christ's precious blood wherein God's justice alone could be satisfied and His wrath satisfied.

Mankind had been consigned to justice's demand, in that we were all in the loins of the first Adam in the Garden of Eden and thusly condemned. When he disobeyed, we also disobeyed in him, our federal head, thusly the assigned representative of the whole race. We, like Adam, were undone and without hope except that in God's infinite wisdom He designed an acceptable means whereby His own inflexible justice and discretionary mercy could be righteously retained.

This seemingly impossible task was accomplished through Christ on the cross. God's justice fully satisfied and the mercy of God exercised were fully beheld at Golgotha. For those whom the Father had given to His Son from eternity, Christ suffered in His body and soul the Father's infinite vengeance against the sinner. This was of absolute necessity, due to the inflexible nature of God's justice.

The price of sin was death—infinite, eternal death—and Christ paid to the last farthing with His own precious blood, satisfying the justice of God in His flesh and not without the infinite nature of His deity. When He cried, "It is finished" (John 19:30), the required payment had been completed in full, wherein the way to heaven was paved. This is evangelism's foundation, without which no man can be saved.

Such justice was not alone on that cross; mercy also attended. It was God's design and desire to manifest His great love and mercy through His own Son to pay the sinner's debt, though His resplendent character demanded no obligation. As Paul stated in Romans 3:26, "It was to show his righteousness at the present time, so that he might be just and the justifier of the one who has faith in Jesus."

It is not unusual for one to believe that such an extraordinary salvation—as found within the context of the fall of man through the last Adam's substitution—is infinitely superior to a salvation that could have been derived from the first Adam's probationary obedience in the garden, had he not fallen. In other words, the salvation of the lost through Christ's obedience and sacrifice is necessarily of infinite superiority to all other contingencies known to God.

This eventuality alone could provide the most glorious exaltation of the eternal Mediator, Jesus Christ, as well as the blessed Godhead. This is evangelism's ultimate end that is to be supremely exalted in the church of the Living God. When God is extolled above all else in the church, His desired end is ultimately accomplished.

Such faith required by God is His gift given without impurity and improper motives. Faith is not conjured up in man's fallen depravity, but it is produced by Spirit-inspired truth and regeneration. It is assuredly evident to the sinner that what brought him to such faith was previously unknown to him due to spiritual ignorance and unmitigated depravity.

But now God's redemptive purpose has supplied the necessary knowledge where man is illuminated by spiritual conviction. He is also secured by new birth to desire above all else the highest good, which is God glorified and enjoyed forever by His redeemed. Such mighty work produces the necessary conversion, which involves turning away from sin (repentance) and turning to salvation (faith) found in Christ alone. Such solace and peace are eternally established in that soul, which discovers it through grace. He experiences Christ as his own Sabbath rest.

Implicit in faith is the repentance that cannot be neglected for faith, for there is no faith without repentance, and there is no repentance without faith (see Acts 20:20). Both are gifts, and both produce a declared justification by the Father. This justification was secured by the merits of Christ who has bestowed on His elect an alien righteousness, which cannot be rescinded:

> For the gifts and the calling of God are irrevocable (Romans 11:29, ESV).

> Now may the God of peace who brought again from the dead our Lord Jesus, the great shepherd of the sheep, by the blood of the eternal covenant ... (Hebrews 13:20, ESV).

> ... whatever God does endures forever; nothing can be added to it, nor anything taken from it (Ecclesiastes 3:14, ESV).

Such is the glory bestowed in the heart by the warrant of the Holy Spirit that one's desire for others to know of such love flows naturally from the converted. This is the underpinning of all true and fervent evangelistic motives.

Is this end not the greatest end, seeing that God has decreed it? Instead of a manufactured evangelism, which has manifested its evil intent throughout the centuries of Christianity, we see and know a faith founded in truth and inspiring awe in the soul's longing for that remedy, which alone can mend such a loathsome malady.

Candy is sweet to the taste but rots the teeth. Such is the nature of an evangelism that finds little or no foundation in Holy Writ and rots the soul. Milk and meat are necessary to a balanced diet that builds the sinew and muscles of the spiritual man. Some may suggest that we have not enough time to engage in such an extended exercise of consistent feedings of the soul, for the night of judgment is rapidly approaching.

Could it be to our favor to teach a man half the truth in a day rather than teach a man all the truth in a lifetime? What good is a half-truth conversion in a man whose death has been assigned to this day? This is not the ranting of a mad man, for I have William Carey, the father of modern-day missions, as my witness. Who among us knows not of Carey's appellation? Furthermore, who has forgotten his long labor of love in India—a labor that strove through a long and arduous seven years before the first conversion was bestowed upon his labor?

Of course, we live in the days of ATMs, plastic cards and fast-food restaurants. We are into shortcuts and quick-fix solutions. How foolish is it for us to strive in gaining more converts through half-witted measures than to gain true converts through laborious sacrifice and persevering proclamation of sound doctrine?

If you mistakenly read into such practices—properly maintained by our spiritual forefathers—that there should be no sense of urgency in soul-winning, you miss the point. Both urgency and patience are required, but when one usurps the other, it usually produces unexpected, unfruitful consequences. To persuade the uninformed with newly contrived measures is to multiply their ignorance. To patiently inform the uninformed while waiting on the Lord to accomplish the work that only He can do is supremely wise and fruitful.

Urgency must attend to our patient instruction, but it must not usurp it. Nor may patience usurp biblical urgency. "Today is the day of salvation" is urgency declared (see 2 Corinthians 6:2). But to pray as a watchman over the souls of men, though their conversion is often delayed, is the bounty of their godly perseverance. Both are biblical and necessary in God's providential dealings with His creatures.

It is quite interesting that Christ's three-year ministry, which included miracles, mighty works and previously unrevealed truths, resulted in only 120 believers praying in an upper room—after He had died and arisen from the dead. Today, most "experts" in evangelism would likely call that discouraging, unfortunate and unfruitful. It shows the wise that Christ was patient with sinners and that His model should be exampled in His followers.

Forget not, that after such patience was satisfied, 3,000 were suddenly converted through necessary knowledge and Holy Spirit conviction. The lot of each was not an altar call but the question of conscience: "Men and brethren, *what shall we do* [to be saved]?" (Acts 2:37, NKJV, emphasis added).

The subject of evangelism causes much division regarding its place and priority in the church. Unfortunately, much of it is produced by human pride and an overwhelming desire to be praised by our peers as fruitful. When a man is driven by such motives, dangerous consequences usually follow. If numbers, buildings, prestige, money and position are moving us to evangelize the unsaved, the glory of God is lost in such improper motives.

Consequently, the methods of evangelism are engineered according to such motives. When the glory of God is our true motive in evangelism, that desire serves as a guardian against hidden agendas and unscriptural methods.

Christ is an example of proper motives and methods in evangelism. His pure message often supplied more departures from His mercies than converts. He drove away a rich man who, in our day, would have willingly repeated the sinner's prayer and most likely helped pay for the church's new facility. On many occasions, he also supplied such necessary truth that even His few disciples questioned their own responses while watching thousands leave His side, never to follow Him again. Seminaries and churches today would not be able to practice Christ's approach to the lost, as quintessential evangelism is practiced today. His would not meet the standards of our prevalent quick-fix religious culture.

Please understand: when a preacher is most interested in building the church (which Christ alone can do) and less interested in glorifying God through cross-bearing faithfulness, he is much more susceptible to passing fads which engulf many congregations on a regular basis. In such a context, biblical Christianity is usually sacrificed on the altar of pragmatism and self-promotion. This leads to numerous instances of false conversions, as well as congregational confusion.

It must be stated succinctly that biblical evangelism is the greatest means whereby the glory of God—the greatest end—is made known here on earth. It is not my intent to subvert evangelism. It is my desire to promote it to the heights to which Christ has already promoted it. But the evangelism practiced today does not necessarily meet that standard.

Our goal of promoting soul-winning through the incessant demand for the ascendency of evangelism over the glory of God is the very death of it. Look around. Is this not, in fact, the general reality in our churches today? It is amazing that we live in a time when there are, more than ever before, a myriad of books about evangelism, numerous conferences, countless seminars and sermons trying to stir our people to engage in evangelism. Yet, we are all aware of the general dearth of true evangelism in our churches. What does that say of our new-found approaches? When was the last Great Awakening in your town, city or country? Sadly, we all know the tragic answer to that question.

Could it be that we have placed this means above the very person of God? Could it be that we have forgotten that true religion is to have a true knowledge of God and His Beloved Son through whom a saving mediation alone rescues the lost and dying? I think it is so with the common persuasion of the masses that profess Christianity.

It is not my hope and prayer alone, but of many, that God's rightful place requires all other elements as subservient to God alone. Evangelism is temporal, but God is eternal. Let us live as though we actually believe it to be so. Perhaps God may be merciful to such pitiful and unfruitful servants and pour another mighty spiritual awakening upon our dull, hardened hearts.

May God have mercy on our souls and on our churches! May He be glorified above all our means, programs, principles, goals, ad nauseam, Amen!

15

Missions and the Doctrines of Grace

David Sills

God is saving sinners all over the world today, granting them repentance and faith to believe on the risen Christ and bringing them to fall before Him in worship. Although He needs nothing outside of Himself, He chooses to use men and women, churches, and mission agencies, and all of their sacrificial efforts in the process. This complex whole of philosophies, missiologies, strategies and methodologies is what we refer to as missions.

The foundation of all missions efforts flows from the heart of our missionary God. He Himself came to Adam and Eve when they had sinned and were hiding in contrition and shame. God shed the first blood to cover their sin (Genesis 3:21) and pronounced the *protoevangelion* that one day One would come through the seed of the woman to defeat the serpent and his work (Genesis 3:15). Throughout the Old and New Testaments, we see God's missionary heart in His sending prophets to the nations, receiving foreign-born God-fearers and so loving the world that He sent His only-begotten Son.

The Necessity of the Gospel

The gospel is the only hope of salvation for the people groups of the world; there is no salvation apart from hearing the gospel and being born again. The world's peoples are not spiritually neutral beings who hear the gospel and become lost if they reject Christ; they are condemned already. Psalm 19:1–4 and Romans 1:18–20 teach that from general revelation everyone knows that there is a Creator. Romans 2:14–15 teach that God has given us consciences, reasoning minds, and His law on our hearts so that we know that we have sinned against Him. This is the reason that every culture in the world has devised some form of religion; it is an effort to reestablish their relationship with the deity that their conscience tells them they have offended. Yet, general revelation is not sufficient to teach them how they may know God and be born again for their salvation. Therefore, God has revealed Himself in His Word and it is with this special revelation that we learn of Him. God gave us His Word that we might know Him and make Him known, and that is the heartbeat of missions—knowing God and making Him known.

Many passages in the Bible teach about the missions task, but few so clearly as the Great Commission (Matthew 28:18–20). In this passage, Jesus announces that all authority in heaven and on earth has been given to Him. Therefore, missionaries should not fear to go into all the world to preach the gospel. No closed, or creative-access, country will be able to withstand His work through His Word and His church. He commands the church primarily to make disciples, for this is the only imperative verb in the Great Commission passage. He reveals how we are to do this work, explaining that we are to teach them to observe everything He commanded. The participle "go" at the beginning of the commission may not be in the imperative form, but it is an important part of the command, because He further defines where we are to make disciples—"of all nations." This, of course, is *panta ta ethne* in the Greek, which clarifies that the recipients are to be all the ethnicities (or people groups), not geopolitical entities like China, Chile, or Canada. Jesus also commands His church to baptize them, and since baptism is a church ordinance, this shows that we are not only make disciples but also to form them into churches for worship, fellowship and mutual edification. Finally, the passage shows that this missions effort was not intended only for those who stood there listening that day; Jesus promises to be with us in the process until the end of the age. Certainly, there are many other passages of God's Word that inform the entirety of the missionary task, yet the unavoidable truth is that the bare-minimum essentials of missions are that we are to be reaching (making disciples) all the people groups (of all nations) and teaching them (everything He has commanded us). The Great Commission and other missions passages are in the Bible of every missionary, yet some have found more ministry fruit, longer tenures and left healthier churches behind them than others have.

Missiology, Theology, and Philosophy

One of the primary differences among missionaries is the understanding of what God sends missionaries to do. Some missionaries have emphasized gospel preaching, Bible translation and education, while others have focused more on mercy ministries such as medicine, orphanages, feeding the hungry, digging wells or rescuing the oppressed. Even those who focus on preaching and evangelizing divide into two groups: those emphasizing the sovereignty of God and those stressing the responsibility of man. Clearly, what a missionary believes matters because your philosophy drives your methodology and your ecclesiology drives your missiology; or as another has said, ideas have consequences. This has never been more evident than when the theological system and biblical worldview known as the doctrines of grace are engaged in missions to the nations. We have seen a small sampling of what God's Word sends missionaries into the world to do, but what motivates them to go?

Some missionaries have gone to the mission field driven by a profound desire to rescue the perishing and as quickly as possible. The Bible is clear that those who have never heard the gospel are cut off from God and eternal life. Their sin has condemned them and their only hope of salvation is to hear the gospel of forgiveness and redemption. These missionaries and their agencies recruit missionaries and donor funds by stressing the urgent need to reach the unreached.

Other missionaries are motivated out of sheer obedience to the commands of the Bible in passages such as Ezekiel 3 and 33. Their missions conferences urge listeners to make Jesus' last command their first priority. After World War II, many servicemen and women returned to foreign countries as missionaries after processing out of their branches of military service. Some were driven by an awareness of the needs of the world they had not known before traveling the world, others perhaps out of guilt from wartime activities, but many others wrote of a new awareness and appreciation of the fact that the commands of Christ must be obeyed. Wartime service had taught them that soldiers were to obey commands without thought to personal sacrifice. Nate Saint, who was martyred in the jungle of Ecuador in 1956, challenged listeners in an HCJB radio sermon,

> During the last war we were taught to recognize that, in order to obtain our objective, *we had to be willing to be expendable....* This very afternoon thousands of soldiers are known by their serial numbers as men who are expendable....We know there is only one answer to our country's demand that we share in the price of freedom. Yet, when the Lord Jesus asks us to

pay the price for world evangelization, we often answer without a word. We cannot go. We say it costs too much.[1]

Eschatological positions drive others into missions. The interface of a "last days" mentality and the role of missions shapes their philosophy and methodology. Various consequent missiologies result from such thinking. For instance, the combination of a concern to rescue the perishing and the knowledge that Jesus could return at any time urges some to reach the lost before it is too late. Other missionaries are burdened to rescue the perishing, but believe from Matthew 24:14 that Jesus cannot return until we have reached all of the people groups according to our definition of reaching and as we count them. However, other missionaries hold to a partial preterist view that believes that the events in the Olivet discourse surrounding Matthew 24:14 primarily concerned the AD 70 destruction of the temple in Jerusalem. It is obvious that godly men and women who love the Lord and the lost and long to see them saved interpret these passages differently. Indeed, the brilliant missionary to Burma, Adoniram Judson, was postmillennial in his views and even sought to promote a fund for a permanent missions effort in Israel to win the Jews.

Rather than focus on subordinate, and often controversial and competitive motivations for missions, we should focus on the primary motive for missions, which is the glory of God. Virtually all of the other motivations can coexist when ordered beneath this overarching reason for missions. Indeed, we should embrace both a love for the lost and its subsequent desire to rescue the perishing as well as seek to be obedient to the clearly revealed command of Christ. As John Piper has proclaimed throughout his sermons, books, and three decades of ministry, just as the chief end of man is to glorify God, so the chief end of missions is the same. Christians long to see the nations repent and turn to the Living God, worshiping Him, delighting in Him, knowing Him and making Him known.

A love for God's glory, sacrificial obedience and a desire to rescue perishing souls are not only not mutually exclusive, they are in perfect harmony with each other and God's Word. These concerns of every evangelical Christian find a welcome home in the biblical doctrines of grace. Indeed, this doctrinal system brings clarity to understand the Bible, counsel for engaging the heart of man wherever the missionary finds him, hope for fruitful ministry and guidance in living out the missionary life.

---

[1] Elisabeth Elliot, *Through Gates of Splendor* (Chicago, IL: Tyndale, 1981), 60.

The Doctrines of Grace in Missions

Considering the basic tenets of the doctrines of grace and their missiological implications, one wonders how those who are unaware of these doctrines or have rejected them find hope for missionary service in today's gospel-hostile world. From the beginning of Baptist missions efforts, the doctrines of grace have been the guiding theology to spur their missionaries on. Nettles reminds us in *By His Grace and For His Glory*, "Nor did the rise of modern missions come as a result of shaking off the fetters of Calvinism, but instead issued as the necessary expression of it."[2] William Carey, a bivocational pastor known today as the father of modern missions, embraced these doctrines and the clear responsibility to follow God's call to the heathen. Carey's fellow Baptist ministers in London rebuffed his exhortation to consider foreign missions to save the heathen. Yet, his burden continued and his subsequent prayer and searching to know God's will led him to write *An Enquiry into the Obligations of Christians to Use Means for the Conversion of the Heathen* (1791) to challenge Baptists to consider launching out in missions. Carey was convinced that while God is sovereign, men and women are responsible for taking the saving Gospel to the heathen.

After introducing Andrew Fuller, William Carey's contemporary, and demonstrating Fuller's adherence to the doctrines of grace, Nettles wrote, "In short, Andrew Fuller not only championed the cause of foreign missions but strongly defended the Doctrines of Grace. The modern foreign-mission movement was founded upon the thoroughgoing commitment to the absolute sovereignty of God, coupled with uncompromising insistence upon the full responsibility of man."[3] Indeed, the doctrines of grace fuel the hope of missionaries to survive and thrive under the gracious hand of God and see Him advance His kingdom through their human efforts—all for His glory. The missionaries embracing the doctrines of grace have left unmistakable testimonies to their beliefs. Nettles describes Judson's beliefs: "One can clearly see that Judson operated on the basis of the doctrines of total depravity, unconditional election, effectual calling, substitutionary atonement, and perseverance of the saints."[4]

---

[2] Thomas J. Nettles, *By His Grace and For His Glory: A Historical, Theological, and Practical Study of the Doctrines of Grace in Baptist Life* (Grand Rapids, MI: Baker Book House, 1986), 31.

[3] Ibid., 129.

[4] Ibid., 154.

Exclusivity of Jesus Christ

Pluralists and inclusivists increasingly attack the belief that there is only one Savior and that you must be born again. Missionaries who held to the doctrines of grace throughout history also embraced this truth as the foundation of the missionary enterprise. Timothy George summarized what William Carey believed in the matter: "Personal faith in Jesus Christ is the only way of salvation for all peoples everywhere, and those who die without this saving knowledge face eternal damnation."[5] Erroll Hulse describes Adoniram Judson's position, "Supreme in Judson's mind was an unwavering belief that all those who die in their sins outside of Christ will suffer eternal misery in hell."[6] Practically speaking, to believe that there is any other way to salvation and eternal life except through faith in Christ cuts the nerve of missions. Biblically speaking, to believe that there is any other way than through Jesus Christ is to dismiss its clear teachings.

Total Depravity

There is a vast difference between the ministries of missionaries who embrace this understanding of man and those who do not. One approaches a lost indigenous man, believing him to be fallen and depraved in every aspect of his being and believing. The other views him as a good man who is simply yet to be convinced. In a world of God-haters, the missionary does well to understand that while pagans are not as wicked as they could possibly be, there is no part of them that does not require redemption, nor is there any part that is not affected by the Fall. This thoroughgoing depravity precludes the possibility of missionaries learning the language and culture well enough to persuade lost peoples to turn to God.

While missionaries must study to learn languages and culture, they know it is not in their power to change the heart. Tom Nettles writes of Judson's belief in this doctrine, "No romanticism encouraged his hopes about the conversion of the heathen. He knew full well that only the efficacious working of omnipotent power could bring one into saving obedience to Christ. Total depravity was a living doctrine to Judson."[7]

---

[5] Timothy George, *Faithful Witness: The Life & Mission of William Carey* (Birmingham, AL: New Hope, 1991), 172.

[6] Erroll Hulse, *Adoniram Judson and the Missionary Call* (Leeds: Reformation Today Trust, 1996), 45.

7 Nettles, *By His Grace and For His Glory*, 151.

Unconditional Election

Missionaries who have embraced the doctrines of grace are none-theless emboldened that even though the pagans will not choose God, God has chosen some of them. The missionary knows that while all will not accept Christ, some will. God has His remnant in every people, "you were slain, and by your blood you ransomed people for God from every tribe and language and people and nation" (Revelation 5:9b), and He will bring them in, "After this I looked, and behold, a great multitude that no one could number, from every nation, from all tribes and peoples and lan-guages, standing before the throne and before the Lamb, clothed in white robes" (Revelation 7:9). The hard hearts of his hearers that refuse the grace held out to them do not defeat the missionary. Christ's sheep will hear His voice and come to Him.

Detractors have often labeled the doctrine of election anti-missionary. Nettles countered such thinking: "The doctrine of election is the promise of success for the power of the gospel. This was the promise that prompted the entire modern missions movement. Has the contemporary Baptist world lost sight of its origin? Do the names of Carey, Fuller, Pearce, and Ryland no longer mean missions for the glory of the sovereign God?"[8] It is the assurance that God has elected some to salvation that enables per-severance in the missionary task when fruit is slow in coming. Adoniram Judson clearly embraced this doctrine of election. Hulse wrote, "In creedal statements prepared by Judson for the Burmese Church the doctrine of election is clearly stated, 'God send the Holy Spirit to enable those to be-come disciples who were chosen before the world was.'"[9]

Particular Redemption

The missionary of grace trusts that Christ shed not a single drop of blood in vain, no moment of suffering was wasted, no divine intention thwarted. God will not require pagans to pay for their sin for eternity in hell if Christ has paid their debt in full. The specific redemption Christ accomplished for them encourages the missionary working among people with blind eyes, deaf ears and hard hearts. However, even though they are chosen and Christ has purchased their redemption, the elect are not born saved, but rather elect unto salvation. The truth is that they must be born again (John 3:7). Hulse wrote of Judson's belief, "He believed that the

---

[8] Ibid., 400.
[9] Hulse, *Adoniram Judson and the Missionary Call*, 48.

gospel clearly preached was the means used by the Holy Spirit to save the elect (Romans 10:14–15)."[10]

Irresistible Grace

Here again, the missionary who understands these truths finds strength to continue plodding through the hard days of no visible fruit. They may resist his foreign interference and strange religion, but he knows that the Holy Spirit will continue to draw God's own to Himself with irresistible influence, making Christ appear lovely to former haters and replacing the heart of stone with the heart of flesh. Indeed, no one comes to Him unless the Spirit draws him, and when He begins to draw, He will continue it to fulfillment (Philippians 1:6). Familial and societal bonds are hard to break, and even once broken, the pull back into native religions and former ways is strong.

Perseverance of the Holy Spirit Through the Saints

Modern missions history is working on its third century. Many of the heathen that Carey so longed to reach have heard the gospel. Judson's trials and sufferings in Burma resulted in churches there also. Indeed, in Carey and Judson's wake and all over the world, there are believers who evangelize, disciple, teach and remain faithful. History confirms what the Bible taught all along; the Holy Spirit perseveres through true believers to keep them so.

Unfortunately, countless believers have joined churches on the missions fields of the world for a variety of reasons that are not noble or pure. Some joined for the advantages that friendship with the missionary brought, such as medicines, money, modern conveniences, jobs in the missionary compound, education for themselves or children or access to food, clean water or transportation. Such "rice bag" Christians do not endure, especially in times of persecution. They are ubiquitous illustrations for sermons on the Parable of the Soils.

However, the fact that the church has continued in the generations following missionaries who first went to reach and teach demonstrates that some remained faithful. The faithful believers often suffered persecution, and doubtless the temptation to revert to the former ways was strong, but the Holy Spirit kept them strong. Missionaries believing this doctrine rest in their sovereign God that the work He began through their hands will survive and thrive.

[10] Ibid., 45.

The Sovereignty of God

Missionaries who have embraced the doctrines of grace are characterized by a soul-deep belief in God's sovereignty. A fervent belief in the sovereignty of God both undergirds their lives and saturates their letters; it sustains their hopes and fuels their passions. Responding to the source of strength he found to endure his trials, Judson responded, "If I had not felt certain that every additional trial was ordered by infinite love and mercy, I could not have survived my accumulated sufferings."[11] Judson's missionary colleague Luther Rice also held firmly to these doctrines. Timothy George wrote that Rice believed divine grace had blessed him to believe this theology, which should instill patience toward scoffers: "How absurd it is, therefore, to contend against the doctrine of election, or decrees, or divine sovereignty. Let us not, however, become bitter against those who view this matter in a different light, nor treat them in a supercilious manner; rather let us be gentle towards all men. For who has made us to differ from what we once were? Who has removed the scales from our eyes? Or who has disposed us to embrace the truth?"[12] Without doubt, a missionary zeal coursed through the veins of this Baptist missionary, preacher, and mobilizer. Rice wrote in his journal, "This day I am thirty years old. I renewedly give myself to the Lord, renewedly devote myself to the cause of missions, and beg of God to accept me as his, and particularly as devoted to the missionary service."[13] These two emphases on the sovereignty of God and the responsibility of man in missions reverberate in the hearts of missionaries of grace. George wrote of William Carey, "It was not in spite of, but rather because of, his belief in the greatness of God and His divine purpose in election that Carey was willing 'to venture all' to proclaim the gospel in the far corners of the world."[14]

Certainly, these men and women in missions history accepted the responsibility of man, but in its proper perspective. Faith in God's sovereignty fostered unshakable faith in the promises of God in His Word. The doctrines of the sovereignty of God and predestination, far from bringing a stifling immobility or despair, bring peace and assurance. They assure that there is order in the seeming chaos of the world, and underneath every-

---

[11] Quoted in Eugene Myers Harrison, *Giants of the Missionary Trail* (Chicago, IL: Scripture Press Foundation, 1954), 7.

[12] James B. Taylor, *Memoir of Rev. Luther Rice: One of the First American Missionaries to the East* (Baltimore, MD: Armstrong and Berry, 1841), 293–94.

[13] Ibid., 120.

[14] George, *Faithful Witness*, 171.

thing are the arms of One who provides this order, and He loves His own more than we love ourselves.

High View of God's Word

All of these doctrines of grace and their concomitant extensions flow from a high view of Scripture. Indeed, all we can know in detail about God comes from His Word. The Bible is God's direct revelation and is authoritative, inerrant, infallible and inspired by the Holy Spirit. While there is general revelation about God in creation, this is insufficient for man's salvation. Missionaries of grace have always focused on the Bible in their ministries. Timothy George wrote of Carey, "Nowhere is Carey's kinship with the Reformation tradition more clearly seen than in his role as a translator, publisher, and distributor of the Bible. Like Wycliffe, Luther, and Tyndale before him, Carey believed that everyone should be able to read the Scriptures in their own native language."[15] Indeed, Carey and the Serampore trio are credited with the translation of over forty translations of the Bible and developing grammars and dictionaries in many languages.

Similarly, John Piper wrote of Adoniram Judson, "Judson was a lover of the word of God. The main legacy of his thirty-eight years in Burma was a complete translation of the Bible into Burmese and a dictionary that all the later missionaries could use.... The Bible was a friend closer and more lasting than his wife. When the bottom fell out some years later and he struggled with the darkest spiritual depression, he disappeared into the tiger-infested jungle to live alone. But he did not leave his Bible behind. The unbreakable attachment to the Bible saved his life and defined the final outcome."[16]

The Missionary Message

God is perfectly holy. To Him, His holiness is of paramount importance and therefore should be to us as well. He has also commanded us to be holy for, "I the LORD your God am holy" (Leviticus 19:2). Holiness signifies at least two things. First, it means absolute moral perfection. God is holy and does not have a hint of sin or impurity in His holiness. Second, it means that He is separated from everything that is not holy. The three-fold repetition of this divine attribute highlights its importance in both

[15] Ibid., 173.

[16] John Piper, *Filling Up The Afflictions of Christ: The Cost of Bringing the Gospel to the Nations in the Lives of William Tyndale, Adoniram Judson, and John Paton* (Wheaton, IL: Crossway, 2009), 89.

Isaiah 6:3 and Revelation 4:8. The Bible declares that He is "Holy, holy, holy," and nothing that does not have this level of holiness may come into His presence, otherwise such communion would taint Him with this sin and impurity.

The problem created by this truth causes great consternation on the part of men and women when convicted of their sinfulness (Romans 2:14–15; 3:23) Man is a sinner, and as such, he is both separated from God and powerless to do anything about his condition. Even if he were able to achieve sinless perfection, this would not alter the fact that he has sinned repeatedly in the past. Man needs an answer to this problem or he will remain separated from God forever, and by His grace, we have an Answer.

Jesus Christ came to live a perfect life and fulfill all righteousness, obeying all of God's commands without exception. When He suffered on the cross, He purchased the great exchange that is the hope of every believer; He took our sins on Him and gave us His perfect righteous, the righteousness that is required to enter into His presence both now and in the world to come. Yet, these for whom Christ died do not receive the benefits of the great exchange automatically and unconsciously; they must be born again.

Missionaries, especially those who embrace the doctrines of grace, preach the truth that the sins of mankind have separated them from God and that God sent His Son to die on the cross for the salvation of His people from their sins, but all must repent and place faith in Christ. They do not teach that this faith is a good work that accomplishes or even adds to salvation, but it will always be present in genuine new birth. Spurgeon likened the workings of the elements of salvation to spokes on a wheel.

> From the moment that we trusted in Jesus, a new life darted into our spirit. I am not going to say which is first, the new birth, or faith, or repentance. Nobody can tell which spoke of a wheel moves first; it moves as a whole. The moment the divine life comes into the heart we believe: the moment we believe the eternal life is there. We repent because we believe, and believe while we repent.[17]

The new birth that is essential for men and women to enter in a right relationship with God receives great opposition on the mission fields of the world. The enemy of our souls commands the opposing forces in every quarter of societies as well as the demonic realm. Although spiritual warfare lashes Christian missionaries daily, it is merely angry spewing

---

[17] Charles Haddon Spurgeon, "A Sermon for New Year's Day," Sermon No. 1816, Delivered on Thursday Evening, January 1st, 1885, Metropolitan Tabernacle, Newington.

from the unbowed heart of a defeated foe; but the battle has been decided (Colossians 2:13–15). The Holy Spirit makes the foolishness of preaching powerful and effective as He unstops ears to hear the hope of forgiveness and life.

Opposition to the Gospel

Opposition to the preaching of the word, persecution of evangelical missionaries and their new believers, centuries-old systems of pagan religions and competing worldviews are daunting challenges to the missionary who ventures forth in his own strength. Many cultures of the world are based on group orientation where individuals find identity only as a member of the group. One never expresses decisions without consulting with family, friends and elders for wisdom and consensus. The gospel often challenges the beliefs and customs of family and society. Some people fight to retain their family members and prevent their loss to a foreign religion. Indeed Adoniram Judson stated of the Burmese Buddhists among whom he served, "When any person is known to be considering the new Religion, all his relations and acquaintances rise *en masse*; so that to get a new convert is like pulling out the eyetooth of a live tiger."[18]

One of the reasons that opposition is so much fiercer on traditional mission fields than in the West is the perceived shame a family feels when one of their members converts to another religion. Missiologists have noted that the cultures of the world may be divided using the three realities that entered the world in the Fall: fear, shame and guilt. They characterize individualistic Western societies as oriented by guilt and innocence. A guilty member may suffer for his guilt but it does not necessarily affect the rest of his community. Animistic cultures are characterized by fear and power, living in constant fear. Accepting a new religion and the subsequent abandonment of the old spiritual allegiances upsets the balance and harmony in the minds of animists, which is a terrifying prospect that all want to avoid.

Many cultures in the Near, Middle and Far East are characterized by shame and honor. A breach of honor, such as marrying someone other than the arranged spouse or converting to another religion, brings shame on the family and entire community. The only way to restore honor is to destroy that which brought the shame. Honor killings are no more prevalent than they have ever been, but there is much greater awareness through international news and the globalization of our world. For many cultures,

[18] Francis Wayland, *A Memoir of the Life and Labors of Rev. Adoniram Judson*, vol. 2 (Boston, MA: Phillips, Sampson, and Company, 1853), 13.

a hybrid blend of these worldviews holds them in the trap of traditional religions.

All religious shifts, whether from Arminianism to Calvinism, or from Islam to Christianity, require rejecting old theology. This rejection also means rejecting the old theologians, and for many these were often mother and father, grandparents or the man who baptized you. It further signifies one's belief that all family and culture members have been wrong—perhaps for centuries—and that this foreigner alone has the truth. It is little wonder that preaching in and of itself is weak when placed against the monolithic religions of pagan lands.

Evangelical missionaries serving in predominantly Roman Catholic countries find that in many staunchly conservative Catholic areas, persecution against evangelicals persists. Priests sometimes announce that they will excommunicate all who attend evangelical meetings, precluding burial in the Catholic Church cemetery and masses for the deceased. At other times, drunken mobs escalate the expressions of persecution against believers.

A missionary to Muslims reports that as far as he is aware, that radicals have martyred every person he has ever led to Christ. Tragically, his research found that in one North African Muslim country the average life expectancy of a new Christian was forty-five days. Who is sufficient for these things? What missionary could venture forth into such a context and hope that his preaching would be even a faint hope against such hostility?

The Hindu context is also a difficult setting for Christian evangelists because of both the pockets of violent persecution and the malleable, amorphous nature of its doctrines. Such a statement appears contradictory at first glance, but martyrdoms occur in some Hindu areas of the world due to hatred for what they perceive to be arrogance in Christianity's only-one-way belief. Others in Hinduism hold that one can be a good Hindu and follow Christ at the same time; there are more than 330,000,000 Hindu gods. Hindus feel that the absence of Hinduism's concept of karma demonstrates that Christianity is simply a Western religion that treats wrongdoing too lightly. Many Hindus hold that all paths lead to God and that there is no absolute truth.

Stephen Neill estimates that forty percent of the world is animistic.[19] Indeed, all world religions have syncretized animism in with their religious practice and belief to some degree. Animism, the belief spirits, magic, mystical power and veneration of ancestors, is one of the most permeable of the predominant religions in the world since it affects all of life. Since

[19] Stephen Neill, *Christian Faith and Other Faiths* (New York: Oxford, 1970), 125.

animism lives in the shadow of constant fear and the powers of seen and unseen beings and spirits, any threat to the spiritual balance is threatening.

The missionary who goes to serve in his or her own strength, wisdom and resources in any of these worldviews will soon taste defeat from the one who prowls about like a lion seeking whom he may devour. The god of this age has blinded men and women all over the world and deceived them with false religions and superstitions. They serve him in their religious systems, whether openly or unwittingly they serve him all the same. General revelation reveals that there is a Creator and that all have sinned and come short of His glory. Indeed, all already know this and for this reason every culture in the world has created their religion. This religion has been held by their people for countless generations, but has saved no one. Still, their worldview and religion explain the world for them—until the missionary arrives.

The missionary entering this realm is a foot soldier entering hostile territory. Let Christ's missionaries go forth with ambassadorial rank, announcing the King's demands, yielding not an inch as they do. The food that sustains their spirits will be sound theology and biblical truth, and there is none like the precious doctrines of grace to fuel their efforts to glorify God in His world.

Contemporary Theological and Historical Missiological Challenges

The modern missions era began with the sailing of William Carey, a Calvinistic Baptist, called by God to serve in India. Others gripped by the same doctrines and calling followed in Carey's wake. A long list of men and women sacrificed everything, leaving pastorates, university posts, seminary faculty positions, secure lives in lifelong comfort zones and the warmth of loving families to go and die for Christ's sake. Others willingly went forth to labor in anonymity and buried in obscurity the whole of their lives. Notwithstanding disparaging comments to the contrary, they did not go in spite of the fact that they held to the doctrines of grace. In fact, it was these doctrines that led them to embrace God's missionary call to love the lost and glorify Him by going and making His glory known among the nations.

Churches today must learn the lessons Baptist missions history can teach us. These missionaries went out to the uncontacted, unengaged, unreached parts of the world at the beginning of the modern missions era in much the same way that Baptist missionaries are reemphasizing reaching the remaining unreached people groups today. In missions history we see

God's faithfulness to sustain these men and women, their faithfulness to Him, and how important these doctrines were to them. We must not overlook an important and oft neglected lesson they taught us.

Jesus commissioned His church to reach every ethnic group in the world with the gospel (*panta ta ethne*), make disciples of them and then to teach them everything He commanded us. The Great Commission was the core of their ministries. Carey's five-pronged missiological method was widespread preaching of the gospel, translation and distribution of the Bible in the local languages, church planting, studying to understand the non-Christian religions and ministerial training in a comprehensive program.[20] He recognized the truth that when church growth outstrips trained, godly, biblically qualified church leadership the work is headed for heresy and disaster. Adoniram Judson emphasized a similar approach. Hulse wrote, "Judson's method was preaching and church planting followed immediately by the recognition, training and equipping of indigenous pastors."[21] Their methodologies were not identical but they held to a common emphasis on evangelism, discipleship, ministerial training of biblically qualified men and church planting. The Great Commission shaped these missionaries and their methods.

May God's missionary call and the precious doctrines of grace be heard and embraced by a new generation of men and women who will spend and be spent for the glory of His name around the world. May they go out, walking the ancient paths, preaching gospel truth, teaching teachers and training trainers, reaching and teaching the nations for Christ's sake.

[20] Stephen Neill, *A History of Christian Missions* (Baltimore, MD: Penguin, 1964), 263.

[21] Hulse, *Adoniram Judson and the Missionary Call*, 47.

16

"An Ingenuous Unfolding of Our Principles"

CONFESSIONALISM AMONG 17TH CENTURY PARTICULAR BAPTISTS

James M. Renihan

The Holy Scripture is the only sufficient, certain, and infallible rule of all saving knowledge, faith, and obedience.

With these words the *Second London Baptist Confession of Faith* begins its traverse through the landscape of Christian theology. The Baptists assert that Scripture and Scripture alone deserves the unique place of authority in a proper system of doctrine. But the wise reader will notice that these words are contained in a *human* document—a confession of faith. While they properly express a foundational teaching revealed in Scripture, they nonetheless are contained in a document with a far more recent provenance than the Word of God, and thus illustrate the need to wrestle with the question at hand.

Confessionalism is often a controversial subject. For Christians committed to the primacy of Scripture, the suggestion that another document deserves a place of religious allegiance may seem to be highly questionable. Is this substituting a man-made document for the God-given Scriptures?

The subject is difficult to treat, for two reasons. In the first place, there is little positive literature on this matter, especially from a Baptist perspective. While many have said that they accept, or adopt, or even subscribe to a Baptist confession, it is not obvious that there has been common agreement as to what these kinds of phrases intend and imply. In addition, confessional Baptists (those who assert the importance of acceptance, adoption, subscription etc.) are regularly informed that Baptists have not been and are not a creedal people.

In the second place most of the literature that exists from a Baptist perspective is anti-creedal. It may be shown, however, that Baptists have a history of careful and conscientious confessional subscription.

The Scriptures and Confessions

As demonstrated above, Baptists give the preeminent place to the Holy Scriptures. Before considering confessionalism in Baptist history, it will be good to consider what they say about the topic. In fact, the Word of God has much to teach about confessions and the act of confessing. One crucial passage, 1 Timothy 6:12–13, will serve as a helpful guide for consideration.

The Act of Confessing

In these two verses, Paul speaks of two men, Timothy and our Lord Jesus, each of whom made the good confession before many witnesses. What does he mean by these words?

It may be good to begin with verse 13, as we have some Scripture with which we may compare this idea. Paul tells us that the Lord Jesus "witnessed the good confession" before Pontius Pilate. In John 18:33–38, this incident is fleshed out. There, we notice two things: 1) Pilate asked Jesus publicly if he was king of the Jews. Our Savior did not answer this immediately and directly, because to do so would have been misleading. Pilate would have understood him in political terms, and this was not Jesus' intention for himself and his followers. 2) Pilate followed this question with another, seeking to determine why it was that Jesus had been delivered up by his fellow countrymen. At this point, Jesus instructs Pilate plainly regarding the nature of his person and mission. When the circumstance was right and proper, Jesus spoke plainly and truthfully about these two most fundamental aspects of his person and work. In this case, the "good confession" was both accurate and true. It was good because it was accurate: faithful to the necessity of the circumstance—it did not withhold—it testified. And it was good because it was true: in content and intention it reflected the realities of Christ's person and work. Jesus gave to Pilate a precise statement intended to give plain expression to the subject at hand.

In verse 12, Paul speaks of Timothy's confession. Notice that he uses a different verb; this is significant. While Jesus "witnessed," Timothy "confessed." This probably points to a distinction between these two acts. The verb *witness* implies statement; the verb *confess* implies belief. Timothy could not "witness" the good confession in the way that Jesus uniquely could. Timothy confessed this good confession publicly: "before many witnesses," probably at his baptism.[1] Timothy's act was like that of Jesus, a "good confession." While the verb points to the act, the noun points to the thing confessed—as with Jesus, the content of that which was spoken. Timothy's confession was like Jesus'—it was good. It must have been true in content and intention; it must have been faithful to the necessity of the circumstance; it must have given plain and precise expression to the subject at hand. It is even possible that the first phrase in verse 12 "fight the good fight of faith" gives us a clue to Timothy's confession. "Faith" is often shorthand for the body of apostolic doctrine contained in the Scriptures. Whatever Timothy confessed, it was a true and accurate expression of his convictions.

The Content of the Confession

It is certain that when Timothy made his confession, he was not simply quoting Scripture. He must have, in some way, expressed in his own words the truths that he believed. But what would the content be?

If we set this notion into its scriptural context we may see clearly that it is the body of doctrine contained in the Word of God. The Bible is full of references to the existence of such a thing. It is not to be equated with any one passage of Scripture, but with the teaching of all of Scripture; it is the system of truth maintained throughout the pages of Holy Writ.

Paul, for example, makes reference to this in 2 Thessalonians 2:15. He instructs the recipients of his letter to "stand fast and hold the traditions" they were taught. These would be the basis for their lives as believers. But what does Paul mean by the term "tradition?"

In the New Testament, the word for tradition (*paradosis*) is used eleven times, in the sense of a received practice or belief with its origin in an authoritative source. It is not simply a custom; it is something that must

---

[1] See for example John R.W. Stott, *The Message of 1 Timothy and Titus: God's Good News for the World*, The Bible Speaks Today (Downers Grove, IL: Inter-Varsity, 2001), 157; William D. Mounce, *Pastoral Epistles*, Word Biblical Commentary 46 (Nashville, TN: Thomas Nelson Publishers, 2000), 356–57; I. Howard Marshall, Pastoral Epistles, International Critical Commentary (Edinburgh: T&T Clark, 1999), 660–61; Jerome D. Quinn and William C. Wacker, *The First and Second Letters to Timothy* (Grand Rapids, MI: Eerdmans, 2000), 519; William Hendriksen, *New Testament Commentary: Exposition of the Pastoral Epistles*, (Grand Rapids, MI: Baker, 1957), 204.

be followed. It has two different senses: negative and positive; i.e. there is good tradition and bad tradition.

In Mark 7:1–9, the traditions of the elders are the established and accepted teachings of the Jewish Rabbis. As they studied Scripture and applied it to their lives and culture, they believed that God's Law required certain practices. These became "traditions." They did not merely come into accepted practice over a period of time; they were prescribed by an authoritative source: the Rabbis.

Paul employed the word in the same way. Notice for example, how the term is used in the following texts: "I advanced in Judaism beyond many of my contemporaries in my own nation, being more exceedingly zealous for the *traditions* of my fathers" (Galatians 1:14, emphasis added); "Beware lest any one cheat you through philosophy and empty deceit, according to the *tradition* of men, according to the basic principles of the world, and not according to Christ" (Colossians 2:8, emphasis added). In each of these cases, tradition equals something received as it was authoritatively taught. It was not a mere custom, but a belief bearing the weight of authority. Now in these verses, tradition is *bad*, because the authority behind it has misunderstood God's revelation, so that the original concept is obscured. The result is that the people of God are expected to submit to this teaching, as if it were God's, when in fact it is man's invention. The tradition itself was authoritative.

This is not, however, the only sense in which we find the word tradition in the Pauline corpus. We need to consider its good sense as well in the following places: "Now I praise you, brethren, that you remember me in all things, and keep the *traditions*, as I delivered them to you" (1 Corinthians 11:2, emphasis added); "But we command you, brethren, in the name of our Lord Jesus Christ, that you withdraw from every brother who walks disorderly, and not according to the *tradition* which he received from us" (2 Thessalonians 3:6, emphasis added). In these places, tradition is good. The Corinthians are praised for their adherence to it, and the Thessalonians are to use it as a standard by which to judge behavior.

In all of these cases, tradition is a pattern of life originating in an authoritative source, and this is exactly its meaning in 2 Thessalonians 2:15. Tradition is a belief or practice sanctioned by authoritative teaching and received as an essential part of religion. Whether it is good or bad depends on the source! This idea is confirmed by our verse—three phrases make this clear:

a.   "Which you were taught"—the source of these traditions was teaching—not habitual practice. They were the fruit and product of instruction.

b. "whether by word"—Tradition may have its source in verbal communication.

c. "or by our epistle"—Tradition may have its source in written communication from Paul, although verse 2 contributes an important caveat for written communication: the source must be genuine.

To summarize, tradition (*paradosis*) is apostolic doctrine. It is tradition in the sense that, resting on divine authority, it is passed on by God's messengers and received by His servants. It therefore does not, and cannot, refer to human teachings sanctioned by some type of religious hierarchy. It refers solely to the doctrines and practices of the apostles as they were delivered, passed on and practiced by the churches.

There are a whole host of similar ideas in the Bible. We will simply mention several, limiting ourselves to the Pastoral Epistles: In 1 Timothy 6:20 and 2 Timothy 1:12, 14 Paul uses the phrase "Guard the deposit," referring to the truth Timothy had received. In 1 Timothy 1:10, 2 Timothy 4:3, Titus 1:9, 2:1 the apostle speaks of "sound doctrine;" and using a similar adjective speaks of "sound words" in 1 Timothy 6:3 and the "pattern of sound words" in 2 Timothy 1:13. The same idea is conveyed when he urges Titus to ensure that the Cretans are "sound in the faith" in Titus 1:13, 2:2; and in 1 Timothy 6:3 uses the phrase "the doctrine which is according to godliness." In all of these cases, Paul refers to a cohesive standard of doctrine, and the men addressed are to hold it, guard it and live by it. It is not just the words of Scripture in themselves, but the doctrine taught by those words, and even more, the system of doctrine taught by those words. He does not tell them to guard the Scriptures, but to guard the doctrine. It is silly to think of the matter in any other terms. This is a warrant for the practice of confessing the faith. We must understand the system of doctrine contained in Holy Scripture, and guard it, defend it, propagate it—confess it—to the glory of God.

17th Century Particular Baptist Confessionalism

The First London Confession

I will begin by examining confessionalism with reference to the *First London Confession*, focusing on two points: its own words about subscription and William Kiffin's convictions about what subscription meant.

The Confession's Own Words about Subscription

When the Particular Baptists first emerged from the paedobaptist separatist churches in the 1640s, they faced strong opposition. Rumors and innuendo tying them to the continental Anabaptists and the disaster in Münster were being disseminated, and they found it prudent and necessary publicly to distance themselves from that sad event and declare their orthodoxy and similarity to the paedobaptist churches around them. They did this by publishing the *First London Confession* of 1644. The preface to that Confession states,

> Wee have... for the cleering of the truth wee professe, that it may be at libertie, though wee be in bonds, briefly published a Confession of our Faith, as desiring all that feare God, seriously to consider whether (if they compare what wee here say and confesse in the presence of the Lord Jesus and his Saints) men have not with their tongues in Pulpit, and pens in Print, both spoken and written things that are contrary to truth;... And because it may be conceived, that what is here published may be the Judgement of some one particular Congregation, more refined than the rest; We doe therefore here subscribe it, some of each body in the name, and by the appointment of seven Congregations, who though wee be distinct in respect of particular bodies, for conveniency sake, being as many as can well meete together in one place, yet are all one in Communion, holding Jesus Christ to be our head and Lord;... Subscribed in the Names of the seven Churches in *London*.[2]

This action had two important facets. First, by publication they desired to make their views, held commonly and unanimously, known to a wide audience of readers. Secondly, by subscribing their names as representatives of the churches, they were publicly asserting that these doctrines were a true representation of the theological views held among them. Much was at stake, especially their ongoing freedom in the face of rising Presbyterian anti-toleration political power. Remember Milton's famous words: "New Presbyter is but old priest writ large." Few of the Presbyterians were for religious toleration, desiring to replace the episcopalian state church with a presbyterian state church. Subscription was not a nicety; it was a sober, serious and public proclamation that they were orthodox Christians.

---

[2] William Lumpkin, ed., *Baptist Confessions of Faith*, rev. ed. (Valley Forge, PA: Judson Press, 1980), 155–56. Spelling and punctuation have been left unchanged from the original documents throughout this chapter.

WILLIAM KIFFIN'S WORDS ABOUT SUBSCRIPTION

The nature of the earliest Baptist understanding of confessional subscription is not a matter of conjecture. We have some explicit testimony to the exact intent of the men and churches involved in publishing the *First London Confession*. The first name on the list of subscribers is William Kiffin.

In the 1690s, Benjamin Keach caused a furor among the Particular Baptist churches by introducing the practice of congregational hymn singing into public worship. A great controversy arose, and in the midst, Keach published a book in which he made some very unfortunate comments about the first churches in the 1640s. Among his assertions was that these churches did not believe that ministers should receive financial support from their churches. William Kiffin, George Barrett, Robert Steed and Edward Man responded to Keach in a 1692 work entitled *A Serious Answer to a Late Book, Stiled, A Reply to Mr. Robert Steed's Epistle concerning Singing*. They showed Keach that the *First London Confession* (which he later admitted he had never seen) contained an article explicitly advocating ministerial support. Listen to their description of the issue:

> [Keach and his supporters] exhibit a very grievous and a very false charge against those of the same Profession, that were more ancient in it than the Authors of this Reply, who vent this Scandal.... When those ancient Brethren were convinced of their duty, That Believers, upon Confession of their Faith, were the only Subjects of Baptism, and accordingly, sate down together in Communion as a Congregation or Church of Christ; and many in the Nation began to enquire into the truth thereof, they met with many harsh Censures and false Charges cast upon them to make the Truth of Christ contemptible, (*viz.*) That they were corrupt in the Doctrines of the Gospel; That they denied Subjection to Magistrates; that they held, that to maintain [i.e. financially support] ministers was Antichristian &c. They to clear themselves, and to take off those false charges, did think it their duty to publish to the Nation a Confession of their Faith; which when drawn up, was read in the Churches, being then seven in number; and consented to by all the Members, not one dissenting, and subscribed by two of each Church in the name of the rest. Which Confession of Faith was five times printed in the year 1644, and from that, to the year 1651, without the least alteration of any one Article of what was last printed: which Confession gave such general satisfaction to most Christians of all sorts of differing Perswasions from us, that it took off from many that Prejudice and Offence that was formerly taken by them against our Profession. What the Judgment of these Churches in their first Constitution, was, concerning the Maintenance of Ministers, may be seen in the 28th Article, in these words, *We do believe that due*

Maintenance of Ministers should be the free and voluntary Communication of
the Church: That according to Christ's Ordinance, they that preach the Gospel,
should live on the Gospel, &c. And accordingly they did then, and we have
ever since made it our Practice, as a Duty required of all the Members
of the Church that are able to give.... Herein we would be understood in
this, that we now assert concerning the Churches, that we mean princi-
pally as they were in the beginning: And we do find, to our great Grief,
that which was then falsly charg'd upon us by those that did not know us,
is now as falsly (with a far greater Aggravation of their Sin) charg'd upon
us by some of us, who might have satisfied themselves, had they perused
our Confession of Faith....

To this Charge we answer, That nothing can be more falsly asserted, or more slanderously uttered: **For if this their Charge have the least**
shadow of Truth against the Baptized Churches in their first beginning
here in *England***; they must needs be the grossest sort of Hypocrites, in**
professing the contrary by their Profession of Faith, and yet believing
and practicing quite otherwise to what they solemnly professed as their
Faith in the matter. [3]

Elsewhere in the context they call these charges "notorious Falshoods
and abominable Slanders," stating that Keach and his cohorts had uttered

a most false Accusation and Slander against the Baptized Churches in
their first gathering, laying that to their Charge as a received Principle
owned by them, which they had openly declared against to the whole
World in their Confession of Faith, which was in those Days Printed
and Published; whereby they stigmatize or brand them with **the deepest**
Hypocrisy that depraved Mortals can be guilty of.[4]

This is strong language. These men viewed the solemn act of adopting,
subscribing, and publishing a confession of faith to be so serious that they
considered anyone who claimed to own it, but practiced differently, guilty
of, in their own words, "the deepest Hypocrisy that depraved Mortals can
be guilty of." For them, confessional subscription was a moral issue. It was
a declaration of one's convictions about the nature of the Christian faith
itself, and so could not be taken lightly. If you said that you believed something, you had better believe it, or you were nothing short of a hypocrite.

What is especially interesting about this material is that it spans five
decades of Particular Baptist life. William Kiffin was present and involved

---

[3] William Kiffin, Robert Steed, George Barrett and Edward Man, *A Serious*
Answer to a Late Book, Stiled, A Reply to Mr. Robert Steed's Epistle concerning Sing-
ing (London: Printed in the Year, 1692), 16–19, emphasis added.

[4] Ibid., 5, emphasis added.

in the adoption and publication of the First London Confession, as also the Second. He and his companions, writing in 1692, looked back to 1644 and made these assertions about subscription. These words apply to his understanding of confessional subscription as it was practiced throughout the first half-century of the existence of our churches. With this in mind, let us turn to their later Confession.

The Second London Confession

Here I discuss four points: The Confession in the General Assembly; The Confession in the Churches; The Confession in the Associations; and The Confession as a doctrinal tool.

IN THE GENERAL ASSEMBLY

When it was first published in 1677, the *Second London Confession* included an interesting preface (as well as an appendix). In the preface, the subscribers explained their reasons for issuing the document. Their words are of great interest:

> There is one thing more which we sincerely profess, and earnestly desire credence in, *viz*. That contention is most remote from our design in all that we have done in this matter: and we hope the liberty of an ingenuous unfolding our principles, and opening our hearts unto our Brethren, with the Scripture grounds on which our faith and practice leanes, will by none of them be either denied to us, or taken ill from us. Our whole design is accomplished, if we may obtain that Justice, as to be measured in our principles, and practice, and the judgement of both by others, according to what we have now published, which the Lord (whose eyes are as a flame of fire) knoweth to be the doctrine, which with our hearts we most firmly believe, and sincerely indeavor to conform our lives to.[5]

For these men, the Confession was an "ingenuous" unfolding of their principles, i.e. it was open, frank, free from reserve, restraint or dissimulation. They were even willing to invoke the Lord as a witness that it was a true statement of the doctrine "most firmly believed" to which they "sincerely indeavored" to conform their lives.

---

[5] *A Confession of Faith* (London: Printed in the Year, 1677), unnumbered pages 6–7 of preface.

At the 1689 General Assembly, the importance of the Confession was manifest. As many as 108 churches were represented or sent communications to the Assembly, and the Confession was endorsed in famous terms:

> We the Ministers and Messengers of, and concerned for, upwards of one hundred Baptized Congregations in *England* and *Wales* (denying *Arminianism*) being met together in *London* from the *3d* of the *7th* Month to the *11th* of the same, 1689, to consider of some things that might be for the Glory of God, and the good of these Congregations; have thought meet (for the satisfaction of all other Christians that differ from us in the point of Baptism) to recommend to their perusal the Confession of our Faith, Printed for, and sold by, Mr. *John Harris* at the *Harrow* in the *Poultrey*; **Which Confession we own, as containing the Doctrine of our Faith and Practice**; and do desire that the Members of our Churches respectively do furnish themselves therewith.[6]

They "own" the Confession, and insist that it is a plain statement of their belief and practice. For them, the Confession was an apologetic tool. Outsiders would be able to read its declarations and recognize that these churches were doctrinally orthodox. We have no reason to think that they meant anything different with regard to the *Second London Confession* than was intended with the adoption of the *First London Confession*. The second name subscribed, after Hanserd Knollys, was William Kiffin.

IN THE CHURCHES

Confessional subscription was considered to be a serious matter among many churches. It was "solemn owning and ratifying," a commitment to a definitive theological system. So strongly were these men committed to the words contained in their Confession that they considered anyone "the grossest sort of Hypocrite, in professing the contrary by their Profession

---

[6] *A Narrative of the Proceedings of the General Assembly Of divers Pastors, Messengers and Ministring Brethren of the Baptized Churches, met together in London, from Septemb. 3. to 12. 1689, from divers parts of England and Wales: Owning the Doctrine of Personal Election, and final Perseverance* (London: Printed in the Year, 1689), 18, emphasis added. It is curious that though the document is commonly known as the 1689 Confession, I can find no bibliographic evidence that it was printed in that year. It was published in 1677, 1688, and 1699. See Donald Wing, *Short-Title Catalogue of Books Printed in England, Scotland, Ireland, Wales, and British America and of English Books Printed in Other Countries 1641–1700*, 2d ed., (New York: The Index Committee of the Modern Language Association of America, 1972), 1:369.

of Faith, and yet believing and practicing quite otherwise to what they solemnly professed as their Faith in that matter."[7]

As an example of the Confession's role in the churches, we may consider one London church. When the Maze Pond Church was constituted in February 1694, it explicitly adopted the Confession in the first article of the church covenant. Their words are these: "We believe the holy Scriptures of the old & new Testament to be the word of God, and a soficient [*sic*] rule of all Saveing knowledge, Faith, and Obedience, further herein we agree with a Confession put forth by our brethren the Baptiss [*sic*] in the year 1688 and signed at a Generall assembly by thirty Seven of them."[8] This document served to identify their theological convictions.

IN THE ASSOCIATIONS

We find a similar emphasis among the various associations. After the separation of the General Assembly into two meetings in 1692, one at Bristol and the other at London, the meeting in the metropolis quickly died. In 1706, an attempt was made to renew the London Association. The Bagnio/Cripplegate Church[9] refused to participate. Their records state:

> Some reasons why we did not send Messengers to ye Association yt mett at Joyners Hall ye 25th March last: nor to ye previous meeting at Mr Deerings Coffee House on ye 18 of ye same
> Humbly offered to ye consideration of all those Baptized Churches wch have or can sign the confession of our Faith printed in ye year 1688 and recommended to ye churches by ye Generall Assembly that met at Broken Wharf in London 1689.[10]

Among their reasons for remaining aloof were the presence of a seventh-day Baptist church which the 1689 Assembly had refused to admit, the presence of "that well known Arminian Church meeting in Barbican," and most importantly,

> Because the solemn owning & ratifying of our so well attested & generall approved Confession of Faith, as transmitted to us in ye full evidence of

---

[7] Kiffin, Steed, Barrett and Man, *A Serious Answer*, 18.

[8] Maze Pond Church Book 1691–1708, The Angus Library, Regent's Park College, Oxford, 1.

[9] Formerly pastored by Hanserd Knollys and Robert Steed successively.

[10] Bagnio/Cripplegate *CMB*, 26. Broken Wharf was the location of this same church when Knollys' was pastor. They were thus the host church of the 1689 General Assembly.

yt word by our late pastors &c in ye general assembly seems to us as it did also to them a thing absolutely nessesary to ye just & regular constitution of all associations: but ye admitting of the above sd churches into Association renders this altogether impracticable.[11]

They then cite the importance that subscription to Confessions had for the 1644 and 1652 London Association, the 1656 Western Association, the first issuance of the Second London Confession in 1677, and at the 1689 General Assembly. Listen to their words as they apply to confessional subscription in associations of churches:

> That it hath been the stated method of our Associations **most religiously to own** ye same confession of faith is evident, for we find that ye association in London in 1644 subscribed in ye name of the churches the confession then put forth & also that Association which met in 1652 did ye same. And moreover in ye year 1656 the churches in Somerset, Devon, Dorset, Wilts, Gloucester, & Bristol met in Association put forth a Confession of their faith agreeable with ye former, on purpose that they might declare their harmony in Faith and practice: Again in ye year 1677 the Elders & Brethren of many churches in London & the country unanimously put forth our present confession of faith, which was approved of & signed by ye generall assembly wch met 1689, which generall assembly thought fitt at ye same time to let all ye churches know that they denyed Arminianism & that they hold that good old Orthodox Doctrine of personal election & final perseverance. And we would particularly note one clause in their preface wherein it is said, "our whole design is accomplished if we may obtain yt justice as to be measured by our principles & practices & ye judgment of both by others, according to what we have now published, wch the Lord whose eyes are as a flame of fire knows to be the doctrine which wth our hearts we most firmly believe, & sincerely endeavor to conform our lives to." Now it's plain that this neither was nor indeed can be spoken of by an Assembly that shall admit [7th day] Sabbarians [*sic*] or Arminians among them.[12]

They express fear that the admission of the seventh day church and the Arminian church was a direct attempt to undermine the influence of the Confession in the associations, and incorporate letters from the Bristol Association and the Bridgenorth, Worcestershire Association in support of their position. Bristol advised them to remain aloof from this doctrinally compromised group, saying of the Confession, "we hope [it] ever shall have a very honorable esteem," and the Worcestershire Association wrote

[11] Ibid., unnumbered page facing page 27.
[12] Ibid., 27, unnumbered page facing page 28, emphasis added.

"it is proper for ye members of ye Baptist associations to subscribe ye Baptist Confession of faith printed 1689 generally owned amongst us before their admission into ye said associations; and that ye neglect hereof is of dangerous consequence."[13] For these associations and the church to which they wrote, a weakened doctrinal basis barred formal communion. They would not join with the revived association simply because it would not maintain the strict theological standard traditionally held among the Particular Baptists.

The Confession as a Doctrinal Tool

The use of the Confession as a doctrinal exemplar is demonstrated by an incident from the life of the Broadmead, Bristol church. In April 1682, they required Thomas Whinnell, a member of a General Baptist church who was attempting to join their assembly, to subscribe the Confession, in order to ensure that his views were consonant with their own.[14] The serious differences in the convictions of these theologically diverse groups were settled paradigmatically by means of this personal affirmation. Whinnell went on to become pastor of the Taunton, Somersetshire Particular Baptist church.

Benjamin Keach used the Confession as an apologetic tool in 1694. He was engaged in a debate over the validity of infant baptism, responding to a question on the status of infants. Asserting that "all infants are under the Guilt and stain of original sin ... and that no infant can be saved but through the Blood and Imputation of Christs righteousness," he refers to the "Article of our Faith," and bluntly says "See our confession of Faith" (which, by the way, does in the original incorporate the word "elect" prior to the phrase "infants dying in infancy"). For Keach, the doctrine contained in the Confession was a handy means by which to refute the notion of "habitual [infant] faith" held by his opponent.[15]

---

[13] Ibid., 27, unnumbered page facing page 28, emphasis added.

[14] Roger Hayden, *The Records of A Church of Christ in Bristol, 1640–1687* (Bristol: Bristol Record Society, 1974), 241. The records actually state that he "professed to believe ye principles contained in ye Baptist Confession of Faith, 1667." The modern editor states "No Confession of Faith of this date is known. It is likely that Terrill [the author of the *Records*] is referring to the Particular Baptist Confession of Faith for 1677, which was a standard test of orthodoxy among Particular Baptist Churches of the time."

[15] Benjamin Keach, *A Counter Antidote to purge out the Malignant Effects of a Late Counterfiet, Prepared by Mr. Gyles Shute, an Unskilful Person in Polemical Cures* (London: H. Bernard, 1694), 12. Habitual faith is "The God-given spiritual capacity of fallen human beings to have faith." See Richard A. Muller, *Dictionary*

In similar fashion, the Philadelphia Association made use of the Confession. The records state, "in the year 1724, a query, concerning the fourth commandment, whether changed, altered or diminished. We refer to the Confession of faith, set forth by the elders and brethren met in London, 1689, and owned by us, chap. 22, sect. 7 and 8."[16] The confessional Lord's Day Sabbath position was sufficient to answer the question. In 1727, they responded to a question about marriage in the same way. The records tersely state "Answered, by referring to our Confession of faith, chapter 26th in our last edition."[17]

In all of these cases, the Second London Confession played an active and vital role in the lives of the churches and associations. Our brothers understood its importance and made use of it as a helpful resource in many circumstances. It did not fetter them; it truthfully described their common convictions.[18]

---

of Latin and Greek Theological Terms (Grand Rapids, MI: Baker, 1985), 134. Shute seems to have argued that this habit of faith, apart from the actual act of faith, was sufficient to save infants, and was thus a basis for their baptism.

[16] A.D. Gillette, ed., *Minutes of the Philadelphia Association from A.D. 1707 to A.D. 1807, Being the First One Hundred Years of Its Existence* (Philadelphia, PA: American Baptist Publication Society, 1851), 27.

[17] Ibid., 29. The reference to chapter 26 is an indication that the Philadelphia Association had already adopted the additional chapters on Singing and Laying on of Hands.

[18] Significant evidence exists for a study of General Baptist confessionalism as well. In 1660, just two months before the Restoration, forty leaders issued a confession "in the behalf of themselves, and many others unto whom they belong, in London, and in several counties of this nation, who are of the same faith with us." In that work, they articulate principles similar to those of their predestinarian cousins (e.g. "these things… we verily believe to be the Lords will and mind"). See *A Brief Confession or Declaration of Faith set forth by many of us, who are (falsely) called Ana-Baptists. To inform all men (in these days of scandal and reproach) or our innocent belief and practice; for which we are not only resolved to suffer persecution, to the loss of our goods, but also life itself, rather than to decline the same* (London: Printed by G.D. for F. Smith, at the Elephant and Castle, 1660), 3, 11. A few years later, Thomas Grantham reprinted a slightly amended version of the same confession, for the same purpose. See Thomas Grantham, *Christianismus Primitivus* (London: Printed for Francis Smith, 1678), Book Two, 61 (second pagination). A third example is found in Thomas Monck's anonymously published *An Orthodox Creed, or a Protestant Confession of Faith* (London: NP: 1679), unnumbered page 11 of "To the Impartial Reader"; more directly see page 77 where Monck states concerning these articles that he and the others "most heartily and unfeignedly own, believe, and profess."

Conclusion

Confessions played an important role in the life of the early Baptist churches. Subject to rumor, innuendo and threat, these congregations employed the common method of careful and extensive doctrinal articulation as a means of demonstrating their orthodoxy to the world. The stakes were high—in fact in publishing the *Second London Confession* based upon the earlier *Westminster* and *Savoy Confessions*, the Baptists were inviting further persecution. They understood the implications of their actions, and recognized that a straightforward, an" ingenuous" declaration of truth, was essential to both their survival and growth. It is churches united in common faith that advance.

Nearly two hundred years later, C.H. Spurgeon nicely stated the point. Here are some of his comments about confessionalism in relation to the Downgrade Controversy. They reflect exactly the sentiments of the earlier Baptists.

> To say that "a creed comes between a man and his God," is to suppose that it is not true; for truth, however definitely stated, does not divide the believer from his Lord. So far as I am concerned, that which I believe I am not ashamed to state in the plainest possible language; and the truth I hold I embrace because I believe it to be the mind of God revealed in his infallible Word. How can it divide me from God who revealed it? It is one means of communion with my Lord, that I receive his words as well as himself, and submit my understanding to what I see to be taught by him. Say what he may, I accept it because he says it, and therein pay him the humble worship of my inmost soul.[19]

Spurgeon's argument is not unlike his predecessors. Careful and conscientious adherence to a detailed confession of faith reflects a vigorous commitment to Scripture. Given his well-known love for the puritan era, it is no surprise to find that he reflects the convictions of his theological fathers.

For centuries, confessionalism has had a long and noble history among Baptists. May it continue to be so. It is a pleasure to remember that Dr. Nettles has been a vigorous advocate of confessionalism throughout his own ministry. The contemporary recovery of truth among Baptist churches owes much to his labors. For this, we thank God.

---

[19] Cited in H. Leon McBeth, *A Sourcebook for Baptist Heritage* (Nashville, TN: Broadman, 1990), 202.

17

On Catechizing

Jim Scott Orrick

The Velveteen Rabbit is a well known children's story about a stuffed, toy rabbit that is transformed into a live rabbit. This miraculous transformation takes place because the little boy who owns the rabbit loves it so much. Before the rabbit is made alive, however, he has already been made real through the love of the boy. Being *made real* before becoming truly alive is a tricky concept, (and this conundrum is not unique to children's books), so it is a good thing that the wise, old Skin Horse that lives in the nursery with the Velveteen Rabbit instructs him further about being real: "It doesn't happen all at once," says the Skin Horse. "You become. It takes a long time. That's why it doesn't often happen to people who break easily, or have sharp edges, or who have to be carefully kept. Generally, by the time you are Real, most of your hair has been loved off, and your eyes drop out and you get loose in the joints and very shabby." Eventually the Rabbit does become real, and the evidence of his realness is that the rabbit has been carried around so much, and played with so much that he becomes threadbare with wear.

I have been blessed with a wonderful library. I was called to the ministry at a young age, and for many years I devoted a significant portion of my income toward buying books. I enjoyed the guidance of a pastor/father who is a reader of good books, so I never made very many book purchases that I later regretted. I have also been privileged to inherit more than one theological library from older ministers who were astute book lovers. But, alas, I am a relatively slow reader, and so I have a great many books in my library that are good books—books that I thought I would read when I added them to my library—that I will probably never get around to reading. They remain on my bookshelves, gleaming in their flawless dust jackets, tantalizing me with their promising titles and sagacious authors. When I am dead, someone will probably put them up for sale on the internet, and the seller will describe them as being in unmarked, pristine condition.

There is one book in my library, however, that will be worthless on the resale market. If wear and tear is evidence of being loved, this book must be the most loved book in my whole collection. It is a paperback, and its brown cover is creased and tattered. When the cover fell apart, I taped it back together with packing tape. When it further disintegrated, I covered it with a clear lamination that wraps around the whole cover. Pages that have fallen out have been taped back in. The edges of the pages are frayed, and they bear a brown smudge that marks the place where I have put my thumb thousands of times to flip to a specific location in the book. It has been stained with some liquid, but I cannot guarantee that it was water. It has been around children a lot. It is marked profusely, and I will say more about the markings later. The cover reads, "*Baptist Catechisms: To Make Thee Wise Unto Salvation*, by Tom J. Nettles."[1] It may be worthless as far as resale value is concerned, but it is unspeakably precious to me.

It is precious to me, firstly, because it represents the commencement of one of the most cherished friendships of my life. I acquired this book not long after I entered Mid-America Baptist Theological Seminary, where Tom Nettles was then on faculty. I believe that it was in the second semester of that same year that I took a class that Dr. Nettles taught: *Baptist Confessions and Catechisms*. Like most Baptists of the late twentieth century, I had only a vague notion of what a catechism was, and my suspicion was that it was a tool utilized by dead or heretical denominations. As I recall, I took the class not primarily because of the subject matter, but because I had already begun to love and admire Dr. Nettles. Our relationship was strictly that of professor and student, and I grimaced disapprovingly at the cheek of the brash young man in our class who went to the same church as Dr. Nettles and who cavalierly referred to him as "Tom." I would not dream of calling him by his first name. I respected Dr. Nettles as an astute thinker, a thoroughgoing scholar, and a hard teacher. I had already taken his Church History class, and I had not made a good grade, but that notwithstanding, I had learned a lot in the class, and I had learned so much from Tom Nettles as a person. He was so patient, yet he could dissect a fallacious argument with the skill of a benevolent surgeon. He was so humble, yet he taught with the confidence that comes from a lifetime of assiduous

---

[1] Tom J. Nettles, *Baptist Catechisms: To Make Thee Wise Unto Salvation* (Fort Worth, TX: Published by Tom Nettles, 1982).

study of God's Word. I resolved to take as many of his classes as I could, for I innately embraced what I now know: the heart of theological education is being in the same room with a man of God who loves his subject and loves his students.

Some years after I was his student, through his example and his advice, Dr. Nettles encouraged me to pursue further graduate studies. We occasionally corresponded during the years that I was a pastor, and when I was asked to join him on the faculty at The Southern Baptist Theological Seminary, his counsel again meant much to me. For nearly a decade now we have been on the same faculty, and I count him one of my dearest friends. At his insistence, I now dutifully call him "Tom," but I still regard him with a respect that only deepens with the passage of time. It all really commenced with that tattered, little, brown book.

I love the book, secondly, because of what it has meant to my own personal spiritual development. There are a number of catechisms included in the book, but two of them have been especially meaningful to me. The first is *The Baptist Catechism*, also known as *Keach's Catechism*. It is essentially *The Westminster Shorter Catechism* with biblical upgrades on the questions having to do with baptism. It is a magnificent piece of work. What beauty of language! What logic! What economy of language and logic! And best of all, what systematic and biblical theology! My basic theological perspectives were already formed when I first read *The Baptist Catechism*, but my perspectives might be compared to a well-furnished workshop that needed organization. *The Baptist Catechism* came into the workshop and said, "Let's get this place in working order. First, what does God require humans to believe? Next, what does God require humans to do? Here is a pegboard to help you organize what the Bible teaches about The Ten Commandments. Here is a shelf to help you fully utilize The Lord's Prayer in your prayer life." I immediately began committing *The Baptist Catechism* to memory. Day after day, as I meditated on the exchanges of the catechism, I found that some of the reliable old tools in my workshop needed sharpening. For example, I basically knew what justification was, but I could not give a complete, concise definition of it. I probably would have said something like, "Justification is when God declares us 'not guilty' because we believe in Jesus." How much sharper and glorious is the definition given in the catechism: "Justification is an act of God's free grace wherein he pardoneth all our sins and accepteth us as righteous in his sight only for the righteousness of Christ imputed to us and received by faith alone." There is not a bit of rust on that definition; it is all gleaming, burnished steel.

Similarly, the catechism has been a great aid in my personal devotional life. I commonly utilize The Lord's Prayer as an outline for my daily praying. What do I mean when I pray, "Thy will be done on earth as it is in heaven?" The catechism guides me: "In the third petition, which is Thy will be done on earth as it is in heaven, we pray that God, by his grace, will make us able and willing to know, obey, and submit to his will in all things as the angels do in heaven." That is a rich understanding of the third petition, and it is a petition that I need to offer every day. Sometimes, as an aid to confession of sin, I will pray through the Ten Commandments. Again, the catechism has helped me to understand what is required and what is forbidden in each of the commandments. My understanding of God's moral law and of my own moral condition has been richly informed by the catechism.

Besides *The Baptist Catechism*, the other catechism that I have used extensively is *The Catechism for Boys and Girls*. This catechism reminds me of a third reason why that old, brown book is precious to me: it has helped me to teach my family. I remember many happy hours surrounded by my little children as I taught them the catechism from that tattered, old book. How thrilled my wife and I were as our little firstborn answered the first question: "Who made you?" Answer: "God made me." (As every parent who has tried to teach the catechism knows, it takes about three months for the child to progress from answering, "God," to "God made me). As God blessed us with more children (all six girls) and another little girl would stammer out, "God *made me*," the rest of the family would clap and encourage her with our admiration and laughter. Happy, happy days. Scattered throughout the pages of *The Catechism for Boys and Girls* I have made notes in the margin denoting how far into the catechism each child had memorized by her sequential birthdays.

No amount of good teaching will guarantee that our children will embrace Christ as their Lord and Savior; salvation is of the Lord. But we are responsible to teach our children the truth of God's word, and a catechism can be a wonderful aid to us as we endeavor to do our duty. When God accomplishes the supernatural work of regeneration, he utilizes information that has been learned through natural means. He persuades and enables us to embrace Jesus Christ freely offered to us in the gospel, and receive and rest upon him alone for salvation; we believe the truth about Christ and we trust Christ. It is God who makes us willing in the day of his power, but the act of faith *per se* is not a supernatural act. Faith comes by hearing, and hearing by the word of God.

Not long ago I sat in the room of a hardened old sinner who was staring eternity in the face. I tried to reason with him, and I pleaded with him to repent and believe on Christ. The thought occurred to me that his already-failing mind must be in a muddle as to what it meant to believe in Christ, and he was even more clueless about who Christ is. We are saved, not by believing the right doctrines but by trusting in the right person: the

Lord Jesus Christ. But that Christ is known through doctrines. Bless God, a person does not need to be a theologian to believe in Christ; a person does not need to have memorized the catechism to believe in Christ; but a person must know the truth about Christ in order to believe in him. And so, in the darkened room of my dying friend, I went over the basic facts of the gospel in hopes that the God who raises dry bones would do his miraculous work again. We must urge our children to believe. Through teaching them a good catechism we inform them about the Lord in whom they must believe.

Some time ago I heard that a young man who had been in one of the churches I pastored had come to Christ in faith. He had been reared in a good family and had been taught the catechism, but he had been troubled for years, never resting in Christ. His conversion is a delightful story—too long to relate here—but here is a general retelling of one part of our conversation about his conversion.

He said, "And so, I decided that I would embrace the Bible as true."

I asked, "And it was not long after that that you received Christ?"

He answered, "Oh, it was virtually concurrent, for, you see, I knew what the Bible taught about Christ and the way of salvation through him."

This exchange illustrates the benefit of having been taught the Holy Scriptures from childhood. When the crisis comes; when the heart is softened; when the will is subdued; when God's eye diffuses that quickening ray and the dungeon flames with light; the sinner opens his long-blinded eyes to behold a full, robust Christ who is known to be Prophet, Priest, and King.

I know another young man who gave many evidences of being an earnest believer, yet he was plagued with doubts about his salvation. A wise counselor walked him through the section of the catechism that explains the offices that Christ executes as our Redeemer (that of Prophet, Priest, and King), and the counselor proceeded as follows:

"Here is what the Bible teaches about Christ as a prophet. Are you willing to have Christ teach you the will of God for your salvation?"

"Yes."

"Here is what the Bible teaches about Christ as Priest. Are you willing to receive Christ's sacrifice on behalf of sinners as sufficient to satisfy Divine justice and to reconcile you to God? Are you willing to rest upon Christ's intercession for sinners?"

"Yes, with all my heart!"

"Here is what the Bible teaches about Christ as King. Are you willing to submit to Christ as your King, to be subdued by him and ruled by him, and to have him restrain and conquer all your enemies and all his enemies?"

"Yes," I answered, for I was the young man, and William Guthrie, who was the wise counselor responded, "In what other way beyond this can you receive Christ?" I saw that I had received Christ, and my doubts were laid to rest. Though this experience antedates by several years my acquaintance with *The Catechism*, I later understood that this was Guthrie's method in his book, *The Christian's Great Interest*.[2]

A fourth reason why Nettles' compilation is precious to me is because it has helped me in my public ministry. When I was pastoring in West Virginia, four adult men professed faith in Christ within a few days' time. None of them had received much substantial teaching; only one of them had even been a church attender, and a couple of them were almost completely ignorant of the Bible. For their benefit, I commenced a new members' Sunday School class, which I taught. Our literature was *The Baptist Catechism*. It took us about two years to get through the catechism, and during that time the Lord added many others to the class. When the class was over, one of the original four had made unusual progress in his knowledge of the Scriptures. Although he had enjoyed only limited formal education and had been a Christian for only a couple of years, his knowledge of the Bible and his Christian maturity were advanced beyond others who had been members of the church for many years. He acknowledged his debt to the catechism, observing that the catechism really taught the whole Bible.

Countless times, as I have been preaching or teaching, I have recalled what the catechism says about a particular doctrine that appears in the text I am preaching or that is relevant to the subject we are discussing in class. Again and again, when I have quoted the catechism in preaching or have written a catechism answer on the board in class, I have observed careful listeners and students writing down what has been said. They recognize

---

[2] William Guthrie, *The Christian's Great Interest: Or the Trial of a Saving Interest in Christ and the Way to Obtain It*, ed. Thomas Chalmers (1825; reprint, Whitefish, MT: Kessinger, 2008).

the quality and usefulness of the doctrinal summary they have encountered from the catechism.

I have been privileged to personally disciple a number of young men who were preparing for the ministry. My standard procedure is to require them to memorize *The Baptist Catechism*. Covering the catechism with them insures that we will have opportunity to talk about every essential doctrine of Christianity.

When I sit on ordination councils, and especially if I have the responsibility of interrogating the candidate, I always use the catechism as a template for my questions. I do not expect the candidate to have memorized the catechism, but it does serve as a reliable standard of orthodoxy.

When I was pastor in Kansas City, our church utilized *The Baptist Catechism* in the teaching of our teens, while younger children were taught *The Catechism for Boys and Girls*. The elders determined that we would commence teaching *The Baptist Catechism* in our first grade classes and encourage our families to require their children to memorize it. While I was in hearty agreement with this educational step, I also realized that memorizing *The Baptist Catechism* would be quite an arduous undertaking for a six-year-old. To help the children, I decided that I would attempt to set to music every answer in the catechism and then record it so they could listen to it at their leisure. The response was very encouraging, and through the years I have received many emails and notes of appreciation for the recording of *The Baptist Catechism Set to Music*.[3] Several have testified that through studying and singing the catechism, their children have been converted. I have heard that the recording is quite popular at one of the Presbyterian seminaries that requires memorization of *The Shorter Catechism* as a prerequisite to graduation. In the margin of my creased and tattered copy of *The Baptist Catechism*, beside each exchange, I penciled in the date on which I set that answer to music.

It would be safe to say that besides the study and memorization of Scripture itself, nothing has been more beneficial to me in my public ministry than has the memorizing of *The Baptist Catechism*.

A few years after I acquired my copy of Nettles' *Baptist Catechisms*, he issued another collection of catechisms, *Teaching Truth, Training Heart: the Study of Catechisms in Baptist Life*.[4] It includes *The Baptist Catechism*, *The Catechism for Boys and Girls*, as well as several other catechisms. The

---

[3] *The Baptist Catechism Set to Music* can be purchased from Founders Press, available online at http://www.founderspress.com/shop/store.php (accessed February 9, 2011).

[4] Tom J. Nettles, *Teaching Truth, Training Heart: the Study of Catechisms in Baptist Life* (Amityville, NY: Calvary Press, 1998).

newer book also contains revisions and expansions of some of the material contained in the older volume that I have come to cherish. His introduction to *Teaching Truth, Training Hearts* is a wonderful history and defense of using catechisms. I encourage anyone interested in catechesis to procure and read that book. I have a copy. It has an attractive cover, and the pages are clean. Dr. Nettles inscribed it and signed it for me. I value it. But I prefer the old, tattered, brown book. It is like an old friend. It represents the commencement of a blessed friendship. It has enriched me personally, in my family life, and in my public ministry.

It is said that John Owen, the great Puritan theologian, once pulled from his pocket a small copy of William Guthrie's book, mentioned above, *The Christian's Great Interest*, and Owen declared, "That author I take to have been one of the greatest divines that ever wrote. It is my *vade mecum*." *Vade mecum* is Latin for "go with me." The phrase has made its way into English, and it refers to a useful thing that a person constantly carries with him, or it refers to a book, such as a guidebook, used for ready reference. Tom Nettles' *Baptist Catechisms: To Make Thee Wise Unto Salvation* is my *vade mecum*. Like the Velveteen Rabbit, its tattered condition indicates how much it has been used and how much it has been loved. It is the most real book in my library.

18

Recovering Regenerate Church Membership

Tom Ascol

When the Southern Baptist Convention convened in Indianapolis, Indiana in June 2008 the messengers adopted the following resolution by an overwhelming majority.

> WHEREAS, The ideal of a regenerate church membership has long been and remains a cherished Baptist principle, with Article VI of the Baptist Faith and Message describing the church as a "local congregation of baptized believers"; and

> WHEREAS, A New Testament church is composed only of those who have been born again by the Holy Spirit through the preaching of the Word, becoming disciples of Jesus Christ, the local church's only Lord, by grace through faith (John 3:5; Ephesians 2:8–9), which church practices believers' only baptism by immersion (Matthew 28:16–20), and the Lord's supper (Matthew 26:26–30); and

> WHEREAS, Local associations, state conventions, and the Southern Baptist Convention compile statistics reported by the churches to make decisions for the future; and

> WHEREAS, the 2007 Southern Baptist Convention annual Church Profiles indicate that there are 16,266,920 members in Southern Baptist churches; and

WHEREAS, Those same profiles indicate that only 6,148,868 of those members attend a primary worship service of their church in a typical week; and

WHEREAS, The Scriptures admonish us to exercise church discipline as we seek to restore any professed brother or sister in Christ who has strayed from the truth and is in sin (Matthew 18:15–35; Galatians 6:1); and now, therefore, be it

RESOLVED, That the messengers to the Southern Baptist Convention meeting in Indianapolis, Indiana, June 10–11, 2008, urge churches to maintain a regenerate membership by acknowledging the necessity of spiritual regeneration and Christ's lordship for all members; and be it further

RESOLVED, That we humbly urge our churches to maintain accurate membership rolls for the purpose of fostering ministry and accountability among all members of the congregation; and be it further

RESOLVED, That we urge the churches of the Southern Baptist Convention to repent of the failure among us to live up to our professed commitment to regenerate church membership and any failure to obey Jesus Christ in the practice of lovingly correcting wayward church members (Matthew 18:15–18); and be it further

RESOLVED, That we humbly encourage denominational servants to support and encourage churches that seek to recover and implement our Savior's teachings on church discipline, even if such efforts result in the reduction in the number of members that are reported in those churches, and be it finally

RESOLVED, That we humbly urge the churches of the Southern Baptist Convention and their pastors to implement a plan to minister to, counsel, and restore wayward church members based upon the commands and principles given in Scripture (Matthew 18:15–35; 2 Thessalonians 3:6–15; Galatians 6:1; James 5:19–20).[1]

The political maneuvering and theological wrangling that preceded the adoption of that resolution included arguments that at times were completely contrary to historic Baptist principles. Nevertheless, with the

---

[1] http://sbc.net/resolutions/amResolution.asp?ID=1189 (accessed May 23, 2010).

final vote, Southern Baptists went on record reaffirming one of the most fundamental convictions that gives strength to their ecclesiology, namely, regenerate church membership.[2]

The belief that only those who have been regenerated by the Holy Spirit are qualified for church membership has been historically one of the foremost ecclesiological distinctives of Baptist churches. It is not that Baptists are the only ones who have believed and defended this principle, but few have held to it as tenaciously and tried to apply it as consistently as they have. When the history of this teaching is considered, Baptists are the ones who emerge as its main champions.

Definition of the Principle

The word "regeneration" is used only twice in the New Testament. In Matthew 19:28 it refers to the final consummation of the kingdom of Christ, but in Titus 3:5 Paul applies it to individuals to describe the Spirit's work of inward renewal. It is in the latter, salvific sense that the word has been employed by Baptists to describe the qualifications for church membership. It is closely associated with the language of new birth employed by Jesus in his conversation with Nicodemus in John 3.

A regenerate person, then, is one who has been born of God's Spirit. He is a recipient of the new life that is found in Jesus Christ. He has been enabled not only to see but to enter the kingdom of God through faith and as such is a believer. A regenerate person is a disciple of Christ, which means simply that in the truest sense of the word, he is a Christian (Acts 11:26; cf. 26:28). Though it is common today to qualify the designation "Christian" with "born-again," the Bible knows no other kind.

Few evangelicals would deny that membership in the universal church (the people of God throughout all ages and all places) consists and has always consisted of only those who are regenerated or will be regenerated. No one will get to heaven without the new birth and all who are born again will get there. The principle of regenerate church membership insists that such persons are the only ones qualified to be numbered among the covenanted members of a local church.

---

[2] For example, in an earlier attempt to pass a similar resolution in 2006, the chairman of the Resolutions Committee, Pastor Tommy French, spoke against the proposal by arguing that if churches removed all their members who are inactive and never attend then they would lose some of their best prospects for evangelism. See Tom Ascol, "The Resolution Failed," Founders Ministries Blog, posted June 14, 2006, http://blog.founders.org/2006/06/resolution-failed.html (accessed January 15, 2011) and Wyman Richardson, *On Earth as it Is in Heaven* (Cape Coral, FL: Founders Press, 2011).

The New Testament teaches that the local churches that were established by the apostles were also composed of regenerate members. Apostolic letters sent to first century churches variously describe the recipients as "saints," "faithful in Christ Jesus," "sanctified in Christ Jesus," "God's chosen ones" and "believers" (Ephesians 1:1; 1 Corinthians 1:2; Colossians 3:12; 1 Thessalonians 2:12). After noting this fact John Dagg rightly concludes that, "No doubt can exist that these churches were, in view of the inspired writers who addressed them, composed of persons truly converted to God."[3]

The idea of regenerate church membership, then, comes from the biblical teaching that local churches are to be comprised of those who can legitimately lay claim to designations that are restricted to recipients of the new birth. All efforts to see churches grow and increase in membership should be governed by this principle so that the integrity of God's saving power in the gospel can be maintained before a watching world. In other words, if their churches are to follow the pattern of those described in the New Testament, then Baptists must insist that only genuine Christians are qualified to be members.

Historical Background

This principle that only Christians are qualified to be church members has come down to modern Baptists through that recovery of New Testament Christianity that took place during the Protestant Reformation of the sixteenth century. In the radical wing of the reformation, the evangelical Anabaptists rejected the idea that the church of Christ locally is comprised of all the members of what was supposed to have been, and was commonly called, a sacred or sacral society. Instead, they

> held that the New Testament Church is comprised of believers. It is a voluntary community, they said, of individuals who have been transformed by the working of the Holy Spirit in their lives, through an experience of grace, and they also taught and believed that baptism is "the symbol and the seal of the faith of those who have been so regenerated."[4]

Peter Rideman was an Anabaptist missionary sent out from the Hutterites of Moravia. In 1540 he published a confession comprised of ninety

---

[3] John L. Dagg, *A Treatise on Church Order* (Harrisonburg, VA: Gano Books, 1982), 79.

[4] William L. Lumpkin, *Baptist Confessions of Faith* (Valley Forge, PA: Judson Press, 1969), 13.

articles called, *Rechenshaft unserer Religion, Lehre, und Glaube (Account of our Religion, Teaching, and Faith)*. Its opening article exemplifies the Anabaptist impulse on this issue by defining a church as consisting of Christians only.

> An assembly of children of God who have separated themselves from all unclean things is the church. It is gathered together, has being, and is kept by the Holy Spirit. Sinners may not be members unless they have repented of their sins.[5]

The idea that a church is a gathered community comprised only of converted persons rather than an institution defined geographically or by the members of the society, is one that did not spread widely among Protestants of the sixteenth and seventeenth centuries. Within the Puritan movement the Independents and later Separatists did have among their number those who adhered, at least theoretically, to regenerate church membership. John Owen, who closely identified with the Independents and is regarded as the most rigorous of the Puritan theologians went so far as to say that "the letting go of this principle, [that] particular churches ought to consist of regenerate persons, brought in the great apostasy of the Christian Church."[6]

It became increasingly apparent to some within the Independent and Separatist movement that the practice of infant baptism is inconsistent with adherence to regenerate church membership. The effort to reconcile this inconsistency in a biblically faithful way is what gave rise to the modern Baptist movement in the early seventeenth century.

Those early Baptists separated into General (Arminian) Baptists and Particular (Calvinistic) Baptists within a generation. Nevertheless, they both maintained a firm commitment to the idea that a church is comprised of members who have been baptized as believers.

In 1609, John Smyth, the preeminent leader of the first General Baptists affirmed in his *Short Confession*, "That the church of Christ is a company of the faithful; baptized after confession of sin and of faith, endowed with the power of Christ."[7] Three years later General Baptists confessed in Article 64 of their *Propositions and Conclusions*, "That the outward church visible, consists of penitent persons only, and of such as believing in Christ, bring forth fruits worthy of amendment of life."[8]

---

[5] Ibid, 40.

[6] Cited in Iain Murray, *Jonathan Edwards, a New Biography* (Edinburgh: Banner of Truth Trust, 1987), 332.

[7] Ibid, 101.

[8] Ibid, 136.

The first associational confession of the Particular Baptists was published by London churches in 1644. In Article 33 the principle of regenerate church membership is expressed in the affirmation of the nature of the church.

> That Christ hath here on earth a spirituall Kingdome, which is the Church, which he hath purchased and redeemed to himself, as a peculiar inheritance: which Church, as it is visible to us, is a company of visible Saints, called & separated from the world, by the word and Spirit of God, to the visible profession of the faith of the Gospel, being baptized into that faith, and joyned to the Lord, and each other, by mutuall agreement, in the practical injoyment of the Ordinances, commanded by Christ their head and King."[9]

Churches are to be comprised of those who have been "called and separated... by the Word and the Spirit." In other words, those who make up local churches are to be regenerated.

Ecclesiology became a point of great contention among Protestants in the late sixteenth and early seventeenth centuries. By the time the Westminster Assembly was gathered in England from 1643–49 the nature of local churches was a very hot topic. The Assembly was comprised primarily of Presbyterians. The few Independents who joined them were called the "Dissenting Brethren." This decided minority argued for the church being defined and recognized locally as consisting of regenerate people. Their views were not well received. In fact, many in the assembly charged them and their convictions with promoting spiritual pride and false assurance in their churches. As William Maxwell Hetherington, a Presbyterian historian of the Westminster Assembly writes, the "Independents held the theory of admitting none to be members of their churches except those whom they believed to have been thoroughly and in the highest sense regenerated or, in the language of the time, 'true saints.'"[10]

The Presbyterian view of the church won the day and is reflected in chapter 25 of the Westminster Confession of Faith. Section 2 of that chapter states, "The visible Church,... consists of all those throughout the world that profess the true religion, together with their children,..."[11]

---

[9] Ibid, 165.

[10] William Maxwell Hetherington, History of the Westminster Assembly of Divines (Edmonton, AB Canada: Still Water Revival Books, 1991 reprint edition), 193–94.

[11] *The Westminster Confession of Faith; the Larger and Shorter Catechisms, with the Scripture Proofs at Large: Together with the Sum of Saving Knowledge* (Glasgow, Scotland: Free Presbyterian Publications, 1983), 107–8.

Baptists stood starkly against this Presbyterian view of the church and by the time the Particular Baptists of London published their second associational confession in 1689 they were able to articulate their distinctive convictions in discriminating language. The second paragraph of chapter 26 of that confession states,

> All persons throughout the world, professing the faith of the Gospel, and obedience unto God by Christ according unto it, not destroying their own profession by any Errors everting the foundation, or unholyness of conversation, are and may be called visible Saints; and of such ought all particular Congregations to be constituted.[12]

The last phrase is a notable advance beyond not only Presbyterianism but also beyond the views of the Independents and demonstrates a clear commitment to the ideal of a pure church comprised of regenerate members.[13] It is inherent in true Baptist identity to insist that only professing believers who demonstrate the sincerity of their professions by holy lives, thereby showing that they have been born of God's Spirit, should be welcomed as members of a local church.

Some Presbyterian theologians have taken strong exception to this principle and to those who have espoused it. Some even condemn it as unbiblical, unrealistic, presumptuous and naive. For example, both Charles Hodge and James Bannerman agree that a "credible profession" of faith is required before allowing anyone to become a communicant member of the local church. They go on to argue, however, that if a man says he believes and does not have an immoral life, then his profession must be judged credible. A verbal profession, coupled with a life that is not scandalous is enough for membership. Hodge argues against the principle of a regenerate church membership by contrasting his own view with it.

> According to the one view the church is bound to be satisfied in its judgment that the applicant is truly regenerated; according to the other, no such judgment is expressed or implied in receiving any one into the fellowship of the Church. As Christ has not given his people the power to

---

[12] Lumpkin, *Baptist Confessions*, 285.

[13] The Congregationalist Savoy Declaration of 1658 obviously provided a basis for the 1689 Baptist statement on the church. The last phrase of the section quoted, "and of such ought all particular Congregations to be constituted," is a unique addition by the Baptists. See Philip Schaff, ed. *The Creeds of Christendom*, Volume 3, *The Creeds of the Evangelical Protestant Churches* (Grand Rapids, MI, Baker Book House, 1983), 721–22.

search the heart, He has not imposed upon them the duty which implies the possession of any such power.[14]

He is certainly correct that God has not given to the church the ability to search human hearts. However, this is not at all what is being asserted when Baptists insist that churches are to be comprised of only regenerate people.

Baptists argue that a credible profession of faith involves more than just a verbal agreement to either a set of facts or doctrines or a profession that has been spelled out, coupled with a life that is not scandalous. Rather, they insist that such a person must also give evidence of a work of grace in the inner life that is in keeping with the biblical teaching on Christian character and conduct. Only the one whose profession includes a life oriented to and empowered by the gospel of Jesus Christ is qualified to be a member of a local church.

Hodge goes on to say that "the Church is not called upon to pronounce a judgment as to the real piety of applicants for membership" and any attempt to do so is an encroachment on God's prerogatives." Baptists respond to that by saying that this is precisely what every church is called to do—to make a judgment about applicants for membership. Whenever any person is received into the membership of a Baptist church that local body is declaring that he or she is a follower of Jesus Christ, a saint, a chosen one, a believer, etc. Not only does a church have the right to make such judgments, it has a responsibility to do so.

Hodge's charge that those who hold this principle are judging men's hearts is a false accusation. It is not a person's heart that is judged but his profession that he knows and follows Jesus Christ. This is precisely what Scripture commands us to do. "Whoever says 'I know him' but does not keep his commandments is a liar, and the truth is not in him, but whoever keeps his word, in him truly the love of God is perfected" (1 John 2:4–5). The same careful judgment that is required of a church when it must remove a member is required when it comes to admitting members. "Is it not those inside the church whom you are to judge?" (1 Corinthians 5:12). John Dagg makes this distinction in his *Treatise on Church Order.*

The churches are not infallible judges, being unable to search the heart; but they owe it to the cause of Christ, and to the candidate himself, to exercise the best judgment of which they are capable. To receive any one

[14] Charles Hodge, *Systematic Theology*, Volume 3 (Grand Rapids, MI: Eerdmans Publishing Company, 1981), 545; cf. 577–79.
    Ibid, 576.

on a mere profession of words, without any effort to ascertain whether he understands and feels what he professes, is unfaithfulness to his interests, and the interests of religion.[16]

By contending for the principle of a regenerate church membership Baptists have conscientiously staked out a minority position in Christian ecclesiology. They have done so, not out of hubris but rather out of clear convictions that the nature of the church arises out of the nature of salvation itself. Only those who have experienced the latter are qualified to be members of the former.

Biblical Foundation

Why have Baptists defended and attempted to order their churches according to the principle of regenerate church membership? What are the biblical arguments for this view? There are four lines of argument from the New Testament that support the Baptist case for their position.

First, the members of the churches in the New Testament are consistently designated by terms that are appropriate only for those who have been born by God's Spirit. Apostolic letters sent to first-century churches variously describe the recipients as "children of God by faith," "saints," "faithful in Christ Jesus," "sanctified in Christ Jesus," "God's chosen ones" and "believers" (Galatians 3:26; Ephesians 1:1; 1 Corinthians 1:2; Colossians 3:12; 1 Thessalonians 2:12). After noting this fact John Dagg rightly concludes that, "No doubt can exist that these churches were, in view of the inspired writers who addressed them, composed of persons truly converted to God."[17]

Those who live contrary to the standards commensurate with such designations are exposed as interlopers who should be separated from the church. Thus the members of the Corinthian church are commanded to deal decisively in removing a sexually immoral member from the membership. "You are to deliver this man to Satan for the destruction of the flesh, so that his spirit may be saved in the day of the Lord" (1 Corinthians 5:5). Furthermore, Paul says, "Purge the evil person from among you" (1 Corinthians 5:13). Similarly, the Lord Jesus directly chastises the church at Thyatira because they "tolerate that woman Jezebel" whose godless teachings led believers astray (Revelation 2:20). Christ expects his churches to be comprised of people who genuinely know and follow him.

---

[16] Dagg, *A Treatise on Church Order*, 269.
[17] Ibid., 79.

A second reason to affirm regenerate church membership comes from recognizing what a person had to experience in order to be included in a New Testament church. In Acts 2 the church at Jerusalem was begun through Peter's preaching at Pentecost. On that occasion the hearers "were cut to the heart" (v. 37). They were affected inwardly with something that caused them to have not only an outward profession and agreement with certain truths or facts but also to reorient their lives in radical ways. They "received his [Peter's] word," evidencing a work in the heart, and "were baptized" (v. 41). Luke closes out his summary of that event by noting that "the Lord added to their number day by day those who were being saved" (v. 47). Only those who had experienced salvation were being added to them by the Lord.

The same is true of the church at Philippi. When Paul first was called to Macedonia, Lydia met him by the side of the river and listened to the word that he taught from the Scriptures. As she did so "the Lord opened her heart," after which she was baptized (Acts 16:14–15). She believed the things that were said, came to faith in Jesus and began to obey his commandments. These are the actions of a regenerated person.

Though the details are different the same testimony is given by the jailer who also became a part of the church at Philippi. After Paul preached the gospel to him in the aftermath of an earthquake, Scripture says he was "trembling" and "believed" with rejoicing (Acts 16:29, 34). These are descriptions of an inward work of the Spirit of God.

A third way the New Testament teaches regenerate church membership is by describing the requirements for entering the Kingdom of God. Church members are repeatedly referred to as citizens of the Kingdom of God as in Colossians 1:13 where Paul describes the members of that church as having been "delivered… from the domain of darkness and transferred… to the kingdom of his beloved Son" (cf. 1 Thessalonians 2:12, 2 Thessalonians 1:5, 2 Timothy 4:18, James 2:5, 2 Peter 1:11).

In order to become a citizen of the kingdom one must be regenerated. As Jesus taught, no one enters the kingdom of God unless he has been born of God's Spirit. In fact, not only is it impossible for a person to enter the kingdom of God without a new birth, one cannot even see the kingdom without this inner change (John 3:3, 5). Since members of the churches in the New Testament are characterized as being citizens of God's kingdom it stands to reason that they are regenerate.

Finally, consider the nature of the spiritual requirements that the New Testament sets before church members. The apostles instruct churches to live in ways that necessitate spiritual life. The New Testament letters written to churches are filled with admonitions to cultivate faith, love, joy, and hope. How could the recipients of those letters be expected to cultivate such virtues if they are void of spiritual life? Such qualities are the fruit of the Spirit's work in a believer's life. The apostles expected the churches to whom they wrote to be comprised of people who were inhabited by the Spirit. Apostolic churches are churches with a regenerate membership.

To hold to the principle of regenerate church membership does not mean that we must therefore believe that there are no unregenerate members in local churches. That is simply not true. The church on earth is fallen and fallible. Sometimes even the most careful church makes mistakes in judging the character and testimony of its prospective members. The Scripture tells us that Satan himself masquerades as an angel of light, and so do his ministers. They look like the authentic article, but they are not.

The apostle John recognized this and speaks of those who "went out from us, but they were not of us; for if they had been of us, they would have continued with us. But they went out, that it might become plain that they all are not of us" (1 John 2:19). Such people profess true religion, have an outward conduct that helps their profession appear credible, and have been received into the church. Then, through the character of their lives as they depart the faith and go their own way, they demonstrate that despite their profession and reception into the church they are not genuinely part of community of regenerate believers. They are intruders and the presence of intruders and unconverted people in a local church in no way overturns the principle of a regenerate church membership.

It is folly to acquiesce to the exception as grounds for giving up the principle. John gives us the right perspective on those who infiltrate the church yet refuse to follow Christ at all costs. Though they look real for a while, they never were part of the faithful members of the church. Though among us, "they were not of us."

The Second London Baptist Confession of 1689 recognizes this inevitability when it states that, "The purest churches under heaven are subject to mixture and error." Local churches will always be afflicted with false believers and unconverted members. Though they are present, they do not belong in the church. Under the ministry of the Word of God in the context of the people of God who are genuinely seeking to live lives of faith and obedience, such intruders are often either converted or exposed.

The fact that there are unconverted people in the church does not mean that there ought to be unconverted people in the church. The principle of regenerate church membership affirms that "oughtness." Because the New Testament teaches that local churches should be comprised only of believers, Baptists have insisted on and defended this principle.

There are several theological corollaries which extend from this principle. Since a person must be sovereignly born of God's Spirit before he is qualified for church membership, all efforts physically or officially to coerce any such church identification are illegitimate. Consequently, religious liberty (and beyond that, the principle of separation of church and state) extends from the belief in a gathered church voluntarily comprised of born again believers. There are others, as well, but two particular corollaries merit special consideration because they are more immediately and absolutely inherent in regenerate church membership. Specifically the practice of believers' baptism and the practice of church discipline both extend from a commitment to a regenerate church and serve to protect and preserve it.

As a church sacrament, or ordinance, baptism is to be administered to all who are covenanted together in a local church. Since only the regenerate are to be church members then baptism is reserved for those who through the new birth have become believers. Without limiting baptism to believers alone a church will inevitably encourage the unregenerate to join its ranks. This is precisely what happens through the practice of paedobaptism.

Historically Baptists have regarded baptism as the outward, ceremonial sign of the inward, spiritual reality of new birth. Both have been required for church membership. These two requirements are complementary and each works to uphold the other. As Tom Nettles rightly notes, when believers' baptism is practiced as an extension of regenerate church membership it "protects the purity of the church and provides a safeguard to that principle. Allowing none but professing believers into the membership of the church through baptism promotes the New Testament ideal of responsible church membership."[18]

Another practice that walks hand-in-hand with a regenerate church is church discipline. Although many paedobaptist communions also believe in church discipline their practice of it is made more complicated than necessary by their rejection of regenerate church membership. Receiving unbelieving children into the church (even as "non-communicant" members) works against the goal of encouraging and maintaining holiness throughout the membership. The tragic eighteenth-century example of Jonathan Edwards at Northampton illustrates this.

The new birth results in a life that is committed to growth in holiness. A church comprised of regenerate people is to be a holy communion. As John Dagg writes, "To be visible saints, a holy life must be superadded to a profession of the true religion; and they who do not exhibit the light of a holy life, whatever their professions may be, have not scriptural claim to be considered members of Christ's church."[19] Just as no regard for holiness

---

[18] Tom Nettles, *Believers Baptism by Immersion* (Nashville, TN: The Historical Commission of the Southern Baptist Convention, 1989), 7.

[19] Dagg, *A Treatise on Church Order*, 123.

disqualifies one from becoming a member of a church so also unwillingness to live in holiness disqualifies one from remaining a member of a church.

Church discipline is usually divided into two categories: formative and corrective. The former consists of working to see Christ formed more and more in the lives of church members through the means that God has ordained in his Word. This is accomplished primarily through faithful proclamation and application of Scripture.

When the normal means of grace are disregarded and a church member begins to live disorderly in belief or practice, then corrective discipline must be implemented. Many passages in Scripture teach how correction is to be administered to wayward church members (Romans 16:17; 1 Corinthians 5; Titus 3:10; 2 Thessalonians 3:6, 14), but our Lord's instructions in Matthew 18:15–20 is the classic one. Only if a member remains recalcitrant in the face of increasingly weighty calls to repent does Jesus command a church finally to remove such a one from membership.

That sad and final step of corrective discipline is in one sense simply an application of regenerate church membership. Just as one must have a credible testimony of being born of God's Spirit in order to be received into membership so he must maintain such a testimony to remain in membership. Edward Hiscox states the matter very directly in his *New Directory of Baptist Churches*.

> If our churches are to fulfill their mission, remain true to their traditions, and honor their apostolical pretensions, they must insist, with unabated vigor, on *a regenerated membership*. Nor must they insist on it in theory only, but take every precaution to maintain it in practice.[20]

The statistics cited in the 2008 resolution on regenerate church membership adopted by the Southern Baptist Convention reveal how far away from this historic Baptist principle modern Baptists—particularly Southern Baptists—have drifted. For decades the Annual Church Profiles compiled by the Southern Baptist Convention reveal that a typical Southern Baptist church can expect fewer than 40% of its members even regularly to attend Sunday worship services. If this minimalist approach is used to evaluate the presence of spiritual life in church members then the conclusion is unavoidable that the great majority of those on the membership rolls of Southern Baptist churches give no sign of being converted. This condition is not an anomaly. It is the norm.

---

[20] Edward T. Hiscox, *The New Directory for Baptist Churches* (Philadelphia, Pennsylvania: Judson Press, 1894), 64.

If Baptists from the earlier centuries were here to evaluate this current condition they would have much to say by way of rebuke and instruction to modern Baptist churches whose memberships appear to be dominated by unregenerate people. Hiscox's admonition to his fellow Baptists in the nineteenth century still applies today. "The character of the persons who are to constitute the churches and hold membership therein, is fixed and prescribed by Christ Himself, and is to remain permanent and unchanged."[21] Neither congregation nor pastor is free to lower the standard of membership. In fact, Hiscox goes on to warn,

> Those pastors make a grave mistake, and are grievously in fault, who hurry persons into the Church without giving the body a fair and full opportunity of gaining evidence of their regenerate state. They may ask a few leading questions themselves, which anyone, saint or sinner, could answer, and … call a vote on their reception, to which a few will respond and many remain silent. No fellowship is accorded by the body, since no evidence is obtained. The Church may seem to be prosperous, because baptisms frequently occur; but the moral strength of the body is weakened, rather, and disorder introduced where order should prevail.[22]

Movement beyond a mere theoretical affirmation of regenerate church membership will require churches to be more thoughtful than is typically the case in receiving members. There must be a clear understanding on the nature of salvation and the marks of regeneration as well as adequate opportunity to discern if the candidate for membership gives evidence of being born of God's Spirit. Williams Rutherford, a professor at the University of Georgia, lamented the lack of care some demonstrated in receiving new members Baptist churches in the late nineteenth century. In his *Church Members' Guide for Baptist Churches*, he writes,

> Churches are not careful enough in receiving members on profession of faith. It frequently happens that persons apply for membership under excitement and without due consideration. In this way many are received who have not been truly regenerated, and remain in an unregenerated state in the Church, very much to the injury of the cause of true godliness. No one should apply for membership in a Baptist Church who has not experienced such a change of heart, by the operation of the Holy Spirit, as to make him anxious to abandon all sin and live a pious and godly life.[23]

[21] Ibid, 62

[22] Ibid, 72–73.

[23] *Church Members' Guide for Baptist Churches* (Atlanta, GA: James P. Harrison, 1885), 103.

The Baptist ideal of a church cannot be pursued without a serious, practical commitment to a regenerate membership. Believers' baptism will be reduced to assenters' baptism and congregational polity will degenerate into carnal anarchy. Formative church discipline will be eclipsed by programs that merely attempt to motivate, if not manipulate, members to do what genuine Christians should desire to do. Corrective discipline will not be tolerated and will ultimately disappear. The end result is that a Baptist church will be weakened, its purity compromised and its mission undermined without a rigorous adherence to a regenerate membership.

As Baptists have recognized throughout their history, Scripture calls them to order their churches under the lordship of Christ, who is the head of every local congregation. In order for his body to be healthy and function according to his will, each member must be regenerate. That is the standard that Baptists have found revealed in God's Word and it is a goal that Baptist churches must pursue in order to remain true to their principles.

19

Believer's Baptism
ITS NATURE, PRACTICE AND IMPORTANCE

Fred Malone

It is an honor to contribute to this *festschrift* honoring Dr. Tom Nettles. He is the epitome of what a Christian and professor should be. I have been blessed with a longtime friendship with him since 1980. At that time, he was teaching at Southwestern Baptist Theological Seminary, where I had just moved to enroll in the PhD program. Dr. Nettles' gracious kindness to me has often encouraged me in the ministry, while his great knowledge of Baptist history and theology has often instructed me. I know of no one in Baptist life to whom both the resurgence toward inerrancy and the increased understanding of historic Baptist theology owes more … in one person. I believe that thousands of students, pastors and laymen would add to my testimony.

It has been assigned to me to dedicate a chapter to Dr. Nettles on that core Baptist distinctive, the baptism of disciples alone. I have titled this chapter "Believer's Baptism: Its Nature, Practice and Importance." In his own right, Dr. Nettles has contributed much to this subject in his various writings. He penned a small pamphlet on baptism in the Foundations of Baptist Heritage series published by the SBC's Historical Commission during the 1980s; thousands of Southern Baptists have read this little summary.[1] He also contributed a chapter in *Understanding Four Views of*

---

[1] Tom J. Nettles, *Believer's Baptism by Immersion*, Foundations of Baptist Heritage (Nashville, TN: The Historical Commission of the Southern Baptist Convention, 1989).

Baptism, representing the historic Baptist position.[2] A personal favorite of mine is his short article on believer's baptism written for *Modern Reformation*.[3] Dr. Nettles has defended well the nature, practice, and importance of believer's baptism in many venues.

A further contribution of Dr. Nettles to the theology of baptism concerns its place in the past and current debates over Baptist identity. For the past one hundred years there has been both a historical revisionism about this issue by moderates in the SBC as well as a reformulation of modern Baptist identity by conservatives. This has brought both confusion and division within SBC ranks. Dr. Nettles three-volume *The Baptists* is his *magnum opus* (so far), which is both historically accurate and prophetically needed today.[4]

I dedicate this chapter to Dr. Nettles on the nature, practice and importance of disciples' only baptism. I hope that he will be pleased with my intent, content and the implications which its meaning carries for regeneration, conversion, sanctification, glorification, ecclesiology, Baptist identity… and for biblical reformation in our beloved Baptist Zion!

The Nature of Believer's Baptism

There is more to believer's baptism than immersion in water. There is more to believer's baptism than just obeying a command of Christ to be baptized. Many truths of Scripture are attached to the nature and meaning of this ordinance. Baptists today need to rediscover the full meaning of believer's baptism.

Baptists have not generally held with other denominations that baptism is a "seal" of salvation, simply because the Holy Spirit, not baptism, is so designated in the New Testament (Ephesians 1:13–14, 4:30; 2 Corinthians 1:21–22). They have tried to avoid any sacramental efficacy or *ex opere operato* understanding of baptism and the Lord's Supper. However, most Baptist confessions give a fuller meaning to believer's baptism than just the immersion of a believer.

---

[2] Thomas J. Nettles, "Baptist View: Baptism as a Symbol of Christ's Saving Work," in *Understanding Four Views of Baptism*, ed. John H. Armstrong (Grand Rapids, MI: Zondervan, 2007), 25–41.

[3] This article is reprinted at The Reformed Reader website. See Tom J. Nettles, "Baptists and the Ordinances," The Reformed Reader, available online at http://www.reformedreader.org/bao.htm (accessed February 8, 2011).

[4] Tom J. Nettles, *The Baptists: Key People Involved in Forming a Baptist Identity*, 3 vols. (Fearn, Ross-Shire, UK: Christian Focus, 2005–2007).

The *1689 Second London Baptist Confession* (SLBC) was a formative influence upon Baptists in England and early America. Both the Philadelphia and Charleston Confessions were almost identical to the SLBC. Therefore, we must assume that our early Baptists (Northern and Southern) agreed to the SLBC's definition of baptism as an ordinance and sign:

> Baptism is an *ordinance* of the New Testament, ordained by Jesus Christ, to be unto the party baptized, a *sign* of his fellowship with him, in his death and resurrection; of his being engrafted into him; of remission of sins; and of giving up into God, through Jesus Christ, to live and walk in newness of life (Section 29:1, emphasis added).

The more recent *Baptist Faith and Message* (2000) defines the nature of baptism as follows:

> Christian baptism is the immersion of a believer in water in the name of the Father, the Son, and the Holy Spirit. It is an act of obedience symbolizing the believer's faith in a crucified, buried, and risen Saviour, the believer's death to sin, the burial of the old life, and the resurrection to walk in newness of life in Christ Jesus. It is a testimony to his faith in the final resurrection of the dead. Being a church ordinance, it is prerequisite to the privileges of church membership and to the Lord's Supper (Article VI: Baptism and the Lord's Supper).

In some ways, the *Baptist Faith and Message* is a more complete explanation of the meaning of baptism than the SLBC, adding baptism's signification of the bodily resurrection of the dead. It is this broader meaning of believer's baptism which needs to be restored in our Baptist churches.

Having surveyed two Baptist confessions for the robust nature and meaning of believer's baptism, I will now expand the main points of historical Baptist beliefs.

Believer's Baptism is an Instituted Ordinance of Jesus Christ

The basic hermeneutical principle which necessitates believer's baptism alone is the regulative principle of worship. The SBLC defines this principle as follows:

> The whole counsel of God concerning all things necessary for his own glory, man's salvation, faith and life, is *either expressly set down or necessarily contained in the Holy Scripture*: unto which nothing at any time is to be added, whether by new revelation of the Spirit, or traditions of men (Section 1:6, emphasis added).

The light of nature shews that there is a God, who hath lordship and sovereignty over all; is just, good and doth good unto all; and is therefore to be feared, loved, praised, called upon, trusted in, and served, with all the heart and soul, and with all the might. But *the acceptable way of worshipping the true God, is instituted by himself, and so limited by his own revealed will,* that he may not be worshipped according to the imagination and devices of men, nor the suggestions of Satan, under any visible representations, *or any other way not prescribed in the Holy Scriptures.* (Section 22:1, emphasis added).

Baptism and the Lord's supper are *ordinances of positive and sovereign institution, appointed by the Lord Jesus,* the only lawgiver, to be continued in his church to the end of the world (Section 28:1, emphasis added).

Historically, Baptists have held to the baptism of disciples alone on the basis of the regulative principle of worship, therefore rejecting infant baptism because the latter is never mentioned in Scripture. In a sense, believer's baptism by the regulative principle is the defining principle of Baptist ecclesiology.

Yet, sadly, many Baptists (and Presbyterians) have forsaken the regulative principle of worship to add uncommanded elements to worship such as drama, plays, movies, musical extravaganzas, weight-lifting displays and women leading worship (1 Timothy 2:11–12). These uncommanded elements of worship take time away from commanded elements of worship. In so doing, many modern Baptists have forsaken the foundation of their separateness, which is the regulative principle of worship for believer's baptism. Such Baptist churches cease to be Baptist in principle, refusing to apply the sufficiency as well as the inerrancy of Scripture.

In rediscovering the regulative nature of instituted believer's baptism, we find not only the hermeneutical principle for reformation in Baptist worship, but also the foundational principle for building a true Baptist church.

Believer's Baptism is a Symbol or Sign of the Crucifixion, Burial and Resurrection of Jesus Christ.

As He faced the immediate threat of the Cross, our Lord told His disciples, "You do not know what you are asking. Are you able to drink the cup that I drink, or to be baptized with the baptism with which I am baptized?" (Mark 10:38). Our Lord's characterization of the crucifixion as a baptism marks forever the act of believer's baptism as a visible symbol and preaching of His atoning work. He was immersed by man and God into death, in order that He might put death to death in His resurrection.

Because baptism is a visible sign of Jesus' death and resurrection, it must never be relegated only to a brief ritual we perform in bare obedience to Christ's command. In itself, believer's baptism is a display of the work of Christ which preaches to those observing (both believers and unbelievers) His glorious work of redemption. It preaches the gospel that He is the only way for any to be justified before God; that all must go to the risen Christ, pray to Him, repent of their sins to Him and ask Him to accept them on the basis of His promised Word; that they must let their baptism be the sign of their Savior's redemptive salvation to walk in newness of life (Romans 6:1–11). It must not be performed in a perfunctory or insignificant manner. At such times, it is worthy to rehearse His gospel for the one baptized as well as for those who observe. Let the ordinance of believer's baptism preach to sinners!

Believer's Baptism is a Confession of Personal Repentance toward God and Faith in our Lord Jesus Christ

The baptism of John found him baptizing people who were confessing their sins in (*en*) the Jordan River (Mark 1:5). His was a baptism of repentance unto the forgiveness of sins and of believing in the One to come (Acts 19:4). Our Lord also called all to repent of sin and to believe His gospel before baptism (Mark 1:15; John 4:1–2). And this was the Great Commission baptism practiced by the Apostles on Pentecost and thereafter. Only those who repented and received Peter's words by a confessing faith were baptized (Acts 2:38–41; 26:18–20).

This confession in baptism necessarily includes belief in the Trinitarian divinity of Christ as Lord, condemnation for one's sins against God's Law, substitutionary atonement, justification by faith alone in Christ alone, cleansing from sin, the receiving of the Holy Spirit, spiritual union with Christ, commitment to a holy life of obedience to His commandments, union with the body of Christ and the hope of glorification. This is a disciple's confession, and disciples were the only ones whom Jesus and the Apostles baptized. This is why the church is often called "the disciples" (Acts 6:2; 11:26; 13:52).

Could it be that we Baptists have truncated the meaning of baptism to a bare confession instead of a robust confession of repentance from sin and faith in Christ as found in the New Testament? Could it be that this is one reason why it is so easy to see multitudes "get baptized," yet so hard to get them to walk in faith and obedience all the days of their lives? Where are the over 50% of our baptized members? Such baptized ones show neither true repentance nor a faith that submits to Christ as Lord. Perhaps they did not know what they were confessing to begin with.

It would do us well to take the time to make disciples before we baptize them. We must make sure they understand the gospel and its elements as well as the call to a holy life (Romans 6:1–10). If necessary, we should take time to instruct them about the full meaning of believer's baptism before we baptize them. After all, it is a *believer's* baptism.

Baptism is a Sign of Spiritual Union with the Trinity

It is clear from the Great Commission that believer's baptism is a sign of spiritual union with the Trinity: the Father, the Son, and the Holy Spirit (Matthew 28:19–20). Even though the Apostles baptized "in the name of Jesus Christ" (Acts 2:38), this presumes union with the Father and the Son and the Spirit within the Godhead. Christ is the Way into union with the Trinity. Baptism itself does not unite us to the Godhead *ex opere operato*, as some might say, but it testifies to the believer that he has been united to the Trinity through faith alone in Jesus Christ alone. Believer's baptism is a confession that one believes in our Trinitarian God.

Leonard Riisen is helpful on this point:

> Therefore when the pastor says, I baptize thee, it is the same as if he were saying, I declare in God's name that this water in which I wash you is a symbol of your admission into God's covenant and His Church; that the Father accepts you as a son, the Son as a member of His body and a brother, and the Holy Spirit as a host with whom He is willing to dwell for ever; and that you worship Father, Son and Holy Spirit, in virtue of the terms of your duty to the triune God, with worship and obedience, and consecrate yourself wholly to the worship of the Trinity for ever.[5]

Perhaps this is one reason why we see such a low level of commitment in our church members today. They have not been taught the glorious truth that baptism is a sign of our spiritual union with the Father as His adopted child, with the Son as our mediating blood brother, and the Holy Spirit as our indwelling Comforter. Let us teach the wonderful truth of Trinitarian baptism to our people, so that they may rejoice in what their baptism represents.

Baptism is a Sign of a Regenerate Church

Believer's baptism is both a sign that one has been born again by the Holy Spirit and that he is being baptized into the concept of a regenerate

---

[5] Heinrich Heppe, *Reformed Dogmatics*, trans. G. T. Thompson (Grand Rapids: Baker, 1978), 615.

church (John 3:3–8; 1 Corinthians 12:13). All Baptists know and agree that not everyone who has been baptized as a confessing believer has truly been born again by God's Holy Spirit. We know that the Scripture speaks of apostasy and false conversion (Matthew 7:22–23; 1 John 2:19). However, with good faith, we trust that the confessor has been brought to this point of baptism by Holy Spirit regeneration. So what should we teach the candidate and the congregation?

The kingdom of God is entered into by the regenerating work of the Holy Spirit, resulting in the confession of repentance and faith (John 3:3–8; Acts 10:47; see also the *Baptist Faith and Message* [2000], Article IV: Salvation). Believer's baptism is a confession that one has been born again into the kingdom of God (Titus 3:5–7). As a result, the local church of Jesus Christ is to be a body of confessing believers, testifying that they have been born again to a living hope in Christ alone. This is the foundation of Baptist ecclesiology.

Therefore, believer's baptism must be explained and practiced in terms of the confession giving evidence of regeneration and the foundation of the local church. If we would see the building of a regenerate church of faithful members, Baptists must return to a robust understanding and teaching of baptism as a sign of regeneration and the foundation of a regenerate church. This continual teaching is essential to build a faithful church membership, as well as to gain the congregation's understanding of loving church discipline to win the straying brother (Matthew 18:15–17). Baptist reformation begins with a robust understanding of believer's baptism as a sign of regeneration.

Baptism is a Sign of Commitment to an Obedient Life

Believer's baptism, of necessity, testifies of one's commitment to an obedient life to Jesus Christ as Lord (Matthew 28:19–20). For the last one hundred years, the teaching of "the carnal Christian doctrine" has weakened the concept of an obedient life among Baptists. Teaching the separation of Jesus as Savior from Jesus as Lord, the early dispensational and "higher life" teachers undermined the concept of baptism as a commitment to an obedient life according to the Ten Commandments and the other commandments of the New Covenant. The low level of biblical holiness in our local churches testifies to the damaging effects of this teaching.

If Baptists wish to see churches filled with believers committed to an obedient life, we must restore the Great Commission commitment to obedience in believer's baptism (Matthew 28:19–20). How many candidates for baptism today are taught the Ten Commandments of Jesus Christ as a standard for holy living before they are baptized? How many are taught the other commandments of Christ and His Apostles as the goal of a Christ-like life? Paul's haunting words to King Agrippa reflect his commission from Jesus Christ about how to preach the gospel before baptizing a convert:

> So, King Agrippa, I did not prove disobedient to the heavenly vision, but kept declaring both to those of Damascus first, and also at Jerusalem and then throughout all the region of Judea, and even to the Gentiles, *that they should repent and turn to God, performing deeds appropriate to repentance* (Acts 26:19–20; emphasis added).

Is this the gospel call we make to sinners today as Baptists? Thankfully, many times it is. But, sadly, many times it is not. Calls to believe in Jesus Christ as Savior often contain little or no reference to His Lordship in living according to "all that I commanded you." If we wish to build the faithful Baptist churches which our forefathers built before "carnal Christianity" infected our churches and preaching, we must return to the robust call of bringing forth "the deeds appropriate to repentance" before we baptize someone on confession of their faith.

Baptism is a Sign of the Future Resurrection

There is no doubt that believer's baptism is a visible sign of death to sin's dominance and resurrection to newness of life ... in this life (Romans 6:1–11). However, the resurrection of Jesus Christ also was a promise to the believer that he shall be raised from the dead bodily someday (1 Corinthians 15:20–22). *The Baptist Faith and Message* (2000) recognizes this meaning of baptism with these words: "It is a testimony to his faith in the final resurrection of the dead (Chapter VII)."

A believer's baptism by immersion signifies his future resurrection of the body from the dead. It is a sign of future glorification! For all those whom God foreknew, He predestined to full conformity to the image of Christ. And all those whom He predestined, He also called effectually to that salvation. And all whom He called, He also justified. And all whom He justified, He also glorified. Believer's baptism signifies all these things. The baptized believer awaits the final resurrection of the dead and full conformity to the image of Christ. Baptists need to restore this understanding to the candidate and to the watching the congregation. What rejoicing there would be!

All of the blessings mentioned above constitute a full understanding of believer's baptism. If we wish to see our people living in the light of God's full salvation, it must begin with a robust instruction and administration of believer's baptism.

The Practice of Believer's Baptism

Our Baptist forefathers gave much attention to the proper practice of believer's baptism. This is refreshing in light of the diminishing importance of believer's baptism in many of our churches. For we often see that baptism is practiced at the beginning or end of our worship services in a perfunctory manner, often with little or no explanation or instruction about it to the candidate or congregation. Further, it is also most grievous to see some Baptist pastors and churches, along with some Bible churches, accept believer's baptism by sprinkling or pouring, or even infant baptism, as sufficient for church membership. This issue touches the question of the practice of Baptist distinctives for true Baptist identity.

Many questions have been asked about baptism by Baptists. Should only ordained pastors baptize? Should Baptist churches accept into membership immersed believers from non-Baptist churches and/or administrators? Where and when should baptism be administered? And, finally, should Baptists require church membership of those whom they baptize? Or is that a completely separate issue? Those who tend to dismiss these issues as minor and unimportant belittle the persecution our forefathers endured for searching the Scriptures on these points.

The following discussion of the Baptist practice of believer's baptism as an instituted ordinance of Jesus Christ will reflect the regulative principle of worship previously discussed. It is out of this principle that Baptists have endeavored to practice the biblically authorized mode, subjects, administrators, and church membership.

Mode—The Requirement of Full Immersion

The New Testament use of *baptizo* in its contexts conforms well to its common lexical meaning of "to dip, to immerse, to dye." However, our paedobaptist friends, arguing for the possibility of pouring or sprinkling, often have ignored the verb forms of *baptidzo* which require immersion instead of other modes.

In the passive forms of *baptidzo*, the subject of the verb is baptized. That is, people are baptized (dipped or immersed), not the medium of water (poured or sprinkled). There is no instance in the New Testament description of baptisms in which water is the subject of the passive form of *baptizo*, which would be necessary if it means pouring or sprinkling. As A.

H. Strong says, "The absence of any use of [*baptidzo*] in the passive voice with 'water' as its subject confirms our conclusion that its meaning is 'to immerse.' Water is never said to be baptized upon a man."[6]

For instance, Mark records the imperfect passive: "[they] were baptized by [John] in the Jordan River" (Mark 1:5). No mention of water is made as the receiver of the action of the verb. John baptized (dipped) the people, not baptized (poured) the water upon the people.

Another example is the aorist passive of *baptidzo* in Mark 1:9: "Jesus ... was baptized (dipped or immersed, not poured or sprinkled) by John into (*eis*) the Jordan River." Again, no mention is made of water as the subject of *baptidzo*. It is ridiculous to think of Jesus Himself, as the receiver of the action of the verb, being poured or sprinkled in or into the Jordan River by John. Rather, He Himself was immersed in or into it. To accept the literal and historical meaning of *baptidzo* as "to dip or to immerse" is the most natural reading of the passive verbs.

Baptists must not yield to the mode of baptism as unimportant in the modern day. It is true that, relatively, it is not as important as justification by faith alone in Christ alone. But the mode of baptism must be formed by its command and example in Scripture alone. Immersion is necessary for Baptist practice.

Subjects – The Requirement of Disciples Alone

John 4:1–2 is very instructive in the active form of *baptizo*: "Jesus was making and baptizing more disciples than John (although Jesus Himself was not baptizing, but His disciples were)...." Disciples were first made then baptized (Matthew 28:19–20; Acts 2:41). Neither infants nor those ignorant of the gospel and the demands of discipleship may be baptized. Our Lord described a disciple as one who denies himself, takes up his cross daily, and follows Him (Luke 9:23; 14:27). A disciple is a committed follower of the Lord Jesus Christ who understands His gospel and understands the kind of holy life to which he is committing in baptism.

Paedobaptists readily admit that there is neither command nor clear example of infant baptism in the entire Bible. However, through "good and necessary consequence" from the Abrahamic Covenant of circumcision, it is claimed that the infants of believers should be baptized. Again, this is a violation of the regulative principle of worship. If an ordinance is not instituted by revelation, it is not to be practiced in the worship of the church.

---

[6] A. H. Strong, *Systematic Theology*, vol. III (Valley Forge, PA: Judson, 1907), 935.

If we Baptists would see a reversal of the lack of commitment by baptized church members, it would behoove us to first make disciples before we baptize them.

Administrators—The Requirement of Church Administration for Believer's Baptism

There has been disagreement among Baptists as to who should baptize. However, the SLBC says that baptism is a church ordinance to be performed by the properly called:

> Baptism and the Lord's supper are ordinances of positive and sovereign institution, appointed by the Lord Jesus, the only lawgiver, to be *continued in his church* to the end of the world (Section 28:1, emphasis added).

> These holy appointments are to be administered *by those only who are qualified and thereunto called, according to the commission of Christ* (Section 28:2, emphasis added).

The Great Commission of Christ was given to His Apostles to establish the church. We see them doing the baptisms in the book of Acts (Acts 2:41), except for Philip the Evangelist (also an ordained deacon). Others mentioned include Apollos, an apostolic servant of Paul (1 Corinthians 1:12). The point is that the only evidence of who baptized was either Apostles or one of their close cohorts. We do not see anyone in the congregation baptizing, nor fathers baptizing family members. The performance of baptism requires the ordained authority of Christ through the church. Therefore, most Baptists have only allowed pastors to baptize except in extreme circumstances.

Church membership—The Requirement of Baptism for Church Membership and the Requirement of Church Membership after Believer's Baptism

John the Baptist and Jesus baptized individuals, calling them to be faithful in their lives (Matthew 3:8; Luke 3:10–14). There was literally no organized church to unite oneself to at that time. After Pentecost, all who were baptized ordinarily were either added to the church or helped form a church (Acts 2:41–47; 11:19–30). While some baptisms may not mention a church present or formed in the context, the Great Commission itself requires the forming and joining of a church. After being baptized, the new

Christians are to be taught to do all that Christ commanded the Apostles (Matthew 28:19–20). The Apostles passed on that work to ordinary elders as the churches were established to carry on the Great Commission after they were gone (Acts 14:22).

The Great Commission baptism would include the necessity of being identified as a Christian in submission to a church body for instruction and church discipline, both formative and corrective (Matthew 18:15–17). Further evidence for church membership following baptism is implied in the commands to be subject to the elders, "Obey your leaders and submit to them, for they keep watch over your souls as those who will give an account. Let them do this with joy and not with grief, for this would be unprofitable for you" (Hebrews 13:17). How can the elders know for whom they are responsible to God unless there is a visible commitment to their leadership and authority in the local church membership?

Those who decry the principle of church membership itself, or the necessity for the baptized to join a local church, show a prooftext mentality requiring every New Testament baptism to result in stated church membership. Such hermeneutics overlook the didactic passages such as the Great Commission and those mentioned above.

Away with the individualistic ecclesiology plaguing America which minimizes baptism and church membership, leaving Christians the freedom to float around without feeling responsible to a pastor or a church. Such an attitude feeds the antinomian spirit we see growing today. Yet, the whole teaching of the NT is that Christians need the ministry of a committed body of believers (church membership) which baptism calls them to. Church membership is required after baptism and believer's baptism is required for church membership.

The Preparation for Believer's Baptism

Ordinarily in the New Testament, believer's baptism was performed immediately after the confession of repentance toward God and faith toward our Lord Jesus Christ (John 4:2; Acts 2:41). Therefore, some Baptists have advocated immediate baptism of all who say that they have been saved, followed by immediate church membership.

However, there are some extenuating circumstances to the New Testament which are not present today. Those baptized by John, Jesus and the Apostles (on the day of Pentecost) were Jews and Gentile God-fearers who usually had a much deeper understanding of God's Word than the average person today. They were familiar with the Old Testament God of Israel (Acts 2:22–37; 8:27; 10:2), the Ten Commandments, the issue of sin, the need of atonement by blood sacrifice, the need of repentance toward God, the concept of a people of God in covenant with Him, the need of righteousness before God, the call to a holy life, etc. (Ephesians 2:12; Romans 9:1–5). In our society, one is hard-pressed to find even many church members who understand these basic things or who can list all Ten Commandments.

To immediately baptize those who are ignorant of the gospel, have little idea of the Ten Commandments they are committing to obey, and who may be confused about grace versus works for salvation is not the same situation as the New Testament examples we have. We need to make sure people understand the gospel and the call to discipleship before we baptize them. This may necessitate a brief delay of baptism to instruct them. Such an approach is not a contradiction of the biblical examples in Acts, simply because our Lord commanded us to "make disciples" before baptizing them. If we believe that a person is saved before baptism, yet still ignorant of the basics of discipleship, there is nothing lost to make sure their baptism is with real knowledge of Christ and His gospel.

One word about baptizing children. We believe that God can save at any age. However, we must be careful of baptizing little ones who are simply trying to please their parents or to become part of a group. We must require the same knowledge of Christ and the gospel, repentance from sin, faith in Christ, and the desire to live a holy life that we require of older ones, only at a child's simple level. Both parents and pastors must work together to do good to the souls of our children.

In summary, the proper practice of believer's baptism is a fundamental building block for a committed church membership. Our concept of building a regenerate church membership based upon a good confession of Christ and a commitment to live faithfully for His glory requires carefulness at this point. May God bring reform and a restored importance to our practice of believer's baptism. The future of sound and fruitful Baptist churches depends upon it!

The Importance of Believer's Baptism

There are many practical implications to belief in believer's baptism, the baptism of disciples alone. Only two will be covered in this discussion: the importance for ecclesiology and the importance for Baptist identity.

The Importance of Believer's Baptism for Ecclesiology.

In order to give more space to the second issue of Baptist identity, I will simply list the principles of believer's baptism for Baptist ecclesiology gleaned from the discussion above:

1. First, the New Testament church is called repeatedly "the disciples" (Acts 6:1–7, 9:26; 11:26); biblical churches must be composed of those made disciples, then baptized (John 4:2; Acts 2:41).

2. Second, the baptism of disciples alone affects evangelism; we must make sure the candidate for baptism knows what it means to be a disciple of Christ beforehand (Matthew 28:19–20).

3. Third, the church as an assembly of baptized disciples demands that the worship and teaching ministry of the church on the Lord's Day be geared toward disciples, not "seekers"; the Great Commission requires that baptized disciples be taught expositionally "to do all that [Christ] commanded [His disciples]" as the basic foundation of Christian worship "in spirit and in truth (John 4:24)."

4. Fourth, the church as an assembly of baptized disciples demands that the priority and autonomy of the local church be emphasized over denominationalism; the local church is the only authorized instrument of Jesus Christ on earth, each with Him as Head (Revelation 2–3); associational connections are voluntary and associational employees are servants of the churches, not masters.

5. Fifth, the church as an assembly of baptized disciples must recognize the priesthood of the baptized believer as he approaches God through Christ alone; yet each church must require some body of beliefs for membership and unity.

6. Sixth, the church as an assembly of baptized disciples requires the practice of church discipline (Matthew 18:15–17); disciples need fellowship, correction, and accountability.

7. Seventh, the church as an assembly of baptized disciples requires the church to practice biblically regulated worship; the Great Commission of Christ requires the church "in spirit and in truth," not "in spirit and in creativity," according to the commandments of Christ (John 4:21–24; Matthew 28:19–20).

The ecclesiastical importance of believer's baptism is not insignificant. It is formative to the establishment of biblical Baptist churches that will stand before the next generation holding forth the biblical gospel of Jesus Christ. We pray that God will raise up a new generation of historic Baptist churches that will stand in the front line as outposts of the Kingdom of God, as cities of light for the lost and as cities of refuge for the weary believers who are looking for Bunyan's House Beautiful as a spiritual haven and armory for battle.

The Importance of Believer's Baptism for Baptist Identity.

There is much more to Baptist identity than the distinctive of believer's (confessor's) baptism. In the early 1990s, when the Cooperative Baptist Fellowship was forming, I heard a sermon by Dr. Bill Leonard which seemed to say that the foundation of Baptist unity is that we have all been baptized. To require more is creedalism, he implied. This kind of reductionistic view of Baptist identity to believer's baptism, soul competency and the separation of church and state was a smokescreen used by many during the Inerrancy Controversy to oppose biblical inerrancy as another Baptist distinctive. Such historical revisionism was exposed well by Drs. Russ Bush and Tom Nettles during that period in their book *Baptists and the Bible.*[7]

In his three-volume masterpiece, *The Baptists*, Dr. Nettles argues that there are two major camps among modern Baptists with differing views concerning Baptist identity:

> This [inerrancy] controversy reveals not only a fissure among Baptists in their understanding of the nature of biblical authority, but more broadly reveals two fundamentally disparate views of Baptist identity. One party in the discussion argues for a narrow, reduced definition of Baptist identity. This group focuses on the distinctives related to liberty and independence; they minimize the importance of positive doctrinal affirmations. Doctrinal definition intruded into Baptist life from fundamentalism and eventually neo-evangelicalism but was alien to the original Baptist ethos, so they say. They view a serious confessionalism as contrary to Baptist witness because objectivity in doctrinal formulation tends to overpower subjective experience and individual perceptions of truth. Liberty of conscience, the key to Baptist life, cannot co-exist with the broad and objective doctrinal emphasis of confessions. Many testimonies advocating this

---

[7] This modern classic, first published in 1980, has been revised and republished in recent years. See L. Russ Bush and Tom J. Nettles, *Baptists and the Bible*, rev. and expanded ed. (Nashville: B&H, 1999).

view of Baptist life may be found in the volume published by Smyth and Helwys entitled *Why I am a Baptist*. E. Y. Mullins emerges as the single most influential theologian for this understanding of Baptist Identity. Mullins used the phrase "the competency of the soul in religion: to isolate the unique Baptist contribution to Christian thought. His view has been massaged to a different shape and abstracted from its theological context and has emerged from this makeover as the single most significant point in Baptist identity. Because of the particular emphases and alteration placed on Mullin's concept, I will sometimes refer to those who hold this view as the 'soul-liberty party'.

On the other hand, another group seeks to demonstrate that distinctive tenets of freedom and *voluntarism* would never produce a Baptist church apart from a broader foundation of theological, Christological, and soteriological truths. This group sees Baptist identity not only in terms of its distinctive emphasis on freedom and individual choice. Just as important is the body of revealed truth upon which faith fastens itself. Baptists must be Christian and Protestant evangelical before they can be Baptist. Sometimes I will refer to this as the 'coherent-truth party'. This book is written to argue that this view of Baptist identity more closely corresponds to a contextually responsible interpretation of the documents than the soul-liberty view.[8]

I believe Dr. Nettles' analysis of the two-party divide among Baptists to be accurate. However, oddly, some Conservative Resurgence defenders have opposed his comprehensive view of Baptist identity. Holding to the fundamentalist-evangelical theology of the twentieth-century, which still is a confession of faith, they have failed to look beyond those fundamentals to the robust Protestant-Reformed theology of the original Baptists. So, the present Baptist identity discussions today present a confusing debate to the person in the pew.

Dr. Nettles clarifies his position in these discussions by outlining four Baptist distinctives necessary for evaluating true Baptist identity. After a thorough historical argument in the first chapter to demonstrate his four-principle view, Nettles outlines these four principles in chapter two:

> The framework suggested below, therefore, seeks to establish a broad definition of Baptist identity based on the theological self-consciousness reflected in Baptist confessions. This coherent-truth model is consistent with, though more extensive than, [Stan] Norman's Reformation tradition. Four categories provide the framework for this interpretation of Baptist identity: orthodoxy, evangelicalism, separateness (that is, a theologically integrated ecclesiology), and conscientious confessionality. Each

[8] Nettles, *The Baptists*, 1:12–13, emphasis in original.

category will be illustrated from early and irreproachable representatives of Baptist commitments. *The Second London Confession* (1677, 1689) became the single most formative theological influence on Baptist life in England and America. The highly influential Philadelphia Association endorsed its language and chapters as the standard by which churches in the Association were received, disciplined and advised; it was adopted early on by the First Baptist Church of Charleston, South Carolina, and became the theological guidepost of the Charleston Association. The Southern Baptist Theological Seminary, founded in 1859 and initially located in Greenville, South Carolina, adopted an abstract of this document, *The Abstract of Principles*, as its theological formulary.[9]

Heartily agreeing with Nettles' four categories as a framework for Baptist identity, one place to begin in Baptist reformation is to restore the robust meaning of baptism to Baptists demonstrated in this chapter. Having observed many baptisms over the years, it has concerned me how its meaning often has been truncated or unexplained altogether. I have observed baptisms with no explanation of its meaning to the congregation or to the candidate. Others only mentioned that it is an act of obedience to Christ. Still others seemed in a hurry to finish so that they could get on with the rest of the service. I wonder how many Baptists really understand the meaning and importance of their baptisms?

Yet, believer's baptism is a microcosm of Baptist identity. The Bible gives a broad meaning to baptism which incorporates Nettles' framework for historical Baptist identity. The baptism of disciples alone must be orthodox, evangelical, separate and confessional. Each of these categories is attached to the meaning of baptism in the Bible. For biblical reformation in Baptist churches, we must restore the robust meaning of baptism which our forefathers held and often suffered for. Baptist identity for them was often written in blood, not just water.

Conclusion

In this chapter, I have endeavored to present a brief overview of the nature, practice and importance of believer's baptism for Baptist reformation. It is my hope and prayer that it will produce a greater commitment to believer's baptism in our churches and a more robust teaching about the meaning of believer's baptism at those times we practice it, both for the disciple to be baptized and the congregation which observes the ordinance. I believe that if we Baptists would do that, we would see more committed

---

[9] Nettles, *The Baptists*, 1:36.

disciples in our churches, and spiritually stronger churches, than we do at this time. To God be the glory!

Dr. Nettles' many contributions to this distinctive essential for Baptist churches have been noted. His incorporation of a robust theology of believer's baptism in his arguments for Baptist identity form a way ahead for future Baptist reformation and true revival. It is my prayer that as he approaches the latter years of his work, he will continue to write and teach for biblical Baptist reformation. May God so bless his efforts, that after the Lord takes Him to glory, it will be said: "he, being dead, still speaketh." Again, to God be the glory!

20

Baptists, Worldview and Focal Practices

Ben Mitchell

Many contemporary Christians may find it curious that Baptists, including Southern Baptists, did not engage in a protracted discussion of worldview until the 20th century.[1] This is not to say that Baptists did not have a worldview or did not form believers to think "worldviewishly." In fact, to accuse early Baptists of not attending to the notion of Christian worldview would be anachronistic since the origin of Baptists preceded the idea by at least several generations, if not centuries, depending on how one defines "worldview" and when one marks Baptist beginnings.

Prussian philosopher Immanuel Kant coined the term *Weltanschauung* in 1790, in his *Critique of Judgement*, but did so in a purely philosophical sense, and in a context unlikely to impact directly many European Baptists of the period. After all, Baptists had only recently ceased literally running for their lives when Kant wrote. Wrangling over philosophical epistemology was perhaps not their highest priority.

In this chapter I will argue that early Baptists taught their worldview not primarily using philosophical apologetic methods, as they most often

---

[1] Among Southern Baptists, E. Y. Mullins may have been the first seriously to take up the themes typically associated with worldview thinking in his sparring with the Modernists in *Why is Christianity True?* (Philadelphia, PA: American Baptist Publication Society, 1905). For a brief discussion of Mullins's contribution to that debate see Tom Nettles, *Ready for Reformation? Bringing Authentic Reform to Southern Baptist Churches* (Nashville, TN: Broadman & Holman, 2005), 115.

do today, but through living life together in covenantal communities. Further, I will argue that formative practices underwrote and informed their doctrinal affirmations at least as much as the other way around. Worldviews are shaped not only through the intellect, but also through embodied focal practices.

Do Baptists Have a Worldview?

In his encyclopedic volume, *Worldview: The History of a Concept*, David Naugle demonstrates that the contemporary Christian worldview discussion owes its genesis to Calvin and the Reformed tradition, with Scottish Presbyterian minister and theologian, James Orr, establishing a benchmark in the late nineteenth and early twentieth century.[2] Among twentieth century Baptists, it was Carl F. H. Henry who provided the most erudite, compelling and comprehensive example of Christian worldview thinking.[3]

In one of his last essays on the subject, Henry defined Christian worldview as "a theistic system exhibiting the rational coherence of the biblical revelation."[4] Whatever the assets or deficiencies of this definition, it points clearly to the fact that for a Christian worldview to be distinctly Christian it must find its basis in the Scriptures of the Old and New Testaments. Furthermore, a worldview must describe and define how a Christian makes sense of, or, inhabits the world. At least one way of understanding a worldview is as a frame of reference, a lens through which one understands one's experience in the world. C. S. Lewis famously said, "I believe in Christianity as I believe the Sun has risen—not only because I see it, but because by it, I see everything else."[5] For Christians, God's revealed truth is the lens through which everything else is understood.

However, Beeson Divinity School professor of theology, Graham Cole, asks, "has Christianity a worldview?" He answers with both a yes and a no. "As for the Yes," he says, "there is a cluster of touchstone propositions at the heart of an intellectual account of Christianity: propositions about the Creator, the creation, the fall, the rescue, and the restoration."[6] "As

---

[2] David K. Naugle, *Worldview: The History of a Concept* (Grand Rapids, MI: William B. Eerdmans, 2002), 5 and *passim*.

[3] Not only was this true of his magisterial six volume work, *God, Revelation, and Authority* (Waco: Word) published over a seven year period from 1976–1983, but also of numerous volumes written for a popular audience.

[4] Carl F. H. Henry, "Fortunes of the Christian Worldview," *Trinity Journal* 19 (1998), 163.

[5] C. S. Lewis, "Is Theology Poetry?" in *C. S. Lewis: Essay Collection* (London: Collins, 2000), 21.

[6] Graham A. Cole, "Do Christians Have a Worldview?", 21.

for the No," he maintains, "... Christianity is first of all news of a person and his significance and not views about the world."[7] Christianity is not a philosophy but a religion with objects of worship, not frames of reference *per se*. There is a real sense, then, in which worldview is a modern concept, while Christianity is a pre-modern or supra-modern religion.

This way of characterizing worldview goes a long way to explaining why Baptists did not enter the discussion until the late-modern period. As a people shaped by biblical revelation—"people of the Book"—and formed by the gospel of the risen Christ, they typically did not appeal to philosophical categories. Worldview language was, as it were, a different genre from gospel language.

Still, within the scope of biblical revelation and gospel affirmation, there is that cluster of theological propositions about the nature of reality, anthropology, history and the future: creation, fall, redemption, and restoration, for instance. Although Baptists have always appealed to theological categories such as these for understanding their place in the world, I maintain that their worldview was not shaped solely by theological assent.

How Were Baptists' Worldviews Formed?

Calvin College professor James K. A. Smith has recently critiqued Christian higher education for its "rationalist" anthropology, the view of the human person that appeals exclusively, or at least functionally so, to the intellect to account for and shape human behavior. In other words, the intellectualist educator believes that if he or she can convince a person to affirm certain truths, the rest will follow. What this has meant for Christian colleges and universities, asserts Smith, is that the emphasis has been placed on helping students "develop a Christian worldview" to the neglect of the affective nature of human beings. Putting on worldview lenses usually has meant framing and reframing conceptual categories—getting one's head right. "What if," he asks, "education was primarily concerned with shaping our hopes and passions—our visions of 'the good life'—and not merely about the dissemination of data and information inputs as inputs to our thinking? What if the primary work of education was the transforming of our imagination rather than the saturation of our intellect? And what if this had as much to do with our bodies as with our minds?"[8]

In response to these questions, Smith calls for a re-visioning of Christian education that focuses on formation, which by all means includes information input, but is also attentive to the formation of desires through

---

[7] Ibid.

[8] James K. A. Smith, *Desiring the Kingdom: Worship, Worldview, and Cultural Formation* (Grand Rapids, MI: Baker Academic, 2009), 18.

what individuals love and do, through what they desire and how they be-
have. To make his case professor Smith exegetes the average American
shopping mall, suggesting that the mall is both a pedagogical and liturgical
institution, and a very effective one at that.

> Indeed, the genius of the mall religion is that actually it operates with a
> more holistic, affective, embodied anthropology (or theory of the human
> person) than the Christian church tends to assume! Because worldview-
> thinking still tends to focus on ideas and beliefs, the formative cultural
> impact of sites like the mall tends to not show up on our radar. Such
> a heady approach, focused on beliefs, is not really calibrated to see the
> quasi-liturgical practices at work in a site like the mall. An idea-centric
> or belief-centric approach will fail to see the pedagogy at work in the
> mall, and thus will also fail to articulate a critique and counter-pedagogy.
> In order to recognize the religious power and formative force of the mall,
> we need to adopt a paradigm of cultural critique and discernment that
> thinks even deeper than beliefs or worldviews and takes seriously the
> central role of formative practices—or what I'll describe in this book as
> *liturgies*.[9]

The shopping mall shapes the shopper's desires through the experience of shopping. So what Smith prescribes is that education should help
reorder the desires of the learner through alternative liturgies from those of
the mall since, as he puts it, "liturgies—whether 'sacred' or 'secular'—shape
and constitute our identities by forming our most fundamental desires and
more most basic attunement to the world. In short, liturgies make us certain kinds of people, and what defines us is what we *love*."[10] That is to say,
our liturgies—our practices—shape our desires and inform our beliefs as
much as the other way around.

Although Smith develops a very elaborate discussion of the relationship between liturgies, practices and rituals, his central task is "to argue for
a more affective picture of the human person that situates and relativizes
the importance of the intellect and instead places (renewed) emphasis on
the 'heart' as the affective, embodied, pre-conscious core of the human
person that drives and shapes our action and behavior."[11] He offers a coun-

---

[9] Ibid., 24. This probably also helps explain how Christians can affirm orthodox doctrines and so often remain conspicuous consumers. The head is too far
from the wallet to control spending.

[10] Ibid., 25.

[11] Todd C. Ream, Perry L. Glanzer, David S. Guthrie, Steven M. Nolt,
John W. Wright, and James K. A. Smith, "Review Symposium: Desiring the
Kingdom: Worship, Worldview, and Cultural Formation by James K. A. Smith,"
Christian Scholar's Review XXXIX:2 (Winter 2010), 230.

terbalance to what he perceives to be an overly rationalistic, intellectualized orientation to evangelical Christian worldview thinking. He argues that practices, ritualized behavior and community expectations have a much greater impact on worldview than most have acknowledged. What we think with our minds informs what we do with our bodies, *and* what we do with our bodies informs how we think. Orthopraxy contributes to orthodoxy.

Another way to make the case for a more holistic anthropology and, therefore, a more holistic view of thinking about worldview, is to examine the roles of *focal things* and *focal practices*. Building on the work of philosopher Albert Borgmann, theologian Brent Waters, distinguishes between focal things and focal practices. A focal thing is "an objective reality that shapes the values and behavior of those whose attention is seized by its presence. A focal practice consists of acts that express and perform the values and behavior that are formed by those devoted to the focal thing."[12]

According to Borgmann and Waters, a family meal is an example of a focal thing, a reality that shapes the behavior of those who participate in it. Family meals are not merely about the consumption of calories, but about gathering as family, sharing a common history, traditions and conversation. The meal unites individual members to a larger network of social relationships. The family meal has a temporal beginning and end; it is a focal *thing* in that sense. Focal *practices* are those behaviors that underwrite, facilitate and inform a focal thing. Careful preparation of the meal, proper setting of the table, the giving of thanks for the bounty and convivial conversation are examples of those practices. Moreover, the family meal is (or was) the place where the story of the family is told, where the moral and religious values of the family are expressed and where the expectations of the family are shaped in embodied relationships.

Just as with Jamie Smith's liturgies, focal things and practices do not as much pick out specific intellectual affirmations as they shape human behaviors, activities and rituals. Children, for instance, do not learn first about the philosophical facts of the family as an institution, they first enjoy the experience of the family. They are not first taught an abstract definition of "family" as a social institution, they themselves and their ideas of family are formed primarily by the experience of living in a family.

---

[12] Brent Waters, *From Human to Posthuman: Christian Theology and Technology in a Postmodern World* (Burlington, VT: Ashgate Publishing Limited, 2006), 147. Borgmann first offered these concepts in *Technology and the Character of Contemporary Life: A Philosophical Inquiry* (Chicago, IL: University of Chicago Press, 1984) and later in *Power Failure: Christianity in the Culture of Technology* (Grand Rapids, MI: Brazos Press, 2003).

What does this have to do with Baptist history, theology and world-view? Well, to paraphrase Smith, what if being a Baptist historically was primarily concerned with the shaping of hopes and passions—visions of 'the good life'—and not merely about the dissemination of data and information inputs as inputs to Baptist thinking? What if being Baptist was not only—or even always first—about certain intellectual affirmations and, instead, about a complex web of behaviors, relationships, liturgies and focal practices?

I would not want to ignore or diminish the cognitive dimension. From the beginning Baptists have been a confessional people. One glance at William Lumpkin's catalogue of confessions, *Baptist Confessions of Faith*, would convince even the most obstinate skeptic that Baptists have written, owned and affirmed statements of doctrine.[13] Ardent, sacrificial defense of liberty of conscience and freedom of religion notwithstanding, most Baptists have required doctrinal orthodoxy for church membership. To be Baptist meant to believe specific biblical truths. So early Southern Baptist professor of evangelism J. B. Gambrell could proclaim both that "The all-sufficiency of the Scriptures as a guide in religion is a cardinal principle with Baptists. This eliminates the authority of councils, popes, synods, conferences, bishops, etc...." and that "As Baptist principles are peculiar to Baptists, every Baptist church, with all its appointments, from preach-er to Sunday-school teacher, ought to stand, in the community where it holds forth the word, for something different from any other congrega-tion. When a Baptist church thinks of itself as just one of the churches in a community, with no mission above others, it has become a very weak affair."[14] Baptists are therefore obliged to teach Baptist principles.

Having acknowledged that Baptists have been confessional, however, is it possible that the "liturgies" of Baptist churches have had at least an equally formative role in shaping the tacit worldview of Baptists in the past? If Borgmann and Waters are right about focal things and focal prac-tices, might it be the case that Baptist churches have been formed by those practices as much as by their assent to certain doctrinal propositions? And if so, what would that mean for Baptists of both past and future?

In his discussion of worldview and theology in *Ready for Reformation?* Southern Baptist Theological Seminary professor of history Tom Nettles

---

[13] William L. Lumpkin, *Baptist Confessions of Faith* (Valley Forge, PA: Jud-son Press, 1959). Cf., William J. McGlothlin, *Baptist Confessions of Faith* (Phila-delphia, PA: American Baptist Publication Society, 1911).

[14] J. B. Gambrell, "The Obligation of Baptists To Teach Their Principles," in J. B. Jeter, *Baptist Principles Reset* (Richmond, VA: Religious Herald, 1902), 252.

points to the holistic transformative role of Christian doctrine when he says,

> Not only does Christian truth unfolded in biblical revelation challenge the philosophical assumptions that seek to minimize or eliminate the divine component of reality; it also challenges the innate, inbred, and culturally reinforced worldliness of our thoughts. In addition to the philosophical challenge Christians should learn to present to the prevailing intellectual culture, there must be an internal revolution in the way we view ourselves and our neighbors in light of biblical theology. We must learn to see Christian doctrine as so relevant and revitalizing that its implications redefine our entire being.[15]

Yet, how does one "learn to see" the relevance and vitality of Christian doctrine? One might learn some aspects of it when those doctrines are preached with clarity and unction. Other aspects of those truths might be made manifest through catechetical instruction.[16] Still others might be learned through Sunday School classes. But these strategies emphasize only the cognitive elements of worldview formation. Shaping a Baptist worldview is about more than intellectualizing like a Baptist.

The Role of Covenants in Worldview Formation

Historically, Baptists not only authored confessional statements to affirm "the faith once for all delivered to the saints," they also entered into ecclesial covenants. According to historian Charles DeWeese "A church covenant is a series of written pledges based on the Bible which members voluntarily make to God and to one another regarding their basic moral and spiritual commitments and the practice of their faith. A covenant deals mainly with conduct (although it contains some doctrinal elements), while a confession of faith centers more heavily on beliefs."[17] He goes on to observe that "Through the centuries Baptist churches have tended to write and/or adopt church covenants and confessions of faith in tandem as basic constitutive documents of their congregational life. This process has sought a balance between faith and practice, words and deeds, beliefs and behaviors, doctrine and conduct."[18] If confessions focused primarily on

---

[15] Nettles, *Ready for Reformation?*, 116.

[16] See Tom J. Nettles, *Teaching Truth, Training Hearts: The Study of Catechisms in Baptist Life* (Amityville, NY: Calvary Press, 1998).

[17] Charles W. Deweese, *Baptist Church Covenants* (Nashville, TN: Broadman Press, 1990), viii.

[18] Ibid., ix.

doctrine, covenants focused especially on churchly and ethical practice. If catechisms established doctrinal expectations, covenants set expectations for Christian living within the believing community.

For instance, as we see below, church covenants often both prescribed and proscribed specific behaviors and liturgies, establishing and shaping the expectations for those who lived their lives together in the church. Regular attendance at worship was, for instance, often established in the covenant as an expectation of faithful membership. Not only was a theology of the ordinances of baptism and the Lord's Supper set out in the confessional statement of a church, but through the covenant their role was expounded. Covenants also tended to prescribe the daily activities of the individual including their relationships with God, their pastor, their family and their neighbors. The expectations of the covenant were meant to shape the desires of the believer not just to think rightly but to live faithfully.

Space will not permit a comprehensive survey of Baptist church covenants, but a few examples will represent of some of the focal practices of Baptist congregations of the past, one English and one American. The focal things—those important aspects of their life together—were underwritten, reinforced and supported by regular liturgies that shaped the community.

Covenant of the Baptist Church in Horse Fair, Stony Stratford, Bucks, England, 1790

We whose names are underwritten do now declare that we embrace the Word of God as our only guide in matters of religion, and acknowledge no other authority whatever as binding upon the conscience. Having, we hope, found mercy at the hands of God, in delivering us from the power of darkness, and translating us into the Kingdom of His dear Son, we think and feel ourselves bound to walk in obedience to His divine commands. On looking into the sacred Scripture, we find it was common in the first ages of Christianity for such as professed repentance towards God and faith in our Lord Jesus Christ, voluntarily to unite together in Christian societies called churches. Their ends in so doing were to honor God and promote their own spiritual edification. Having searched the written Word, in order that we may know how to act, as well as what to believe, and sought unto God by prayer for divine direction, we heartily approve of, and mean to follow their example. With a view to this, we now solemnly, in the presence of the all-seeing and heart-searching God, do mutually covenant and agree, in manner and form following.

1. To maintain and hold fast the important and fundamental truths of revelation....

2. To seek by all proper means the good of the church with which we stand connected. To this end we engage to attend regularly, as far as we have opportunity, all seasons of public worship, church meetings, and meetings of prayer appointed by the church. When we are absent we will be ready to give an account why we were so, if required. We will diligently watch for the appearances of God's work in our congregation; and if we see any setting their faces Zion-ward (towards Heaven), we will endeavor to instruct and encourage; and having hopeful evidence of the reality of God's work upon their souls, will lay before them the privileges they have a right unto, and the duties they ought to be found in, of following Christ in His ordinances and institutions. If called to the painful work of executing the penalties of Christ upon the breakers of the laws of His house, we will endeavor to exercise it in the spirit of the gospel, without respect of persons. Also we engage that according to our ability, we will contribute our share towards defraying all necessary expenses attending the worship of God. We likewise promise to keep the secrets of the church and not to expose its concerns to the world around.

3. To esteem our pastor highly in love for his work's sake, this we will endeavor to manifest by frequently and fervently praying for him; diligently attending on his ministry; encouraging his heart and strengthening his hands to the utmost of our power in the work of the Lord; freely consulting him as we have occasion and opportunity, respecting our spiritual affairs; treating him affectionately when present, and speaking respectfully of him when absent. As he is a man of like passions with others, we will endeavor to conceal and cover with a mantle of love, his weaknesses and imperfections; also to communicate unto him of our temporal good things, knowing that the Lord hath ordained that they that preach the gospel should live of the gospel.

4. To walk in love toward those with whom we stand connected in bonds of Christian fellowship. As the effect of this, we will pray much for one another. As we have opportunity, we will associate together for religious purposes. Those of us who are in more comfortable situations in life than some of our brethren will administer as we have ability and see occasion, to their necessities. We will bear one another's burdens, sympathize with the afflicted in body and mind, so far as we know their case, under their trials; and as we see

occasion, advise, caution, and encourage one another. We will watch over one another for good. We will studiously avoid giving or taking offenses. Thus we will make it our study to fulfill the law of Christ.

5. To be particularly attentive to our station in life, and the peculiar duties incumbent on us in that situation. We who are husbands or wives will conscientiously discharge relative duties towards our respective yoke-fellows. We who are heads of families will maintain the daily worship of God in our houses, and endeavor to instruct those under our care, both by our words and actions. We who are children will be obedient to our parents in the Lord. We who are masters will render unto our servants that which is just and equal. We who are servants engage to be diligent and faithful, not acting with eye-service as men-pleasers, but with singleness of heart as unto God, knowing we have a Master in heaven. We will in our different places of abode, inquire what we can do for the good of the church to which we belong, and as far as we have ability, we will open or encourage the opening of a door wherever we can, for the preaching of the Word, remembering that we ought to be as the salt of the earth.

6. To walk in a way and manner becoming the gospel, before them that are without, that we may by well-doing put to silence the ignorance of gainsayers. We will practice the strictest honesty in our dealings, and faithfulness in fulfilling all our promises. We will abstain from all vain amusements and diversions, by which time would be foolishly spent, money wasted, our minds carnalized, and we exposed to many dangerous temptations. We engage in a special manner to sanctify the Lord's Day. It shall be our study to keep our garments unspotted by the flesh, and walk as becometh saints.

7. To receive such, and only such, into communion with us we think are born again; have been baptized according to the primitive mode of administering that ordinance, and profess their hearty approbation of, and subjection to, this our solemn church covenant.

These things, and whatever else may appear enjoined by the Word of God, we promise in the strength of divine grace to observe and practice. But knowing our insufficiency for anything that is spiritually good, in and of ourselves, we look up to Him who giveth power to the faint, rejoicing that in the Lord we have not only righteousness but strength. Hold thou us up, O Lord, and we shall be safe! Amen!

Church Covenant, John Newton Brown,
The Baptist Church Manual, 1853

Having been led, as we believe by the Spirit of God, to receive the Lord Jesus Christ as our Savior and, on the profession of our faith, having been baptized in the name of the Father, and of the Son, and of the Holy Spirit, we do now, in the presence of God, and this assembly, most solemnly and joyfully enter into covenant with one another as one body in Christ.

We engage, therefore, by the aid of the Holy Spirit to walk together in Christian love; to strive for the advancement of this church, in knowledge, holiness, and comfort; to promote its prosperity and spirituality and to sustain its worship, ordinances, discipline, and doctrines; to contribute cheerfully and regularly to the support of the ministry, the expenses of the church, the relief of the poor, and the spread of the gospel through all nations.

We also engage to maintain family and secret devotions; to religiously educate our children; to seek the salvation of our kindred and acquaintances; to walk circumspectly in the world; to be just in our dealings, faithful in our engagements, and exemplary in our deportment; to avoid all tattling, backbiting, and excessive anger; to abstain from the sale of, and use of, intoxicating drinks as a beverage; to be zealous in our efforts to advance the kingdom of our Savior.

We further engage to watch over one another in brotherly love; to remember one another in prayer; to aid one another in sickness and distress; to cultivate Christian sympathy in feeling and Christian courtesy in speech; to be slow to take offense, but always ready for reconciliation and mindful of the rules of our Savior to secure it without delay.

We moreover engage that when we remove from this place we will, as soon as possible, unite with some other church where we can carry out the spirit of this covenant and the principles of God's Word.

Conclusion

In light of this discussion, a few concluding observations are in order:

1. A great deal of concerned has been expressed lately about the loss of Baptist identity.[19] Some have even spoken of a Baptist Identity "movement." The erosion of denominational identity has sometimes been the result of doctrinal latitudinarianism. This was the worry that led to the so-called conservative resurgence in Southern Baptist life that began in the late 1970s. But the waning of Baptist identity might also be due to the loss of Baptist focal practices and liturgies. That is, as the worship and congregational practice of Baptist churches begin to reflect a broader low-church evangelical style, flattening distinctively Baptist liturgies, so the way Baptists inhabit the world might become less and less recognizable.

2. Although the preaching and teaching ministry of a Baptist church must receive rigorous attention, faithful execution and hearty affirmation, so must the focal things and focal practices of Baptist life together. If Baptists are "People of the Book" as they often claim to be, then Bible reading ought to have a more focal part in our worship and a more consistent part in our lives. Prayer Book Anglican worship, for instance, is much more Bible-centered in practice than most Baptist worship services. In the Anglican liturgy, at least four passages of Scripture are read every Sunday (from the Old Testament, Psalms, New Testament, and Gospels).

3. The liturgies of the church, in both their formal and informal sense, are important. Many Baptist churches have begun to practice an essentially two part liturgy. There is singing followed by preaching. Baptisms occur as needed and communion is received on a quarterly basis. Although the New Testament certainly allows the liberty to order the worship of a church in this way, pastors and church leaders should consider what focal things might be lost by this minimalistic approach. Whatever the pitfalls of liturgical worship, the focal practice of the liturgy underscores the focal doctrine and practice of the church. Following the seasons of the Christian church year (e.g., Advent, Christmas, Epiphany, Lent, Holy Week, Easter, Pentecost, Trinity Sunday, and Ordinary Time), blends both doxology

---

[19] See, for instance, David S. Dockery (ed), *Southern Baptist Identity: An Evangelical Denomination Faces the Future* (Wheaton, IL: Crossway, 2009).

and narrative. That is, the focal practice of remembering the church year underwrites the focal things, *viz.*, the important doctrines and outlines of the gospel story.

4. Church membership is not only about affirming truth, it is also about life together, in community. Baptists have always been known for their emphasis on fellowship. Whether it is around the fellowship supper, the church reunion, the men's breakfast, or the ladies' mission group, Baptists have found ways to build community. In many ways these liturgies have been healthy (if not always healthful) venues for churches not only to tell their story as a community of believers, but through mission emphases, for instance, to tell the story of the good news of Christ.

5. Just as many Baptists are giving emphasis to Baptist confessions, so they may wish to examine church covenants as a way of re-affirming Baptist identity, building community, exercising formative discipline within the churches and communicating worldview thinking among the congregations.

It remains unclear what Baptists, including Southern Baptists, will look like in the next half-century. There is a great deal of foment in Baptist life. Denominational identity seems to be waning. In some ways this is a welcome development. Meaningful unity of the sort for which Jesus prayed in John 17 is something every genuine believer should seek. At the same time, the loss of distinctly Baptist focal practices seems to be resulting in the loss of Baptist focal things. What this might mean for the way Baptists understand their worldview, only the omniscient God knows. It seems to me that exploring what was gained in the past through the use of covenants might be an effective way to consider what might be lost through the flattening of our life together.

The Writings of Thomas J. Nettles
A BIBLIOGRAPHY

Nathan Finn and Matthew Emerson

Over the course of his distinguished career, Tom Nettles has exemplified what it means to be a *doctor ecclesiae*—a doctor of the church. While he has written for the academy, throughout his career much of Nettles' scholarship has been used in the service of the church. Alongside scholarly articles have been dozens of popular articles, alongside academic book reviews have been numerous pastoral book reviews, and alongside academic monographs have been textbooks and "tracts for the times."

In this annotated bibliography, we have attempted to discover as much of Nettles' published writings as possible. It would have been much easier to contact him and ask for his current *curriculum vitae*, but since this *festschrift* is intended to be a surprise, we have simply dug around and chased leads in an attempt to find as much material as possible. Special thanks to Russ Moore, dean of the School of Theology at The Southern Baptist Theological Seminary, and Dean Moore's administrative assistant, Katy Ferguson, for their assistance. Though we are confident we have included all of Nettles' most important works, it is entirely possible that we have overlooked reviews and essays published in lesser-known periodicals in particular; we apologize for any omissions.

We have chosen to focus upon Nettles' writings, so we have not included sermons, addresses, or lectures. We have included a handful of miscellaneous items, including one audio resource and a couple of oral interviews. While we have noted revised editions of Nettles' books, we have chosen not to mention additional editions of his popular articles, some of which were reprinted in more than one periodical. We hope scholars, students and pastors will find these sources beneficial for years to come.

Dissertation

Nettles, Thomas Julian. "A Comparative Study of the Historical Stimuli Contributing to the Ecclesiological Views of Francis Johnson, John Smyth, and Robert Williams." PhD diss., Southwestern Baptist Theological Seminary, 1976.

Books

Bush, L. Russ, and Tom J. Nettles. *Baptists and the Bible: The Baptist Doctrines of Biblical Inspiration and Religious Authority in Historical Perspective*. Chicago, IL: Moody Press, 1980.

———. *Baptists and the Bible*, revised and expanded ed. Nashville, TN: Broadman, 1999.

Nettles, Tom J. The Baptists: *Key People in Forming a Baptist Identity*: Volume One, *Beginnings in Britain*. Fearn, Ross-shire, Scotland: Christian Focus, 2005.

———. *The Baptists: Key People in Forming a Baptist Identity:* Volume Two, *Beginnings in America*. Fearn, Ross-shire, Scotland: Christian Focus, 2006.

———. *The Baptists: Key People in Forming a Baptist Identity:* Volume Three, *The Modern Era*. Fearn, Ross-shire, Scotland: Christian Focus, 2007.

———. *Believer's Baptism by Immersion*. Foundations of Baptist Heritage. Nashville, TN: The Historical Commission of the Southern Baptist Convention, 1989.

———. *By His Grace and for His Glory: A Historical, Theological, and Practical Study of the Doctrines of Grace in Baptist Life*. Grand Rapids, MI: Baker Book House, 1986. Reprinted by Cor Meum Tibi in 2002.

———. *By His Grace and for His Glory: A Historical, Theological, and Practical Study of the Doctrines of Grace in Baptist Life*. Revised and Expanded 20th Anniversary Edition. Cape Coral, FL: Founders Press, 2006.

———. *A Foundation for the Future: The Southern Baptist Message and Mission*. Cape Coral, FL: Founders Press, 1997.

———. *Growth for God's Glory: A Fiftieth Anniversary History of Broadmoor Baptist Church, Shreveport, Louisiana.* Shreveport, LA: Broadmoor Baptist Church, 1980.

———. *An Introduction to the Southern Baptists.* London: Carey Publications, 1986.

———. *James Petigru Boyce: A Southern Baptist Statesman.* Phillipsburg, NJ: P & R, 2009.

———. *The Patience of Providence: A History of First Baptist Church Brandon, Mississippi, 1835–1985.* Brandon, MS: First Baptist Church, 1989.

———. *Ready for Reformation: Bringing Authentic Reform to Southern Baptist Churches.* Nashville, TN: Broadman & Holman, 2005.

Dictionary Entries

Nettles, Tom J. s.v. "Catechisms, Baptist Use of." Page 80 in Bill J. Leonard, ed., *Dictionary of Baptists in America.* Downers Grove, IL: InterVarsity Press, 1994.

———. s.v. "Edgar Young Mullins." Pages 54–66 in Walter A. Elwell, ed., *Handbook of Evangelical Theologians.* Grand Rapids, MI: Baker Books, 1993.

———. s.v. "Mid-America Baptist Theological Seminary." Pages 187–88 in Bill J. Leonard, ed., *Dictionary of Baptists in America.* Downers Grove, IL: InterVarsity Press, 1994.

———. s.v. "Reformed Baptists." Page 233 in Bill J. Leonard, ed., *Dictionary of Baptists in America.* Downers Grove, IL: InterVarsity Press, 1994.

———. s.v. "Southern Baptist Conference on the Faith of the Founders." Page 253 in Bill J. Leonard, ed., *Dictionary of Baptists in America.* Downers Grove, IL: InterVarsity Press, 1994.

Journal Articles

Armstrong, John, Mark Dever, Tom Nettles, and James White. "Key Points in the ECT Debate." *The Southern Baptist Journal of Theology* 5.4 (Winter 2001): 98–108.

Powell, Josh and Tom J. Nettles. "Shubal Stearns and the Separate Baptist Tradition." *The Founders Journal* 44 (Spring 2001): 16–31.

Nettles, Tom J. "Are Calvinists Hyper?" *The Founders Journal* 30 (Fall 1997): 11–14.

———. "Are Creeds Appropriate for Bible Believing Baptists?" *The Founders Journal* 3 (Fall/Winter 1990–91): 19–25.

———. "Assurance." *The Founders Journal* 58 (Fall 2004): 18–22.

———. "Basil Manly: Fire From Light—The Transforming Power of Theological Preaching (Part 1)." *The Founders Journal* 21 (Summer 1995): 17–24.

———. "Basil Manly: Fire From Light—The Transforming Power of Theological Preaching (Part 2)." *The Founders Journal* 22 (Fall 1995): 9–17.

———. "Boyce the Theologian." *The Founders Journal* 69 (Summer 2007): 10–18.

———. "A Brief History of the Southern Baptist Theological Seminary." *The Founders Journal* 77 (Summer 2009): 1–4.

———. "A Calvinist By Any Other Name." *The Founders Journal* 69 (Summer 2007): 1–8.

———. "Church Purity." *The Founders Journal* 73 (Summer 2008): 1–10.

———. "Confession: A Union of Heart between Sheep and Shepherd." *The Founders Journal* 49 (Summer 2002): 16–22.

———. "The Confessional Convictions of Spencer Cone." *The Founders Journal* 49 (Summer 2002): 23–27.

———. "The Conserving Power of the Doctrines of Grace." *The Founders Journal* 29 (Summer 1997): 24–27.

———. "Curtis Vaughan: A Tribute by Personal Testimony." *The Founders Journal* 60 (Spring 2005): 6–9.

———. "Doctrinal Preaching: The Central Task of the Christian Minister." *The Founders Journal* 65 (Summer 2006): 24–30.

———. "E. Y. Mullins–Reluctant Evangelical." *The Southern Baptist Journal of Theology* 3.4 (Winter 1999): 24–43.

———. "Early Baptists and Easy-Believism." *The Founders Journal* 6 (Fall 1991): 22–28.

———. "Editorial Introduction." *The Founders Journal* 57 (Summer 2004): 1.

———. "Edwards and His Impact on Baptists." *The Founders Journal* 53 (Summer 2003): 1–18.

———. "An Encouragement to Use Catechisms." *The Founders Journal* 10 (Fall 1992): 19–23.

———. "An Encouragement to Use Catechisms (Pt. 2)." *The Founders Journal* 12 (Spring 1993): 18–23.

———. "An Encouragement to Use Catechisms (Pt. 3)." *The Founders Journal* 13 (Summer 1993): 19–22.

———. "Finding the Richest Confessional Treasure." *The Founders Journal* 61 (Summer 2005): 1–3.

———. "The Forgotten Founder—William Williams." *The Founders Journal* 77 (Summer 2009): 19–30.

———. "He Descended Into Hell." *Modern Reformation* 11.3 (May/June 2002): 38–41.

———. "The Health of Confessional Christianity." *The Founders Journal* 49 (Summer 2002): 5–10.

———. "Heels Together, Shoulders Back, Chin Down." *The Founders Journal* 74 (Fall 2008): 1.

———. "Helpful Books." *The Founders Journal* 53 (Summer 2003): 31–33.

———. "How Do We Know Who We Are?" *The Founders Journal* 49 (Summer 2002): 1–4.

———. "The Influence of Jonathan Edwards on Andrew Fuller." *Eusebia: The Bulletin of the Andrew Fuller Center for Baptist Studies* 9 (Spring 2008): 97–116.

———. "James Petigru Boyce: For Christ and His Church." *The Southern Baptist Journal of Theology* 13.1 (Spring 2009): 6–29.

———. "John Clifford (1836–1923): Irrepressible Liberal." *The Southern Baptist Journal of Theology* 6.4 (Winter 2002): 58–81.

————. "John Spilsbury and His Confession." *The Founders Journal* 44 (Spring 2001): 10–15.

————. "Jonathan Edwards: An Appreciation." *The Founders Journal* 53 (Summer 2003): [web edition only] Online. http://www.founders.org/journal/fj53/editorial.html

————. "The Kind of Man God Uses: Samuel Pearce (1766–1799). *The Founders Journal* 57 (Summer 2004): 24–25.

————. "L. R. Scarborough: Public Figure." *Southwestern Journal of Theology* 25.2 (Spring 1983): 24–42.

————. "Missions and Creeds (Part 1)." *The Founders Journal* 17 (Summer 1994): 20–27.

————. "Missions and Creeds (Part 2)." *The Founders Journal* 18 (Fall 1994): 16–22.

————. "On the Other Hand: The Decline of Confessions." *The Founders Journal* 49 (Summer 2002): 11–15.

————. "Once Upon a Time, Four Hundred Years Ago…" *The Founders Journal* 76 (Spring 2009): 2–8.

————. "Patterns of Financial Giving for Missions Support among Baptists." *Baptist History and Heritage* 14.1 (1979): 27–36.

————. "The Posture of Preaching." *The Founders Journal* 74 (Fall 2008): 22–27.

————. "Recapturing the Complementarity of Law and Gospel." *The Founders Journal* 59 (Winter 2005): 14–24.

————. "Ready for Reformation?" *The Founders Journal* 44 (Spring 2001): 3–9.

————. "Retracing Our Steps." *The Founders Journal* 44 (Spring 2001): 1–2.

————. "The Rise and Demise of Calvinism among Southern Baptists." *The Founders Journal* 19/20 : 6–21.

————. "The Role of Confessions in Baptist Faith." *The Founders Journal* 4 (Spring 1991): 16–23.

———. "Smyth and Helwys: The Key to Anabaptist-Baptist Relations." *Southwestern Journal of Theology* 19.1 (1976): 101–104.

———. "Southern Baptists: Regional to National Transition." *Baptist History and Heritage* 16.1 (1981): 13–23.

———. "Southern Baptist Identity: Influenced by Calvinism." *Baptist History and Heritage* 31.4 (1996): 17–26.

———. "Spurgeon's Message of Christ's Atoning Sacrifice, Part 1." *The Founders Journal* 14 (Fall 1993): 7–17.

———. "Spurgeon's Message of Christ's Atoning Sacrifice, Pt 2: The Extent of the Atonement." *The Founders Journal* 15 (Winter 1994): 16–22.

———. "Themes for Research in Southern Baptist History." *Baptist History and Heritage* 14.2 (1979): 15–19.

———. "Transformed by the Renewing of Your Minds." *The Founders Journal* 73 (Summer 2008): 17–25.

———. "A Vision of Theological Education." *The Founders Journal* 32 (Spring 1998): 18–21.

———. "Why Can't They See This?" *The Founders Journal* 11 (Winter 1993): 8–12.

———. "Why Your Next Pastor Should Be A Calvinist." *The Founders Journal* 71 (Winter 2008): 5–15.

Book Chapters and Other Essays

Nettles, Tom J. "Andrew Fuller (1754–1815)." Pages 97–142 in *The British Particular Baptists: 1638–1910*. Vol. 2. Edited by Michael A. G. Haykin. Springfield, MO: Particular Baptist Press, 2000.

———. "Apologetics and Scripture: A Lesson from the Early Church." Pages 47–74 in *Defending the Faith, Engaging the Culture: Essays Honoring L. Russ Bush*. Edited by Bruce A. Little and Mark D. Liederbach. Nashville, TN: B&H Academic, 2011.

———. "Baptist View: Baptism as a Symbol of Christ's Saving Work." Pages 25–41 in *Understanding Four Views on Baptism*. Edited by John H. Armstrong and John E. Engle. Grand Rapids, MI: Zondervan, 2007.

————. "Baptists and Scripture." Pages 323–57 in *Inerrancy and the Church*. Edited by John D. Hannah. Chicago, IL: Moody Press, 1984.

————. "Baptists and the Great Commission." Pages 89–107 in *The Great Commission: Evangelicals and the History of World Missions*. Edited by Martin I. Klauber and Scott M. Manetsch. Nashville, TN: Broadman and Holman, 2008.

————. "Being Baptist: We Must Not Sell it Cheap." Pages 3–18 in *Why I Am a Baptist*. Edited by Tom J. Nettles and Russell D. Moore. Nashville, TN: Broadman & Holman, 2001.

————. "Benjamin Keach (1640–1704)." Pages 95–132 in *The British Particular Baptists: 1638–1910*. Vol. 1. Edited by Michael A. G. Haykin. Springfield, MO: Particular Baptist Press, 1998.

————. "A Better Way: Church Growth through Revival and Reformation." Pages 161–87 in *Power Religion: The Selling Out of the Evangelical Church?* Edited by Michael S. Horton. Chicago, IL: Moody Press, 1992.

————. "Christianity Pure and Simple: Andrew Fuller's Contest with Socinianism." Pages 139–73 in *'At the Pure Fountain of Thy Word': Andrew Fuller as an Apologist, Studies in Baptist History and Thought*, vol. 6. Edited by Michael A. G. Haykin. Carlisle, Cumbria, UK, and Waynesboro, GA: Paternoster, 2004.

————. "Creedalism, Confessionalism, and the Baptist Faith and Message." Pages 143–54 in *The Unfettered Word: Confronting the Authority-Inerrancy Question*. Edited by Robison B. James. Waco, TX: Word, 1987. This book was reprinted by Smyth & Helwys in 1994.

————. "The Enduring Importance and Relevance of 'A Treatise on the Preparation and Delivery of Sermons.'" Pages 176–211 in *John A. Broadus: A Living Legacy*. Edited by David S. Dockery and Roger D. Duke. Nashville, TN: Broadman and Holman, 2008.

————. "God's Purpose of Grace, Election." Pages 19–20 in *An Exposition from the Faculty of The Southern Baptist Theological Seminary of the Baptist Faith and Message 2000*. Louisville, KY: The Southern Baptist Theological Seminary, 2001.

————. "A Historical View of the Doctrinal Importance of Calvinism Among Baptists." Pages 47–72 in *Calvinism: A Southern Baptist Dia-*

logue. Edited by E. Ray Clendenen and Brad J. Waggoner. Nashville, TN: Broadman and Holman, 2008.

————. "How to Lose Your Way: A History Lesson in Confessions." Pages xiii–xxv (Introduction) in *Baptist Faith and Message 2000: Critical Issues in America's Largest Protestant Denomination*. Edited by Douglas K. Blount and Joseph D. Wooddell. Lanham, MD: Rowman and Littlefield, 2007.

————. "Inerrancy in History: Something Old, Something New." Pages 127–54 in *Authority and Interpretation: A Baptist Perspective*. Edited by Duane A. Garrett and Richard R. Melick. Grand Rapids, MI: Baker, 1987.

————. "Influence of the Philadelphia Confession of Faith on Baptists in America." Pages 95–120 in *Baptist History Celebration–2007: A Symposium on Our History, Theology, and Hymnody*. Springfield, MO: Particular Baptist Press, 2008.

————. "John Gill and the Evangelical Awakening." Pages 131–170 in *Life and Thought of John Gill (1697–1771): A Tercentennial Appreciation*. Edited by Michael A. G. Haykin. Leiden: E. J. Brill, 1997.

————. "John Wesley's Contention with Calvinism: Interactions Then and Now." Pages 297–322 in *The Grace of God, The Bondage of the Will: Historical and Theological Perspectives on Calvinism*. Vol. 2. Edited by Thomas R. Schreiner and Bruce A. Ware. Grand Rapids, MI: Baker Books, 1995.

————. "One Holy, Catholic, Apostolic Church." Pages 25–44 in *Roman Catholicism: Evangelical Protestants Analyze What Divides and Unites Us*. Edited by John Armstrong. Chicago, IL: The Moody Bible Institute, 1994.

————. "Religious Liberty," Pages 41–43 in *An Exposition from the Faculty of The Southern Baptist Theological Seminary of the Baptist Faith and Message 2000*. Louisville, KY: The Southern Baptist Theological Seminary, 2001.

————. "Richard Furman." Pages 140–64 in *Baptist Theologians*. Edited by Timothy George and David S. Dockery. Nashville: Broadman, 1990.

————. "The World's Great Soldier: Robert E. Lee." Pages 26–31 in *More Than Conquerors*. Edited by John D. Woodbridge. Chicago, IL: Moody Press, 1992.

Introductions, Prefaces and Forewords

Nettles, Tom J. Foreword to *The Armies of the Lamb: The Spirituality of Andrew Fuller*, by Andrew Fuller and Michael A. G. Haykin. Dundas, Ontario, Canada: Joshua Press, 2001.

————. Introduction to *Asahel Nettleton: Sermons from the Second Great Awakening*. Ames, IA: International Outreach, 1995.

————. Introduction to *The Cause of God and Truth, by John Gill*. The Baptist Faith 3. Paris, AR: The Baptist Standard Bearer, 2000.

————. Preface to *The Complete Works of the Rev. Andrew Fuller: With a Memoir of His Life* by Andrew Gunton Fuller. 3 vols. Edited by Joseph Belcher. Philadelphia, PA: American Baptist Publication Society, 1845; reprint, Harrisonburg, PA: Sprinkle Publications, 1988.

————. Preface to the *Manual of Theology, by J. L. Dagg*. Charleston, SC: The Southern Baptist Publication Society; reprint, Harrisonburg, PA: Gano, 1990.

Edited Works

Nettles, Tom J., ed. *Baptist Catechisms: To Make Thee Wise Unto Salvation*. Fort Worth, TX: Tom Nettles, 1983.

————, ed. *Southern Baptist Sermons on Sovereignty and Responsibility*. Harrisonburg, PA: Sprinkle, 1984.

————.*Stray Recollections, Short Articles and Public Orations of James P. Boyce*. Cape Coral, FL: Founders Press, 2009.

————, ed. *Teaching Truth, Training Hearts: The Study of Catechisms in Baptist Life*. Amityville, NY: Calvary Press, 1998.

———— and Russell Moore, eds. *Why I Am a Baptist*. Nashville, TN: Broadman & Holman, 2001.

Reviews

Nettles, Tom J. Review of Zane Clark Hodges, *Absolutely Free: A Biblical Reply to Lordship Salvation*. In *Trinity Journal* 11.2 (Fall 1990): 242–47.

————. Review of Thomas C. Oden, *Classical Pastoral Care*, 4 vols. In *Trinity Journal* 15.2 (Fall 1994): 278–79.

————. Review of R. B. C. Howell, *The Covenants*. In *The Founders Journal* 8 (Spring 1992): 35.

————. Review of *Defending the Faith: J. Gresham Machen and the Crisis of Conservative Protestantism in Modern America*. In *Trinity Journal* 15.2 (Fall 1994): 279.

————. Review of Marc A. Jolley and John D. Pierce, eds., *Distinctively Baptist: Essays on Baptist History*. In *Journal of the Evangelical Theological Society* 50.3 (2007): 651–53.

————. Review of J. N. D. Kelly, *Early Christian Doctrines*. In *Southwestern Journal of Theology* 21.1 (Fall 1978): 108–109.

————. Review of William A. Dembski, *The End of Christianity: Finding a Good God in an Evil World*. In *The Southern Baptist Journal of Theology* 13.4 (Winter 2009): 80–85.

————. Review of Gerald R. Cragg, *Freedom and Authority*. In *Southwestern Journal of Theology* 18.2 (1976): 103–104.

————. Review of Sinclair Ferguson, *A Heart for God*. In *Criswell Theological Review* 1, (1986): 194–195.

————. Review of Thomas C. Oden, *John Wesley's Scriptural Christianity: A Plain Exposition of His Teaching on Christian Doctrine*. In *Trinity Journal* 15.2 (Fall 1994): 281.

————. Review of *Lutheran Cyclopedia*, rev. ed. In *Southwestern Journal of Theology* 18.2 (1976): 116–117.

————. Review of Terry Wolever, ed., *Minutes of the Philadelphia Baptist Association, 1707–1807*. In *The Founders Journal* 49 (Summer 2002): 28–33.

————. Review of Mark Dever, ed., *Polity: Biblical Arguments on How to Conduct Church Life*. In *The Founders Journal* 45 (Summer 2001): 27–29.

————. Review of James R. White, *The Potter's Freedom: A Defense of the Reformation and a Rebuttal of Norman Geisler's Chosen But Free*. In *The Southern Baptist Journal of the Theology* 5.1 (Spring 2001): 92–98.

———. Review of Monica Furlong, *Puritan's Progress: A Study of John Bunyan*. In *Christianity Today* 22.3 no. 4 (1977): 236–37.

———. Review of William R. Estep, *Renaissance and Reformation*. In *Criswell Theological Review* 1 (Spring 1987): 420–22.

———. Review of Stanley Grenz, *Revisioning Evangelical Theology: A Fresh Agenda for the 21st Century*. In *Trinity Journal* 15.1 (1994): 123–130.

———. Review of Iain H. Murray, *Revival and Revivalism: The Making and Marring of American Evangelicalism, 1750–1858*. In *Trinity Journal* 15.2 (Fall 1994): 278.

———. Review of Greg Wills, *The Southern Baptist Theological Seminary, 1859–2009*. In *The Founders Journal* 77 (Summer 2009): 31–33.

———. Review of Robert D. Culver, *Toward a Biblical View of Civil Government*. In *Southwestern Journal of Theology* 19.1 (1976): 105–106.

———. Review of James M. Renihan, ed., *True Confessions: Baptist Douments in the Reformed Family*. In *The Founders Journal* 73 (Summer 2008): 32–33.

———. Review of Robert Brow and Clark Pinnock, *Unbounded Love: A Good News Theology For the 21st Century*. In *Trinity Journal* 15.2 (Fall 1994): 280.

———. James Slatton, *W. H. Whitsitt: The Man and the Controversy*. In *The Founders Journal* 77 (Summer 2009): 33.

Other Resources

Baker, Robert Andrew, and Tom J. Nettles. *The Oral Memoirs of Robert A. Baker: A Series of Interviews Conducted September 21, 1977 Through October 19, 1977*. Dallas, TX: Baptist General Convention of Texas, 1977.

Holcomb, Rowe C., and Tom J. Nettles. *The Oral Memoirs of Rowe C. Holcomb: An Interview Conducted July 22, 1977*. Dallas, TX: Baptist General Convention of Texas, 1979.

Nettles, Tom J. *Baptists and the Doctrines of Grace*. DVD. Cape Coral, FL: Founders Press, 2004.

Index of People and Places

Index of Scripture References